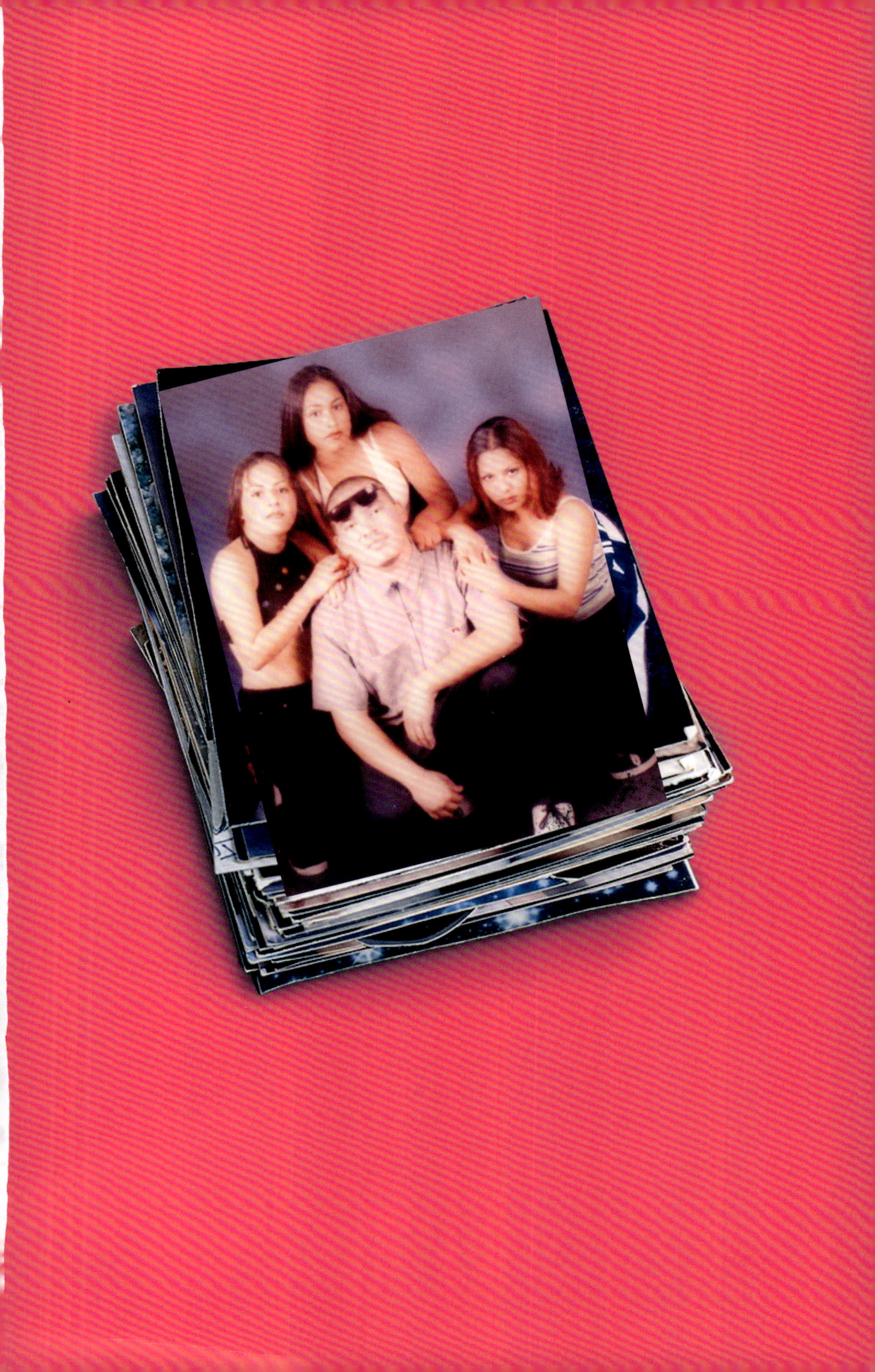

BY

GUADALUPE ROSALES

Map Pointz East of the River

EAST OF THE RIVER

EAST OF THE RIVER

A Memoir of Los Angeles Girlhood

GUADALUPE ROSALES

ONE WORLD · NEW YORK

One World
An imprint of Random House
A division of Penguin Random House LLC
1745 Broadway, New York, NY 10019
oneworldlit.com
penguinrandomhouse.com

Hardcover ISBN 978-0-593-44726-0
Ebook ISBN 978-0-593-44727-7

Printed in China

2 4 6 8 9 7 5 3 1

FIRST EDITION

Book Team: production editor: *Luke Epplin* • managing editor: *Rebecca Berlant* • production manager: *Richard Elman* • copy editor: *Stuart Calderwood* • proofreaders: *Nicole Ramirez, Megha Jain, Tricia Wygal, Al Madocs, Zora O'Neill, Nancee Adams*

Book design by Stephen Serato
Book layout by Stephen Serrano and Barbara M. Bachman

The authorized representative in the EU for product safety and compliance is Penguin Random House Ireland, Morrison Chambers, 32 Nassau Street, Dublin D02 YH68, Ireland. https://eu-contact.penguin.ie

Dedicated to all the women—

mothers, daughters, and sisters—

who remind me of what

strength, love, and memory look like

**“Yo no pedí ser Mexicana,
solo tuve suerte.”**

Contents

SECTION II

Away

SECTION III

Coming Home

EAST OF THE RIVER

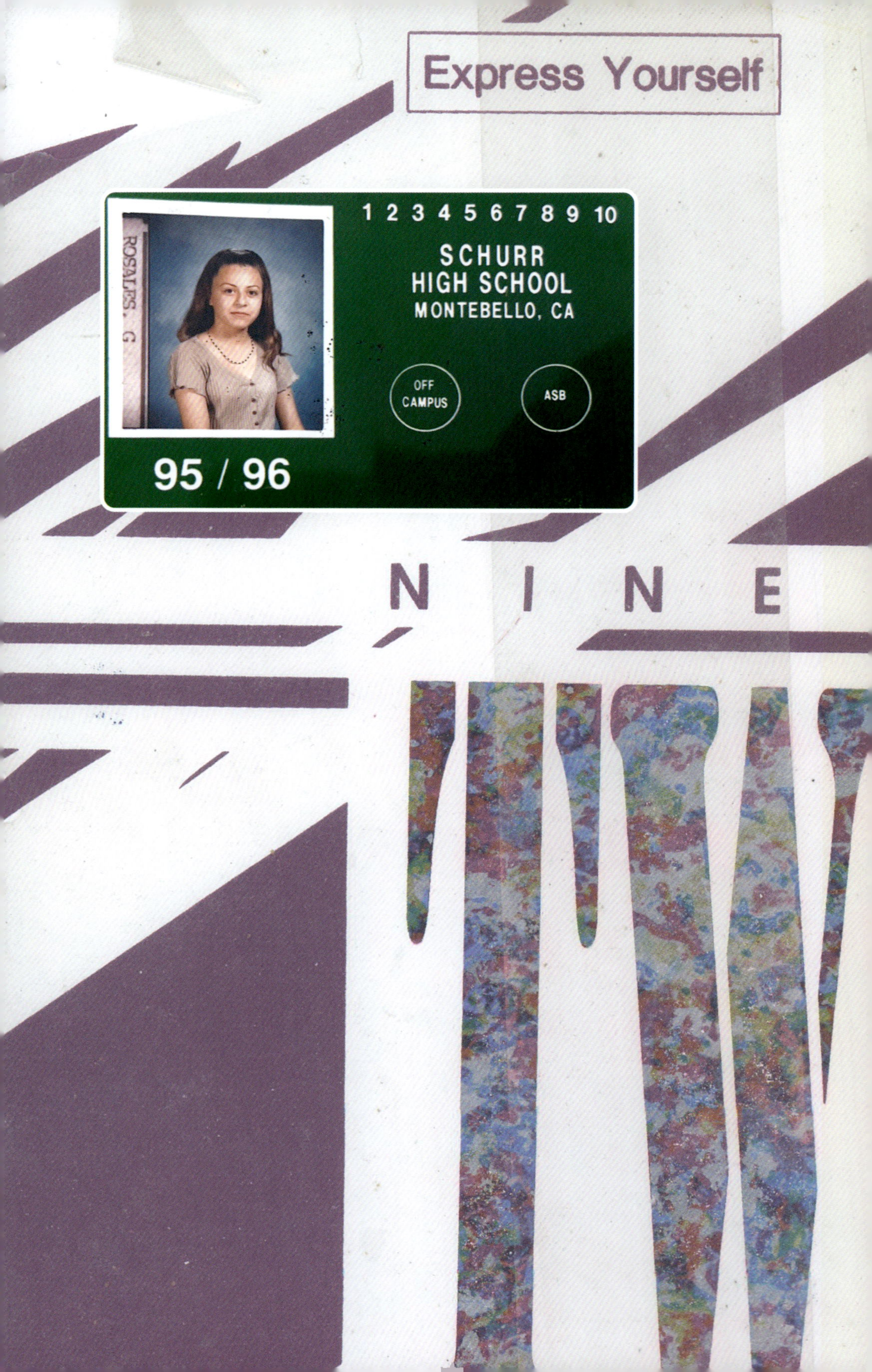

Express Yourself
ROSALES, G
1 2 3 4 5 6 7 8 9 10
SCHURR
HIGH SCHOOL
MONTEBELLO, CA
OFF
CAMPUS
ASB
95 / 96
NINE

INTRODUCTION

When I was about eleven years old, my sister Maria and I, along with our friend Silvia, would walk to the East Los Angeles public library and spend hours there. It was a two-mile walk from our house, and we'd go even if it rained.

We visited the library about three times a week. It was the first space that gave me a way into my imagination through books and other materials I had limited access to otherwise. I didn't know anyone who had a library or a shelf filled with books at home. At the public library, we had free access to books, films, and news articles that helped us give shape to and understand the unimaginable. With the newspaper articles on microfiche we could look through a frame in a way that felt intimate and voyeuristic.

Once we got to the library, we all dispersed and went to find our favorite genres, then came back and huddled around the books we'd selected. My sister and Silvia loved the Beatles and pop culture. I was obsessed with Jim Morrison, the *Titanic* tragedy, and the Bermuda Triangle conspiracies.

I loved the mystery of not knowing whether these stories were real or made-up. When I looked at the images of the *Titanic*—the fashion, the decorations in the ballroom, the gymnasium, and the dining area, the people in these spaces—I somehow felt a connection to these eerie photos, even though they were far from my own existence.

All I needed to travel to another dimension were these images and my imagination. I often found myself lost in the pages of books and old photographs, trying to imagine a world that seemed both distant and unfamiliar. I could get lost in the stillness of a black-and-white photograph and in the smell of old books. The text in books, too, was a gateway—filling in the spaces that images couldn't reach.

Without knowing it then, this library was probably my first "safe space" as a kid. I'm not proud to admit that I stole and damaged so many books and magazines—I would rip out pages because I couldn't afford to buy them. The time I spent there was part of my survival as a child. My first obsession with music, art, and history. Every time my mother made it difficult for us to be home, we wound up there.

When we looked at photos from before our time, we were curious to know what it was like to walk on cobblestone streets wearing dress shoes. This is the feeling I want to evoke in this book. There are joy, celebration, eerie and ghostly energies all around us. This is what keeps me inspired as an artist and how I have always understood the world.

There was something magical about a time before smartphones and instant photos, not just in the early 1900s but even when I was a kid in the 1990s—a time when memories weren't so easily captured or shared. I grew up in Los Angeles in the '90s, when life felt like it had to be lived in the moment. The families with a little more money who could afford camcorders and cameras were rare. When I look at old video footage, I'm grateful to the people who carried those big cameras around—the kind with a bulky VHS tape inside.

We, on the other hand, were the kids with disposable cameras, those little plastic boxes you'd pick up at Thrifty drugstore, packed with twenty-seven shots, each one a calculated risk. The anticipation was part of the magic—the way you'd hold the camera in your hands, wondering what the picture would look like once the film was developed. The images had imperfections—over- or underexposed, light leaks, or that faint flash of light caught in the wrong moment—but that was part of their charm, just like scars, wrinkles, and beauty marks on our bodies. There was no "delete" button, no retake; what you took was what you got.

And yet, in that imperfection, there was truth. We didn't yet realize how much we would come to crave instant access to our memories—especially the difficult and tragic ones, which we often wish to forget, even as a part of us struggles to hold on. How quickly we'd forget someone's scent and laughter or what it felt like to wait for a photograph to be developed or a letter to arrive in the mail.

Waiting was part of the experience, and maybe that's why those moments feel so much richer now: It was a promise that time, as fleeting as it seemed, would somehow come back to us, not in the form of a notification or a selfie, but as a tangible, fragile reminder of where we were, who we were, and how we saw the world.

I want to paint a dreamlike image for those who read this book. Whether the book is read today or a hundred years from now, the world I am painting does not exist anymore, but there are residues these pages pick up on, like that familiar scent or perfume that reminds us of a person or place. Some might recognize these images; some might feel like they've been here before.

This is a time capsule that will take us back while standing here (and still) in the present moment, but that also connects that past with this present. It starts with my youth in East Los Angeles, through tragedy to my exile in New York City, and back to Los Angeles, transformed. It's not just my story: It's the story of my family and my community, and the people who have become my community by sharing their stories with me and with the world. In those years without smartphones, without instant documentation, I began to materialize the moments of my life—not through photos, but through feeling. And through that feeling, I began to humanize the world around me, to breathe life into Los Angeles in ways that could never be captured by a lens or the click of a button.

In that same way, I looked at the moments of my own life and the streets of Los Angeles through images, not through the lens of a camera or a screen, but through the feeling of *being* in them. Without photographs to freeze them, I had to bring them to life with my imagination.

Now, looking back, I sometimes wish I could relive those moments, not just through the pictures, but through the feeling of being there. So I make work that materializes my feelings evoked by the conversations I have with friends and family and sometimes people I meet on social media by using photography, sculpture, and even soundscapes I record and use in my installations. As an educator and mentor, I encourage others to consider the importance of self-preservation and to rethink their own personal histories, to preserve their stories and personal collections of photographs, letters, and ephemera.

Our stories and histories, particularly those of marginalized communities, deserve to be preserved. I also want to inspire people to reconnect with the physical aspect of archiving. There's something irreplaceable about holding tangible objects—an old photograph or a handwritten letter—that a digital file cannot replicate.

In these pages, I revisit the places and moments that shaped me—from East L.A. in the 1990s to New York in the 2000s, and the memories that led to *Veteranas and Rucas* and *Map Pointz*. What begins as a story about growing up becomes one about healing, belonging, and the power of remembering. I am often recognized for my work on social media, but my story doesn't begin there. Before the archives lived online, they lived in real places—our homes, parties, and backyards, and in the East Los Angeles public library, my second home. Before I ever posted an image, I was that kid lost in the stacks, touching history through the scent of old books and the glow of microfiche. Those aisles were my first feed.

Creating this book feels like returning to that space, making something physical that might one day live on those same shelves. A place for memory to breathe, to be held, to be passed from hand to hand. On Instagram, captions are brief and fleeting. Here, I get to slow down, to share the stories behind the images, memories from my life and from my community, alongside photographs from those eras. Together they reveal the nights and days that shaped my work as an artist and archivist, so you can feel the rhythm and the pulse that shaped us. This is the beginning of a journey through memory, of what it means to grow up between two worlds, to lose and to rebuild, to turn pain into archive and archive into art. It is also about what it means to do this collectively—to gather strength in shared stories, to remember together, to honor what might otherwise be lost. Step into this world with me.

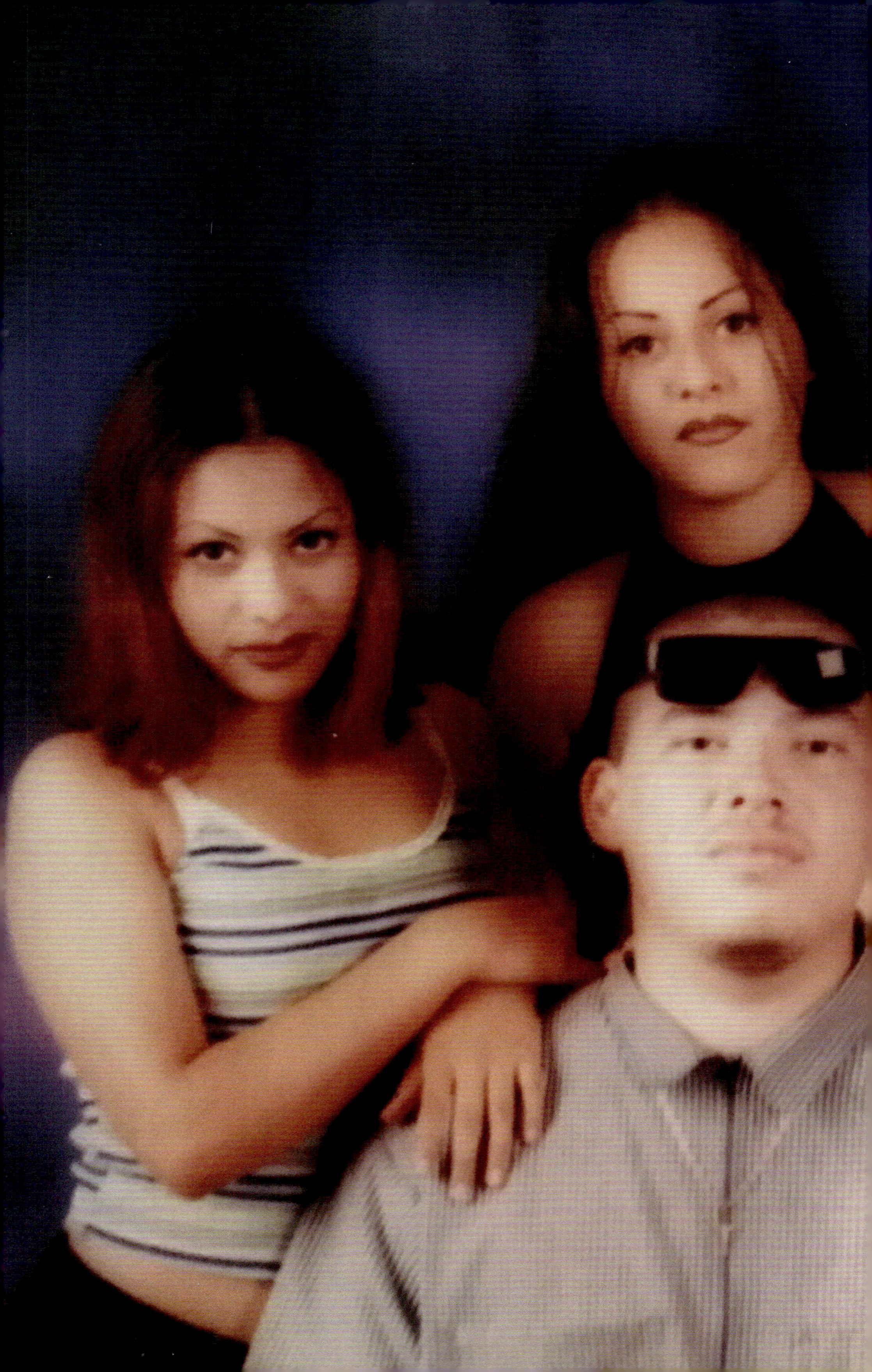

SECTION I

Home

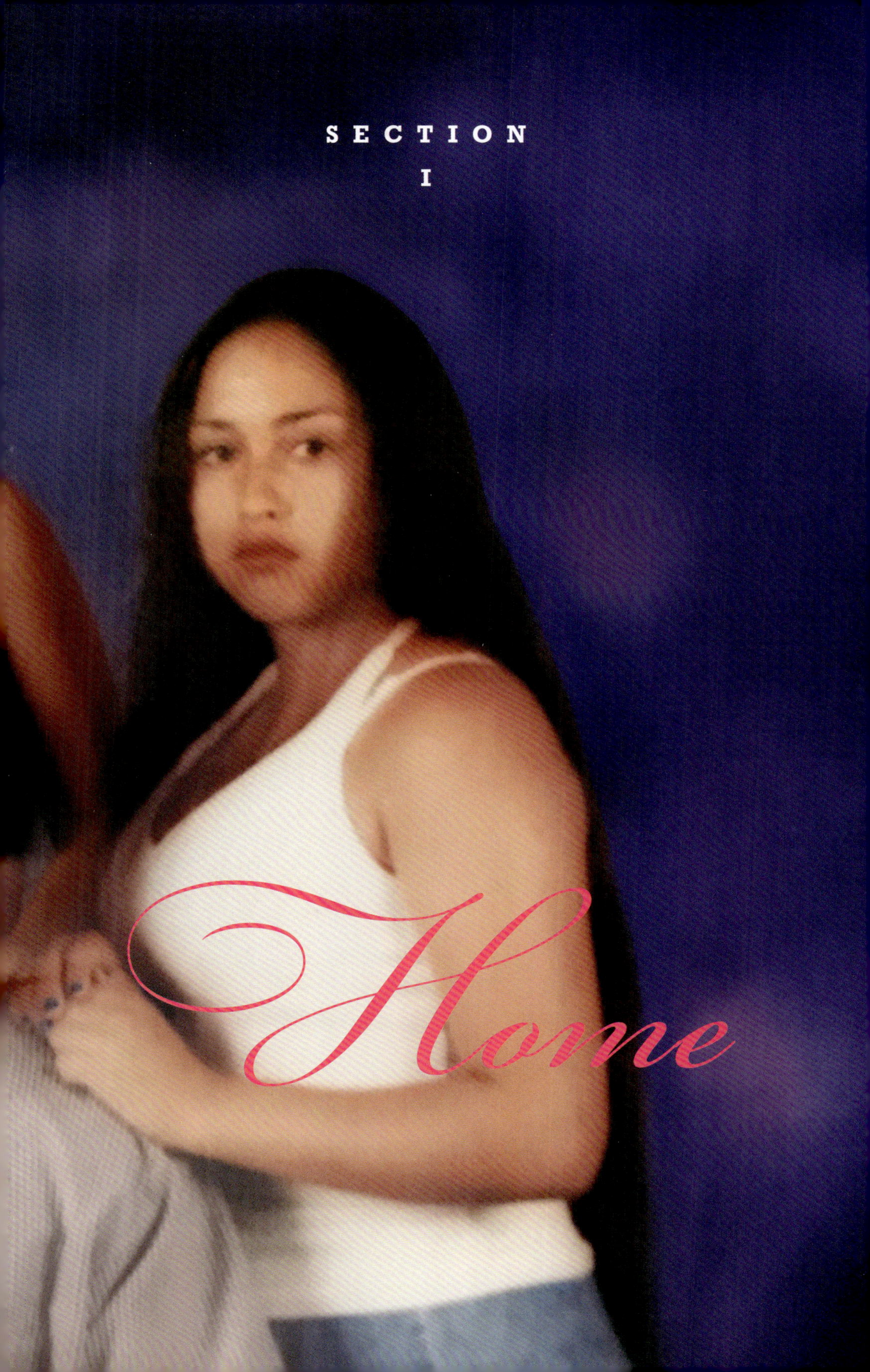

RIGHT: My sister Maria and me in Redwood City, CA, 1983

BELOW: My sisters, Maria and Yesi, and me in Redwood City, CA, circa 1983

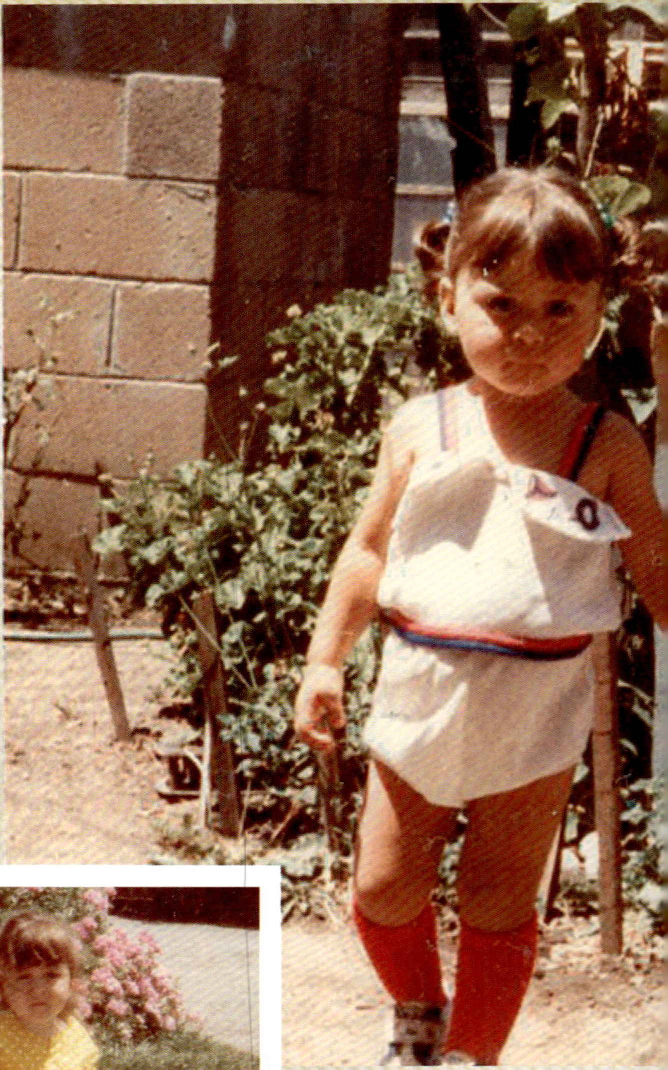

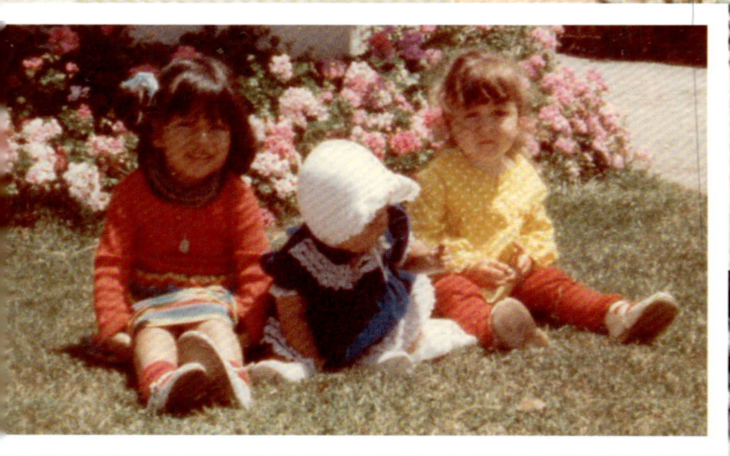

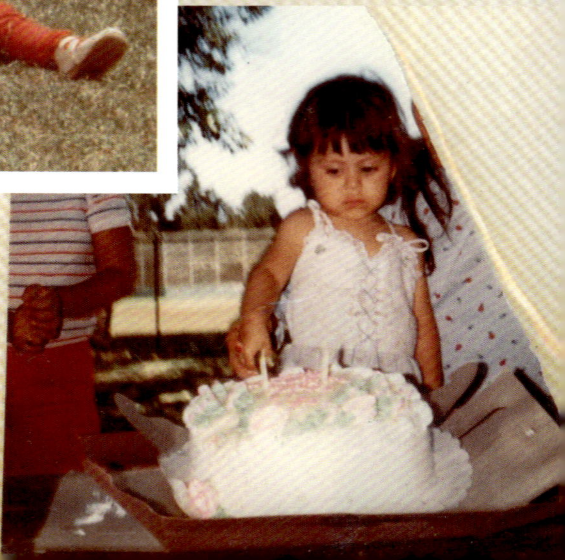

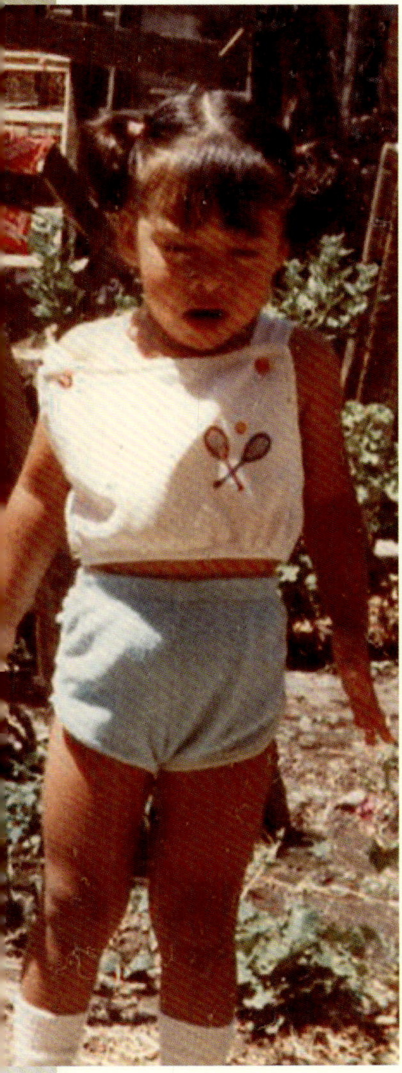

ALMOST TWINS

THE SUN ALWAYS BOTHERED MY SISter Maria. When I saw her squinting, I'd step in without thinking and cup my hands above her eyes, just enough to block out the light but still letting her see through my fingers. I started doing this when I was about three years old.

In nearly every childhood photo of her, you'll find her closing her eyes from the sunlight, or her face hidden behind me, seeking shade. This small gesture stayed with me over the years, evolving as we grew. When we got older, I would often go with her when she snuck out of the house, just to make sure she was safe. Nothing mattered more than wanting to be by her side, even if the circumstances were dangerous. There were many nights when we ran from the police together. It was always about keeping her company.

Ever since we were little, I played the role of her caretaker. I'd look out for both my sisters, but especially Maria. Maria and I are ten months apart. She's older. For two months each year, we're the same age, technically twins, and we joked about it. I'd remind Maria that during those two months, she couldn't boss me around because we were the same age. It became a running joke between us as we grew older.

To some degree, I always looked up to her—and I also looked out for her. She's rebellious, social, fun to be around. She taught me how to carry myself, how to do my eyeliner, and she helped me escape when our home no longer felt safe. The first rules we broke were there, with my mother. Then with the law. As she got older, she became even more rebellious.

Maria snuck out of the house at night more than I can remember. She always invited me to come with her. I declined the invitation many times, but eventually I gave in. Nothing else can give you that first rush from making sure we

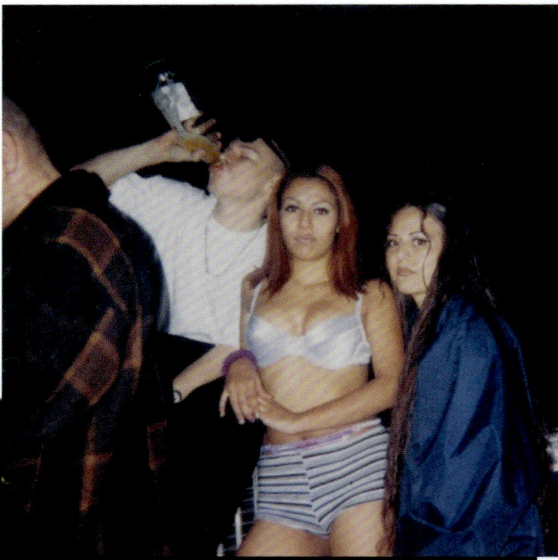

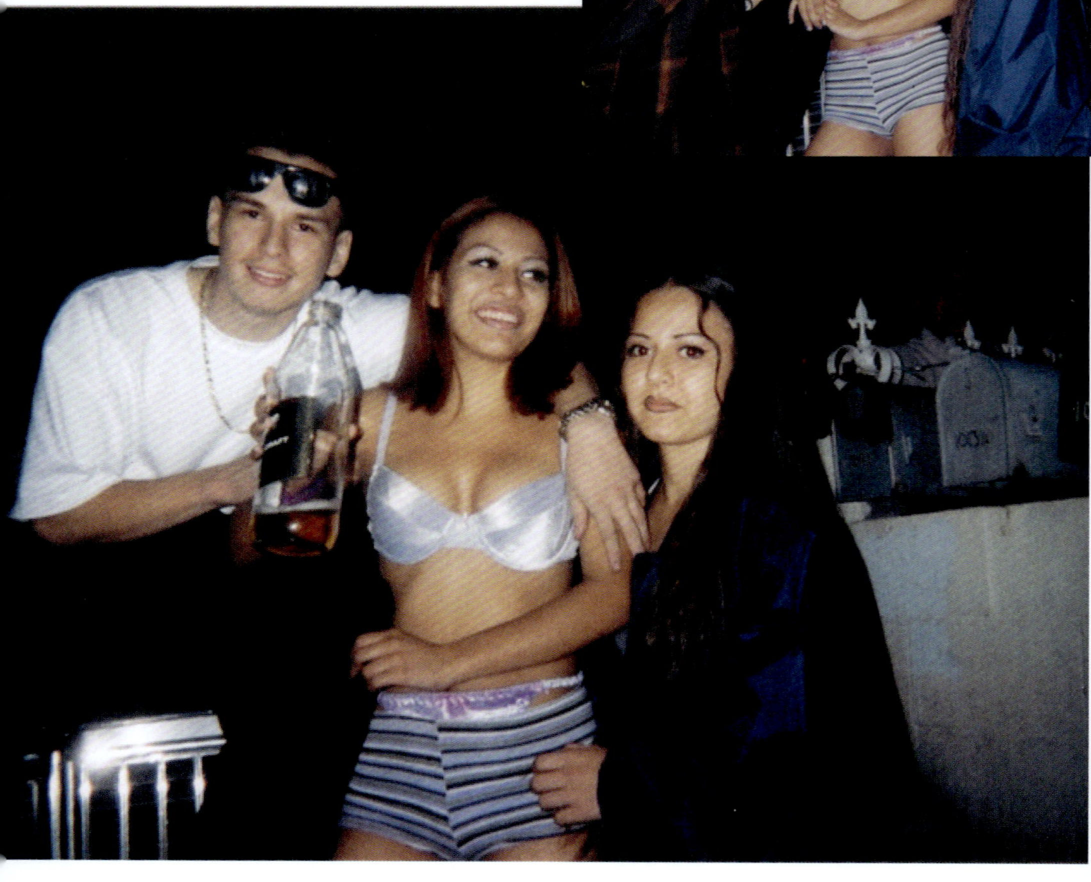

didn't make any noise and the adrenaline pumping in our veins as we prepared to leave the house.

Then came the excitement as we slid into our ride, stealing glances out the window at the dark alley and the house, making sure no light flicked on. Many nights, from midnight to 4 A.M., it was Maria, me, and our friends Silvia and Gina, riding in a friend's car—usually with Carlos and his crew. When Gina came along and her dog was left outside at night, locked into the gated area of the house, one of us would distract him so he wouldn't bark. We'd toss pieces of bologna or hot dog sausages over the fence, feeding him just enough to keep him quiet.

We were adventurous and daring together, sometimes driving through Turnbull Canyon with the headlights off, letting the darkness swallow us. Other nights, we'd cruise down Atlantic Boulevard to Cascade Park in Monterey Park, where we'd hang out near the old Art Deco–style fountain. It glowed under the streetlights, its cascading tiers glimmering through the city darkness.

We were just there to catch a quiet night under the humid, hazy night air. That place felt dreamy—like a backdrop for secrets, for being young, and feeling like the whole city was quietly ours. And maybe part of the thrill was knowing we had just snuck out—sometimes with friends our mom liked, and sometimes with others she wouldn't approve of. That mix, the risk and the secrecy, made everything feel even more electric.

If I didn't sneak out with Maria, I stayed in bed and looked out for her like a guardian angel. I stayed awake or got a light sleep so I could be ready for a knock on the window. Looking out for her was not a choice, it's an instinct. There were many times when I could hear Mom open the door to our room to check up on us in the middle of the night, and I felt like my heart stopped every time this happened and I knew Maria was out somewhere.

At first the bedroom felt empty without her, but I slowly got used to it. I never stopped worrying about her, and I never stopped being ready to open the window when she finally tapped. In many ways, she was my model and my mentor: the person who showed me how to push the limits that were imposed on us both.

OPPOSITE: Maria and me at a gangster party in City Terrace, circa 1996

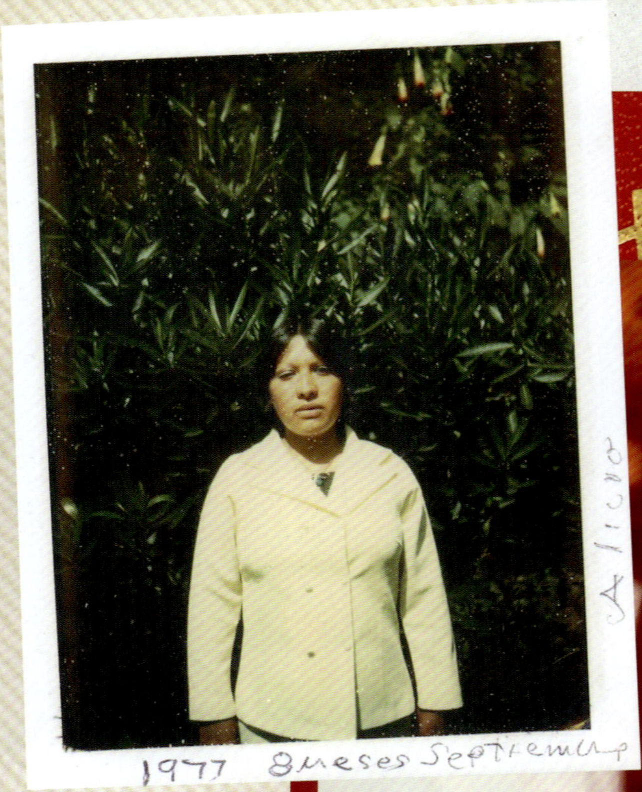

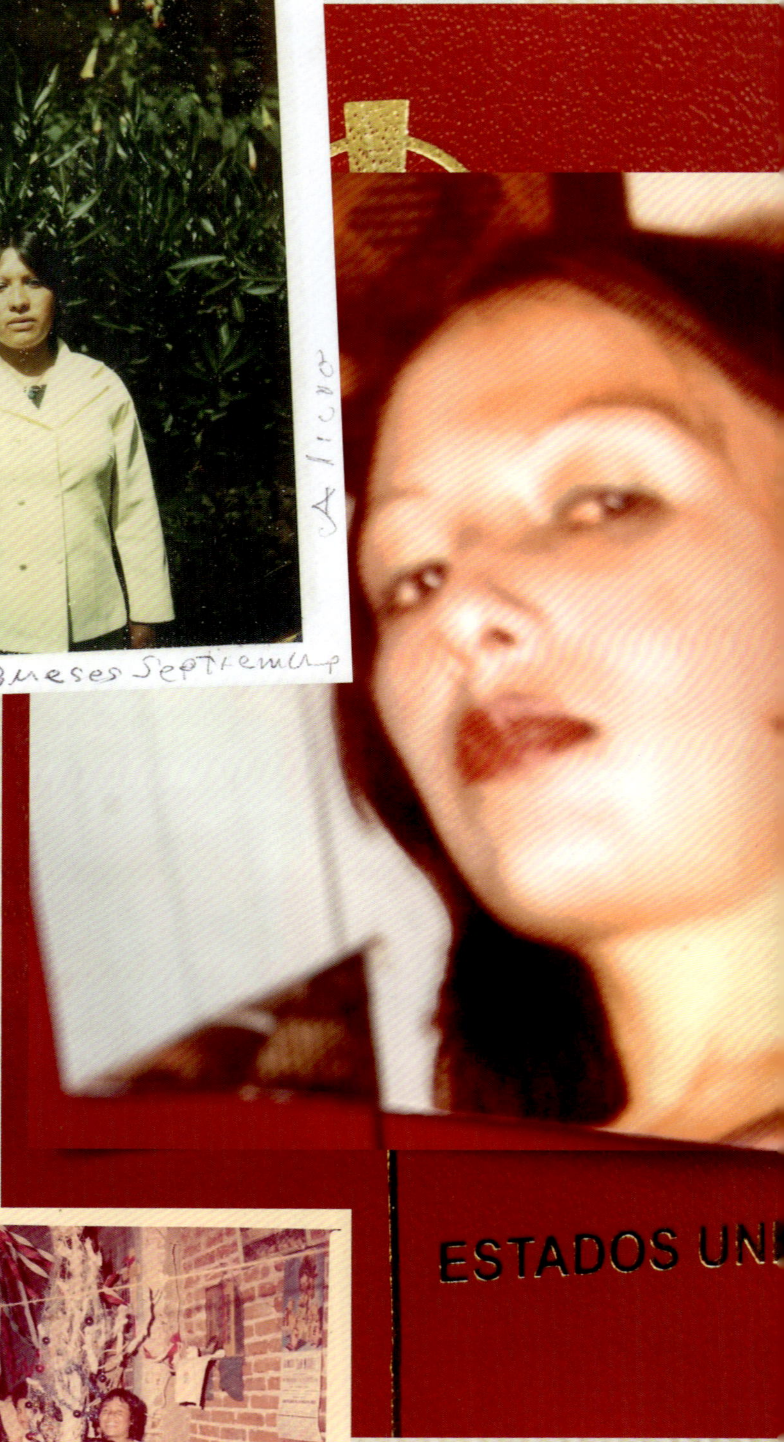

ABOVE: Mom, eight months pregnant in 1977, in Michoacán, Mexico

RIGHT: Mom in Redwood City in the '70s

BELOW: Mom in a yellow dress with her siblings during Christmas in Michoacán, Mexico, 1971

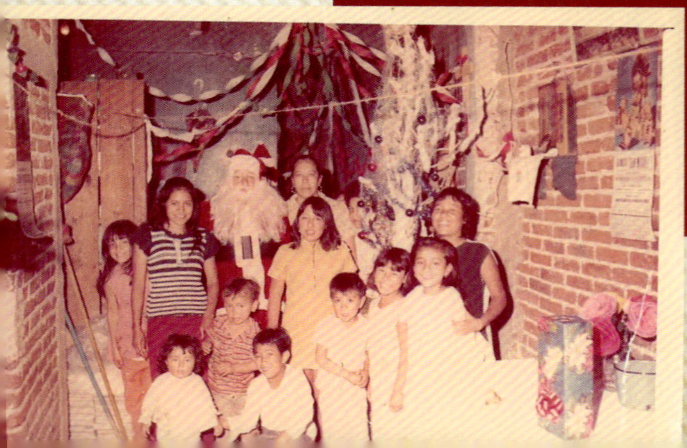

MOM

MY MOTHER IS A SMALL, PETITE WOMAN, pretty much the same height as me and Maria. (Our little sister is shorter.) She has black hair and shaved her natural eyebrows to paint them on with a thin pencil line. When we were kids, her nails were always long and painted red. She is private, quiet, and reserved, but with a toughness that held us all together. She is the most beautiful woman I know. She is the constant in our lives. Men are not.

My mom was born in Uruapan, Michoacán, part of a large family—eleven siblings in all. She was the middle child. She had her first baby, my brother Gus, at the age of twenty in 1977. Gus's dad left Mom when he found out she was pregnant, so she had to find ways to make ends meet. She and a friend decided to go to the U.S., and she left Gus with my grandmother. They were going to figure it out in California and then go get my brother. That's when she crossed the border for the first time—like so many others

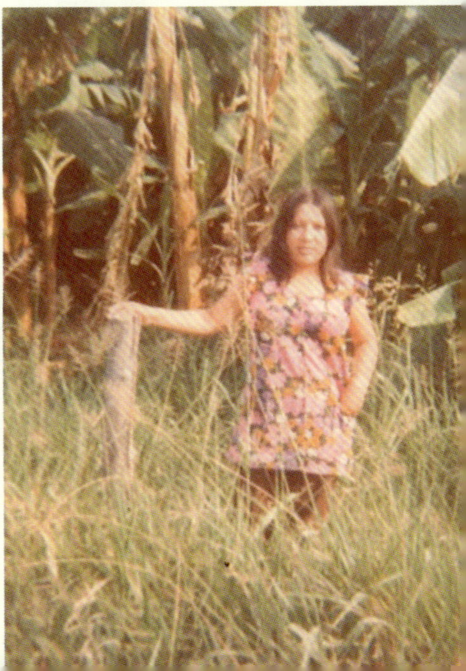

Mom at age sixteen in Michoacán, Mexico, 1973

before and after her. She was looking for something but she didn't know what exactly.

My mom had an uncle from her mom's side in the Bay Area, so she made that her destination: Fresno, California. He knew someone who was renting rooms in a compound of houses and she stayed there for a few months. That's where she met my dad in 1978. At the time, he was working in the fields and was also a janitor at a local school. Mom got a job as a babysitter and did everything she could to save her coins and send money back to Gus. She was a single mother with a young son waiting for her back in Michoacán. Still, she fell in love with my dad, and together they began a new life here in California.

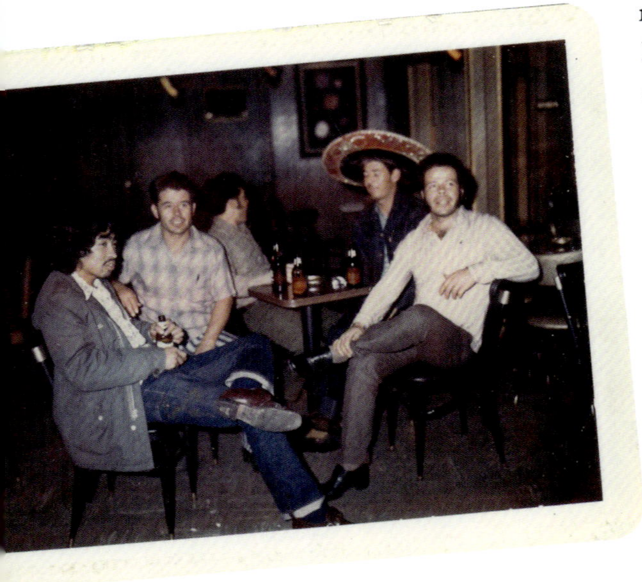

ABOVE: Mi papá on the right with friends, in the Bay in the '70s

OPPOSITE: Money orders and money wires sent by Mom to Michoacán for my brother Gus, circa mid-1980s

My mom had my older sister, Maria (but we called her by her middle name, Toñita, until she was around ten years old), in 1979, then me in 1980, and my younger sister, Gesenia (or Yesi), in 1982—all of us were born in Redwood City. But Mom never forgot her firstborn son. Even while living in the Bay, she kept making that difficult journey across the border to see him—once with me in her belly and Maria in her arms. Much later, when Mom left my father and started a relationship with my stepdad, came three more kids.

My father had family in L.A.—specifically in Boyle Heights and Lynwood—and since neither of them had many ties in the Bay, it made sense to move. So with the little money Mom had saved, they rented a U-Haul and made the drive to Los Angeles. I was just three years old. After we settled in L.A., my mom kept going back to the city of Uruapan, in Michoacán, Mexico, to see my brother. When she couldn't make the

CUSTOMER'S RECEIPT DO NOT SEND THIS RECEIPT FOR PAYMENT KEEP IT FOR YOUR RECORDS

3467413697 5 850419 900231 *95*00

SERIAL NUMBER YEAR MONTH DAY POST OFFICE U. S. DOLLARS AND CENTS

PAY TO FROM

STREET

CITY STATE ZIP

Uroopan Mich

CUSTOMER RECEIPT

This receipt is your guarantee of 100% refund if you ... or stolen, provided you fill in the Pay To and From ... money order in the space provided. No claim fo...

...eceipt ... Please ... order.

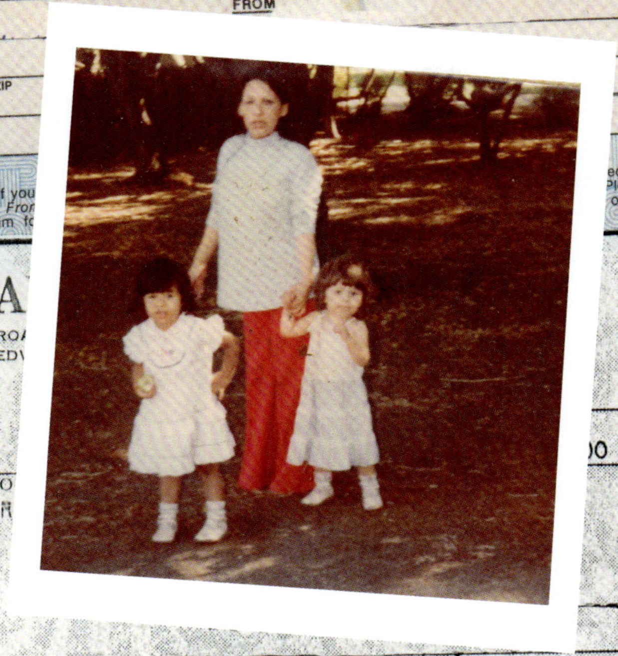

PERSONA...

WOODSIDE ROA...

REDV...

11-24/861
1210 (8)

19 85

THE ORDER OF

NOT GOOD FO...

WELLS FAR...

BANK

STREET ADDRESS

...S FARGO BANK, N.A. CITY STATE

⑆010264⑆ ⑆121000248⑆9861 503027⑈

REGISTERED NO. 327081009

POSTMARK ... NOT SEND THIS RECEIPT FOR PAY... KEEP IT FOR YOUR RECORDS

Post Office Completion			
Reg. Fee	$ 3.60	Special Delivery	$
Handling Charge	$	Return Receipt	$
Postage	$ 22	Restricted Delivery	$
Received by	Clarke	Intl	

Customer must declare Full value $ W

With Postal Insurance ... Without Postal Insurance ... $25,000 Domestic Ins...

...ST be in Ball Point or Typed

LOS A... 25 1986 USPS ... STA

POST OFFICE U. S. DOLLARS AND ...

FROM

STREET

CITY STATE

Los Angeles 9...

COD NO. OR USED FOR

...en, present thi... ...our Post Office

CUSTOMER'S RECEIPT DO NOT SEND THIS RECEIPT FOR PAYMENT KEEP IT FOR YOUR RECORDS

3668755717 1 851224 900231 *40*00

SERIAL NUMBER YEAR MONTH DAY POST OFFICE U. S. DOLLARS AND CENTS

CUSTOMER'S RECEIPT DO NOT SEND THIS RECEIPT FOR PAYMENT KEEP IT FOR YOUR RECORDS

3668842300 4 860124 900231 *50*00

trip herself, she sent money to my grandparents or to her older sister Liduvina (my aunt) or her brother Salvador.

The rhythm of the border became something she knew well. The journey was never easy for her—not the first time, nor the second, nor the third—but somehow, despite it all, she always made it. The desert itself was dangerous: long stretches of heat and cold and dust, the threat of dehydration, of getting lost.

Every crossing was a risk. And as a woman, she also faced the risk of being assaulted or raped—the kind of danger that made each journey even more uncertain. There were a handful of times when Mom was caught and detained by Border Patrol.

One time, she was carrying Maria, still just a baby, in her arms. Exhausted from running through the desert, Mom was out of breath, her body worn down, but Maria was quiet the whole time, as if she knew not to make noise. When the officers finally caught up with her group, they threw them onto a bus to Tijuana. At the Border Patrol station there, one of the officers made a pass at her. My mom broke down in tears, begging him to leave her alone.

He eventually backed off. He offered to help feed baby Maria, who had woken up crying from hunger. Desperate, my mom accepted. She handed him the empty baby bottle she carried in her bag, and he poured in regular milk watered down. About twenty minutes later, Maria started throwing up and had diarrhea. My mom thought he had given the baby spoiled milk intentionally, to punish her for rejecting him. Despite that, they made it back and Maria was okay.

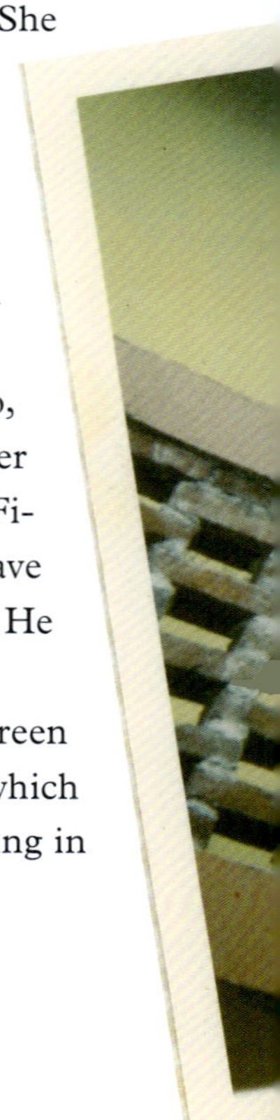

My father knew about the son Mom had left behind in Mexico, and he offered to help bring him to the U.S. In 1986, my mother brought Gus to L.A., and that's when I finally met my brother. Finally we could all be together. I remember how exciting it was to have him home. He was so shy and sweet, and he looked just like Mom. He must have been eight or nine years old then, and I was six.

The final step came in 1986, when my mom was granted a green card through Reagan's Immigration Reform and Control Act, which offered amnesty to undocumented immigrants who had been living in the U.S. since before 1982. She later became a U.S. citizen.

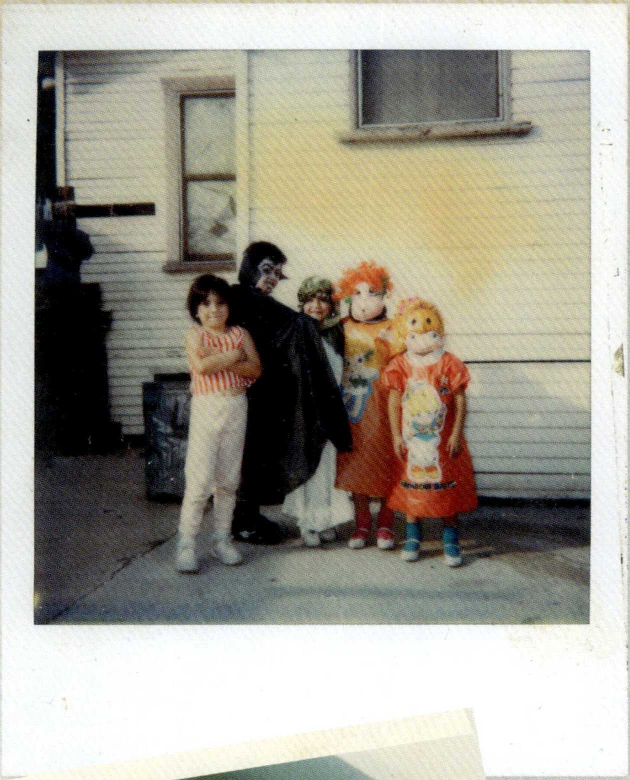

RIGHT: Mom made us Halloween costumes from scratch or bought us the cheap plastic ones from the dollar store, circa late 1980s.

BELOW: Mom and my brother Gus in Michoacán, Mexico, circa mid-1980s

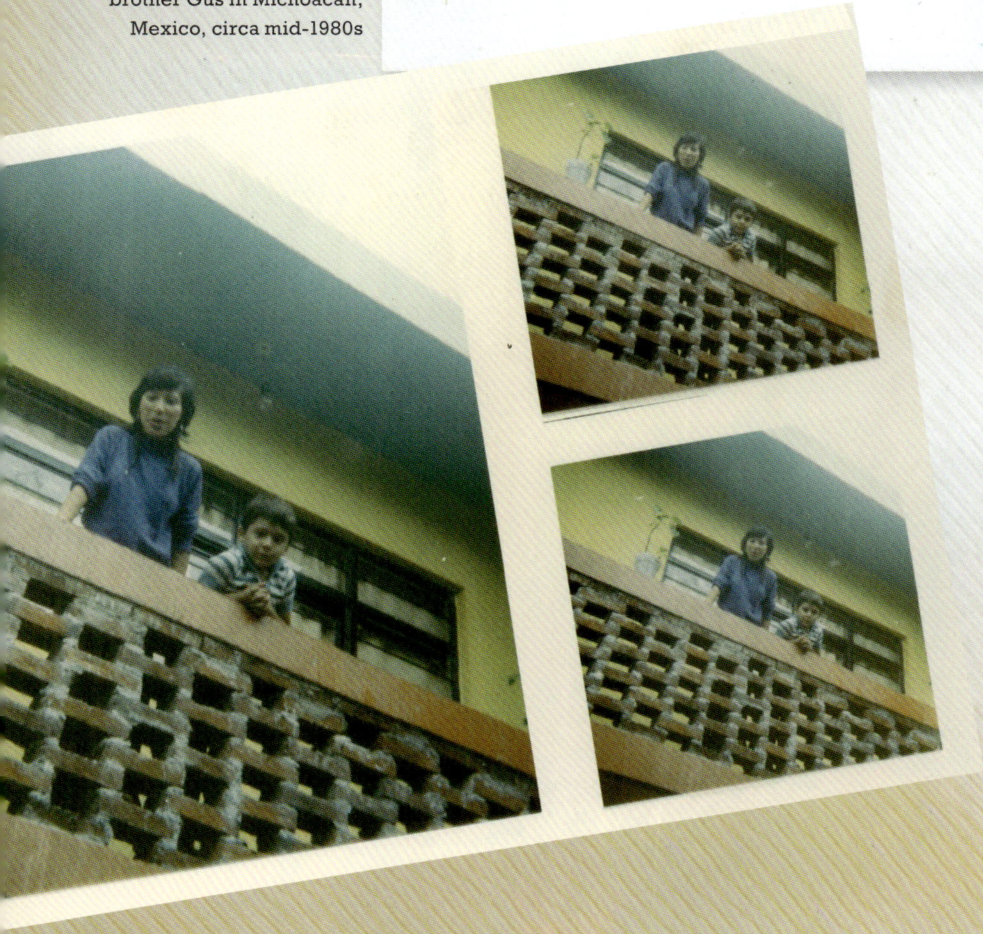

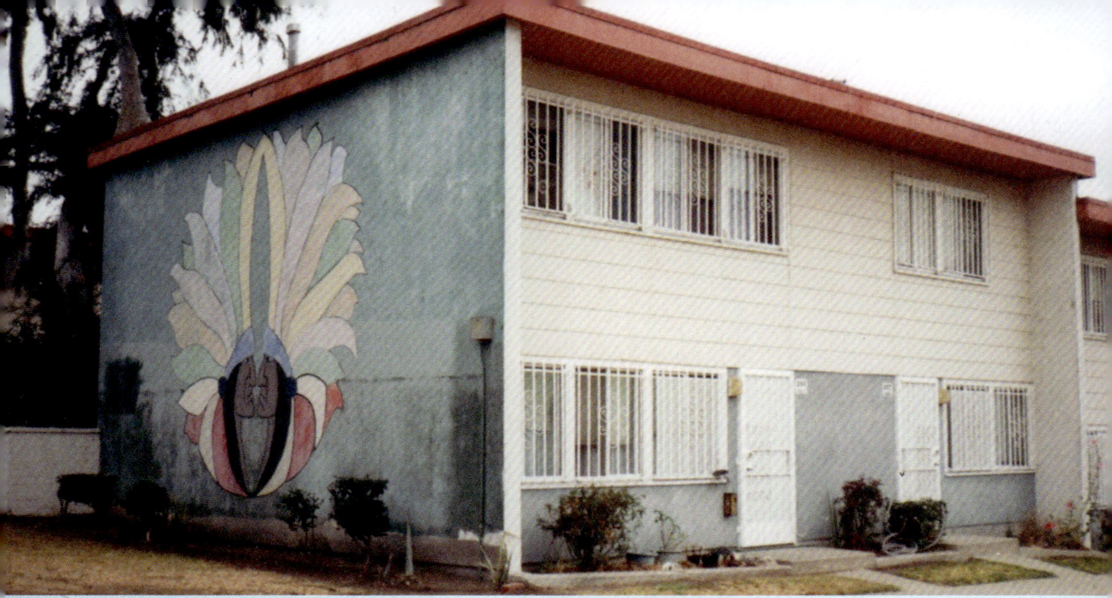

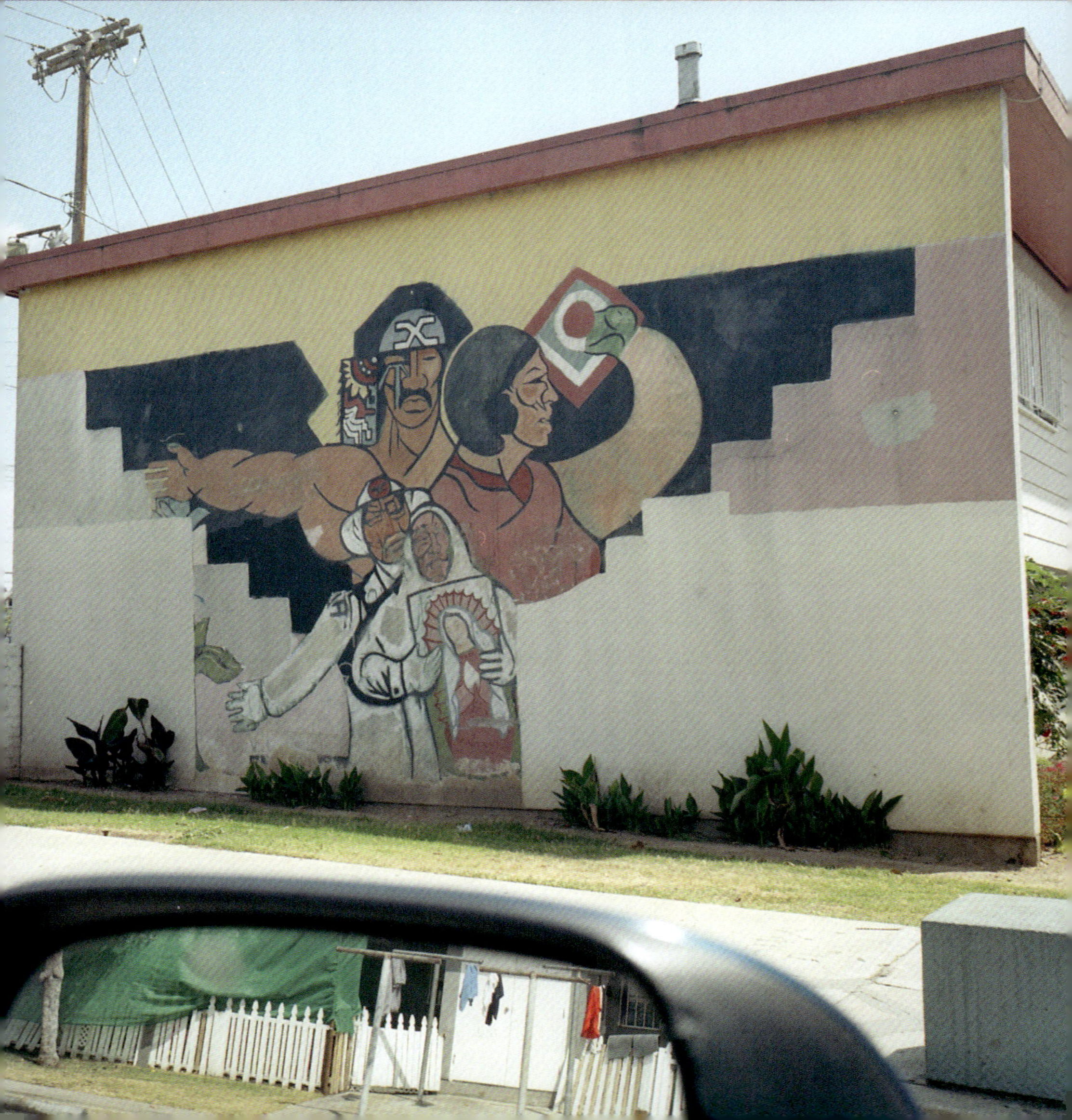

US AGAINST THE WORLD

DAD HAD RELATIVES HERE IN CALIFORNIA, BUT Mom didn't have any family of her own around, so our immediate family felt really close. She made friends easily—she had her comadres from the neighborhood and church. I remember Arcelia, who lived next door from us in Boyle Heights, and Pati, who lived in the Estrada Courts and visited pretty frequently. But it was mostly just us—Mom and her kids—no grandparents or tías nearby on her side. That's how it was from the start: Our little crew stuck together.

Gus reconnected with his biological father and was back and forth between our house and his father's in Orange County; every time he went there, he got into trouble and was sent back to us. Growing up it was mostly me, Maria, and Yesi: the sisterhood. The three of us did everything together, so when someone left, it felt like losing a limb.

Pre-K at Dacotah was the first time I was away from them, but especially from Maria. Those three hours felt like an eternity. For the first week of school I cried so much I made my chest hurt. My sister was a grade older and went to a different school, so each morning I'd get dropped off first before her. I'd grip the chain-link fence as I watched Mom and Maria walk away each morning.

The pain was unbearable for my little body—I can still feel the heaviness in my chest. Some people might say that looking out for someone this much is a good thing, but I

OPPOSITE: Murals in Estrada Courts

often wonder if it comes from a good place or from some sort of attachment I learned at a young age, separation anxiety or attachment disorder. In elementary school, I'd lie and tell my teacher I wasn't feeling well. The nurse would then call my mom so she could pick me up. Eventually Mom caught on and this stopped working.

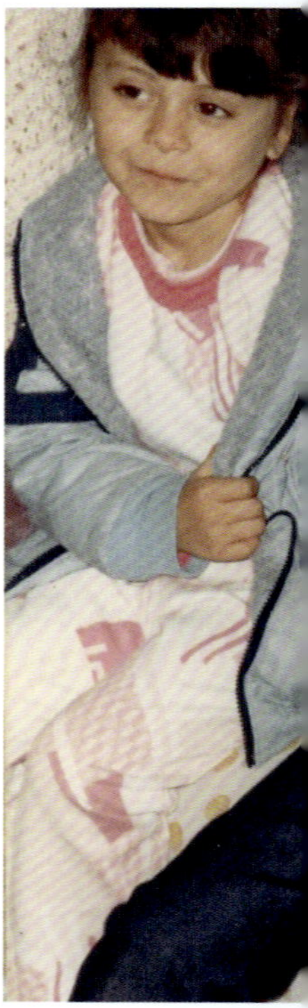

We moved around a lot in the Boyle Heights area in the '80s because Mom couldn't afford rent and Dad stopped working because he spent his days drinking and sleeping. We went from Spence and Siskiyou (I loved this little house because it had a beautiful apricot tree in the backyard that made the property smell sweet) to Hunter Street, between 8th and Spence Street. I went to several different elementary schools, never really settling into any of them except Lorena Elementary.

Our home on Hunter Street had a huge avocado tree that gave us plenty of shade. That's where we threw our birthday and First Communion parties. The house was built with light-blue Sawtelle wooden paneling. The interior was the same color as the outside: light blue, almost white. It was long and narrow like a shoebox but the perfect size for us. The kitchen was big and open, with a hand-me-down stove that felt like it had already lived many lives. One of my favorite things about living there was sitting on the stoop in the summer, watching TV outside in the warm air.

But as my dad's alcoholism worsened, our home became increasingly unsafe and violent. The violence came from Mom due to her frustrations and anger toward Dad, who neglected us and was unreliable. In 1987, when I was seven years old, our mother finally left him. It happened after one of their fights turned physical. My mom had reached her breaking point—tired of him spending what little money they had on alcohol while she held everything together.

Dad wasn't a violent man by nature. When he wasn't drinking and at home—which was rare—he could be the sweetest father anyone could ask for and he loved braiding my hair. It's one of the things I remember—how gentle and patient he was when he separated the strands and then wove them together. But those moments were few and far between. Most of the time he was gone, and when he did show up, he was drunk and passed out on the couch or floor. My mom bore the brunt of everything. She finally made a choice—it was us over him and his alcoholism.

RIGHT: Mom and Dad in our Boyle Heights home on Christmas Eve circa mid-1980s

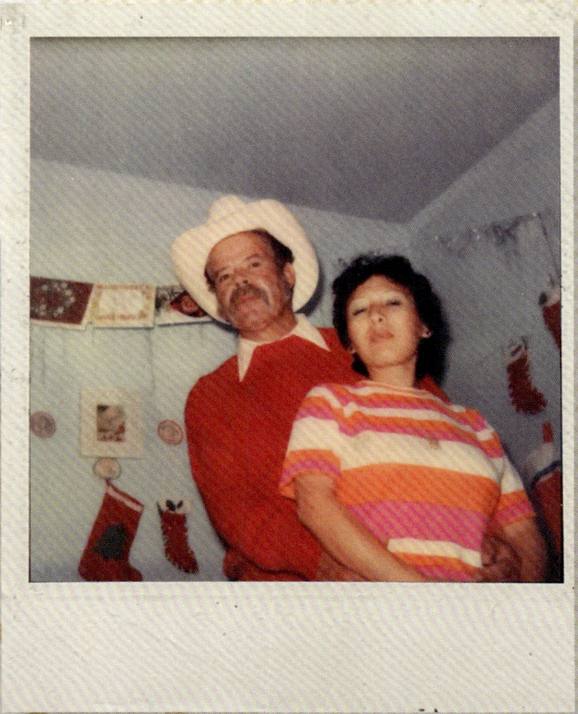

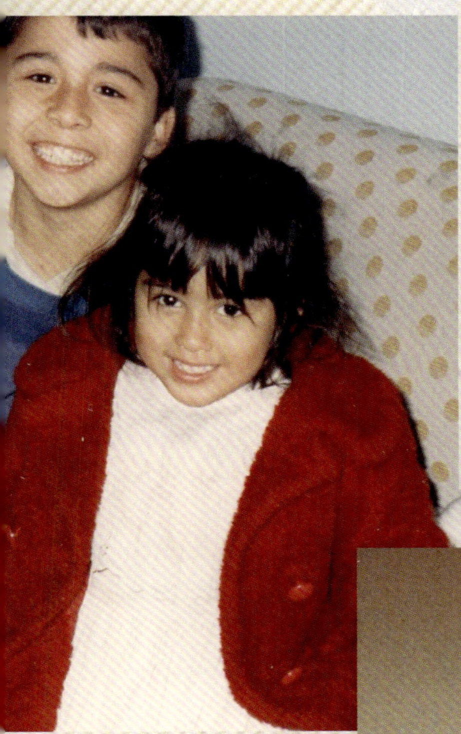

ABOVE: With our brother Gus at home in Boyle heights, mid-1980s. My uncle Manuel had come to visit and drop off Christmas presents.

RIGHT: Mom and Dad after an argument in Boyle Heights around 1986

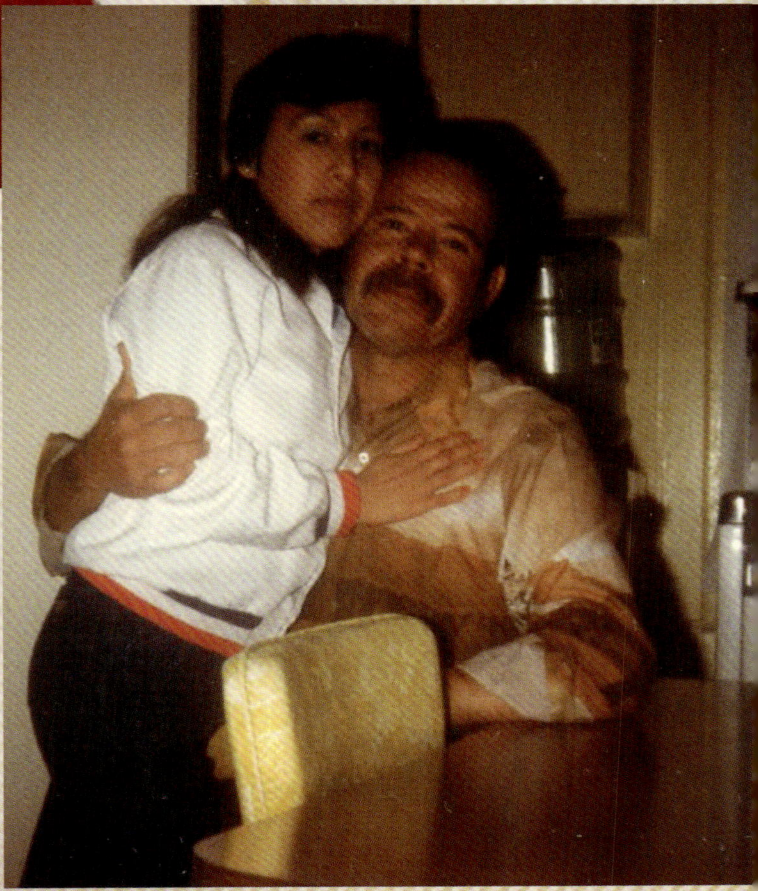

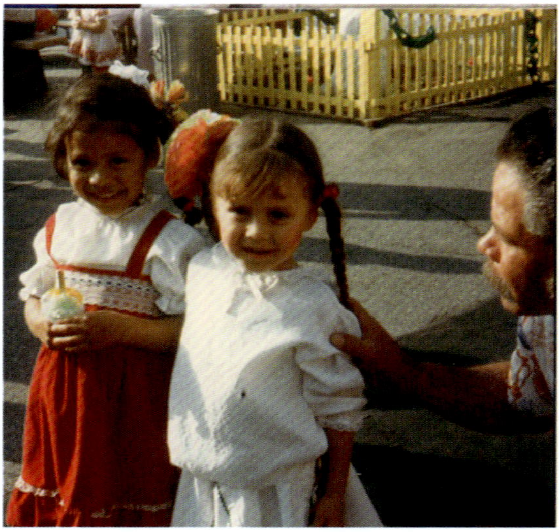

After school on Cinco de Mayo, Lorena Elementary

That day he came home drunk, they started arguing, and her frustration boiled over. She slapped him and stood up against him. He shoved her. She scratched at him with her long red nails, trying to push him off. Blood ran down his arms and chest. Then he called the police and told them she'd tried to stab him with a knife.

That wasn't true, of course, but the cops believed him and arrested our mom immediately right in front of us. She would never stab him no matter how difficult he made her life. I felt horrible, scared, confused. The whole block came outside, and the neighbors were arguing with the cops. Neighbors knew how good a woman she was, which is why they came out to protect her from the police. It was chaos.

My first confrontation with the police happened that day when they arrested my mom and took my two sisters, my brother, and me in a separate police car to the station. On the way there the cops were driving fast to scare us, giving us our first taste of intimidation. We were all sitting in the back, behind the partition, bouncing around on the hard seats. They laughed as they humiliated us; then they took us to McDonald's as a reward for being "tough." When we got to the police department, we saw our mom in handcuffs, crying. Then we all cried and tried breaking the handcuffs off her. My little sister, Yesi, even tried using her index finger to unlock the handcuffs, not knowing how handcuffs even worked, but she tried as tears ran down her face. That was the last time we saw Mom for quite some time. Weeks passed, then months, without our protector.

Being separated from our mother for months felt like an eternity. We all ended up in foster homes scattered around Los Angeles. One of the houses that took us in separated me from my sisters and put us in different rooms. There were nights when I could hear Yesi crying in the room next door, and it broke my heart. I wanted so badly to sneak out of my room and go comfort her, to tell her everything would be okay. But I couldn't because we were told to stay in our rooms and go to sleep. I felt completely helpless, like I couldn't protect her from the hurt she was feeling.

After my mom was released from jail and we all came back home, our bond only grew stronger. She promised us she would never leave us. Those nights, we weren't just kids and a mom—we were a unit. "Nadie les va a hacer daño," Mom would say. Nobody is going to hurt you. "Nosotros contra el mundo." Us against the world. And for a little while, that's exactly how it felt. After leaving Dad, Mom began to blossom, showing us what strength and resilience looked like—no matter what tried to stand in our way.

After Mom left Dad, it was only her and the four of us—Gus, Maria, me, and Yesi (Gesenia). We were like a wolf pack and Mom was the alpha. We would all get in the tub together, pretending it

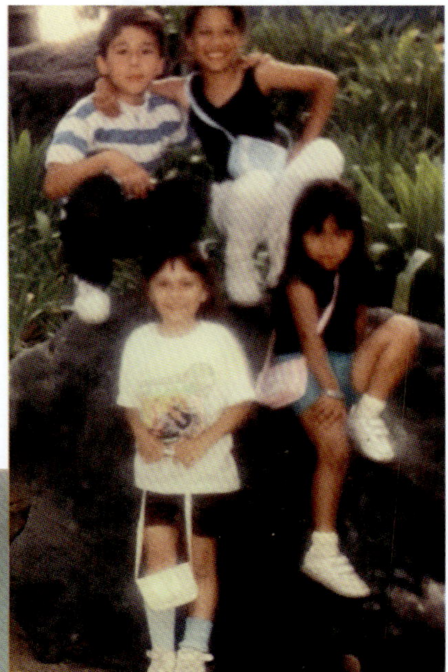

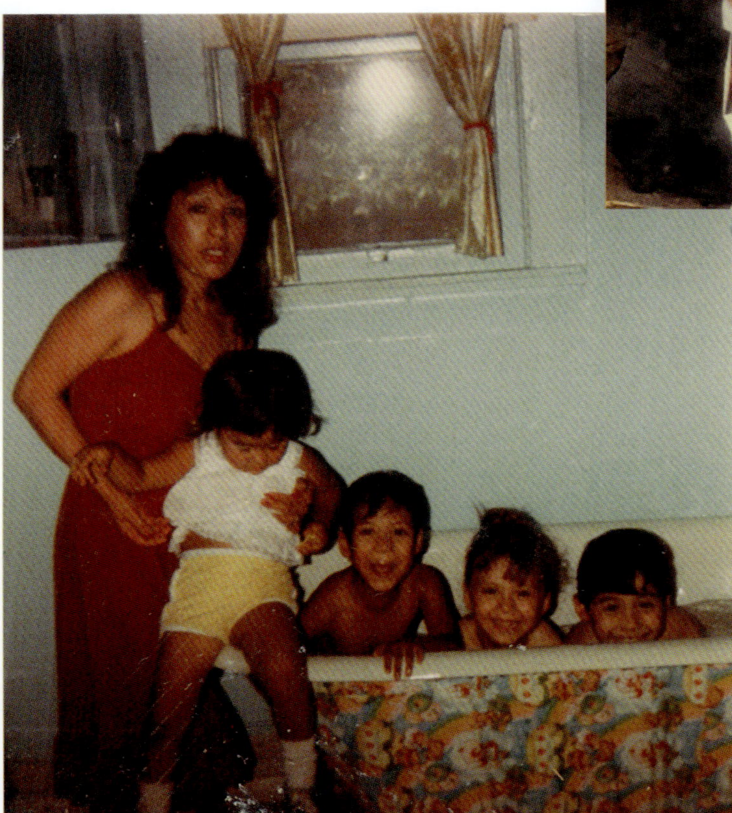

ABOVE: My siblings and me in Commerce. Mom loved taking photos of us, circa late '80s.

LEFT: Gus, Maria, Yesi, and me in the tub with Mom, Boyle Heights, mid-1980s

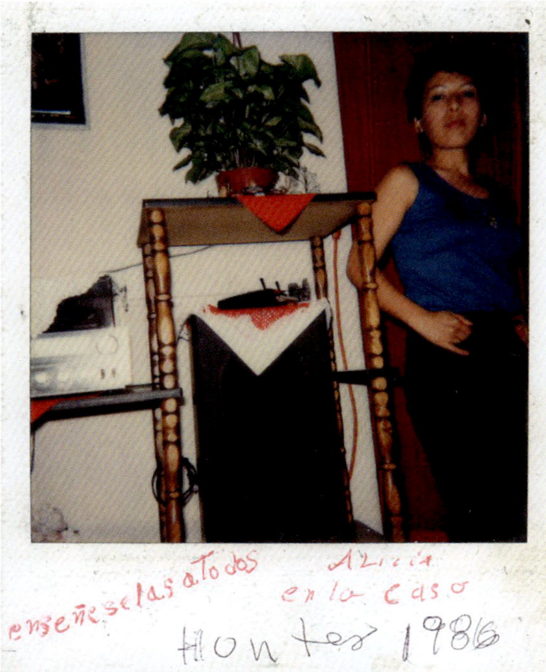

Mom standing proud by her home furniture. She cut her hair off and started to regain her power.

was a pool. We had movie nights and all four of us fell asleep on Mom's bed and nobody complained. Like a five-headed mythical creature. The next day we'd wake up and have cozy mornings in bed all together.

My mom always stayed busy, especially after she left my dad. She worked at a warehouse in City of Commerce packing makeup—lipstick, eyelashes, press-on nails—and took a cosmetology and prosthetic makeup class. She also had a social life. She'd take us to the swap meet (where I saw Chico Che perform a few times) and to local fairs, and she'd have us run errands with her. Before she had a car, she took us everywhere on the RTD bus.

Then she learned how to drive and bought herself a beat-up blue station wagon. That car rocked me to sleep on countless rides, especially in the thick of L.A.'s hot summer rush hour. Even sitting in traffic felt like a beautiful dream—the hum of the engine, the sun pouring in, the world passing slowly by.

At night, she took us with her to adult school at East Los Angeles College because sometimes she couldn't afford a babysitter. We'd wait in the car for a couple of hours in the parking lot, playing and wrestling and beating one another up and watching the night go by until Mom finished her computer and English classes.

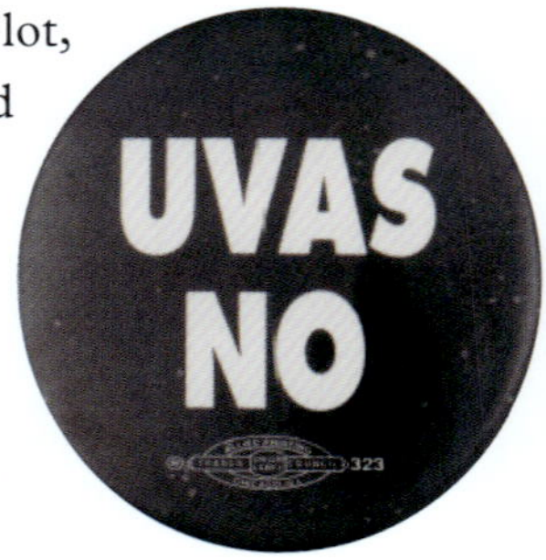

I remember going to protests together—Yesi in a stroller, all of us walking up Broadway, which is now César Chávez Avenue. We'd meet at Cinco Puntos and march all the way to downtown.

It might've been a "No Uvas" protest, part of the boycott against grapes in support of the United Farm Workers, or another march connected to labor rights and immigrant justice. There were many others that I can't remember, but what stuck with me is how great it felt to march with my family.

In the late '80s and early '90s, these movements were everywhere—the legacy of César Chávez and Dolores Huerta was still alive in the streets. The protests were loud, colorful, and full of energy. I didn't understand much of it, but I knew this was one way we spent time together as a family. Being out there with my mom felt like a kind of ritual—holding signs we barely understood but also somehow feeling the weight of what they meant. It was one of the few times we saw our community come together in public, and the beginning of my journey of activism.

Before she met my stepdad in 1989, my mother was very independent, loving but still strict, and we had a lot of respect for her. To Mom's friends, we were very good kids. Then our mom welcomed a predator into our home, and that's when everything changed and so did we. Our stepdad forced Mom to stop working and manipulated her by telling her he would take care of her. She would occasionally take random jobs babysitting but mostly stayed home—we could see she was miserable. We

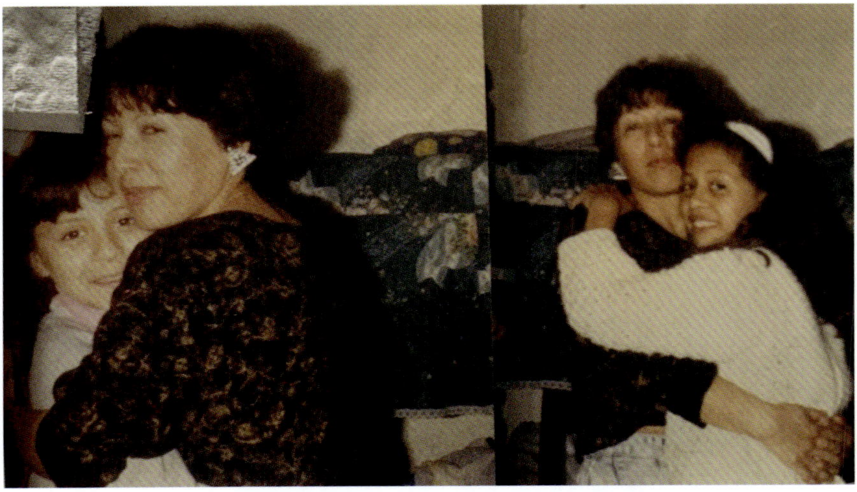

Mom and me (left); Mom and Maria dancing (right), early 1990s in East L.A. We're in our first apartment in East L.A., on Montebello Park Way and Whittier Boulevard, near Simmons Avenue.

witnessed this, and it enraged us. My mom wasn't herself anymore. He had come between us.

A man we barely knew—a stranger, really—had suddenly moved in with us and created chaos in every possible way. He changed our dynamic in creepy ways, and made what had been comfortable, sacred, and easy into uncomfortable and tense. I noticed my sister Maria change. Gradually, she went from being timid and quiet to being an angry teenager.

She stopped respecting our mom, carried resentment, and pushed back in ways I had never seen before. It didn't take long before I followed. I stopped listening to our mom's rules, too. My stepfather's presence forced us into survival mode—fending for ourselves, rebelling, and becoming different versions of who we were.

After my mom and stepdad had Alex in 1990, when I was nine, my stepdad started creating a separation between his kids and us. That same year, Junior, my stepdad's son from a previous marriage, moved in with us after his mother passed away; he was six years old at the time.

With these two new boys in the home, my stepdad would throw verbal jabs at us with the implication that we weren't his kids and he only took care of his own. That created more tension in our home. The bond we had with our mother began to fray.

The friction in our family was especially hard to handle because we had so little room, so little privacy. For a short time, eight of us lived in a studio apartment in East L.A.: my mom, stepdad, me, Maria and Yesi, Gus, Junior, and Alex. In 1992, as the family grew, we moved into a one-bedroom apartment just a block away.

I'll never forget that place: an old, roach-infested one-bedroom. My mom and stepdad were the only ones with a room of their own. The rest of us—Junior, Alex, my two sisters, and I—slept in the living room in bunk beds. (Gus reconnected with his father and occasionally lived with him in Orange County.) Even though this new place was technically bigger, I preferred the studio. It was cleaner. In the one-bedroom, no matter how often we cleaned, mopped, and swept, the roaches never seemed to die.

MOVING AROUND WAS exhausting for all of us, and as we got older, we got more complicated and independent. The groundings and cintarazos just didn't work anymore, and even though we eventually moved into a more spacious house, it wasn't big enough to hold us. My siblings and I were finding a sense of belonging outside our home with new friends in the neighborhood: East Los Angeles was the perfect place for this, as our own home became less safe with our stepdad starting arguments and constantly making us uncomfortable and Mom threatening to call the cops on us to get them to arrest us. These threats were her way of trying to de-escalate the situation. After all, we were all afraid of the police, including her. My life shifted from "My siblings and my mom and me against the world" to "Me and my two sisters against the world."

Almost every weekend, you'd find us and our friends walking down Whittier Boulevard—whether it was chilly or a hot summer night. Across the street from my house was Beto's Market, where we'd pick up snacks—sodas and ice cream, or Flamin' Hot Cheetos to munch on. I loved cherry- or watermelon-flavored Blow Pops, or really anything that would turn our tongues red and sweet.

My cousin Danny was all about orange soda. I'll never forget how I found out that was his favorite drink. It was a Sunday night, and we were bored at home. Danny was about thirteen at the time. He said he was heading over to Beto's Market to grab some Hot Cheetos and an orange soda, and my sister Yesi and I decided to tag along. This is around the time when us three hung out a lot. We walked to the store, grabbed our snacks, and headed back home with big smiles on our faces. Then, as we were crossing the street, a navy-blue Chevy Astro van came up beside us, blocking our way to the alley to go home.

Our house was just a few feet away, which felt like an arm's length, but the van trapped us—a wall behind us and an open view of Whittier Boulevard in front of us. I remember I could see the dark night sky peeking out of the top of the van and buildings in the background. The door of the van slid open, and two big guys got out, walking right up to Danny—just a thirteen-year-old in his Raiders football jersey, Solo pants, Nike Air Maxes, and fresh fade, still a kid.

They started demanding "Where are you from?!" and Danny kept saying "Nowhere." Then, just like that, one of them threw a punch and said, "This is Marianna Maravilla." The next thing we knew, they were jumping him, throwing him to the ground, ripping his Raiders football jersey off, and dragging him on the ground like a rag doll. One guy even took one of Danny's shoes and tossed it over an abandoned building behind us.

After a few punches the gang gave up, realizing my cousin wasn't from a gang because he didn't budge. I feel like that night was what made him consider joining a gang, though. Protection is real, and knowing you are walking in your own territory, even if you get hit up by a rival gang, you feel some sense of protection because you are on your turf. It makes sense that someone would want to protect themselves, you know? People get that sense of security from knowing they have a place to call their own. But it wasn't something that happened every day—not back then, at least.

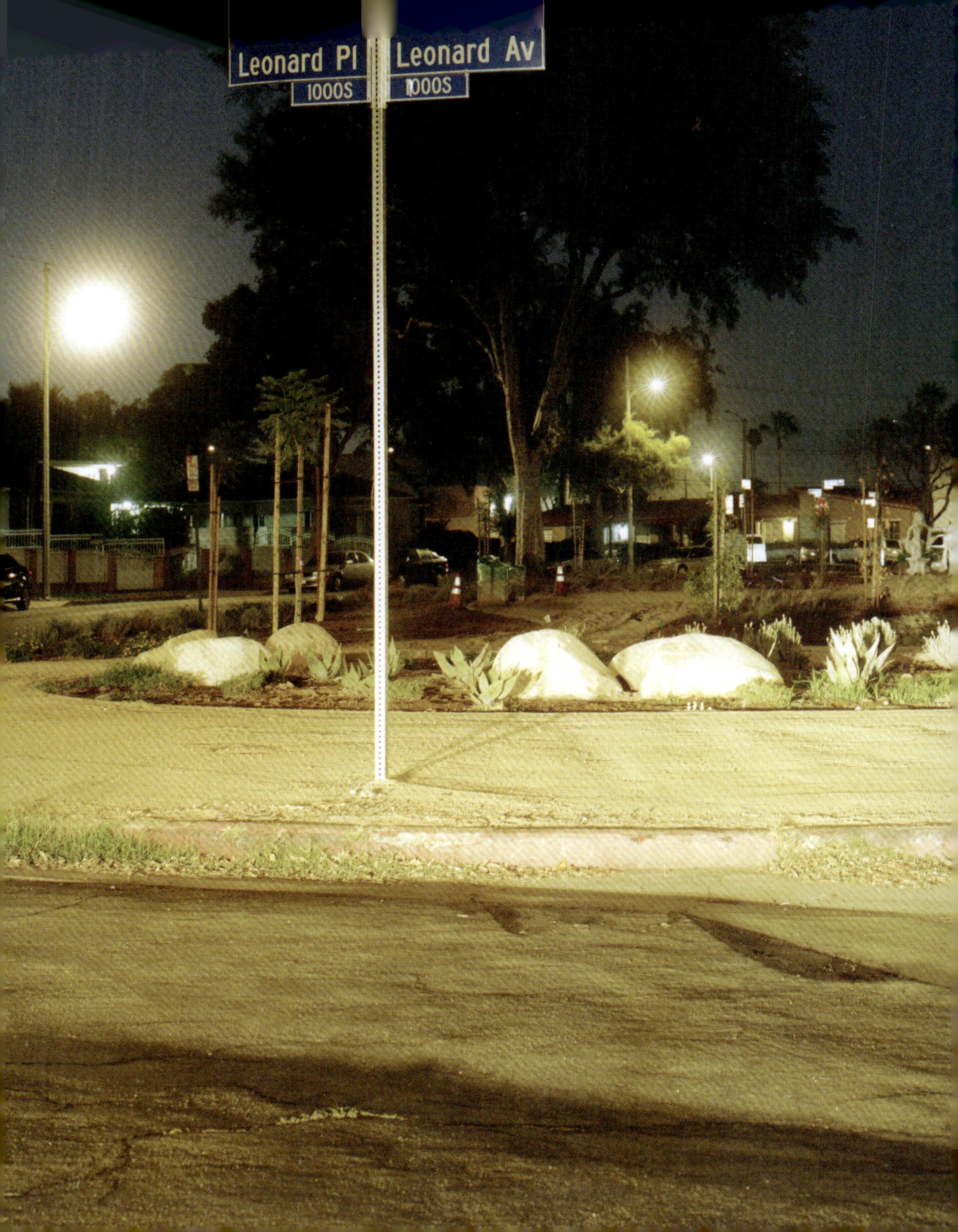
Leonard Pl
1000S
Leonard Av
1000S

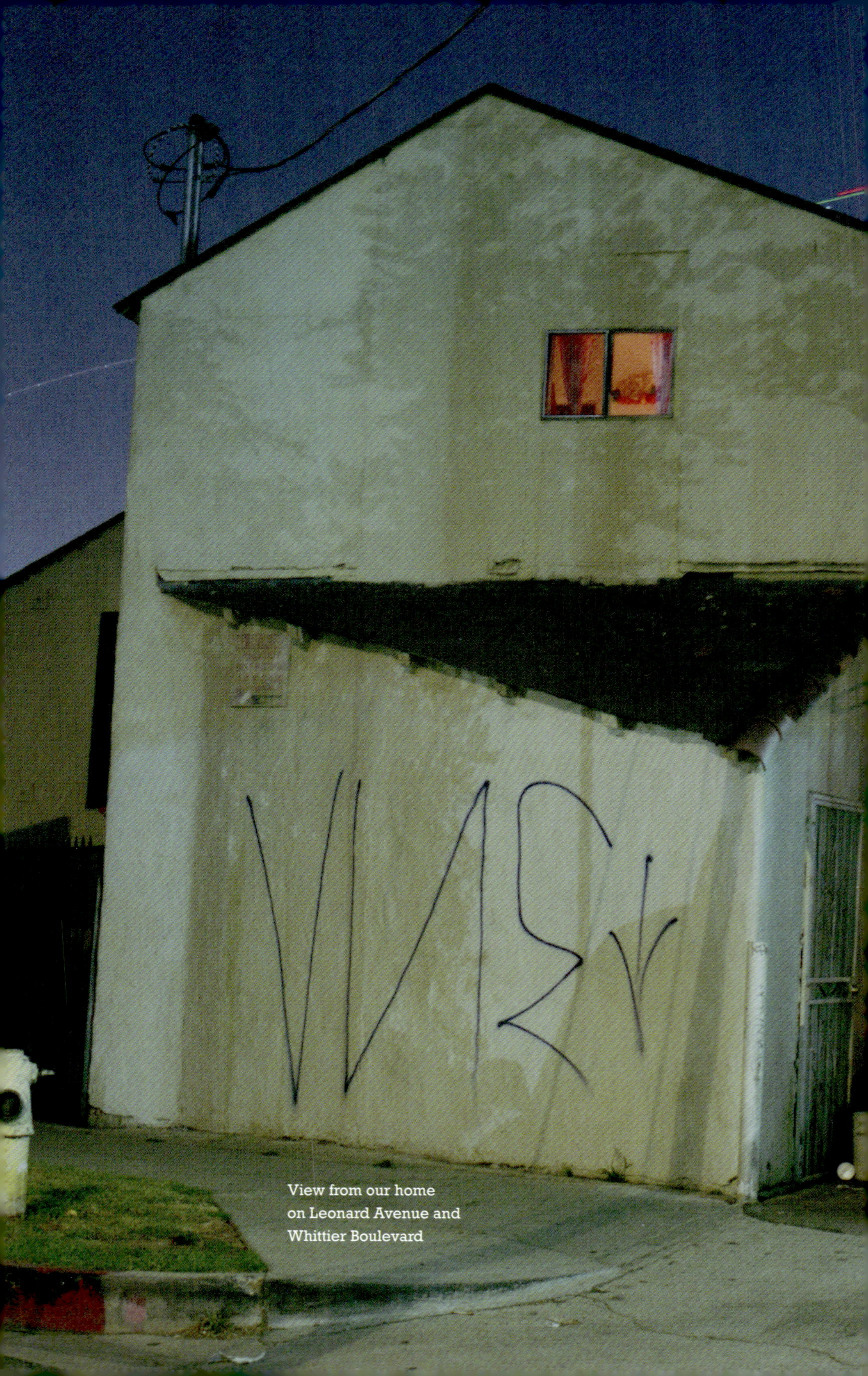

View from our home
on Leonard Avenue and
Whittier Boulevard

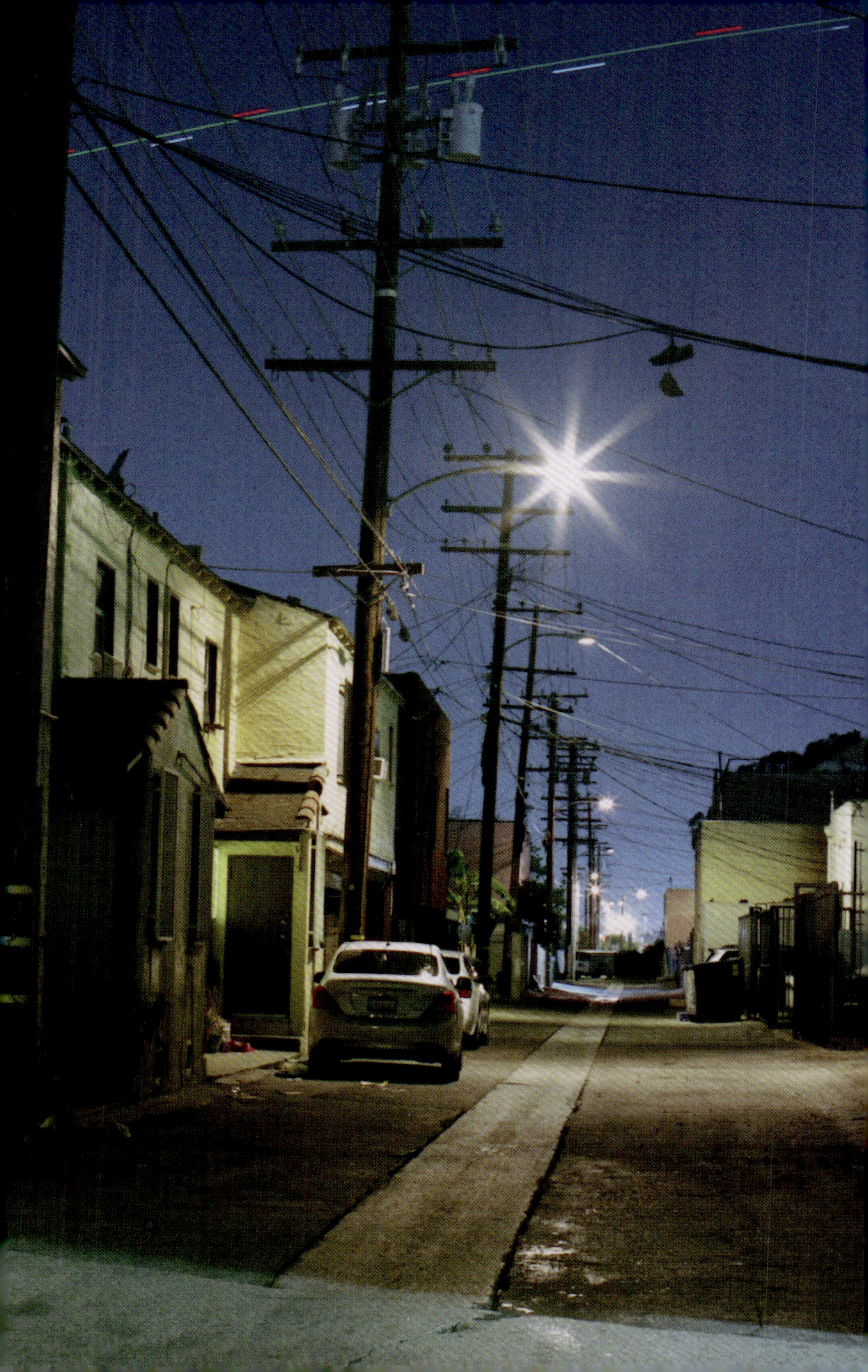

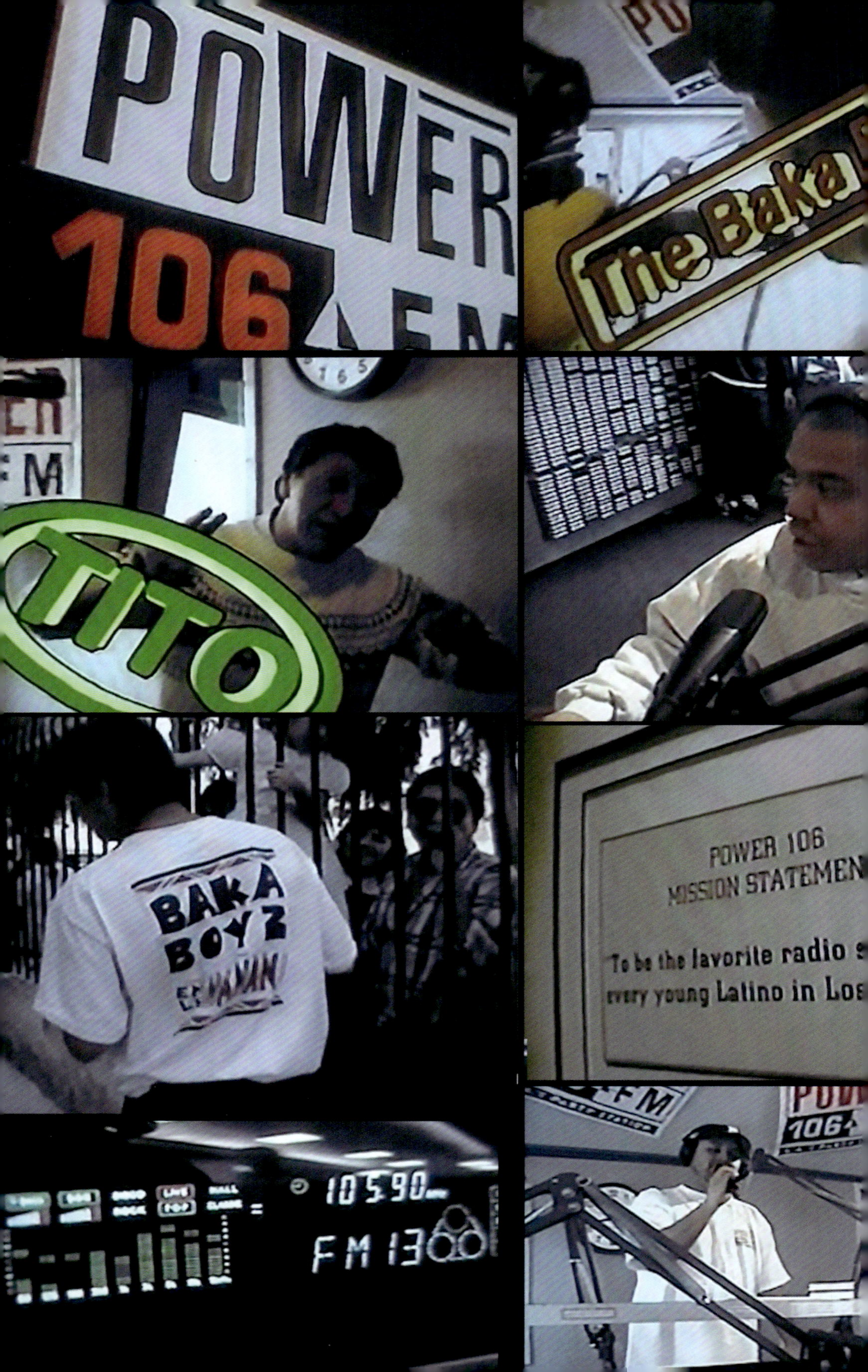

POWER
106
The Baka
TITO
BAKA
BOYZ
POWER 106
MISSION STATEMEN
To be the favorite radio
every young Latino in Los
105.90
FM 13
106

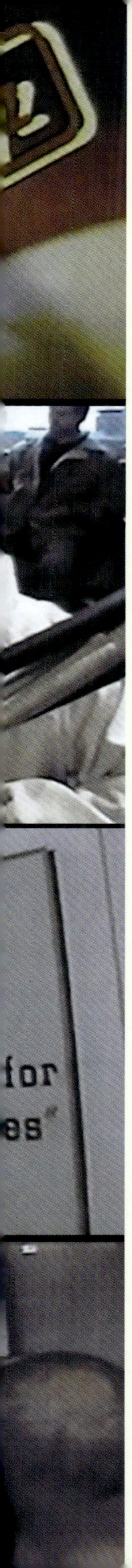

SCHOOL DAZE

MARIA AND I WENT TO THE SAME MIDDLE school in Montebello: Eastmont Intermediate. The school has a 1930s Art Deco architecture and is on Bradshawe and Beverly Boulevard, walking distance to Astro Burger on Beverly. There were so many cool kids at that school—mostly taggers and party-crew kids—and me, an eleven-year-old, wanting either to be like them or at least be their friend. Maria and I were the quiet ones in our circle—she was shier early in middle school—though it took me longer to build a circle of my own. We'd meet between classes and sit together at lunch, and little by little our circles began to overlap—her friends becoming mine, and mine becoming hers.

Still, her friends were different from mine, and even a little different from Maria. They already had boyfriends, were flirty, and were the ones who first taught my sister how to steal. Mine were a little more innocent, a little younger. Maria's friends also taught me a lot because they were little rebels who cracked me and Maria open by always including me in their plans and welcoming me into their circle—I sat with them on our lunch break and hung out with them in front of the school every day before and after school. On middle-school dance nights, I partied with my sister and her friends.

Each morning I watched Maria get ready for school as I lay in bed across from her. Maria had an alarm clock next to her bed set for 6 A.M. Monday through Friday. The alarm went off. The Baka Boyz morning show was playing, overlapped by an irritating alarm beep. It woke up everyone in the house. She'd get out of bed and pull out a Caboodles box full of makeup, scrunchies, and hairpins that she kept safe under her bed. Her showers lasted about an hour, which irritated everyone. Her looks and hygiene came first, and the rest of us made it work. Once she was done, it was time for the rest of us to use the bathroom—to brush our teeth, comb our hair.

Some of us showered the night before, and some had to take quicker showers in the morning. When Maria finally opened the door, the scent of Herbal Essences or VO5 shampoo and conditioner lingered, while Power 106 blared from the radio inside. She teased her bangs with the palm of her hand, working in small, circular motions to add volume. With the other, she sprayed her hair down with a mix of spray and mousse, their fragrance filling the room. She never skipped steps.

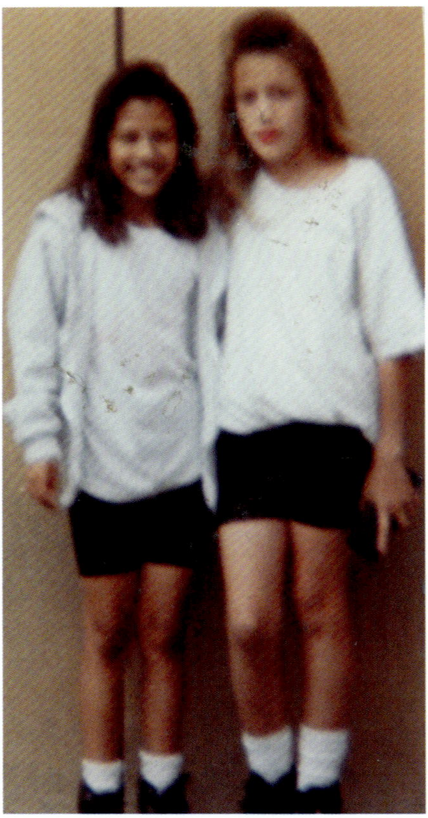

Maria and Silvia on the last day of school at Eastmont Intermediate, 1992. Their shirts were supposed to be a "last day of school autograph shirt," but they got in trouble and their markers were taken away.

In middle school, Maria would pick out her outfit the night before and lay it on her bed. She usually wore leggings or bike shorts and oversized T-shirts; she kept it simple. She planned ahead so she wouldn't be in a rush in the morning.

It took Maria over an hour to get ready. Me, on the other hand, I could be ready in thirty minutes, tops. I rushed through the shower, or sometimes I'd shower the night before. I didn't wear much makeup—I mostly just curled my eyelashes and made sure my face didn't look oily. Mornings were still a temporary chaos, but the minute we stepped outside, the house got quiet like after a storm.

Once Maria was done getting ready, we'd add a splash of CK One, Sunflowers, or a Bath & Body Works spray. Our morning walks were usually a bit chilly and gloomy, and we'd always carry a hooded sweatshirt or windbreaker, since they were in style. We'd grab our Trapper Keeper binders and, with an empty stomach, walk to school.

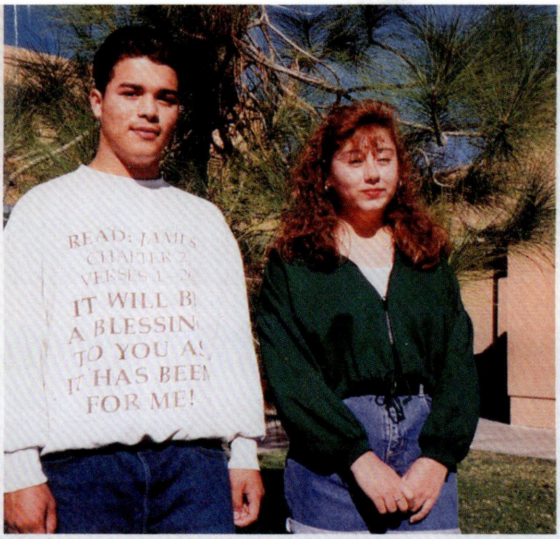

8th GRADE FAVORITES

BEST EYES *BILL PRECIADO AND LISETTE TELLO (above)*

MOST STUDIOUS *STANLY LAM AND TU HUYNH (below)*

NICEST SMILE *BOBBY SOLORIO LUCY ESCANUELA*

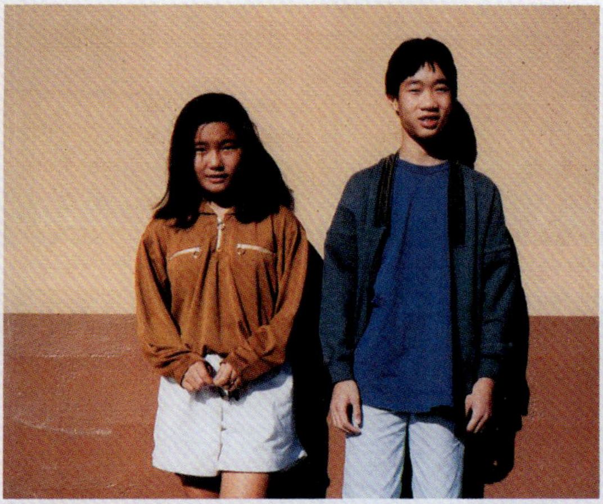

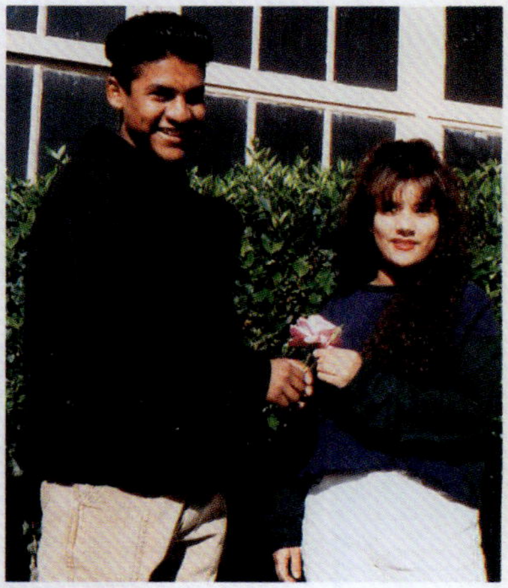

SURVEY

FAVORITE MOVIE	FAVORITE WAYS TO EARN MONEY	FAVORITE WAYS TO SPEND OUR MONEY ON	FAVORITE TYPE OF CLOTHING	WHAT WE WOULD CHANGE IN THE WORLD
1)T.2.	1)ASK PARENTS	1)CLOTHES	1)CASUAL	1)POVERTY
2)BOYZ-N-THE-HOOD	2)CHORES	2)MUSIC	2)HOUSE	2)SCHOOL
3)HOUSE PARTY 2	3)BABY SITTING	3)JUNK FOOD	3)NEW WAVE	3)VIOLENCE

IA AND

REZ

TE T.V.
IE
S
GARTH
DA
H
NA
GATE

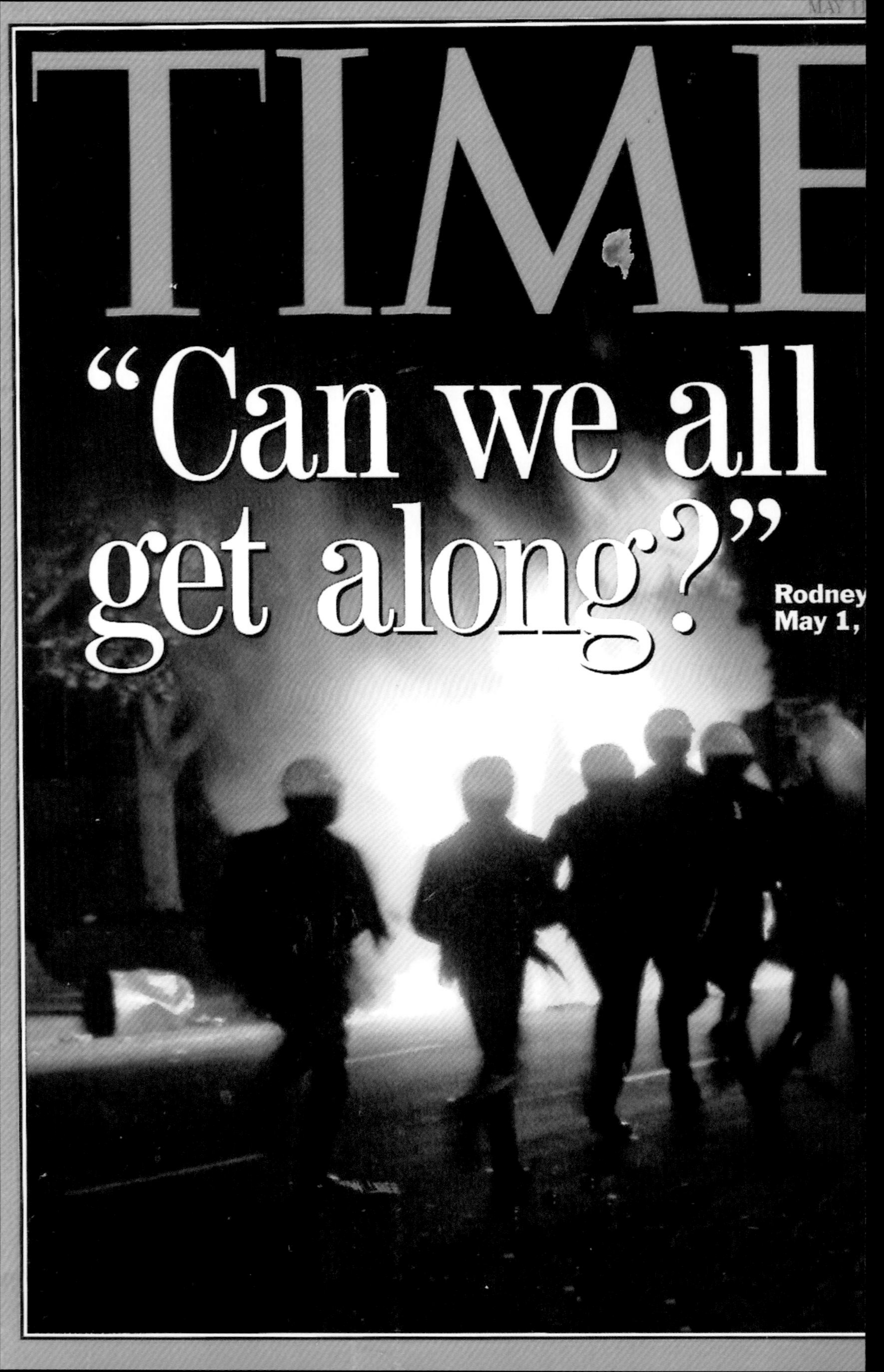
MAY 1
TIME
"Can we all get along?"
Rodney
May 1,

THE WALKOUT

FRIDAY, MARCH 27, 1992, STARTED JUST LIKE any other school day. I dragged myself out of bed, got ready, and walked up Bradshawe to school. Once I got there, the news started spreading fast: Right on the bell for second period, everyone was going to walk out at the same time. At first I wasn't sure if it was true, but two of my friends who were in my class gave me the nod, asking *Should we do it?*

This walkout was organized and led by students from Montebello and Schurr high schools. It was against the Montebello Unified School District's plan to cut our school budget and defund our creative classes and arts programs such as woodshop, drafting, choir—anything that was considered creative. Cutting the school's budget meant that all of our creative curriculum and programs would be taken out, our schools would not get up-to-date and appropriate maintenance, and teachers would lose their jobs.

OPPOSITE: *Time* magazine front cover for the 1992 L.A. uprising

I enjoyed my choir and creative electives, and many kids did, too. Choir was a class that I got to take with my sister and friends from the neighborhood, and where we got to express a different side of ourselves. It pushed us in a creative way.

I had had a difficult time with school since I was in elementary. I wasn't lazy, though. My mind was hungry for knowledge: I carried this feeling as if I wasn't fully satisfied. Besides my own personal struggles and family issues, teachers weren't getting paid enough to take teaching seriously. Many began to care less about the students, and it became more common for them to call in sick. Nothing really felt stable. My classmates would skip class if they knew a substitute was taking over, ignore instructions, talk back, and challenge the rules.

This made it even harder to build trust with our teachers and diminished any respect we had for the school system. That plus the natural disobedience of teenagers in junior high and high school—who just want to hang out with their friends and party—only made things worse.

The relationship that should have been there—one where we could look up to them for guidance, structure, and support—seemed almost impossible to cultivate. Who was left to guide us? If the school system, including our teachers, failed us over and over and showed no respect for us, why should we respect them and their rules?

Despite growing up in an environment where the system itself often felt like it was working against us, many of us still held on to some hope for school. We wanted to believe that it could be a place for growth, learning, friendships, and respect. But the events that were unfolding felt like a tipping point. It wasn't just one thing; it was the culmination of so many small breaks in trust, of promises that were never kept, and of adults who let us down.

So I became one of hundreds of students from my school, Eastmont Intermediate, who walked out to join others from different schools in the area protesting on the streets.

Once I saw kids walking out, that's when I made that decision myself. When we were outside I remember having this feeling of *Oh, shit, I can't believe we just did this.* And we just kept going forward, taking over the streets and marching down to the school district without looking back.

Of course, there were kids who just wanted to rebel and ditch school, but still, it was a pivotal moment—one that made us realize that we had the power to challenge the very system that had let us down. The walkout became more than just an act of rebellion; it was a statement of our unity, our strength, and our refusal to stay silent.

I had never really broken the rules in a big way or gone against the system like some of my friends had. They were the ones who took risks, who ditched class without a second thought. Then there were those who had the courage to speak up when others wouldn't. But this was different. It was no longer just about going against authority for the sake of it—it was about standing up together no matter what the outcome would be. It was about finding my voice and realizing that it mattered.

This moment brought the youth together, no matter what we were into: cholos and cholas, jocks, pretty boys, ravers, punks, skaters, and taggers. And in many ways we learned from one another: The punks and young activists showed us how to reject the system outright—how to not give a damn and speak out. The ravers had already mastered the art of ditching with ease and moved under the radar. And the jocks and studious kids—they walked like they were untouchable. They knew what they *deserved*. Better education was definitely one of those things. All of us had a different relationship to this struggle, but we all showed up. We didn't care about the risks or threats by the school.

Thanks to our protest, nine million dollars in cuts were restored, though the district claimed that they had decided not to make the cuts before we took to the streets. At the time, I didn't realize that we were part of a lineage of Los Angeles students standing up for our rights. That a few decades before, in 1968, thousands of Chicano public-school students had stood up against educational inequalities in the city. That was one of the largest student actions in American history.

The power of youth has echoed through history. Even if many of us didn't know that History, or any history—it still moved around us, quietly shaping who we were, like in 1968, when students from Garfield, Roosevelt, Lincoln, Wilson, and Belmont high schools walked out of class to protest unequal conditions in East L.A. schools. It was usually the youth who started movements, protests, actions, collectives—you name it—in and outside of school.

This was a time of political shifts, uprisings, and protests. In March 1991, the footage of Rodney King being beaten by the police aired on local news, and for the first time, I saw police violence caught on camera and replayed over and over on television. This wasn't a movie, it was real.

A year later, a month after our walkout, the four police officers were acquitted, and Los Angeles erupted in anger and disbelief. Mom told us to be safe and come straight home from school. There was worry in the air. People had been carrying this anger for over a year since the footage was made public, and, historically, for generations.

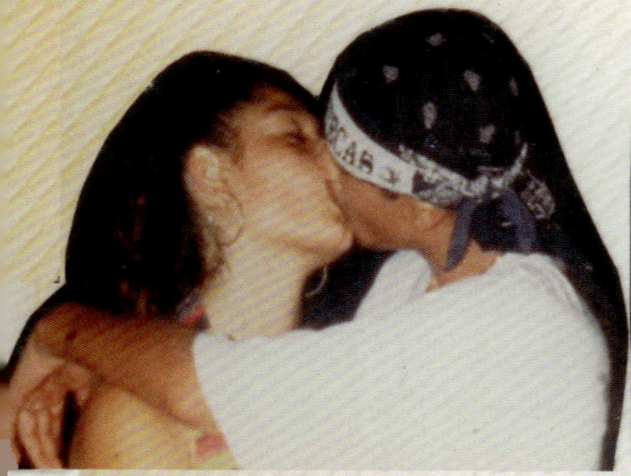

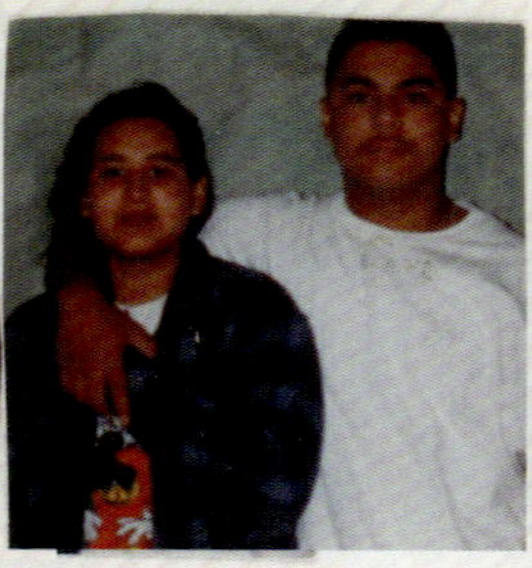

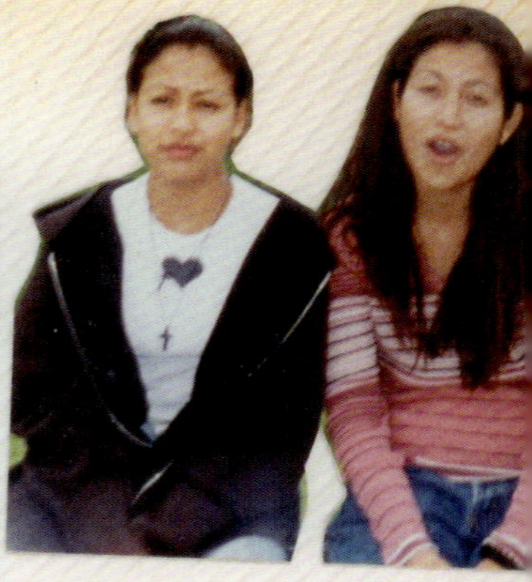

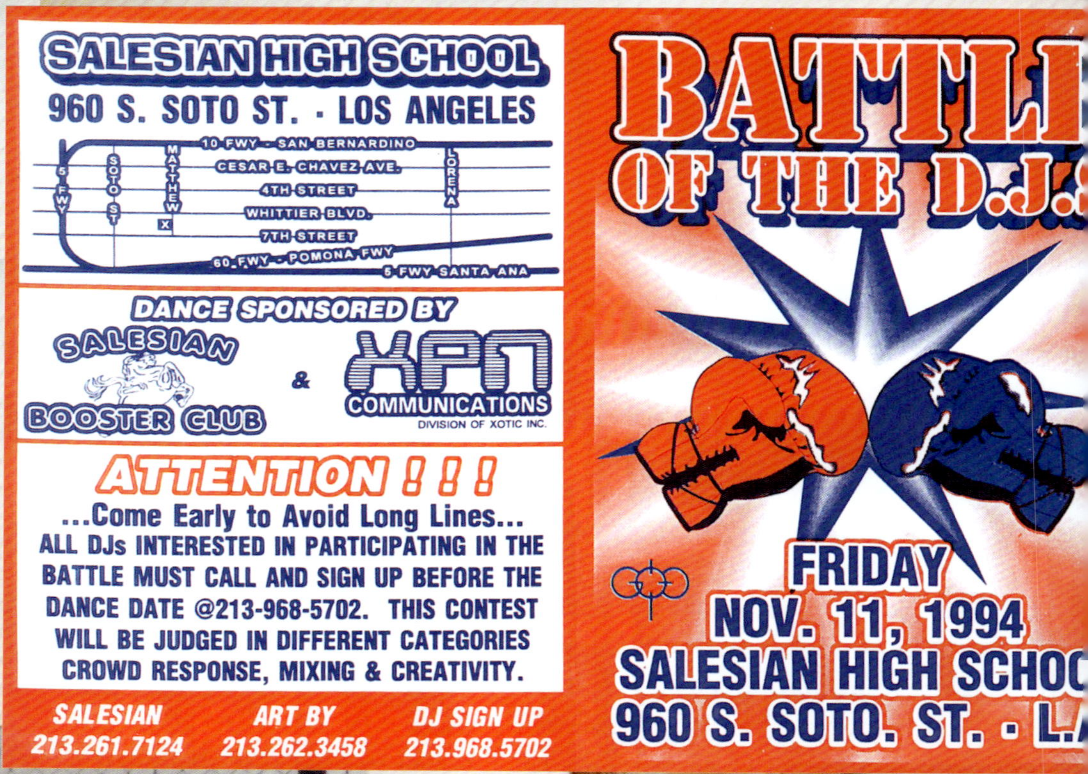
SALESIAN HIGH SCHOOL
960 S. SOTO ST. · LOS ANGELES
10 FWY - SAN BERNARDINO
CESAR E. CHAVEZ AVE.
4TH STREET
WHITTIER BLVD.
7TH STREET
60 FWY - POMONA FWY
5 FWY SANTA ANA
5 FWY
SOTO ST
MATTHEW
LORENA
X
DANCE SPONSORED BY
SALESIAN BOOSTER CLUB
&
XPN COMMUNICATIONS
DIVISION OF XOTIC INC.
ATTENTION ! ! !
...Come Early to Avoid Long Lines...
ALL DJs INTERESTED IN PARTICIPATING IN THE BATTLE MUST CALL AND SIGN UP BEFORE THE DANCE DATE @213-968-5702. THIS CONTEST WILL BE JUDGED IN DIFFERENT CATEGORIES CROWD RESPONSE, MIXING & CREATIVITY.
SALESIAN 213.261.7124
ART BY 213.262.3458
DJ SIGN UP 213.968.5702
BATTL
OF THE D.J.
FRIDAY
NOV. 11, 1994
SALESIAN HIGH SCHOO
960 S. SOTO. ST. · L.

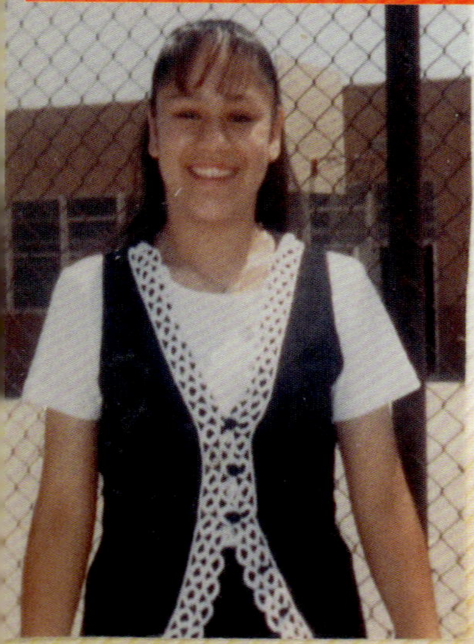

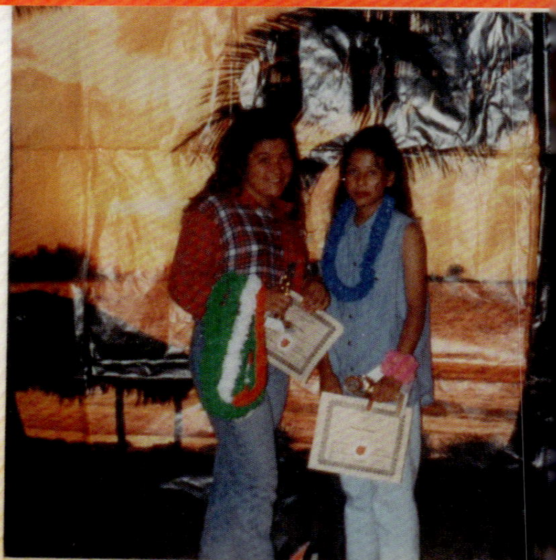

SCHOOL DANCE

WE LIVED IN A TIME OF POLITICAL FLUX, BUT we were also just kids. That school protest was my first experience of the freedom of standing up for what I believed in; soon after I experienced another kind of freedom on the dance floor.

When I think about parties growing up, I fondly remember quinceañeras, weddings, birthday celebrations, bautizos—all the things our parents, godparents, and relatives put together. They were fun, and I enjoyed dancing with my cousins' friends and sisters to quebraditas and cumbias.

At the same time, we had tías and tíos and parents watching over us. At family functions the music was always chosen by the adults, typically the padrinos de música or our parents. Even though we had a blast at these family gatherings, dancing with relatives and catching up with cousins, the vibe was really centered on the adults. The music, the pacing, the whole atmosphere—it was more about what they liked than what we, as teenagers, imagined or desired.

Even when it was supposed to be a celebration for our generation, we didn't have much of a say. If we were lucky, the DJ might take a request, but as soon as the beat shifted from the familiar sounds of salsa or cumbias to something like hip-hop, R&B, or house music, the reactions from the adults were . . . less than supportive. There were those cool relatives who loved to dance and hang with us, the

Flyer promoting a DJ dance at Salesian High School and photos taken at the Eastmont Intermediate School dances, circa 1992/1993 one tío or tía who was the life of the party and danced with us to house music if it was playing.

But some of them would roll their eyes, mutter under their breath, calling our music "cosas del diablo"—things of the devil. They'd take their seats with a cara larga—a long face. You'd think it was their birthday, not ours. They were less about teens' ideas, imagination, and desires.

That's why middle-school dances were so important. There, I was able to spend time with school friends and my sister Maria in a different way, without the usual boundaries of the school day or parents—to dance and feel free on the dance floor.

There is one particular school-dance night that stands out in my memories, one that took place in 1991 at Eastmont Intermediate when I was eleven years old in fifth grade. The dance was in the basketball gym. It was dim and moody, with a few strobe lights.

I knew that high schools were also having their own parties at their schools, particularly Garfield High and Salesian High.

Some were focused on having DJs battle one another to see who was the best. Other parties were organized by radio stations like 92.3 The Beat and Power 106, and their DJs made special appearances and handed out posters and stickers.

This was different from family functions. I experienced something I hadn't felt before: joy, curiosity, excitement, and a little bit of awkwardness all at once. My sister was a year above me, but here we all came together. This night I danced freely with everyone and was in a space with kids around my age.

Like Art Laboe would say, "You pick them, you dedicate them, you get them." The DJs would play whatever we wanted to listen to. Hit songs and Top 40 played all night long.

"One More Try" by Timmy T
"Gonna Make You Sweat" by C+C Music Factory
"I Need Love" by LL Cool J
"The Humpty Dance" by Digital Underground
"Wild Thing" by Tone Lōc
"Bust a Move" by Young MC
"Groove Is in the Heart" by Deee-Lite

OPPOSITE: Garfield High School dance party, around 1994, sourced from *Street Beat Magazine*

GARFIELD
Battle of the DJs

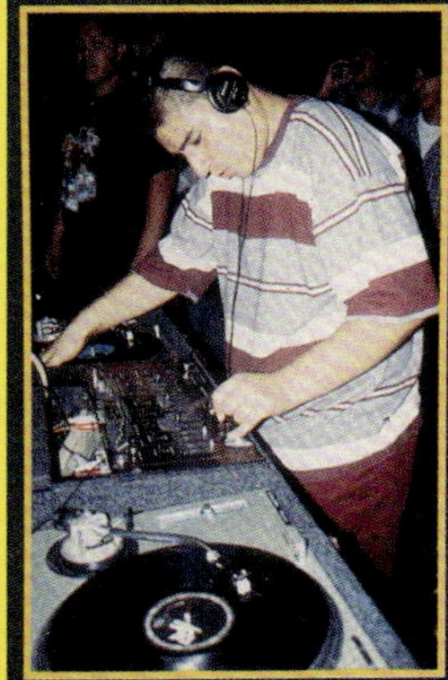

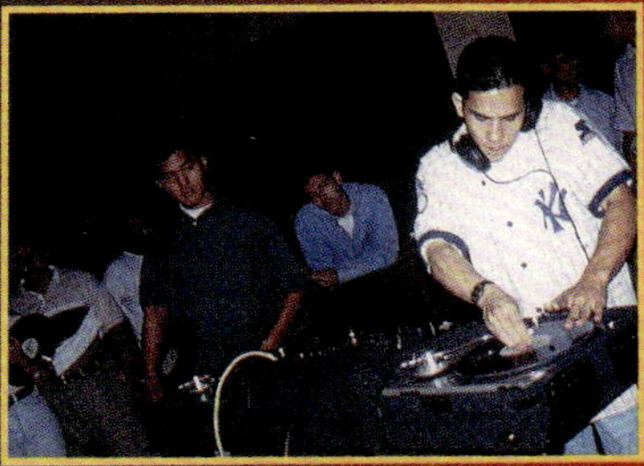

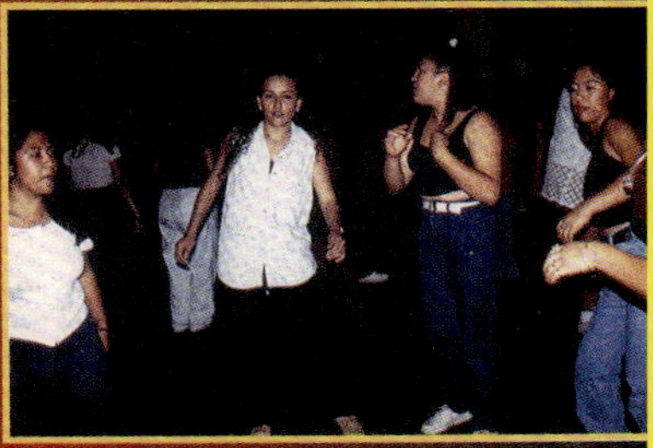

By SB Staff

Putting on a Rave Underground-type setting, East L.A.'s Madness and Garfield High played host to a battle of the DJs, consisting of Magoo, Crow 2, Twkoter-3, Back Draft, Danny G., Mo Cuts (which won the contest) and Troll.

The whole night was filled with hip young people who made it happen for the best. Other crews grooving the night away were The Crooks, Rude Ones, The Khronic, The Violators and Maniacs. Our hats go off to Garfield High and Madness for putting on this event for East L.A. They need more events like these, so let's all work together to make future events happen.

Peace and love for a better world! ❀

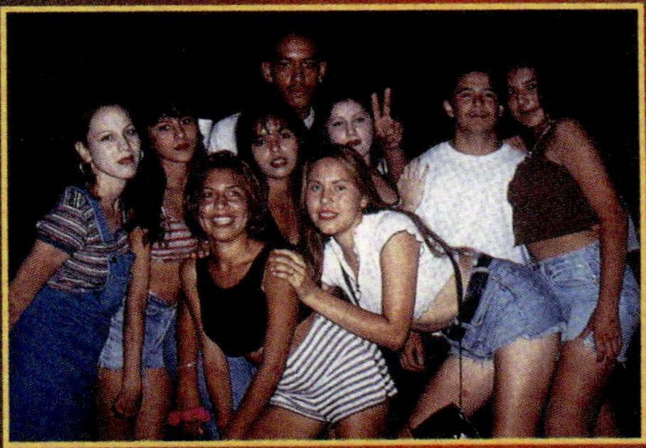

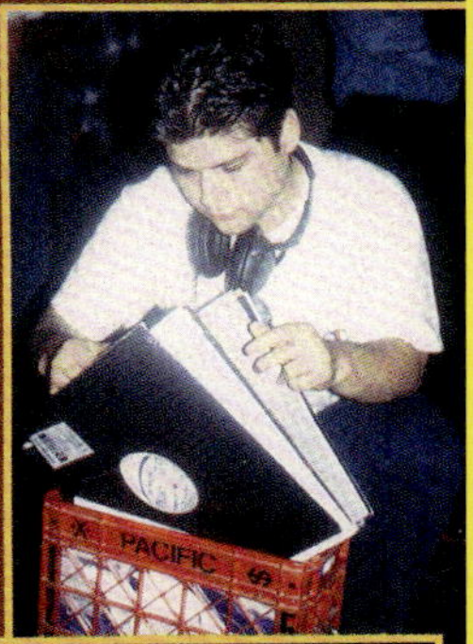

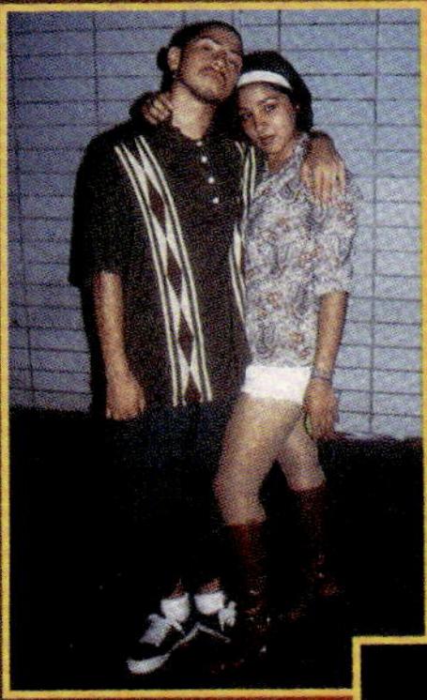

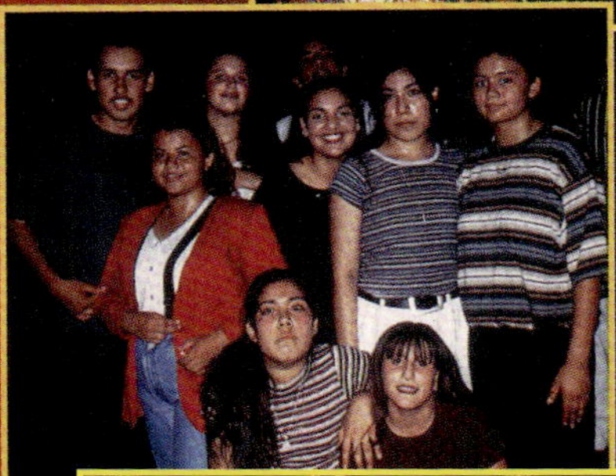

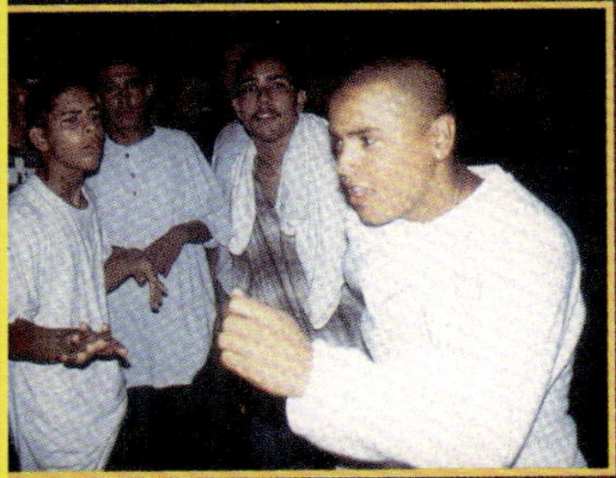

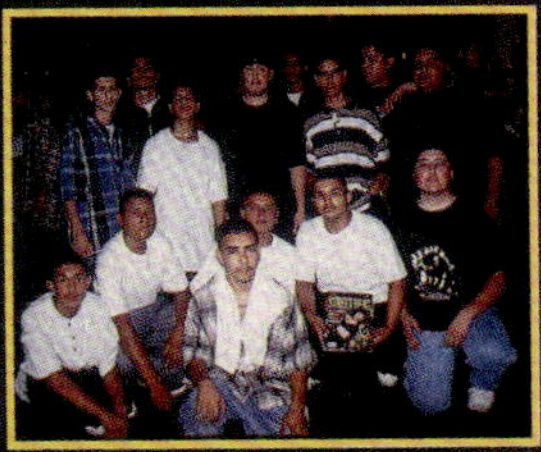

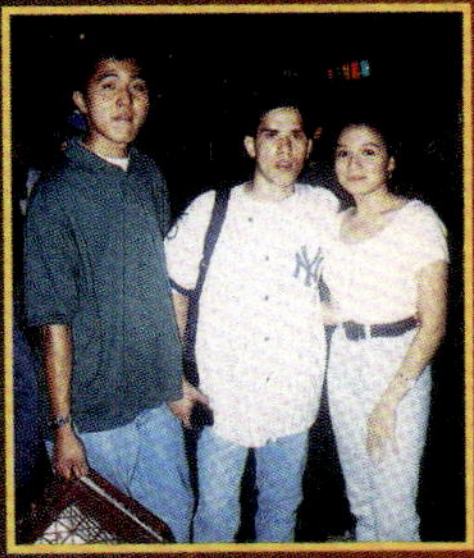

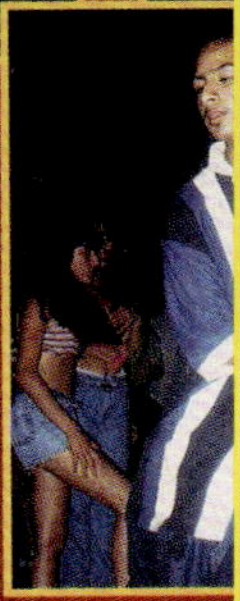

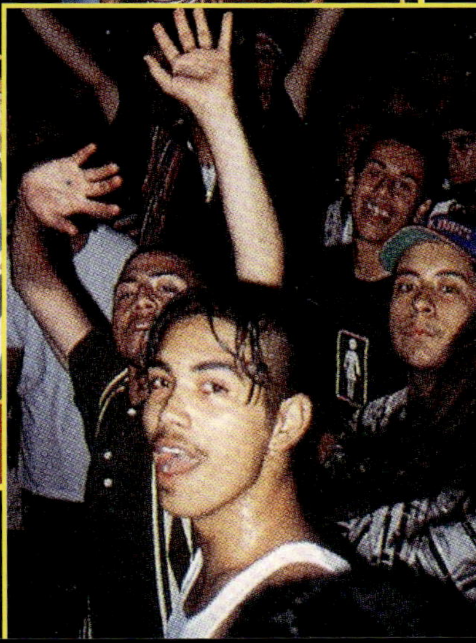

"What Is Love" by Haddaway
"Jump!" by The Movement

Even though they still involved adult supervision (teachers and school staff), students had more say at school dances than back home. The music we requested was played, we proposed ideas for the dance parties, and many students took part in organizing. At these school-dance nights we didn't see adults on the dance floor or trying to control the music unless it had explicit lyrics. The dance floor belonged to us.

Many of my friends who weren't into sports or after-school programs were very committed to dance: They went straight to their garages, their bedrooms, or friends' homes after school and practiced dance moves.

I was surrounded by kids my age for the first time: friends and teenagers I didn't really know but saw around school. The dance floor was packed shoulder to shoulder, and I looked down at my feet and noticed the wooden floor on the basketball court, then people's feet shuffling around in tight circles. I felt so much joy and freedom as we all danced in unison.

We were playful without judgment, circling around one another, taking turns inside the tight circle. Making up new dance moves that had the potential of becoming something cool or perhaps a total failure, but that really didn't matter. We all knew the Roger Rabbit and the Running Man. We were in search of something fun and weird and we taught one another new moves, like one where you hop over your other leg.

The popular kids joined in on the dance floor and showed off their moves—at our school, "popular" wasn't about being football players or cheerleaders; it was more about having style and being a little rebellious. They brought that streetstyle energy and the battling. We were all trying it for the first time. Some danced with their boyfriends or girlfriends; some stood around watching. Others made a circle around the person dancing. Others stood around with their hands in their pockets. The pants were so big you could fit a forty-ounce of beer or a spray can in those pockets.

I'd always been shy, but this night nothing mattered. I was breaking through a barrier I didn't know existed. Music let me be free.

OPPOSITE: Teenage kid practicing dancing in his bedroom, mid-1990s. He's wearing oversized pants and a 187 Hudda shirt with a pair of Adidas shell toes.

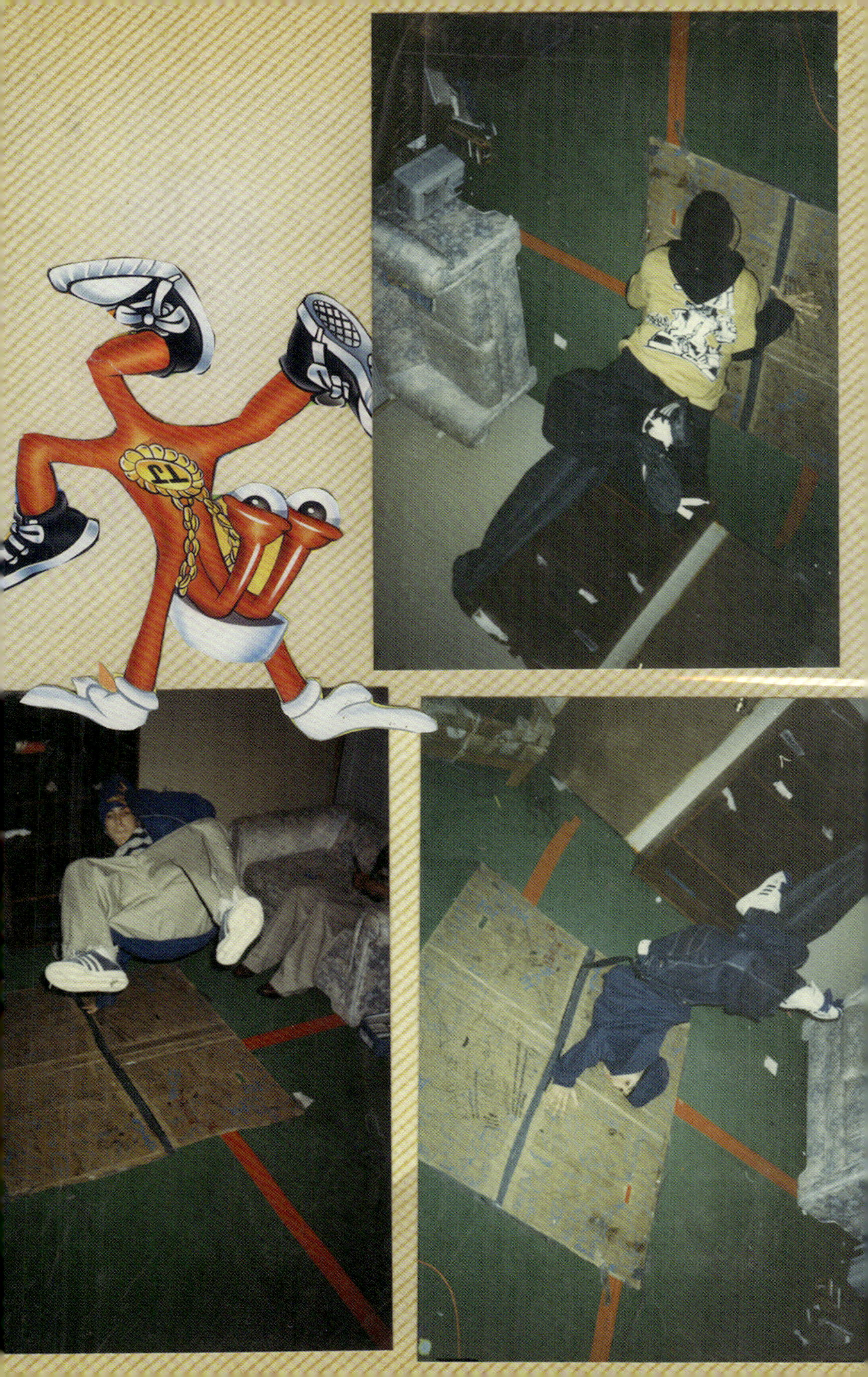

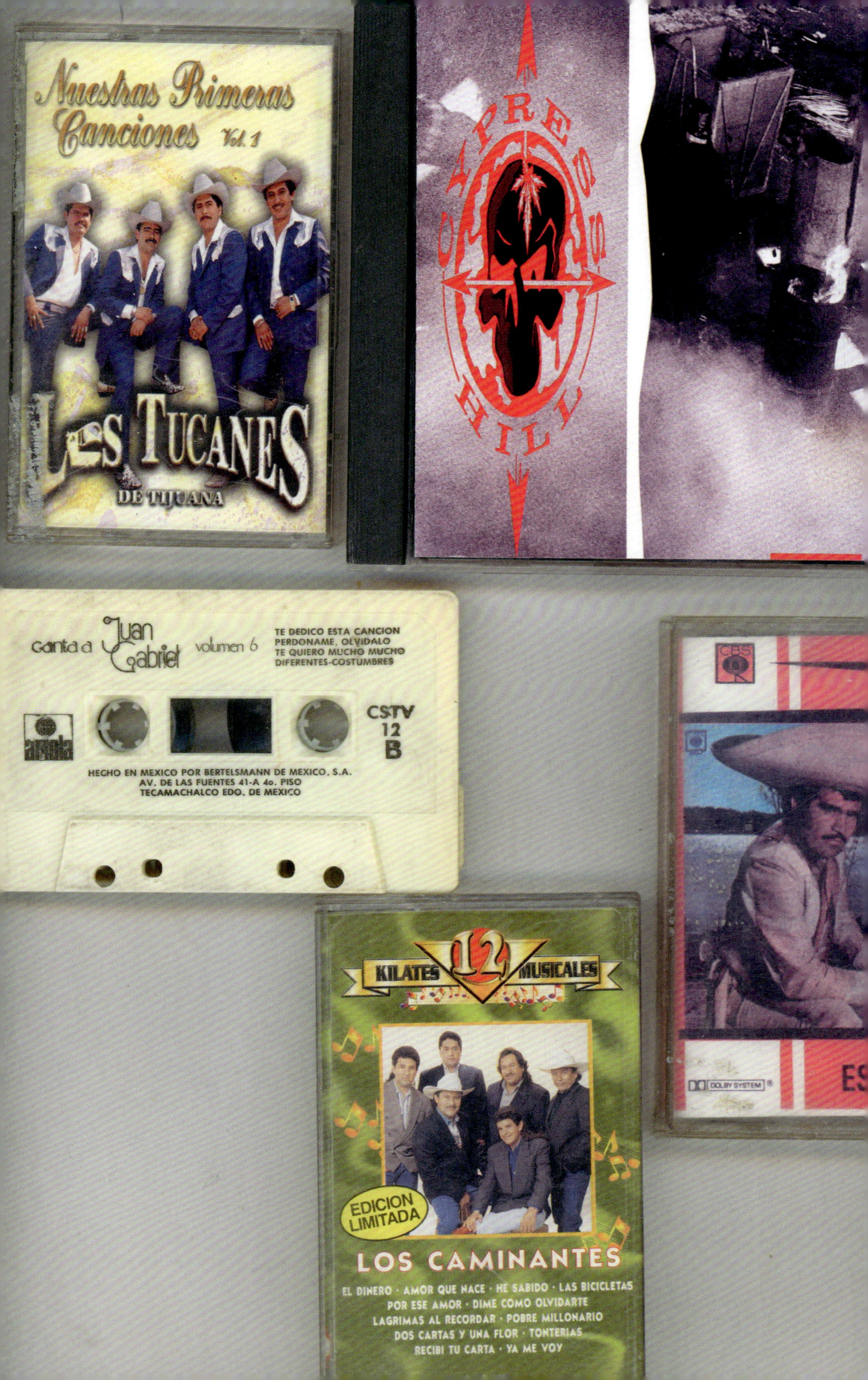
Nuestras Primeras Canciones Vol. 1
LOS TUCANES
DE TIJUANA
CYPRESS HILL
Canta a Juan Gabriel volumen 6
TE DEDICO ESTA CANCION
PERDONAME, OLVIDALO
TE QUIERO MUCHO MUCHO
DIFERENTES COSTUMBRES
ariola
CSTV 12 B
HECHO EN MEXICO POR BERTELSMANN DE MEXICO, S.A.
AV. DE LAS FUENTES 41-A 4o. PISO
TECAMACHALCO EDO. DE MEXICO
CBS
DOLBY SYSTEM
KILATES 12 MUSICALES
EDICION LIMITADA
LOS CAMINANTES
EL DINERO · AMOR QUE NACE · HE SABIDO · LAS BICICLETAS
POR ESE AMOR · DIME COMO OLVIDARTE
LAGRIMAS AL RECORDAR · POBRE MILLONARIO
DOS CARTAS Y UNA FLOR · TONTERIAS
RECIBI TU CARTA · YA ME VOY

LA MÚSICA DE LA CASA

I **GREW UP LISTENING TO DIFFERENT TYPES OF** music and it was always played loud, sometimes not by choice—whether it was the neighbor playing it or my mom or sisters taking over the radio. Whether it was Cypress Hill (my brother Gus's favorite), Keith Sweat (my sister Maria's), Mr. Lil One (Yesi's), or Juan Gabriel and Gerardo Reyes (Mom's favorites), the music blasted through our windows.

The quietest times at home were when my siblings were out on Friday and Saturday nights. Mom could finally relax and watch her telenovelas, but during the day it was always loud. Saturday morning, she was up by 6 A.M., blasting her music to wake us up and start cleaning the house—Juan Gabriel, Vicente Fernández, Ana Gabriel, Cornelio Reyna, and the rest of her playlist. We called it "cleaning music"—our passive-aggressive signal that it was time to scrub, sweep, and mop. There were no weekend breaks, no sleeping in. The house had to be spotless.

To us kids, it just sounded like she was always nagging or complaining. But looking back, I can hear something else in her voice—real frustration, and maybe not even directed at us. It might've been about my brothers, or my stepdad, or everything she was carrying. At any moment, it could spill over. I never knew exactly what was bugging

OPPOSITE: Mom's original cassette tapes and my brother's favorite Cypress Hill album: the soundtrack that filled the house with music

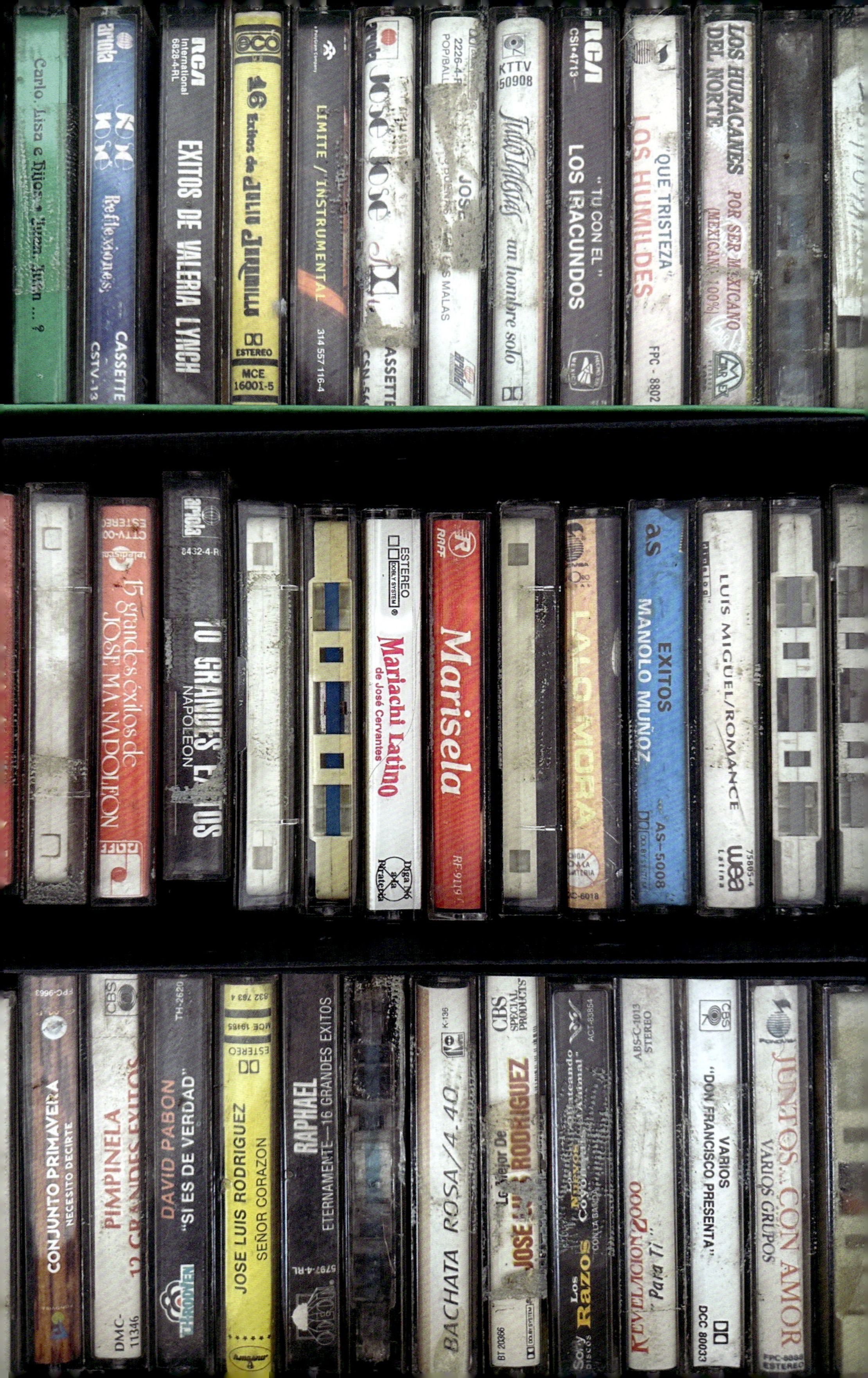

EXITOS DE VALERIA LYNCH
16 Exitos de Julio Jaramillo
LIMITE / INSTRUMENTAL
"TU CON EL" LOS IRACUNDOS
LOS HUMILDES "QUE TRISTEZA"
LOS HURACANES DEL NORTE POR SER MEXICANO
un hombre solo
15 grandes éxitos de JOSE MA NAPOLEON
10 GRANDES EXITOS NAPOLEON
Mariachi Latino de José Cervantes
Marisela
LALO MORA
EXITOS MANOLO MUÑOZ
LUIS MIGUEL/ROMANCE
CONJUNTO PRIMAVERA NECESITO DECIRTE
PIMPINELA 12 GRANDES EXITOS
DAVID PABON "SI ES DE VERDAD"
JOSE LUIS RODRIGUEZ SEÑOR CORAZON
RAPHAEL ETERNAMENTE—16 GRANDES EXITOS
BACHATA ROSA/4.40
Los Razos
REVELACION 2000 Para Ti
VARIOS "DON FRANCISCO PRESENTA"
JUNTOS...CON AMOR VARIOS GRUPOS

her, but you could tell when it was too much: she'd yell—or worse, start banging the pots and pans, hoping we'd finally get the message.

Back then, it felt like torture and we always wanted to leave the house. But now? I look back with gratitude. Those songs—those artists—she shared them with us, and they've stuck with me. She'd play the music so loud that our neighbors probably felt emotion, and we definitely did. In many ways, I think they knew her better than we did.

We could sense what Mom was going through based on the music she'd play. Music was a reflection and expression of her emotions and thoughts. The passion and heartbreaks and sorrows. The music was always dramatic, romantic, and about love and heartbreaks. That is how Mom raised us and this music—cassette tapes of Los Apson, Los Sagitarios, Los Bukis, etc., some dubbed from the radio, some piratería, some original—was all embedded in us.

My mom and stepdad's relationship was off and on, and her cassette collection held clues to where her heart was. Some of the tapes had names written on them with a pen, names of men we got to meet and of strangers we only heard about. I imagine that the songs with a little checkmark next to the title are dedications, or maybe reminded her of a lover, or perhaps they were just her favorite songs. If Mom was going through a heartbreak, we were there with her. If she was in love, we all felt the love in the house. She sang along to Vicente Fernández's "Por Tu Maldito Amor" and Juan Gabriel's "Aunque Te Enamores" and "¿Dónde Estás Vida Mía?," and played them loud and on repeat. We also felt her pain through the music. This is how we learned about love and how to express it: through music.

As we got older, my sisters and I developed our own taste, too. Maria and I listened to the radio on the small black boom box she kept next to her bed, especially Power 106, Art Laboe, KROQ, and KRLA. Power 106 played house music and R&B and there was nothing else like it. We'd spend hours recording our favorite songs that played on the radio. On weekend nights, the radio played house and techno. Sometimes, they had DJ guests from all around Los Angeles and held DJ battles.

Then we had radio stations that played classic rock—The Doors, Janis Joplin—or oldies, and we'd spend hours making our own mixtapes by recording songs straight off the radio. We got good at it, too: Pause, re-

OPPOSITE: Mom's tape collection

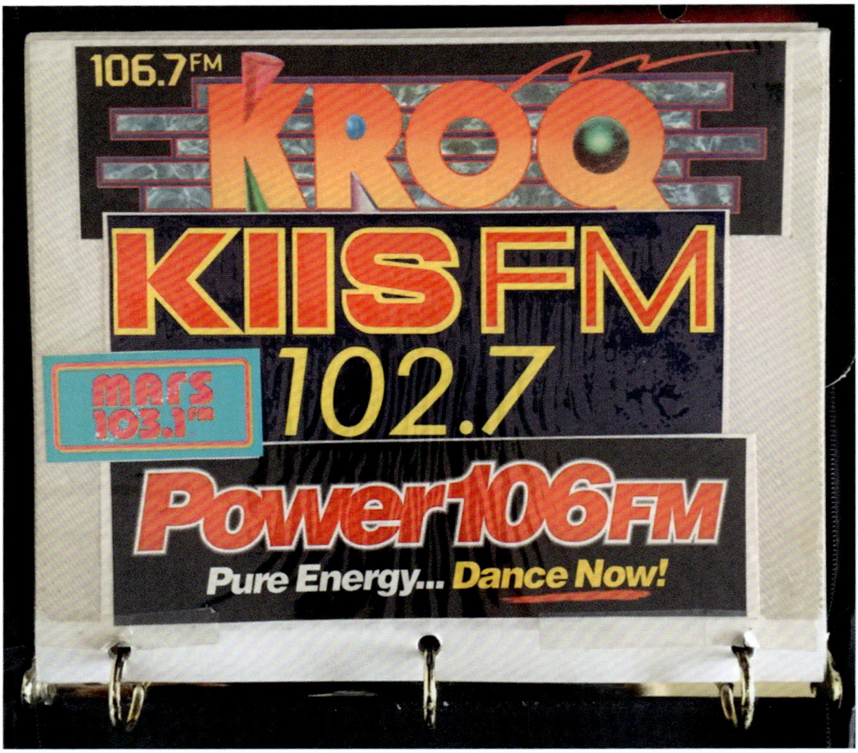

Radio station stickers

cord, stop, repeat. No commercials, only music. If we couldn't afford blank cassettes, we'd raid Mom's collection or grab any tapes we found. Some already had the little record-protection tabs snapped off, so we'd trick the tape deck—stuffing paper or tape into the hole so it would let us record over them. Sometimes I felt so guilty for doing this. At the same time, for us cassette tapes were replaceable.

Eazy-E and Too $hort played the kind of music that you only found at Slauson Mall or a big swap meet. I'd learned about Too $hort through Alfred, Silvia's older brother, who was three years older than me. Silvia was Maria's best friend and lived one block away from us, on Simmons Street. She was always over at our place. Her brother Alfred drove a black Camaro and always talked about moving to Oakland someday. His car didn't have a good sound system, so we'd drive around with a boom box on our laps.

Alfred had a solid tape collection—mostly rap, all underground. This music wasn't on the radio. Too explicit, too sexual, too real. But we found ways to get it. The first time I heard it, I felt how raw and uncensored it was—like watching a movie you weren't supposed to see. Back then, artists like Eazy-E and Too $hort were part of a larger wave of West Coast rap that was just starting to shake the mainstream—unfiltered stories from neighborhoods like ours, told with no apology.

Their music captured street life, sex, police harassment, survival—things we saw around us but rarely heard reflected anywhere else. These weren't just songs; they were soundtracks to a world that felt close, even if we didn't fully understand all of it yet. For me, it was the first time I felt like music could tell the truth—dirty, messy, funny, dangerous truth.

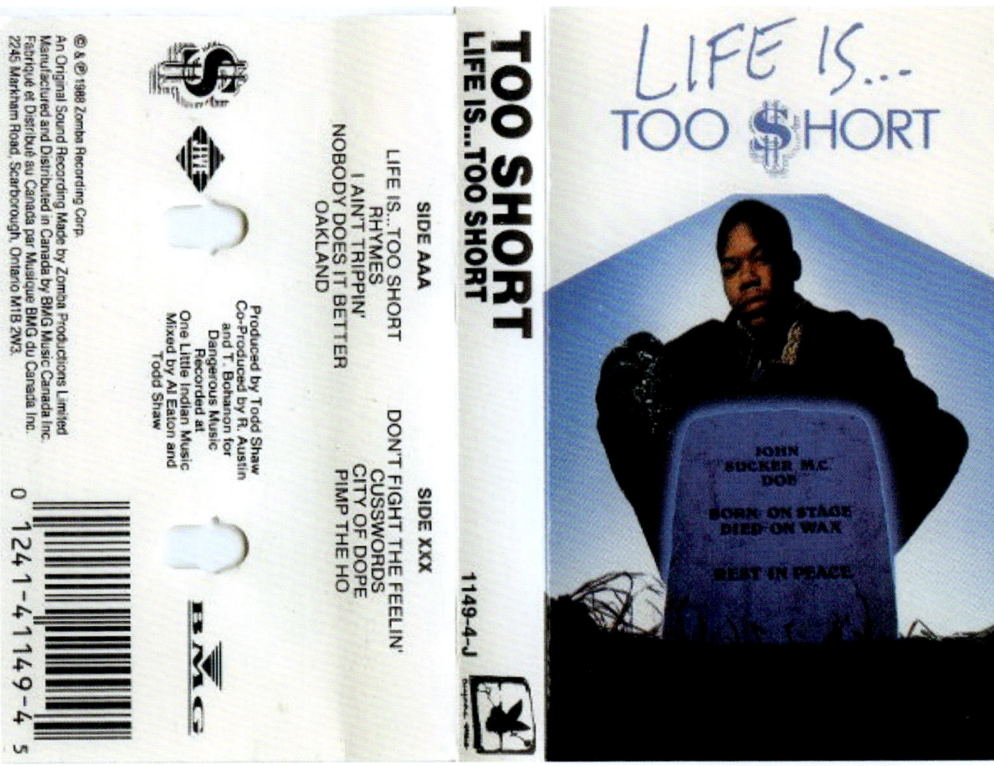

Too $hort tape sleeve, what I would typically listen to in Alfred's Camaro

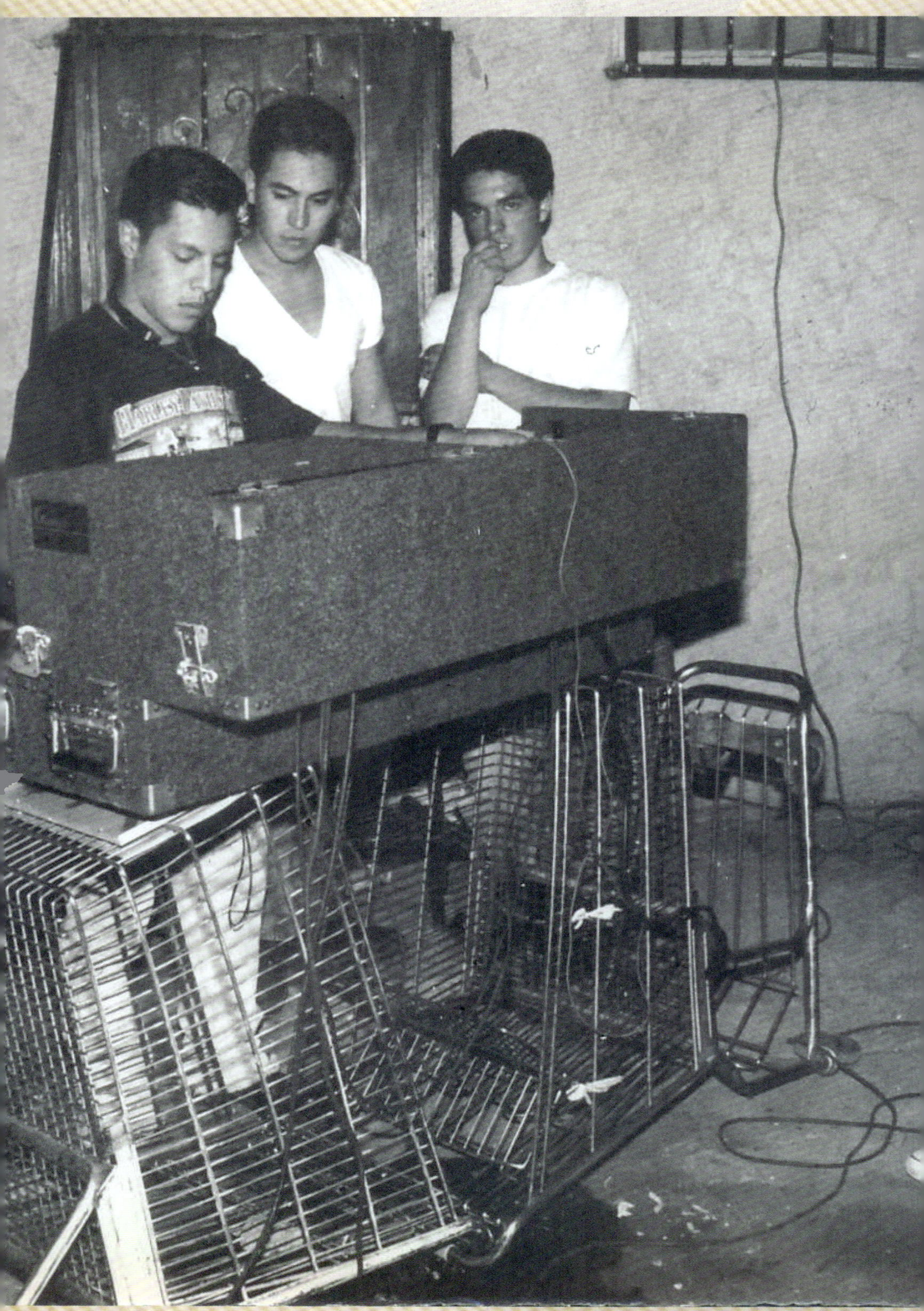

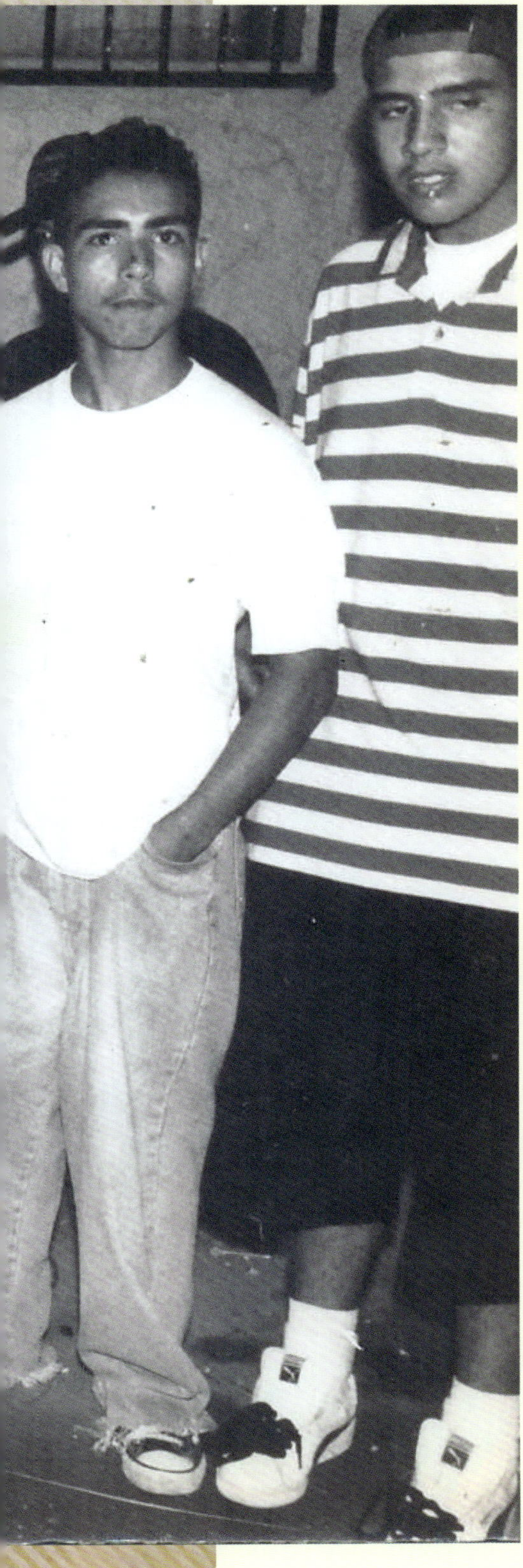

THE PARTY NEXT DOOR

I HEARD THE MUSIC I LOVED on the radio airwaves, in cars, and also out my bedroom window. The first time I learned about a backyard house party was when I was around twelve or thirteen years old. It took place right next door, in my neighbor's backyard on Leonard Avenue. I felt like I was watching a movie on a big TV screen, everything unfolding from my bedroom window.

My house was always loud, but this night was different. It was quiet—quiet like a rare gift. I never took silence for granted, because it was uncommon in our house. There was always someone arguing, music blaring, or my mom yelling at us. But that night, I had the room to myself because my sis-

East LA Madness crew at a backyard house party in the early 1990s ters weren't home. Maybe they were out with friends or their boyfriends. I didn't know, but it felt like the quietest night I'd ever had, so quiet that I could actually hear what was happening outside.

One of the windows in my room faced the alleyway, and the other faced a ten-foot chain-link fence dividing the neighbor's backyard from ours. This was the same fence that kids—me and my siblings included—hopped over when they were running from the cops. The only light that entered my room came from the headlights of passing cars, which cast abstract silhouettes on my walls and ceiling every time they hit the trees, the leaves, or the fences outside.

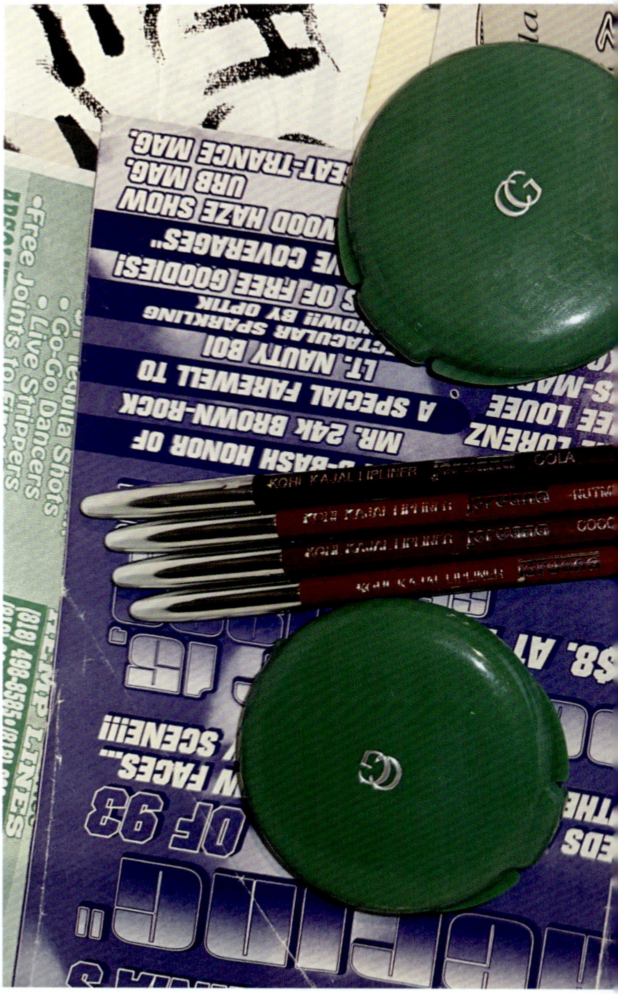

It created an atmosphere that made me feel like I was in one of those moody 1920s movies with fake props and backdrops. It was quiet, but by 9 P.M., I heard a loud thumping sound—the DJ setting up, doing sound checks. Mismatched beats played in and out until the rhythm became consistent. The walls of my room rattled every time the DJ cranked up the volume. I looked out the window. The crowd was getting bigger, and the beats were steadier. The four-on-the-floor of house music mixed so I couldn't tell where one song ended and another began, but I recognized a couple of tracks, maybe one or two that I'd heard late at night on the radio when local DJs spun past midnight on weekends.

When the next DJ took over, he carried a crate full of vinyl records and set it down by the turntables. The music stopped for a split second—just enough for the beat to falter. But then it picked back up again, and nobody seemed to mind the brief silence. I could hear the clink of beer bottles and the murmur of voices as people mingled. It was the sound of a party. I looked out toward the alleyway and saw kids about my age standing in the dark, while others were in the backyard, swaying to the rhythm. Some crowded around the DJ booth, cigarettes dangling from their fingers, clouds of smoke mixing with the beats. Others were gathered around the kegs—one boy gripping the nozzle, ready to spray beer on the girls as a prank.

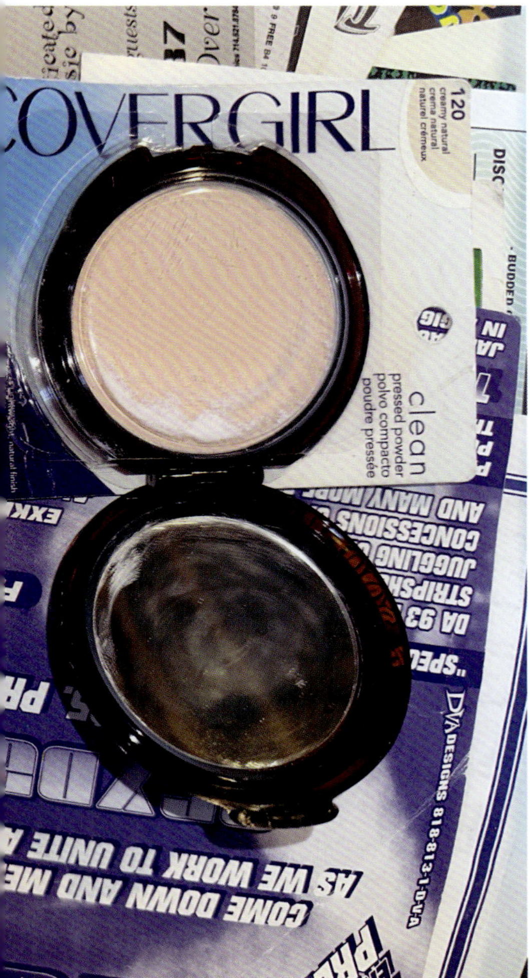

It was dark, and my view was blocked by trees and bushes, but the silhouettes of teenagers dancing were clear as they made clouds of dust. Strobe lights cut through the dust created by their shuffling feet, casting shadows across the backyard. Some girls danced on top of rusted cars that had been there for years, others on go-go boxes made out of plywood. Others climbed onto rooftops, getting the crowd hyped.

The boys wore baseball caps with curved brims, embroidered with Madness, Operation X, L.A. Federation, The Crooks, and The Undertakers—names I would later come to recognize. Most of the boys had baggy clothes and shaved heads or crazy hairstyles. The girls wore crop tops, tight booty shorts, and platform shoes. They doused themselves in body sprays that smelled sweet and flowery.

I didn't know it yet, but that night opened up new possibilities for me and inspired me to see myself in a different light. Hard to describe, but perhaps new possibilities of expression not just through words, but through style, dance, and music. I also noticed the creativity in the party scene—it wasn't just about looking good; it was about making a statement and how one carried oneself. When people think of raves, they think of white kids in London (if that's right) but I grew up during a DIY musical renaissance that was created by underage Chicano kids like myself.

One night at a school dance, flyers were being passed around, and that's when I learned what a party crew was—names like Fusion, Overdose, Hells Rebels, Top Priority, Outsiders, and Sex Mob. They dressed similarly to tagging crews, but instead of claiming turf or marking their names, they were focused on organizing parties. It was a different world, and I realized they weren't about graffiti or street battles.

They were about using space and sound to create a vibe at any time of day. I looked up to them, even though they were about the same age as me. They had something different—something I wanted. Junior high was already buzzing, with new party crews popping up all over, like a virus spreading through the city. And I was ready to join.

The very next day, I was in the girls' bathroom during recess, watching a group of girls—older than me by a year—take over the full-length mirror. They rushed in, throwing their bags to the side, and immediately started reapplying their makeup. Standing in front of the mirror, claiming it as theirs.

They took out their CoverGirl compact powder from their back pockets and Jordana lipliners from their makeup bags, fixing their hair and making sure their looks were fresh for the rest of the day. It smelled like heaven in there: a mix of hairspray, mousse, and CK One perfume. They were all wearing hoop earrings and heavy red lipstick/lipliner and had thin eyebrows.

They wore tank tops and baggy pants with puffed-out front pockets or overalls. Their sneakers—Adidas or Converse Chuck Taylors. Two of the girls wore oversized shirts that hung loosely on their frames, and they had short hair like Demi Moore in the movie *Ghost*. The others wore their hair longer, styled in that wet, wavy look that was so popular, half pulled up with a clip. One took out a travel-size Aqua Net hairspray and mousse, then scrunched up her hair with one hand while spraying her hair with the other.

One of the girls stood in front of the mirror, dancing while singing along to a song. "Dance your ass, ass off, dance your ass, ass off," she sang, her moves perfectly in sync with the lyrics. She was showing her friends new dance moves she'd learned over the weekend. She stood next to one friend to guide her as she caught up to the rhythm while the rest of her friends danced with her, swinging their arms up in the air in a circular motion. I was captivated by their style and dance moves, but most importantly their presence. This moment, which I still think about often decades later, wasn't just about the dance; it was about confidence. They were secure in who they were. The moves, the style, the way they carried themselves—it was magnetic.

Later that day, I was with the boys who had been handing out flyers at our school dance. These flyers weren't just for a regular school event, they were for parties they threw outside of school. I didn't really know what that meant at the time, but it didn't take long to figure it out. I started paying more attention, noticing how everything began to click. Those kids I had observed? I was seeing them in a new light, understanding their world a little more each day.

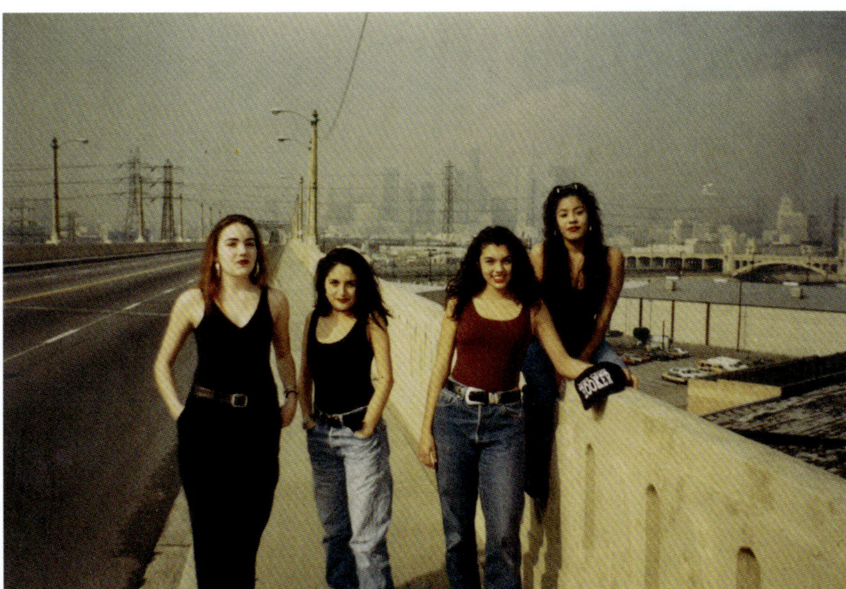

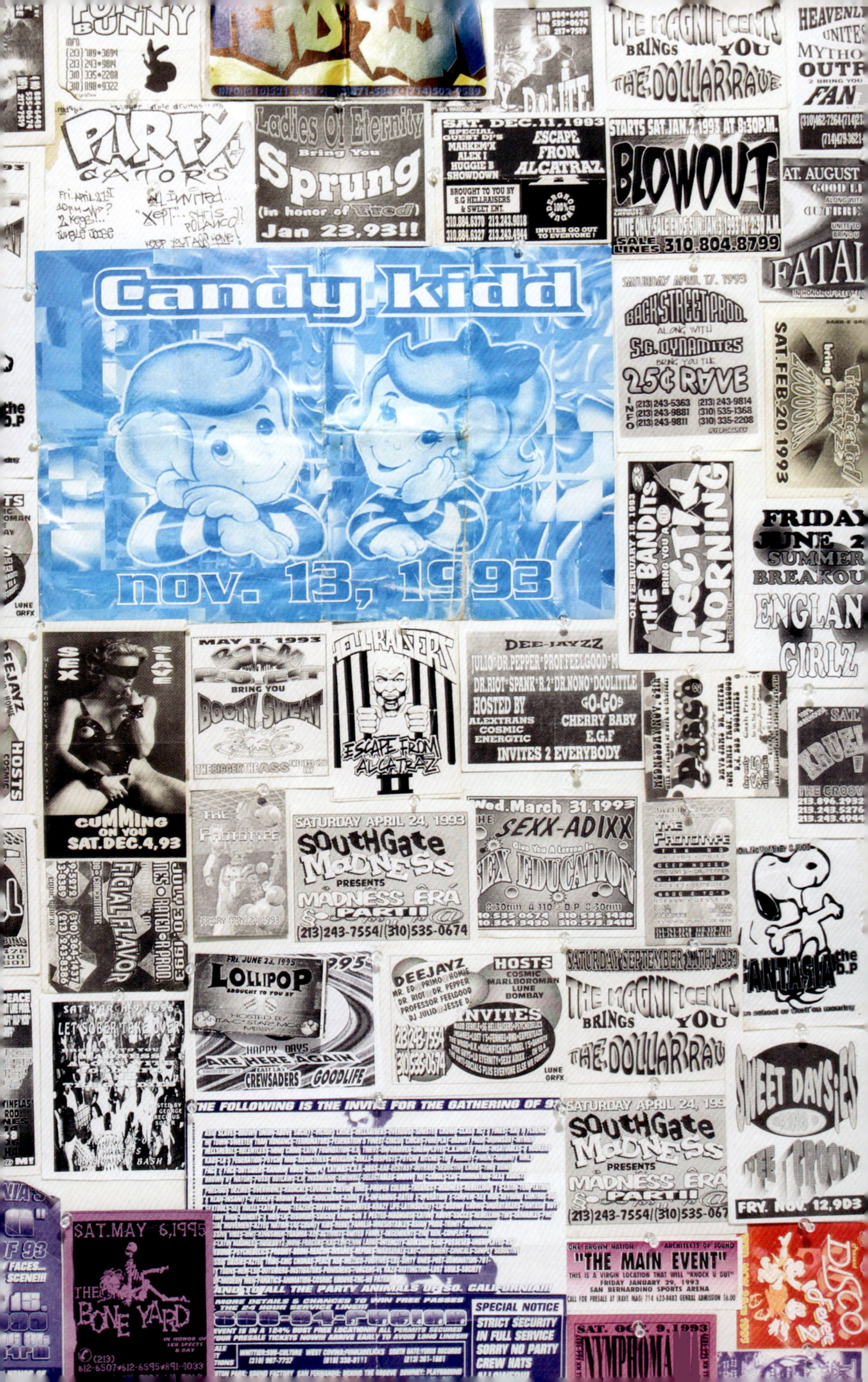
BUNNY
(213) 789-3694
(213) 243-9814
(310) 335-2208
(310) 898-9322
THE MAGNIFICENTS
BRINGS YOU
THE DOLLAR RAVE
HEAVENLY
UNITED
MYTHO
OUTR
FAN
PARTY GATORS
Fri. April 23
ALL INVITED
Ladies Of Eternity
Bring You
Sprung
(in honor of Fred)
Jan 23,93!!
SAT. DEC. 11, 1993
ESCAPE FROM ALCATRAZ
BROUGHT TO YOU BY S.G HELLRAISERS & SWEET ENT.
310.884.5370 213.243.9818
310.884.6327 213.243.4944
INVITES GO OUT TO EVERYONE!
STARTS SAT. JAN. 2, 1993 AT 8:30 P.M.
BLOWOUT
SALE LINES 310.804.8799
AT. AUGUST
FATAL
Candy Kidd
nov. 13, 1993
SATURDAY APRIL 17, 1993
BACKSTREET PROD.
ALONG WITH
S.G. DYNAMITES
BRING YOU THE
25¢ RAVE
INFO
(213) 243-5363
(213) 243-9881
(213) 243-9811
(213) 243-9814
(310) 535-1368
(310) 335-2208
SAT. FEB. 20, 1993
THE BANDITS
BRING YOU A
HECTIK MORNING
FRIDAY
JUNE 2
SUMMER
BREAKOU
ENGLAN
GIRLZ
SEX SLAVE
CUMMING ON YOU
SAT. DEC. 4, 93
MAY 8, 1993
BRING YOU
BOOTY SWEAT
HELLRAISERS
ESCAPE FROM ALCATRAZ
II
DEE-JAYZZ
JULIO DR. PEPPER PROF. FEELGOOD
DR. RIOT SPANK R.2 DR. NONO DOOLITTLE
HOSTED BY
ALEXTRANS
COSMIC
ENERGITIC
GO-GOS
CHERRY BABY
E.G.F
INVITES 2 EVERYBODY
KRUEL
THE GROOV
213.896.2932
213.243.5276
213.243.4944
FICIAL FLAVOR
JULY 30, 1993
THE PROTOTYPE
SATURDAY APRIL 24, 1993
SOUTHGATE MADNESS
PRESENTS
MADNESS ERA
PART II
(213) 243-7554 / (310) 535-0674
Wed. March 31, 1993
THE SEXX-ADIXX
Give You A Lesson In
SEX EDUCATION
THE PROTOTYPE
FANTASIA
FRI. JUNE 23, 1995
LOLLIPOP
HAPPY DAYS ARE HERE AGAIN
CREWSADERS
GOODLIFE
SAT MARCH 9, 1996
LET SOBER TAKE OVER
DEEJAYZ
MR. ED PRIMO HOMIE
DR. RIOT DR. PEPPER
PROFESSOR FEELGOOD
DJ JULIO JESSE D.
HOSTS
COSMIC
MARLBOROMAN
LUNE
BOMBAY
INVITES
SATURDAY SEPTEMBER 11TH, 1993
THE MAGNIFICENTS
BRINGS YOU
THE DOLLAR RAVE
SWEET DAYSIES
THE FOLLOWING IS THE INVITE FOR THE GATHERING OF 93
SATURDAY APRIL 24, 199
SOUTHGATE MADNESS
PRESENTS
MADNESS ERA
PART II
(213) 243-7554 / (310) 535-067
FRY. NOV. 12, 903
SAT. MAY 6, 1995
THE BONE YARD
SPECIAL NOTICE
STRICT SECURITY
IN FULL SERVICE
SORRY NO PARTY
CREW HATS
"THE MAIN EVENT"
SAN BERNARDINO SPORTS ARENA
SAT. OCT. 9, 1993
NYMPHOMA

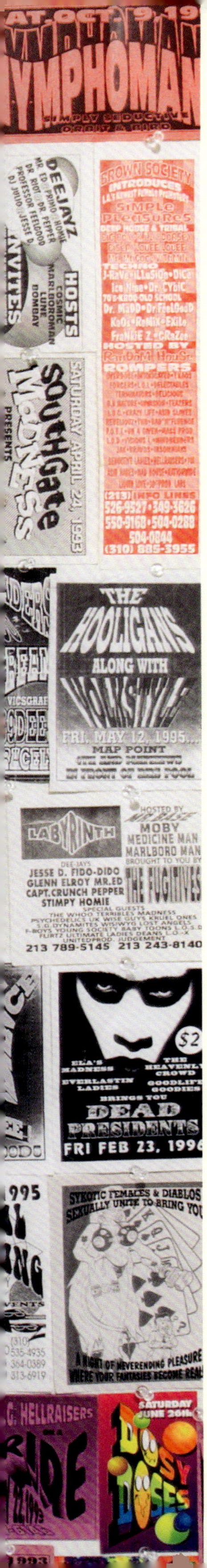

FIRST NIGHT OUT

THE FIRST FLYER PARTY I REMEMBER GOING TO was in 1994, when I had just turned fourteen years old. I was with my sister Maria, Silvia, Silvia's brother Alfred, and a group of his friends I didn't know. Alfred had graduated from Schurr High, so we rolled with him and his friends to celebrate their graduation. They were about three to four years older than us, celebrating the class of 1994. We didn't stay long at the first party. We linked up with others there and then we caravanned or carpooled the rest of the night, especially since the only way we could get ahold of each other was through beepers—I got my first when I was about fifteen years old—and landlines or pay phones.

The party was in the backyard of a home tucked in a dead end in East Los Angeles. The house sat on a sloped street, and to get to the backyard, you had to walk a narrow path along its side. The farther back I went, the darker it got—I could barely see a few feet ahead and had to follow the person in front of me. The music pulled us in, and as we got closer, the backyard seemed to disappear into the dark. I was swallowed by night.

There was a chain-link fence splitting off the neighbor's property. The fence was bent and buckling from its weight because it was old and holding on by its last rusty thread. Many guys were wearing motorcycle jackets and I can still smell the leather. They wore Harley-Davidson boots and greased-up hair combed back. The night was chilly. The boys looked older than me, or maybe it felt like this because I was so shy and short, just five feet.

This is also the first night I had to defend myself from a man on my own. My first time having to push someone off me, respectfully. I say respectfully because I also didn't want to cause a scene or overreact, even if my body knew something wasn't right, because all you can do is freeze. I remember seeing my sister and friends get farther and farther away because I was being pushed to the darkest corner against a fence.

I had to confront so much confusion—reject, but be assertive and polite all at the same time. He was a rebel or greaser. I can still remember what his leather motorcycle jacket felt like—stiff, cold leather. Luckily I pushed him off me and walked away. Being underage was already a risk, but being an underage teenage girl added to the risk. Because no one teaches us how to navigate this and no one talks about this, we brush it off.

But despite that moment, that night was fun. When the party is out in the open, the sound waves travel and bounce off onto the streets, in the alleyways, in the homes, and disappear into the dark. In backyard parties, it was concrete or dirt or a sheet of plywood. The dust and crackling of a record playing at the backyard party has its charm, and nothing can compare to the excitement we get when a group of us walk from the car to the party and hear the music and let it lead us to the night. There is no surveillance, no adults, no policing, and lots of kegs. As you get closer, the music gets louder and clearer. This is when adrenaline hits us like a shock to our bodies. We get anxious and excited at the same time.

After the flyer party, as a nightcap, we ended up at Florentine Gardens, an all-ages club in Hollywood. In the club, the music made us vibrate. When the rooms were empty, the music traveled and echoed in the space. As the room got tighter, we felt it more on our bodies.

The sound was clear at clubs like Florentine Gardens, the Alexandria Hotel, and Baby Doe's and you rarely heard off-beat music transitions. There was that particular smell of a fog machine, sweet and fresh, enclosed in a room. The sound bouncing off the walls and our bodies feels completely different than being outside. I loved how the lights made me feel. I felt like I was taken out of this world. We danced on tile or linoleum or wooden floors, just like at the dance parties at school.

I had smoked a joint; I was so high. On the dance floor the smoke machine and strobe lights made my eyes roll back.

Part of me felt intimidated by everyone in these spaces because it was my first time going out without my mother's guidance and the weed just made me more paranoid. Even though my sister Maria was there, I felt like she needed me to have her back on nights when I lost her in the crowd: Either she'd run off with some guy and I had to hang out with her friends or I'd be alone talking to strangers.

Some people might think that going out without our parents or adults at fourteen years old is too young. Perhaps it is, but almost everyone I knew started going out around that age, possibly even younger. Most of our parents were hustling and making ends meet. Many times, we showed up at home before them since they worked nine-to-five jobs, sometimes longer if they were working overtime or graveyard shifts. Our parents couldn't afford a nanny; we were our own nannies.

Mom tried to be there for us as much as she could, but her priority was to put food on the table, have a job, and keep a roof over our heads. Mom has always worked or stayed busy learning a new skill.

Also, my mom didn't know how to teach us or help us with our homework. We just had to figure it out on our own. Like many parents of kids I knew, my mom didn't graduate from high school, and she wasn't like those fictional parents we'd see on TV who sit with the kid at the table and help them with their math homework.

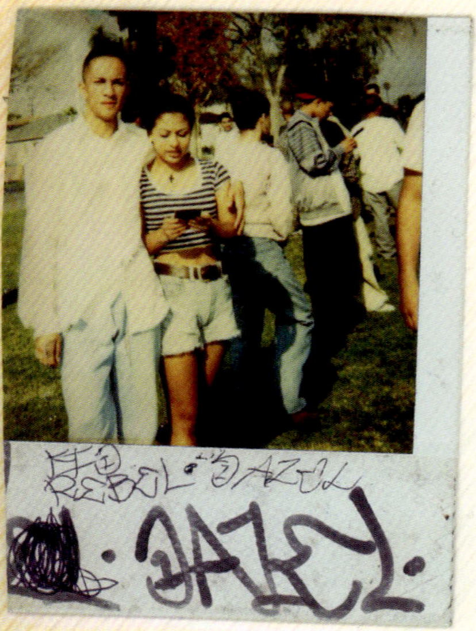

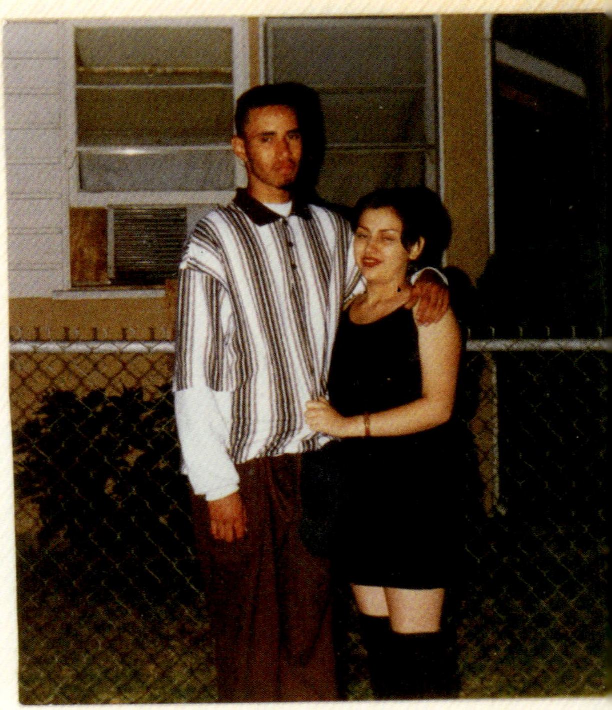

A photo taken during P.E. class right before ditching, and photos of friends taken in front of my house after a party. The top left Polaroid photo is my sister Maria and Kid Rebel in 1995. I am in the back. This was at an East LA Madness party crew meeting in the park.

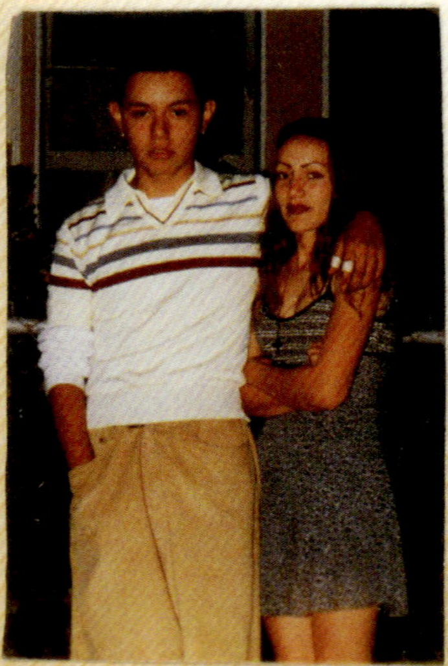

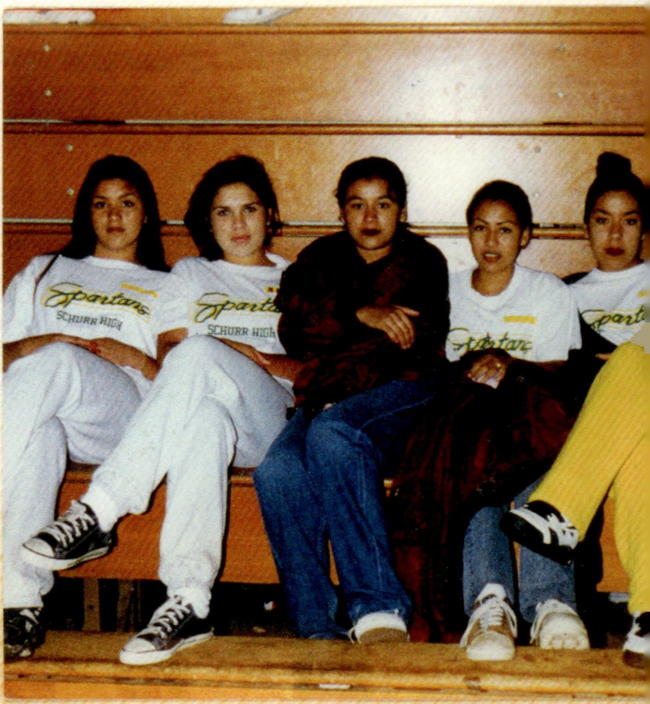

DITCHING

WHEN I WAS IN HIGH SCHOOL, MARIA AND I picked up my friend Miros, who lived on Hendricks, and together we walked up Hay Street, that steep hill we always climbed. We held our heavy books and folders close to our chests. We encountered many creeps along the way. Men pulled up or drove slowly alongside and said inappropriate things to us. Sometimes they parked ahead of us knowing we would walk by them. They rolled down their windows and pretended they wanted to ask us for directions. We looked into their cars and they were touching themselves. This started when I was fourteen. Eventually we learned not to get near these cars or stop if they asked us for help. Many times we didn't look in their direction because we already knew what their intentions were. This is something we couldn't get used to.

Sometimes walking to school felt like an obstacle course. Once we got there, we'd head straight to the cafeteria, hoping to get some breakfast. I loved the classic Los Angeles City School crumb cake and orange juice.

I WAS A freshman and Maria was a sophomore when I started ditching school with her. The first time I ditched was probably the scariest, but the more we did it the easier it got. This was the beginning of so many fun, exciting, scary, and dangerous moments with Maria.

Ditching started off as something easy and silly. Guys from other schools would drive around ours in the mornings, trying to hit on cute girls.

A lot of us would hang out across the street from campus before school started, so it was easy to hop into a car with some cute guys and skip school. Most mornings, Maria and her friends would meet new guys and I'd tag along for the ride.

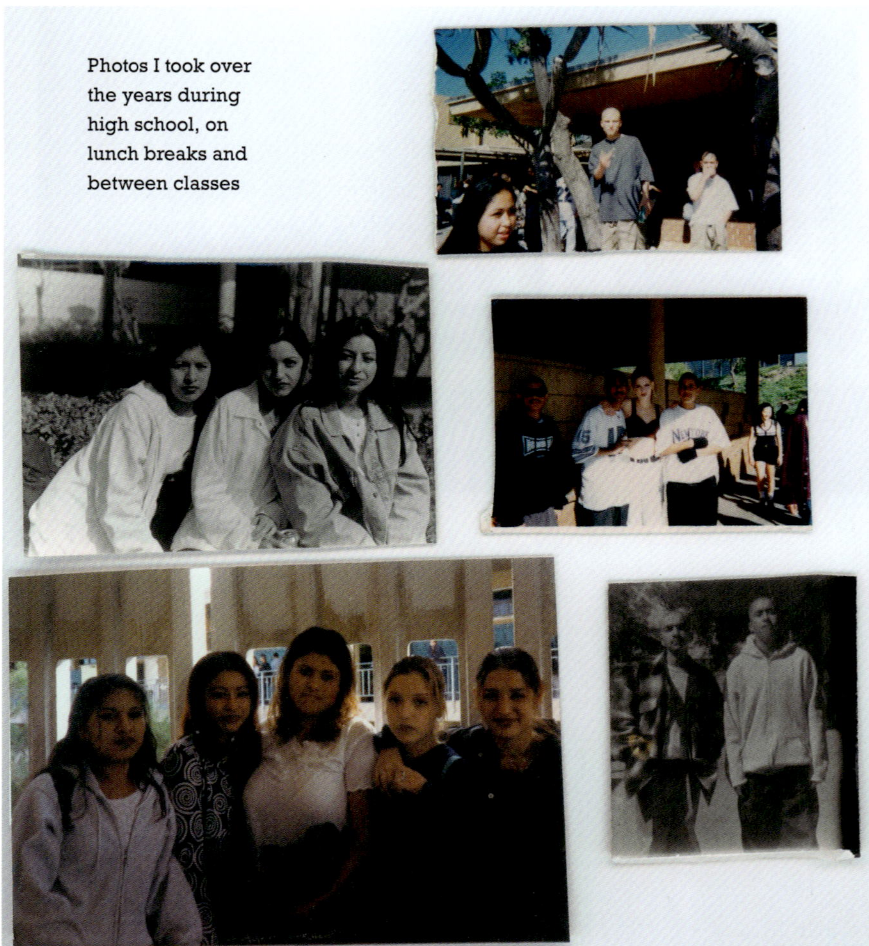

Photos I took over the years during high school, on lunch breaks and between classes

There were these guys from a car club—T-Clan (or maybe it was T-Klan)—who drove fixed-up Hondas and Toyota Tercels with hooked-up sound systems, of course. There was always more than one car, caravanning together. They were older and they had their own auto shop and customized their own rides.

If I didn't go with Maria, she'd come home and tell me all about it—how sometimes they just cruised around listening to music, or got on the freeway to mess around and race each other. Sometimes they'd buy big bags of ice, get back on the freeway, and throw ice at each other's cars. And if any of the girls were really down, they'd moon each other's cars.

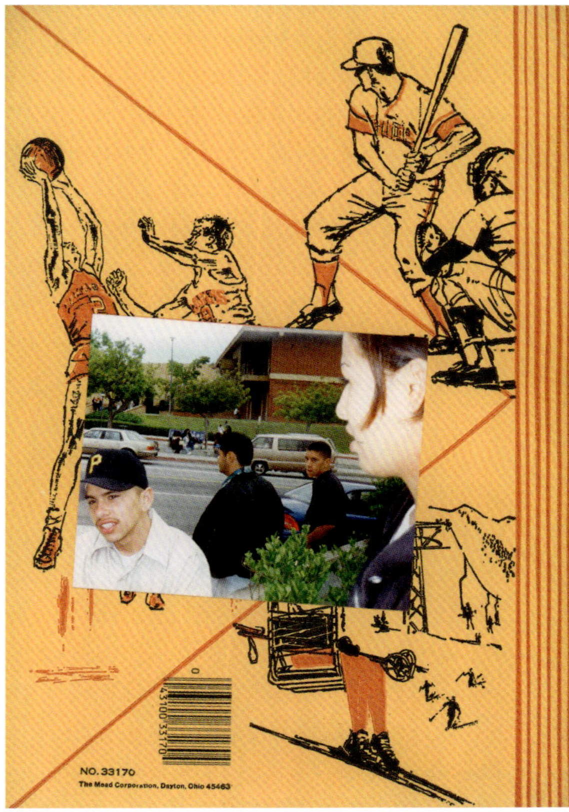

My sister Maria on the right, hanging out with friends across the street from Schurr High, just before class

Then things got a bit more technical, and we got smarter about ditching. The first two years at Schurr High, Maria and I had P.E. in the morning, which made it easier to ditch school. The secret was to never miss first or second period, because we needed to be marked present; otherwise, the school could call our parents. It was also easier to ditch school during P.E. because we were always outside unless it rained.

Our P.E. routine started with a jog around the football field to warm up. Near the field, there was a gate that was usually left open, and if no one was watching, we could slip out or hide under the bleachers by the gate until our ride came. We wore our P.E. clothes—sweatpants and a T-shirt—over our cute outfits, smelling fresh like a Bath & Body Works or a Victoria's Secret body mist. Sometimes this was planned the night before, usually when Maria wanted to party with her guy friends who were older and didn't go to Schurr High. But other times, ditching was spontaneous—my sister would give me the signal just minutes before, usually if I saw her in the locker room.

One chilly morning on our way to school, Maria whispered in my ear that she and a group of friends were going to ditch school during P.E. So nobody would see me putting on my gym clothes over my regular clothes, I quickly made my way to the bathroom stalls to change. Girls might have thought I was weird, or maybe they figured I was just too shy to change in front of people. But the truth? I was about to step out of that bathroom stall and transform into someone else entirely.

In my head, I was a badass—ditching school, joining the Bad Girls Club. Coming out of that stall, I felt bulky with all the layers of clothing, but I played it off like I was comfortable. I made eye contact with my sister and her friends in the locker room and let them know with a smile that my mission was accomplished. Once we were outside with our class, we'd make eye contact again. This time I'd be waiting to catch that little signal. We communicated with our eyes and gestures. As I jogged, I looked out for my sister and her friends to make sure I wouldn't miss them. I'd finally see them hiding under the bleachers waiting for me.

My heart pumped fast from fear and excitement and the unknown. We'd finally made it out together with no teacher or security in sight, though we did know a couple of guards at Schurr who'd look the other way when they saw us. Most of them were young, and some of my sister's friends would see them at backyard parties—like Mike, who was part of a party crew and would always chill with us. Sometimes he'd warn us, "Don't do this again," but we kept ditching anyway. We sped up our walk down the steep street called Westmoreland, not looking back and not knowing if we'd get caught. A white Jeep Cherokee was parked at the corner of Westmoreland and Wilcox—the same car I'd seen circling after school a few days earlier, and again parked outside my house. I realized they were no strangers. Once we got to the car, my sister opened the door and we shoved each other in, rushing to get into the car and out of the area.

My sister introduced me to her friends in the car—Ivan, Tim, and Carlos. Maria and her friend Silvia had met them after school a few months back while Carlos and Tim were driving around the school. It was very common for people, especially boys, to come hang out after school or cruise around the area, because Schurr High was known to have the hottest girls in L.A.

We drove down Westmoreland Drive and made a left on Beverly Boulevard, making our way to the McDonald's drive-through for some breakfast before heading to the kickback. Smaller gatherings were known as "kickbacks." They were usually indoors, at someone's house or garage, turned into a hangout space. No DJ was needed—a boom box did the trick. Kickbacks happened more spontaneously, no flyers, all word of mouth. They'd come together while cruising on the boulevard after not finding a house party or simply when someone just wanted to chill with a small group of friends—or with someone they had just met on the boulevard. They also happened on weekdays when we ditched school.

We drove through East Los Angeles on Whittier Boulevard. Tim hotboxed the car, and I got a subtle contact high, enough to feel relaxed and a bit in a dream state. I rolled down my window to catch some fresh air, letting a cloud of smoke escape. The day was beautiful, with clear skies and a crisp morning breeze. By this time, around 9:30 or 10 A.M., the streets weren't as busy.

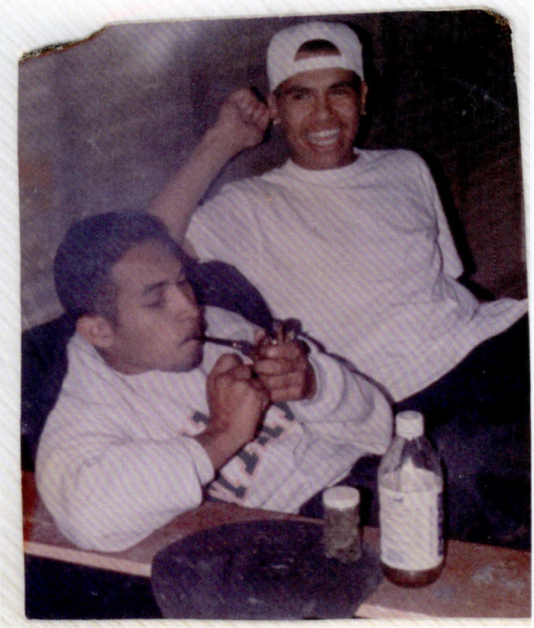

Carlos and Tim, aka Sniper, kicking back and smoking weed

The mood was quiet and relaxed, as we bumped hip-hop, Freestyle Fellowship's *To Whom It May Concern . . .*, Funkdoobiest, and Wu-Tang Clan. I could feel the bass coming out of the subwoofers behind me. Ivan was sitting in the backseat with us and Carlos was driving. Carlos had a strong jawline and dark skin with some acne scars. He wore oversized khaki pants and a white T-shirt with his baseball hat flipped backward. Tim, aka Sniper, was on the passenger side, a quiet guy rolling some joints. I could only see the top of his head—black hair with a short fade and long bangs pushed back, with strands of hair falling down the side of his face.

They all wore clean creased-up, size 40+ Ben Davis pants. Ivan wore a beanie that came down over his forehead, leaving his eyes just enough space to see. They all dressed like tagbangers—big clothes, hair with bangs pushed back, Nike Jordan and Puma sneakers with fat shoelaces. A cross between taggers and gangsters. Tim and Maria were hooking up, information I did not know before this car ride.

We drove around for about forty-five minutes—from Montebello, where Schurr High is, to Boyle Heights, where Ivan lived. We pulled up to Ivan's place, a big apartment building right across from Hollenbeck Park. There was a staircase on the side of the building and we made our way up to the top floor and into the attic. Its gable style and low ceiling made it feel cozy. There were bedsheets and blankets covering the window facing the park. Outside it was sunny with clear skies. Inside, it was smoky and dark but comfy.

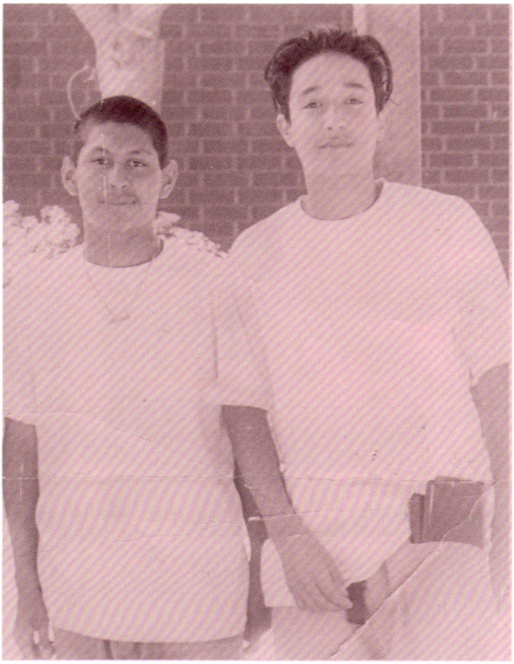
Fax and File. They were known for their looks and cool style in high school.

We all sat around on the floor, and Ivan asked what we felt like listening to. We cracked jokes and forgot we had been asked a question. There was a stereo system—turntables and standing speakers. Carlos finally threw on "Shimmy Shimmy Ya" by Ol' Dirty Bastard from his album *Return to the 36 Chambers: The Dirty Version*. Then he sparked up a joint and passed it around. It was my turn to take a hit.

All of a sudden my mind took a turn and I began to feel like I was in a dream. Everything was echoing and making me laugh. There were moments when I felt stuck and not able to speak. The words just didn't come out, so I closed my eyes and felt the music on my back and legs. The sound of Ol' Dirty Bastard tripped me out and we all began to laugh for an unknown reason. I could see swirls of smoke in the rays of light coming in through the window. There were records on the floor and against the wall and everyone was quiet again.

A few hours passed and we all started to get the munchies. We couldn't decide if we were ready to step out into the world or if we should just hang out 'til the sun came down. We decided to walk to the liquor store across the street and buy Doritos, soda, and water. The sun was glaring on our

OPPOSITE: This is the soundtrack of this time.

IDENTIFICATION CARD FOR FOOD COUPONS AND/OR PUBLIC ASSISTANCE
THE CITY OF BROOKLYN ZOO
Department of Social Services
RETURN TO THE
36 CHAMBERS:
THE DIRTY VERSION
OL' DIRTY BASTARD
Tarjeta de Identificación para Cupones

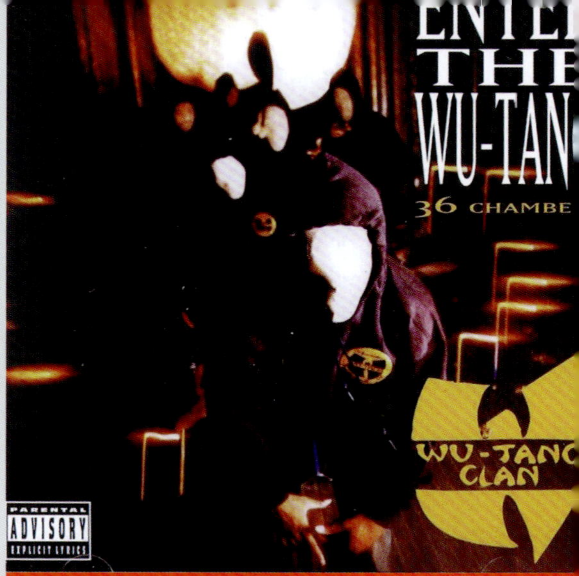
THE
WU-TAN
36 CHAMBE
PARENTAL ADVISORY EXPLICIT LYRICS

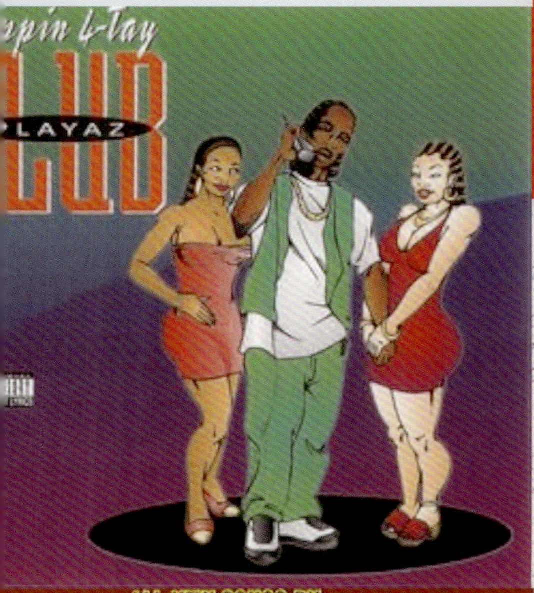
LAYAZ

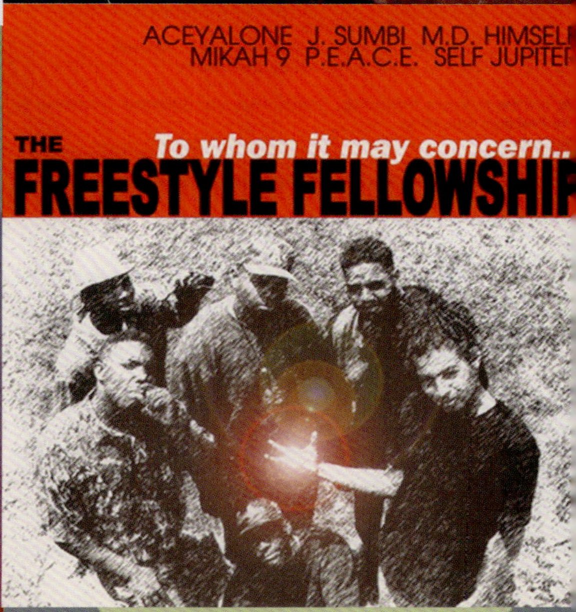
ACEYALONE J. SUMBI M.D. HIMSEL
MIKAH 9 P.E.A.C.E. SELF JUPITE
THE
To whom it may concern..
FREESTYLE FELLOWSHI

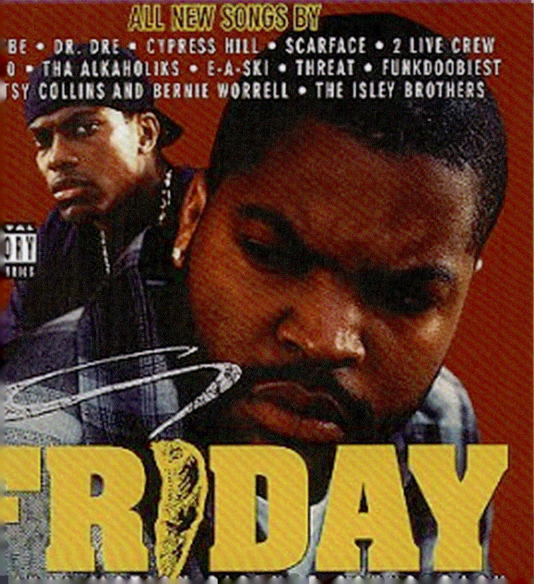
ALL NEW SONGS BY
DR. DRE • CYPRESS HILL • SCARFACE • 2 LIVE CREW
THA ALKAHOLIKS • E-A-SKI • THREAT • FUNKDOOBIEST
COLLINS AND BERNIE WORRELL • THE ISLEY BROTHERS
FRIDAY

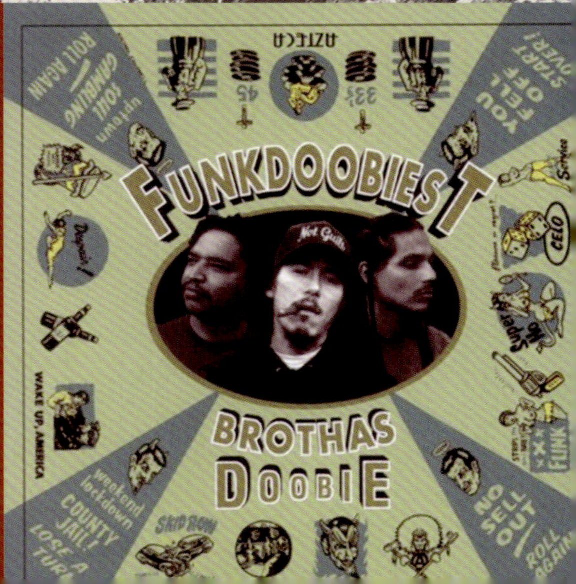
FUNKDOOBIEST
BROTHAS
DOOBIE
YOU FELL OFF START OVER!
NO SELL OUT
COUNTY JAIL!
WAKE UP, AMERICA

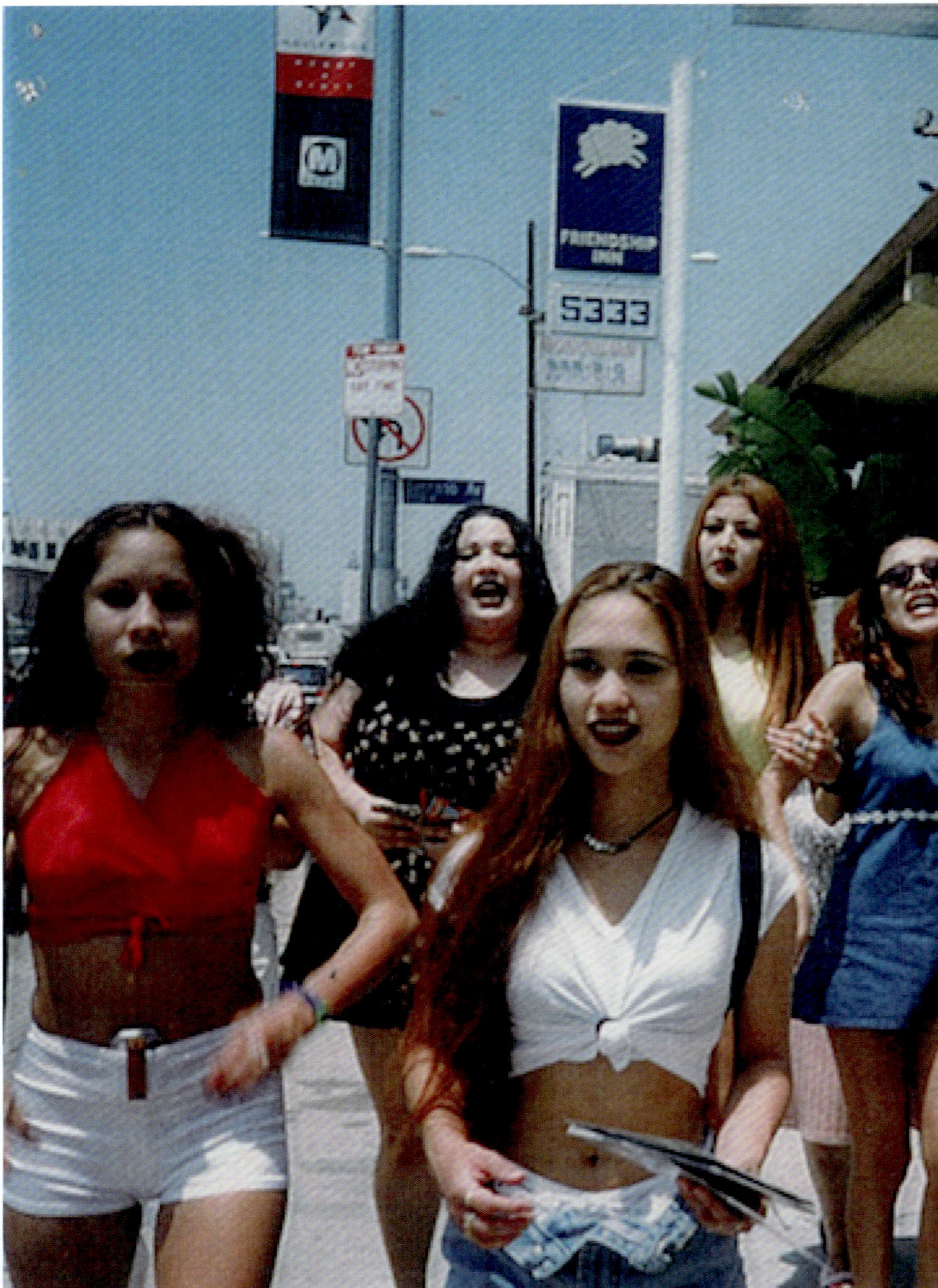

Brown Authority crew walking to Purple Shield in 1996

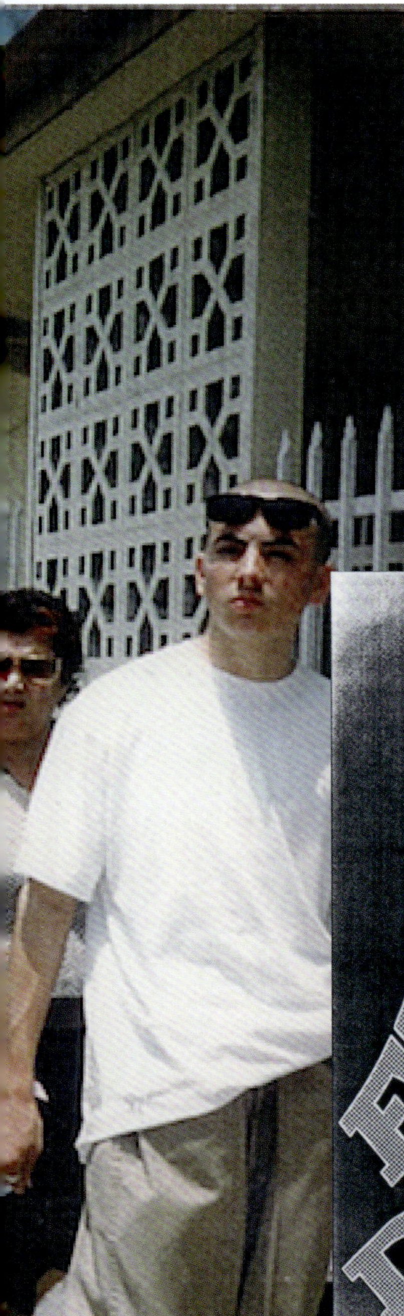

faces and I wished I had a pair of sunglasses. I felt like people were staring at us and wondered if I was just being paranoid.

The sun gave us a second wind. We walked back and threw on another record. This time it was Funkdoobiest's "Superhoes" playing in the background. I began to feel sleepy and maybe a little bored, so I told my sister it was almost 2 P.M., time for us to head back home before Mom found out we'd skipped school. We gathered our backpacks and Carlos took us back to school.

Sometimes Mom picked us up after school. On the days we ditched, we had to

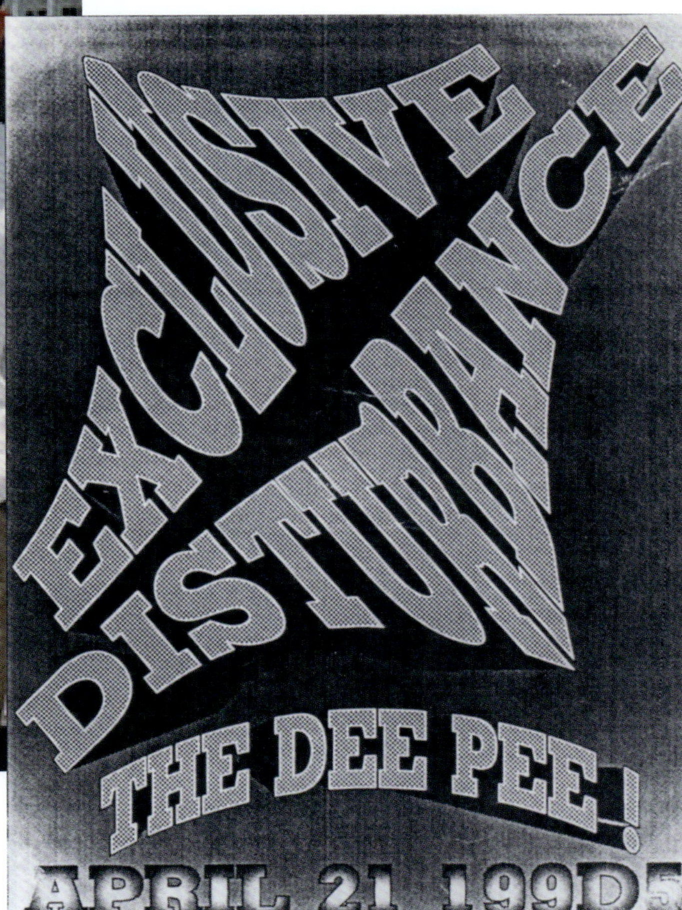

A DP flyer

time it right, heading back to campus just minutes before the bell rang, acting like we'd been there all along. That way, we'd be standing out front, ready for Mom to pick us up. Most days we just walked home, and if we ditched on those days, friends would drop us off a few blocks away so it looked like we were walking back from school.

When ditching in between classes became harder, we'd miss school altogether. In the mornings, instead of going to school, we'd go to the nearest McDonald's and wait for our ride there. Until we got caught. Not once, but twice. The first time was when my sister, my friends, and I got caught at this McDonald's. We saw our school security pulling up so we ran, scared. We all hid in the bathroom. Then we heard a voice, "I know you're all in there. Either come out or I'll get the key and open the door."

They were already keeping an eye on us and knew exactly where we would go every morning before we ditched. The second time, my sister got caught by our stepdad. For him, school didn't matter much. It wasn't about whether we went, it was about finding an excuse to humiliate us and drive a wedge between us and our mom.

He found Maria at McDonald's while she was ditching school. My sister ran out of the restaurant before he saw her inside, but he still managed to make a scene, yelling at her and shoving her around until she was crying, all in front of strangers. This only fueled the anger we had toward him. Our stepdad only wanted her to get in trouble to prove to my mother we weren't good kids. We got caught ditching a few more times and didn't worry about the consequences—from our parents, school, or even the police. By then, Maria and I didn't care much if we got caught; it was all part of the experience.

Sometimes we didn't even bother showing up at all. We'd ditch before school started, around 7:30 A.M., and meet our friends across the street from campus—our usual hangout spot—or sometimes at the McDonald's or Del Taco down the hill. A lot of times we'd head to ditching parties (or DPs, as we called them). Those were always fun, even though they didn't last long—maybe two hours max—but there was always a backup if one got shut down. If there wasn't another DP, we'd go to a friend's house. Low-budget '70s and '80s porn played in the background, or *The Crow* on repeat. Eventually, Maria transferred to Vail High, a continuation school for the "bad" kids. I stayed at Schurr all four years.

. . .

WHEN MARIA WASN'T around anymore, I continued to alternate between going to school and ditching with Yesi and her friend Teresa and sometimes with my friends Miros and Angie. Not having Maria around didn't mean I stopped getting in trouble. Now we either walked to school or caught a ride with a friend on more mornings, which made it easier to lose interest in going to school and just keep hanging out instead.

We were wild kids getting drunk during school hours, and getting into car accidents, fleeing the scene, then later in the day getting home still faded. One morning, Yesi's boyfriend, Hugo, picked us up in a car. What we didn't know was that the car was a G ride (a stolen car). Hugo was completely faded from smoking too much weed, and he had no clue how to drive stick. Not a great combo. As we got close to Schurr High, he spotted a cop clocking cars with a radar gun, and he panicked.

He did the worst thing possible: He hit the gas and burned the clutch as we drove uphill to school. I remember the gestures of the cop trying to get us to stop, swinging his arms in the air. We also panicked and told Hugo to pull over. He said, "I can't because I stole this car." Then everything went into slow motion. Somehow, the car made its way to the front of the school, running only in neutral. We were minutes from the bell. Hugo looked at us, gripped the wheel, and said, "On the count of three, jump out" because he couldn't stop the car.

He counted—"One, two . . . three!"—and we bailed. We hit the ground running. My sister tripped and fell but managed to get up and keep going. We dove into the crowd of students gathering at the front gates as we saw the car crash into a brick fence in front of a house across the street from Schurr High. Above us the skies were gloomy and gray, just like every morning in L.A. before it gets sunny. I saw two helicopters circling around the area. Hugo tried to hide in the bushes but got caught. He was arrested on the spot and wound up in juvenile hall.

Typical East L.A. teenagers, we were in a stolen car, involved in a police chase, and the car crashed in front of our school all before first period. Somehow, we blended into the crowd and made it to class like nothing had happened.

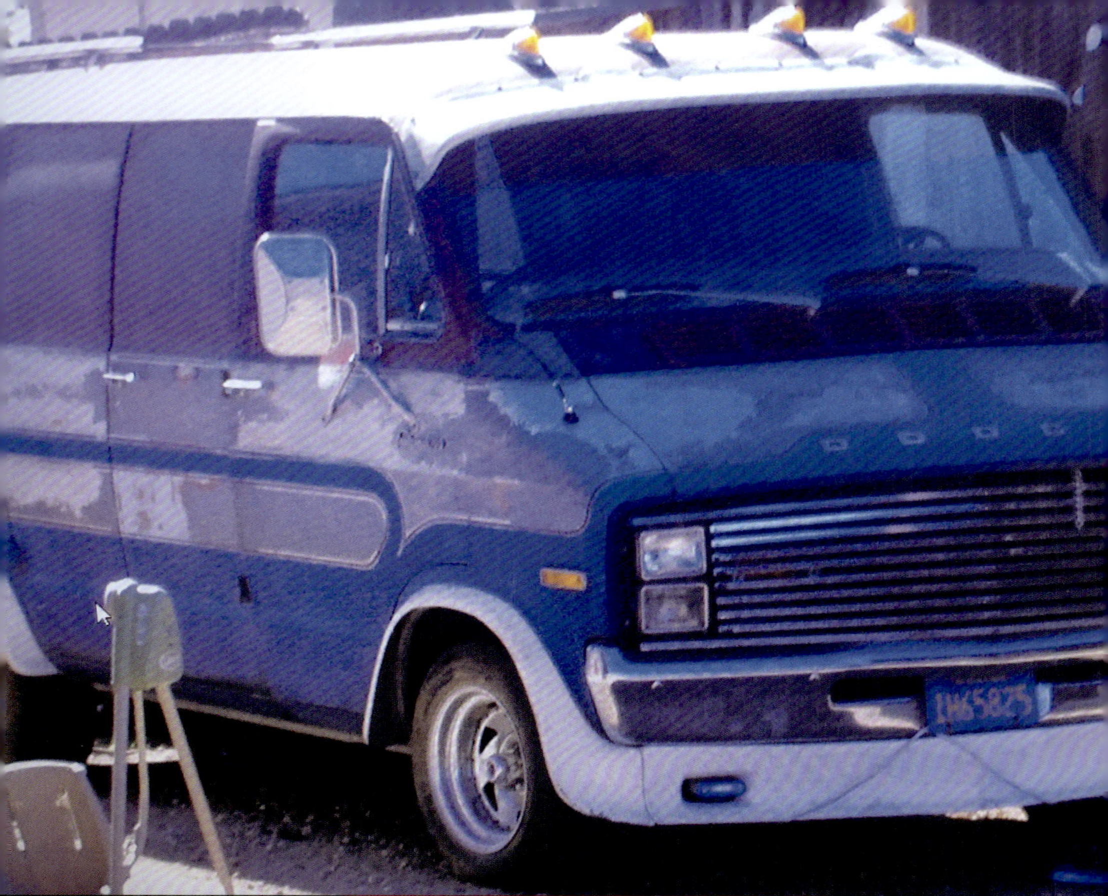

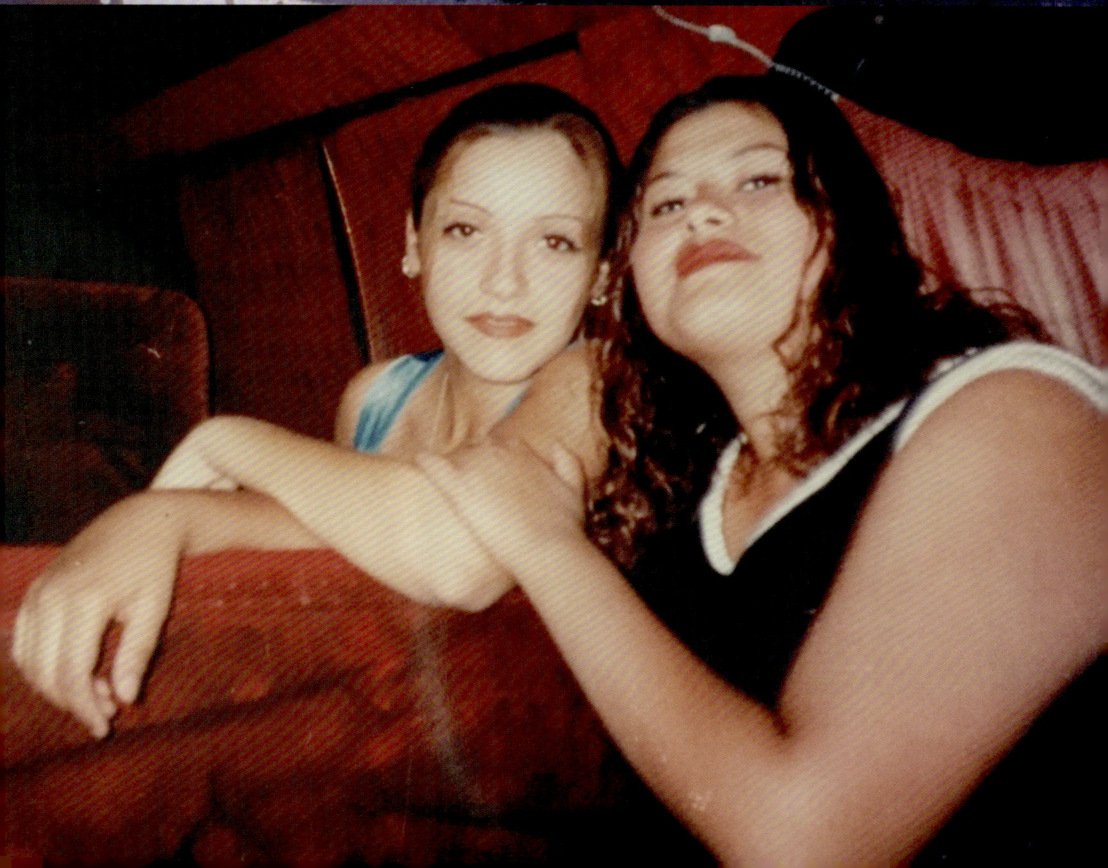

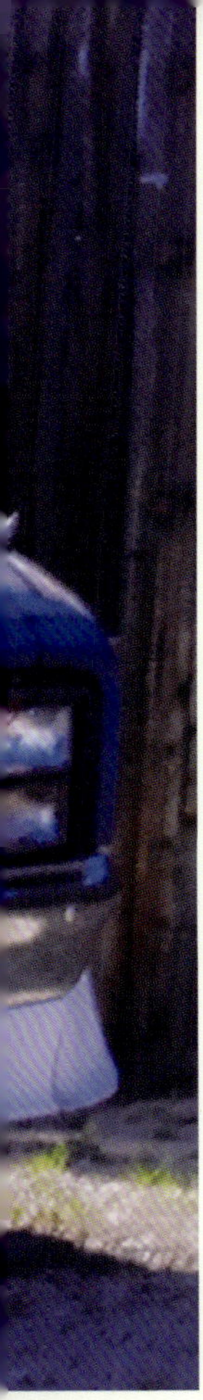

AZTEK NATION

I **MET MIROS IN SEVENTH GRADE AT EASTMONT** Intermediate. I was wearing my black Jim Morrison T-shirt—the one with his face rising out of orange and yellow flames on the front and the lyrics to "Light My Fire" printed on the back. We were inseparable throughout middle school and high school.

One day during class in ninth grade, Miros asked me if I "partied." I answered, "Yes," even though I didn't exactly know what she meant. She said, "Great, I'll pick you up this Friday. We're going to a house party." When Friday came, Miros called my house from hers to let me know she was on her way. She lived about a five-minute drive to my house, but it took her thirty minutes to get to me and she pulled up in a van full of teenagers. Her brothers had an '80s family-style van with a red-wine-colored-upholstery interior that looked like someone's living room. About fifteen people fit in that van—we called it the Aztek van. I got in. Her brothers and cousin ran the Aztek Nation crew, so for me to eventually join was almost a given—it felt like a natural step.

OPPOSITE, TOP: Aztek Nation van. This was our ride to all the parties and could easily fit more than a dozen kids in there.

OPPOSITE, BOTTOM: Angie and Christina inside the Aztek van—wine-colored velvet fabric wrapping every seat and every detail

When we got to the house party, we parked in a dark alley—there was no street parking left. We jumped out of the van chanting "AZ-TEK NA-TION!" and made our way to the party. At the door, the girls got in free and the boys paid three dollars apiece. There were kegs everywhere and people were handing out plastic cups. My

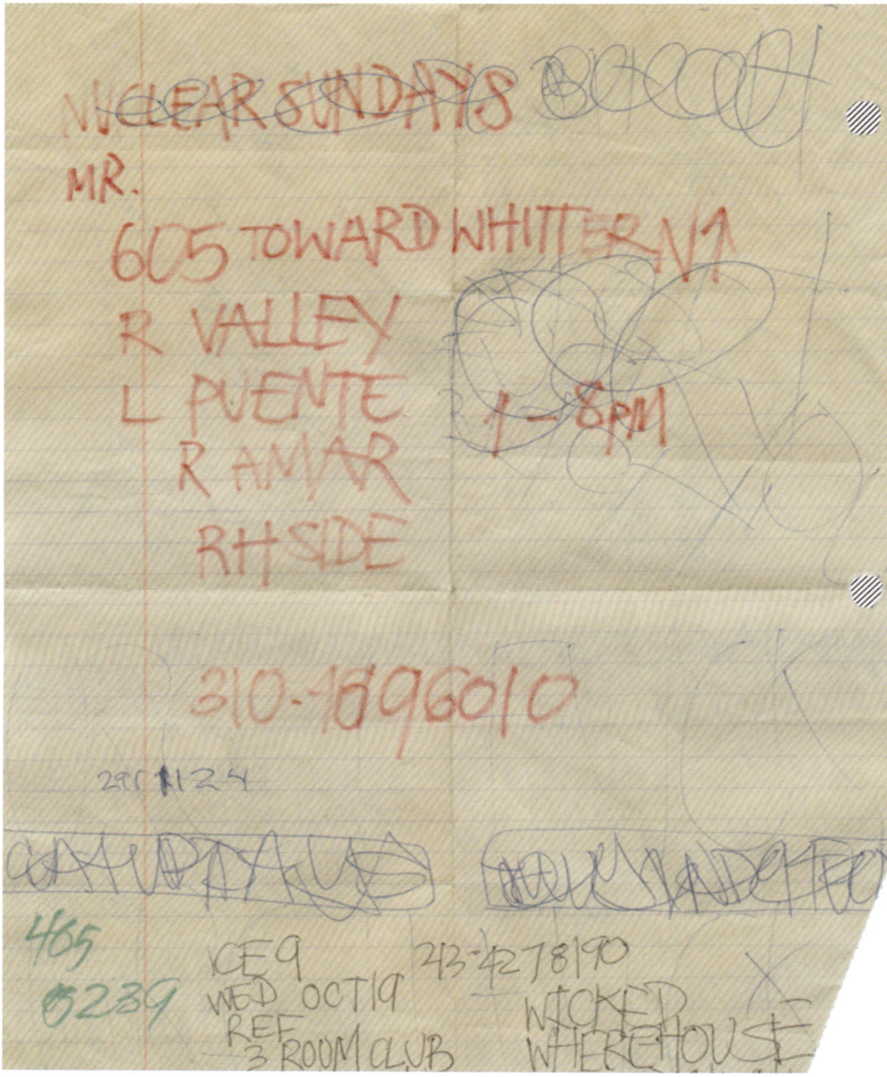

friends Christina and Miros were already drifting toward the dance floor, the music pulling them in.

I carried the sound of bass thumping through backyard fences, a pulse that stayed with me through the rest of my teenage years. This was also the night when Miros asked if I wanted to join the crew. I said yes. I was so happy to be part of something that mattered to me.

Kids in middle school who were around thirteen years old were already organizing raves and backyard parties. I was a couple of years younger than them, but I know that around 1991 or 1992, the rave and party crew scene exploded across East L.A. and nearby cities. By organizing, I mean scouting locations, designing flyers, printing them, paying for production, promoting and distributing the flyers. This was especially common in the summer or even around the holidays, when some kids' parents would go to Mexico to visit family.

Sometimes, though, parents would be home during these parties. This was rare. They'd just stay inside watching their telenovelas, completely uninterested in what was happening outside. Perhaps the parents had lost control of their kids or they would rather have them home than out in the streets. But regardless, it was like they were in their own world while we were in ours. Many times their lovely neighbors called the cops and they'd show up within minutes, but even that didn't stop us—we'd stop the music, pretend it was over or lie and say it was a birthday celebration, then wait for them to leave to start again or hit up another party in the neighborhood.

The best part of being in a crew was putting the party together. Someone who knew a little graphic design would make the flyer, but it was always a group effort—the DJs, friends with gear, everyone pitching in. The flyer usually had a phone number you could call for more info. Promoters would record a voicemail with all the upcoming parties for the weekend, and then update it on the night of the event.

We'd call the number, write the instructions down on a scrap of paper, or look it up in a Thomas Guide to find the map point.

Sometimes the phone numbers and flyers gave full directions to the party, but other times, out of fear of getting raided by cops, they didn't. The info line told you where to meet—a "map point," usually a gas station or grocery store parking lot, where someone from the crew waited to guide the crowd. You'd get a hand-drawn map or another slip of paper with directions and follow the caravan through dark side streets until you finally heard the bass in the distance. Most of the time the info spread by word of mouth.

The parties were all planned out weeks before. We'd talk it through at meetings, throwing out ideas about the theme, what image to use, what kind of vibe we wanted, what DJs we wanted. If the party lined up with a holiday or a member's birthday, it took a few rounds to plan—especially for Halloween or Christmas.

My sister Yesi eventually joined Aztek Nation, but Maria was part of an all-female party crew—East Q-teez. She and her friends started this crew when they were all around fifteen years old and around the time when she was ditching. East LA Q-teez organized parties and were the new it girls in East L.A. They dressed sexy, with platform shoes, hoochie shorts, and crop tops. They were so beautiful. I looked up to them, but mainly I looked up to my sister. She was tough, beautiful, and street-smart, and boys were intimidated by her beauty.

East LA Q-teez loved to party with all sorts of boys—taggers, cholos, ravers, they did not discriminate. As gangs became more prominent and they started to come to our parties (mostly to start trouble), Q-teez began to party more with them. Until my cousin was murdered, during a time when gang violence was on the rise again.

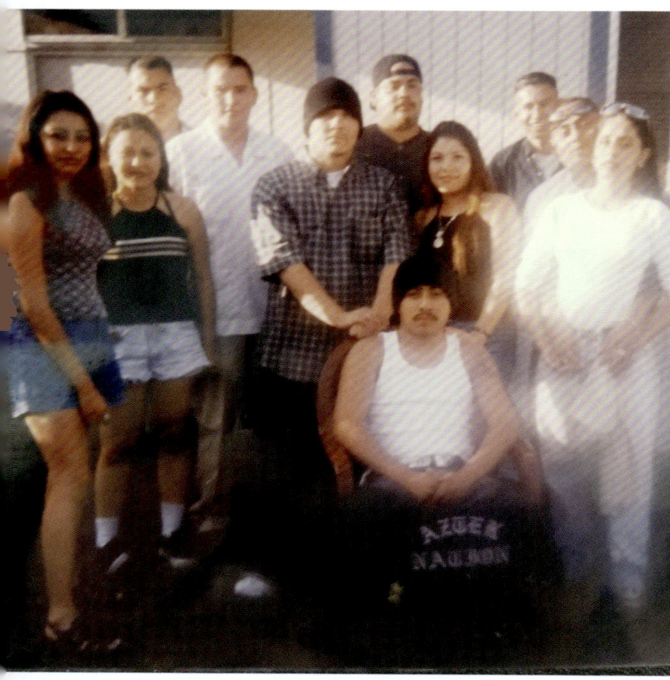

Aztek Nation meeting at Hex's House. Then we BBQ'd.

I remember East LA Madness once named their party "Hallow My Weenie." The flyers had everything—Morrissey photos, Looney Tunes characters, sometimes even pornographic images. That teenage sexual energy just spilled out, no filter.

If your crew was named on the party flyer, you got in for free—but regardless, girls always got in for free. The flyer parties usually took place in someone's backyard and were tucked away from the police and gangs so they wouldn't be interrupted. Even so, that was hard to avoid. The police and gangs always found their way in to mess with us.

Gangs punked and made fun of the rebel boys for their style and the way they danced and sexually harassed the girls. The cops criminalized us. This is why there were so many parties in one night: We knew they wouldn't last longer than a couple of hours before they were broken up.

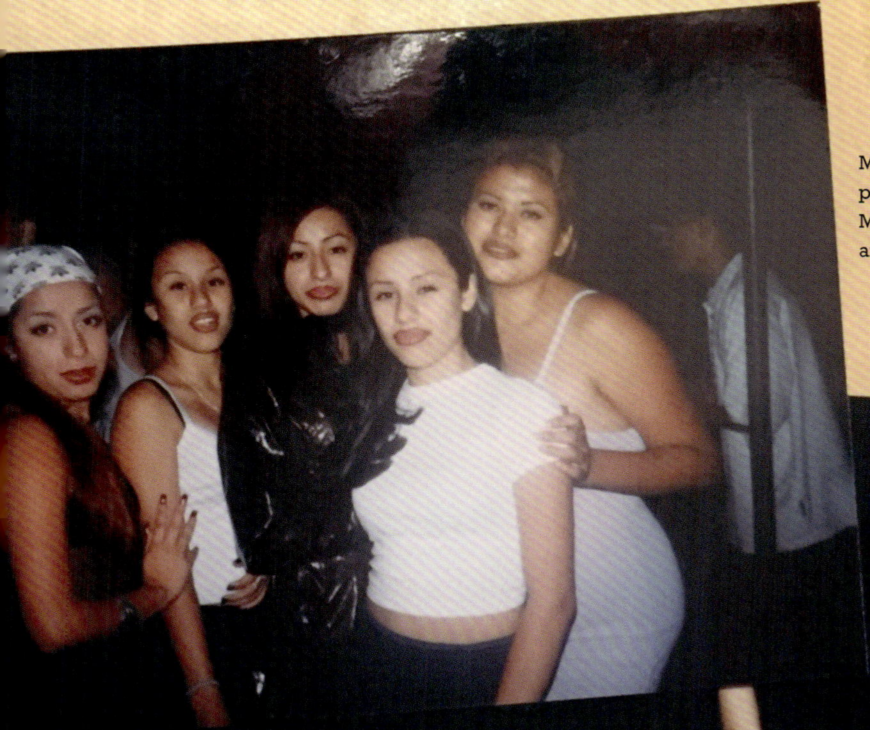

More Aztek Nation photos courtesy of Miros, sometime around 1997 or 1998

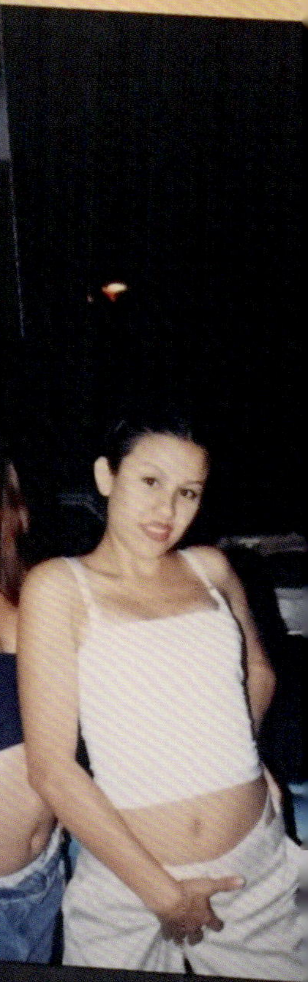

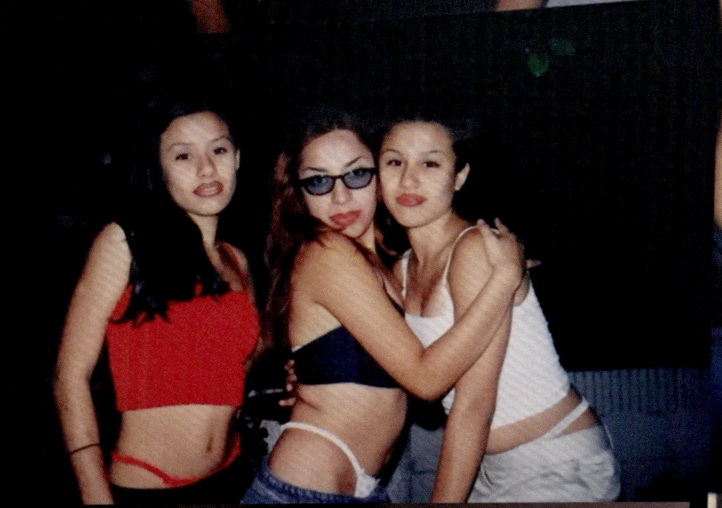

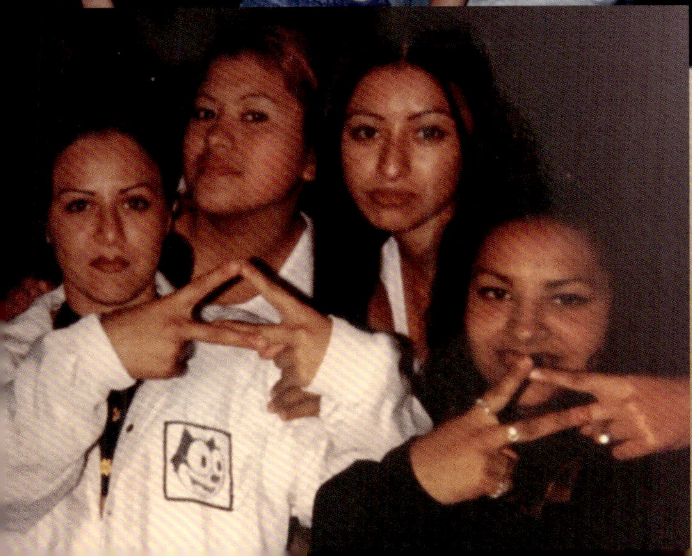

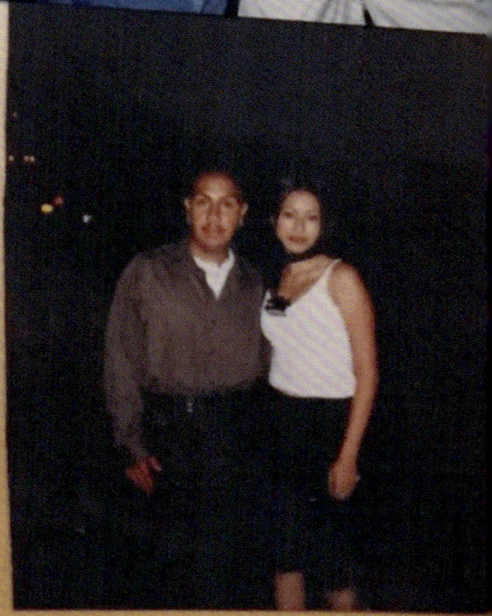

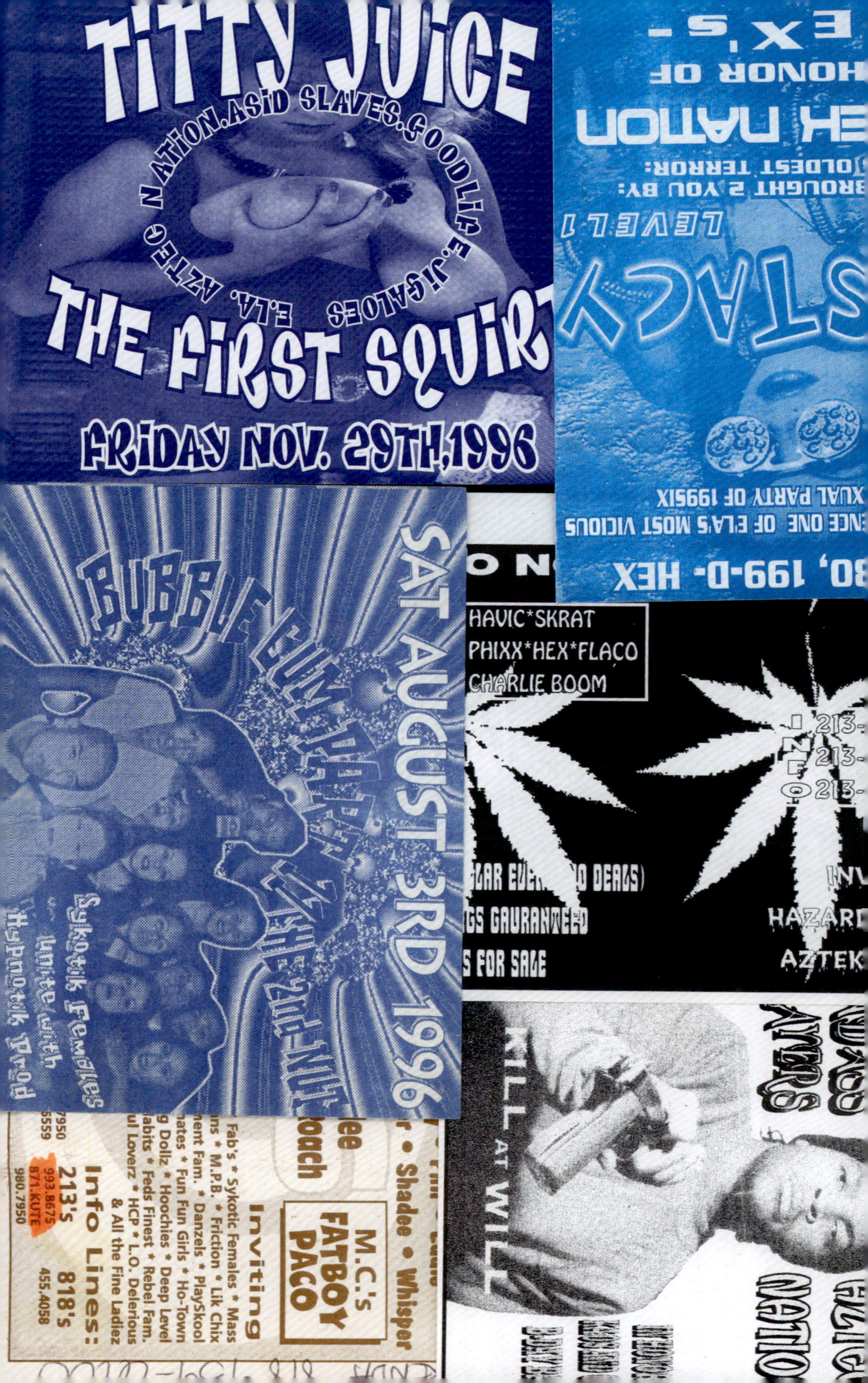
TITTY JUICE
NATION.ASID SLAVES.GOODLIFE.JIGALOES E.LA. AZTEC
THE FIRST SQUIRT
FRIDAY NOV. 29TH,1996
STACY
LEVEL 1
BROUGHT 2 YOU BY:
OLDEST TERROR:
HEX NATION
HONOR OF
EX'S -
ENCE ONE OF ELA'S MOST VICIOUS
XUAL PARTY OF 1995IX
30, 199-D- HEX
SAT AUGUST 3RD 1996
Sykotik Females
Unite with
Hypnotik Prod
HAVIC*SKRAT
PHIXX*HEX*FLACO
CHARLIE BOOM
GS GAURANTEED
S FOR SALE
HAZARD
AZTEK
KILL AT WILL
M.C.'s
FATBOY
PACO
Inviting
Fab's * Sykotic Females * Mass
M.P.B. * Friction * Lik Chix
Danzels * PlaySkool
Fun Fun Girls * Ho-Town
Hoochies * Deep Level
Feds Finest * Rebel Fam.
HCP * L.O. Delerious
& All the Fine Ladiez
Info Lines:
213's
993.8675
871.KUTE
980.7950
818's
455.4058

OPPOSITE: A collection of Aztek Nation flyers that mentioned our party crew as special guests, mid-1990s

This also became part of the thrill: Hit up the next party until we ended up in a random place like the train tracks or at someone's house or garage for a kickback. Kickbacks weren't always fun or safe. Sometimes we'd get there and wonder why we'd come in the first place: We ran the risk of getting stranded with random people and no ride back home, especially if we rode with a boy we liked at a party but didn't like as much afterward.

There were also fights that broke out, especially if we ended up at a kickback with cholos. I've experienced a lot of dangerous kickbacks and spontaneous hangouts with random guys we met on the boulevard or at a party.

Once, when I was with my sisters, Yesi and Maria, and a few friends, we went to Griffith Park with some boys we'd met on the boulevard. A boy started picking on Yesi, commenting on how young she was. (She was around thirteen.) Yesi is someone who doesn't hold back, so she yelled back at him, which created a commotion. The boys had had enough, and they left us there in the dark at the very top of Griffith Park. Like many nights, we had to figure out how to get home. We walked down from the top of the park to one of the main streets nearby, where a

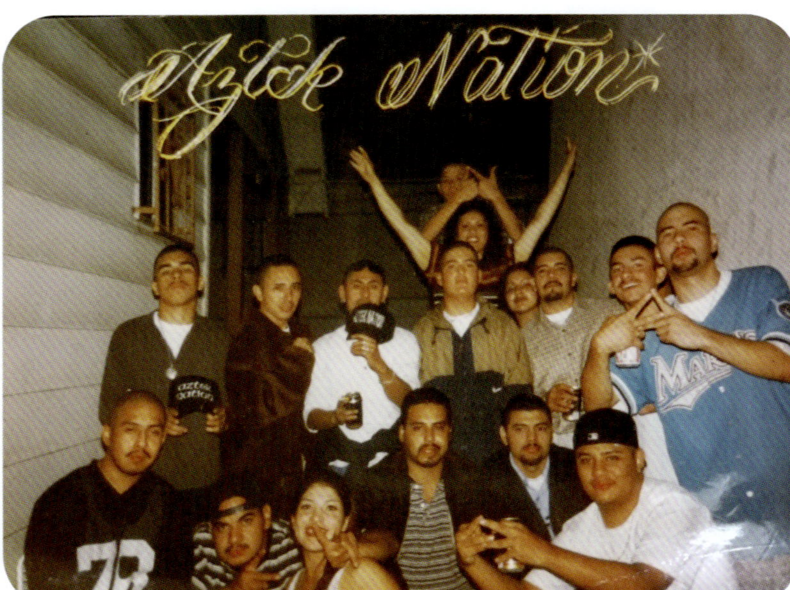

Aztek Nation party crew

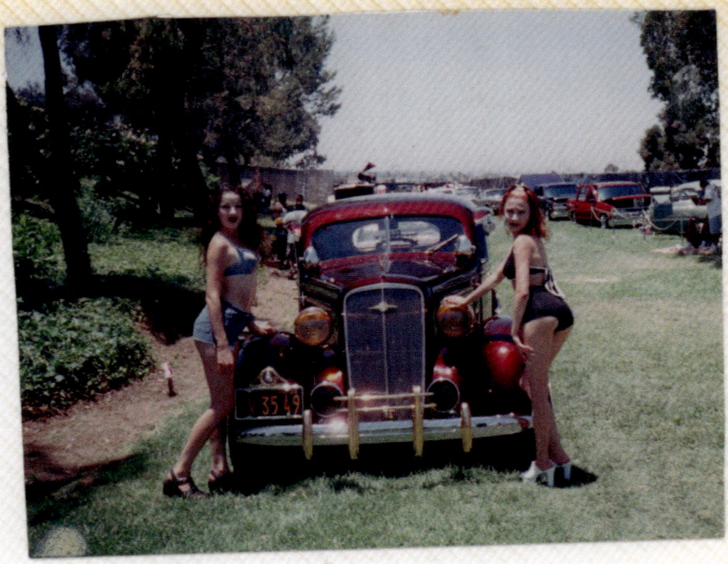
3549

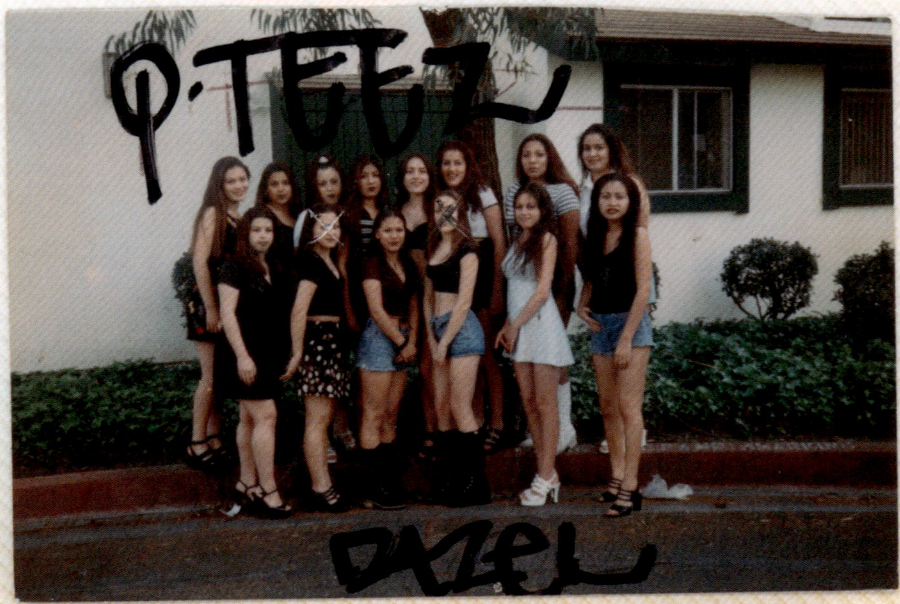
Q·TEEZ

group of boys in a Jeep pulled up next to us and offered us a ride. We hopped in, annoyed at Yesi, and told the boys what had just happened. Eventually we were laughing at the situation. Hitching rides was common. It wasn't safe, but at the time we didn't think about that. We didn't really know what wasn't safe. We were just living.

OPPOSITE: Photos of East LA Q-teez

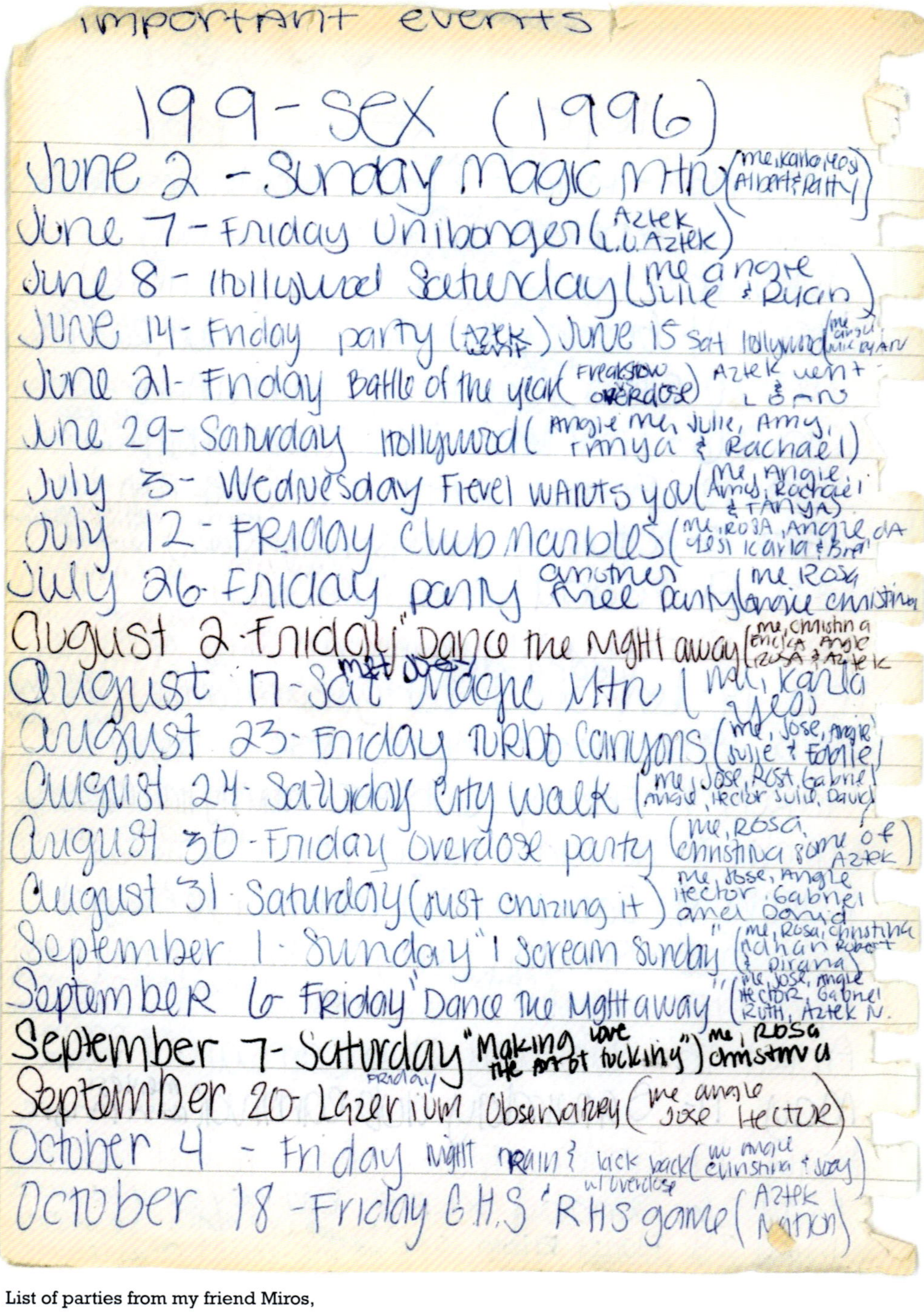

important events

199-SEX (1996)

June 2 - Sunday Magic Mtn (me, Karla, Yesi, Albert & Patty)
June 7 - Friday Unibonger (Aztek L.U. Aztek)
June 8 - Hollywood Saturday (me angie Julie & Ryan)
June 14 - Friday party (Aztek went) June 15 Sat Hollywood (me angie Julie Ryan)
June 21 - Friday Battle of the year (Freakshow vs overdose) Aztek went & Lonnie
June 29 - Saturday Hollywood (Angie me, Julie, Amy, Tanya & Rachael)
July 3 - Wednesday Fievel wants you (me, Angie Amy, Rachael & Tanya)
July 12 - Friday Club Marbles (me, Rosa, Angie, Oa Yesi Karla & Bri)
July 26 - Friday party another free party (me Rosa Angie christina)
August 2 - Friday "Dance the night away" (me, Christina Enrica Angie Rosa & Aztek)
August 17 - Sat met Joe Magic Mtn (me, Karla Yesi)
August 23 - Friday Turbo Canyons (me, Jose, Angie Julie & Eddie)
August 24 - Saturday City walk (me, Jose, Rosa, Gabriel Angie, Hector Julie, David)
August 30 - Friday Overdose party (me, Rosa, Christina some of Aztek)
August 31 - Saturday (just cruizing it) me, Jose, Angie Hector, Gabriel and David
September 1 - Sunday "I Scream Sunday" (me, Rosa, Christina Nathan Robert & Pirana)
September 6 - Friday "Dance the night away" (me, Jose, Angie Hector, Gabriel Ruth, Aztek N.
September 7 - Saturday "Making love the art of fucking") me, Rosa christina
September 20 Friday Lazerium Observatory (me angie Jose Hector)
October 4 - Friday Night Rain & lack back w/ overdose (me Angie christina & Joey)
October 18 - Friday G.H.S & R.H.S game (Aztek Nation)

List of parties from my friend Miros, who kept track of everything we did

1997 events

March 15 - Saturday Kill at will (me, Angie, Hector, Julie Adnan, Rupert, Christina, Corinne, Gabriel & aztek)

March 21 - Friday meeting & Kicking it Cojom

March 30 - Sunday Sweet Sundays me Karla Angie & Hec

May 2 - Bad Examples party Friday (me angie Jojo corinne Christina)

May 3 - Brainwash party Saturday (AZACK)

May 9 - Friday show me what u got club (me angie, Hector & Jose)

May 11 - Venice Beach Sunday (me Karla Yesi angie vernie Adnan Julia Hector)

May 17 - Saturday Brown Cartel Kickback (Brown cartel)

May 31 - Saturday aztek meeting & Feel the vibe (AZTK)

June 8 - Sunday Dysneyland (me, Hex, Roxanne Joey, Cassandra & Bobby)

June 13 - Friday Journey into ~~celtic~~ indian sound (aztek nation)

(I took car)

June 20 - Friday A Fiesta club Richard H vission & Bad Boy Bill (me, Christina & Corinne)

MET SAM (took car)

June 27 - Friday (Mayhem Party) (me Hex Peter & Christina)

July 5 - Saturday Magic Mountain (me Karla Yesi & aunt Patty)

July 12 - Saturday Hula party for Julie at her house

July 16 - Wednesday Magic Mtn (me angie Julie & adnan)

July 18 - Friday Magic Mtn. (me, Angie, Karla, Adnan, Julie, vernie, ...)

July 25 - Friday party badd Examples Exotic Dreams (me, Karla, Yesi Christina Julia adnan)

August 2 - Saturday Hollywood (me Lupe Besenia Maria & Hamm)

August 8 - Friday Club Vynle (me Karla Yesi & Christina)

August 15 - Friday Magic Mtn (me, Karla, angie vernie, & Hector)

August 31 - Sunday Sweet Sundays & arena Pat Hacmer (me Yesi angie & vernie)

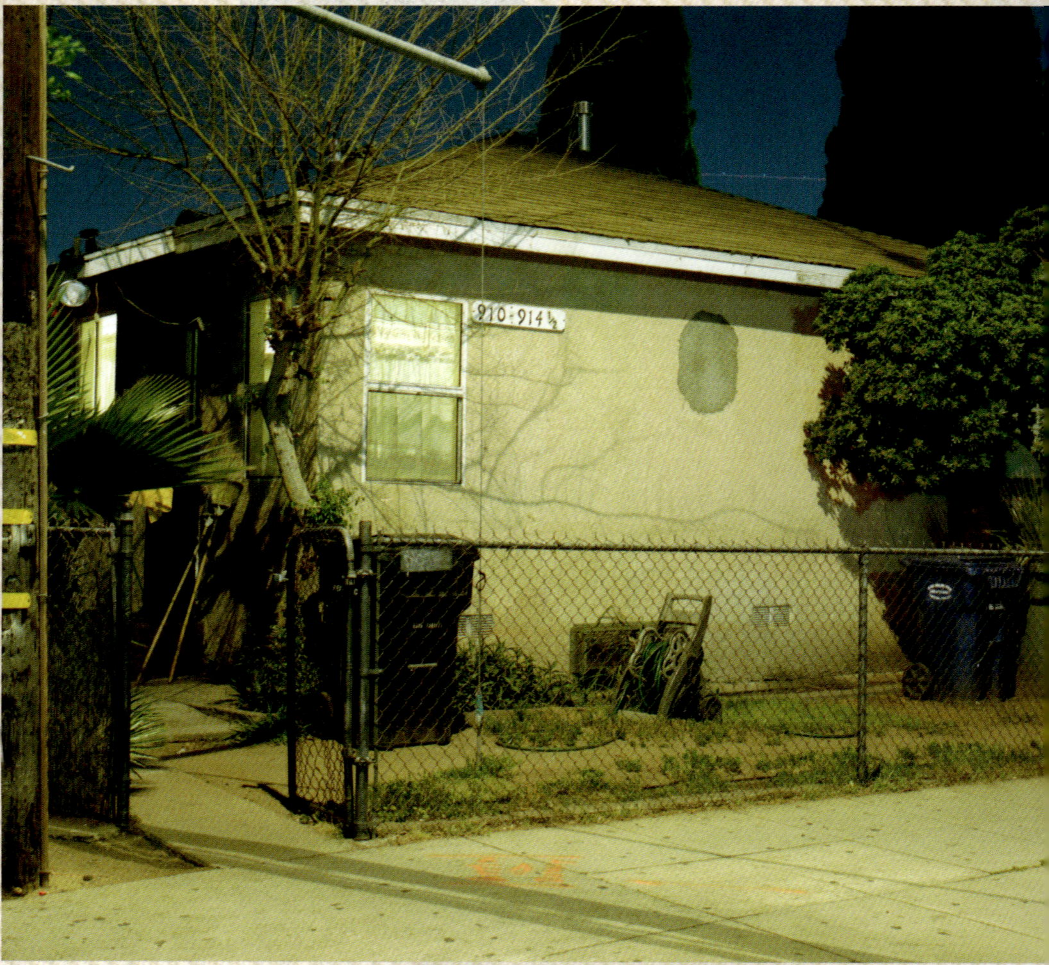

Leonard Avenue apartment compound at night. It sits on the corner of Whittier Boulevard and Leonard Avenue.

THE BOULEVARD

WHEN I WAS FOURTEEN, WE MOVED INTO OUR dream house: The main house on the same lot as the one-bedroom apartment on Leonard Avenue, just off Whittier Boulevard, became available for $700 a month, and my parents jumped at the opportunity. It felt like we had all won the lottery—we had never lived in a place that big. None of us had ever had our own bedroom, but here, we had the most privacy we had ever experienced.

The house was a detached three-bedroom with a long, horizontal layout, with a living room, a dining area, and a small kitchen. None of the furniture matched except three slender, honey-colored shelves with turned wooden spindles that stood in the living room, the tiers carefully arranged with Mom's delicate crystal glasses and a stereo with mismatched speakers.

This is what we carried around to every house we moved into. My mother and my stepdad had their own bedroom, my two brothers Alex and Junior shared one, and my two sisters and I shared the bedroom next to theirs. When my younger brother Jimmy was born in 1995, he slept in Mom's room.

The front of the house was simple: The porch had a red brick stoop worn smooth by time, its surface layered in the remnants of rushed and badly done paint jobs.

This house sat on the back of a compound, with duplex bungalows lined up in front that shared walls. We had to

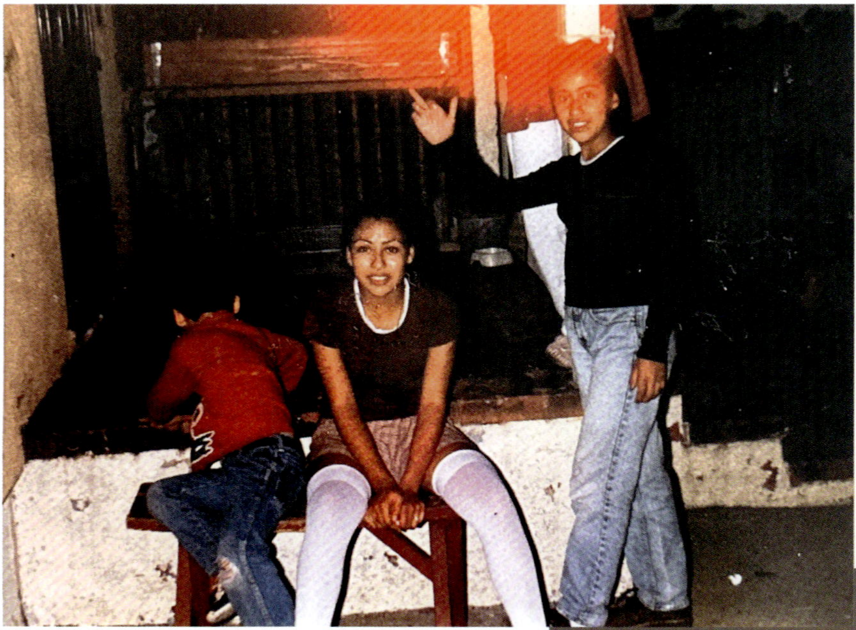

walk along the duplex and down a narrow path through overgrown trees to reach our porch, which felt like our own little world, tucked away from everyone else. We had neighbors on one side and an alleyway on the other.

My house was right in the center of the neighborhood—not far from Montebello. In many ways I had everything I needed. My first kiss, my first real friendships and heartbreaks—they all happened here.

Leonard Avenue in East Los Angeles was my world. Whittier Boulevard was right in front of our house. I could see it from our windows. The minute I'd step out of the house, I was already there. I walked these streets from day to night, until the sun greeted me again. I knew all of East L.A.'s

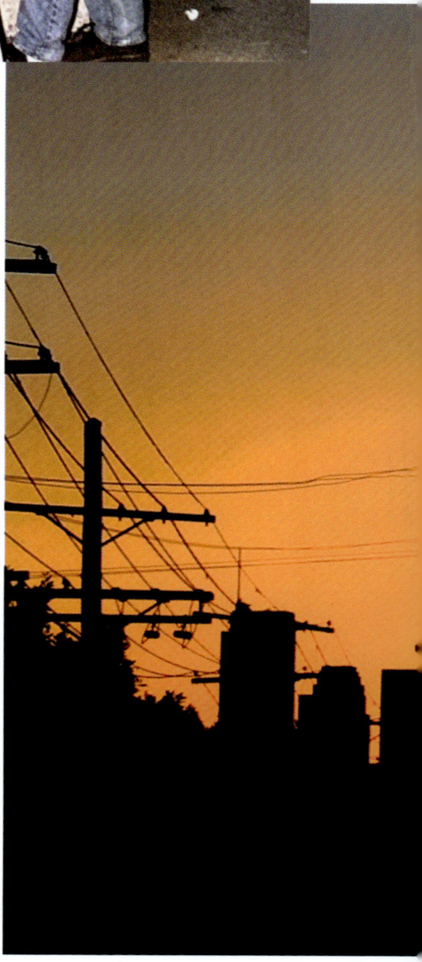

RIGHT: Orange L.A. skies. How it typically is in L.A., especially in the summer.

shortcuts and secret hideaways and the fastest way to get to my neighborhood friends' houses. I knew how to get away from the police when they chased me. I knew how to sneak into the movie theater and watch for free. I knew the codes and secrets of this neighborhood.

Our friends came over and sat with us on the stoop at any time of day or night, sometimes for just ten or fifteen minutes, other times 'til the sun came out again the next day. Many times we'd wander to the front yard and lean over the chain-link fence to chat, laugh, and smoke cigarettes while people passed by on their way to work or school. The neighborhood had its own rhythm. Morning had its rush hour, with a brief lull around 11 A.M., but by 3 P.M. the city noise would pick up again—the thrum of life on Whittier Boulevard just beyond our block.

I'd take in the city noise, the beautiful sunsets, and the luminous nights right from the steps of our house. It wasn't always beautiful: Some-

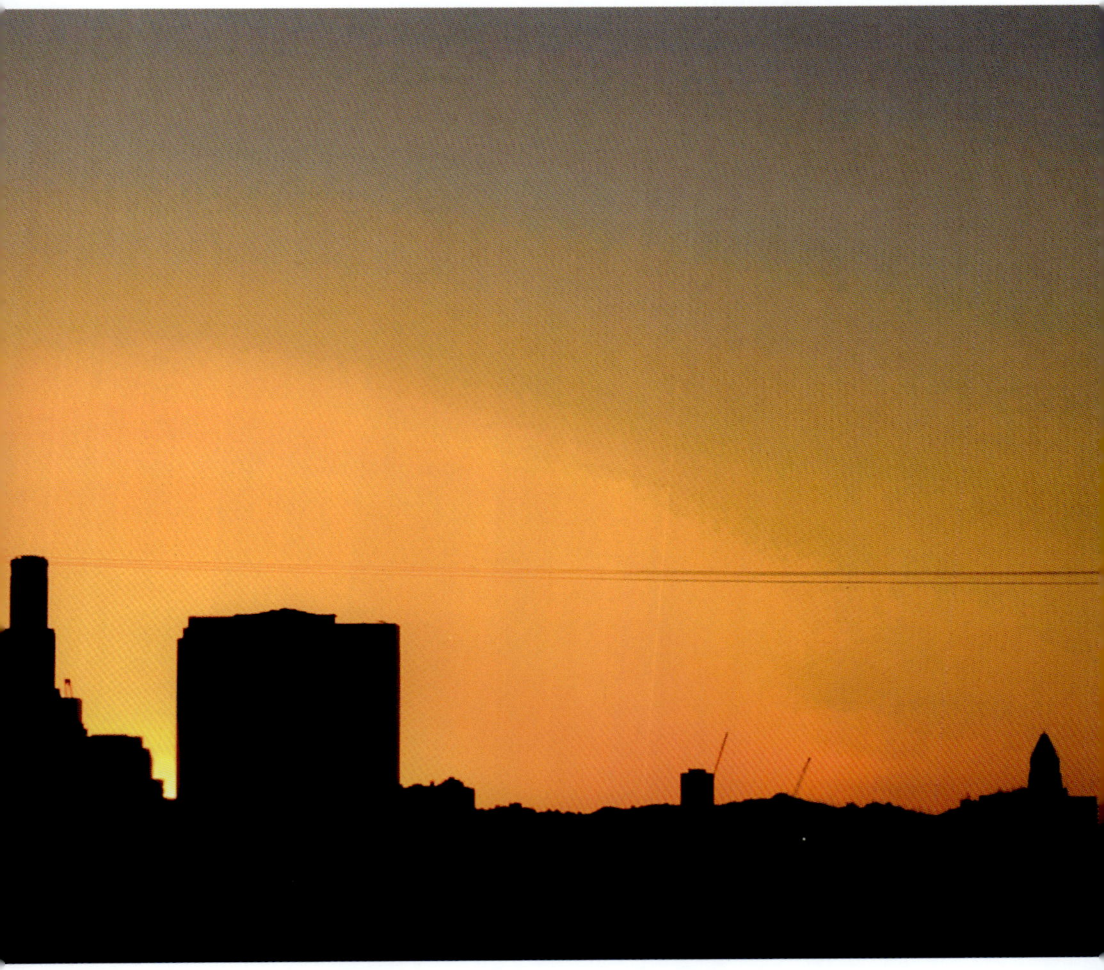

times our house could be a target, just like any corner or street or pay phone in the neighborhood. We didn't question it. But most of the time, I could hear the songs in the cars cruising down the boulevard as they slowly faded away in the air. One car played Barbara Mason's "Yes, I'm Ready," and others played Zapp and Roger's "Be Alright" and Eazy-E's "Real Muthaphuckkin G's."

The sounds in the street overlapped, the paleteros chiming their bells, the cars with their loud sound, voices drifting through the air—all mixing to create a new melody, a rhythm unique to the cityscape fading into night. The night gave me a sense of freedom, although this doesn't mean it was safe, especially for teenage girls. Still, there was something nurturing about the night, like a mother's womb, even though we could feel the complexity of being both free and chased. In this way, night in East Los Angeles has its own reality. A surreality. Like a waking dream.

People don't usually describe Los Angeles as eerie or apocalyptic, but in the summer—with its piercing orange-yellow skies—it could be, day or night. On summer Sundays after a long weekend of festivities, we would all be ready to relax back at the house, take naps while our younger brothers played outside with their friends. We'd have that feeling you get when you go to the beach and lie in the sun all day—relaxed and sun-kissed. Everyone was outside—the ice-cream truck and fruit guy selling treats to the neighborhood kids, mothers and their comadres hanging out on their stoops catching up on the gossip. The neighborhood kids playing with their remote-control cars on their hot concrete patios.

All of a sudden there would

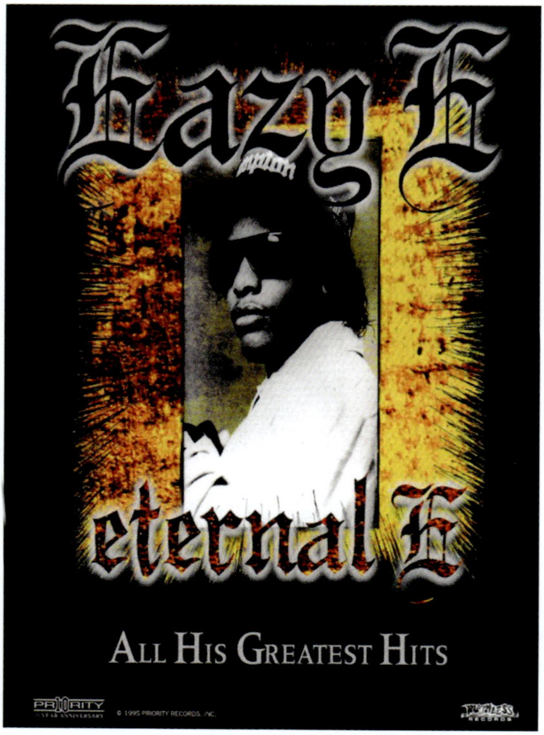

Eazy-E.
We listened to this album on repeat in 1995.

be multiple loud bangs, one after another that echoed in the air, and everything would go silent for a few seconds as if time stood still. Then we'd all come back out from wherever we were hiding, dust off our knees and chests, and continue to chat and play outside as if nothing had just happened. Drive-by shootings were so common that our faces didn't even flinch at the sound of a gunshot. There was a late reaction.

Perhaps we were desensitized to them—they were expected and normal to us. We knew how and when to run for cover, like we could predict the future. There was always an eerie, quiet moment right before tragedy struck. As I got older I could sense it—a quietness that felt different. Some people call it PTSD or paranoia. I call it being street-smart—paying attention to your surroundings and the shift of energy in the city. And yet, every night in late summer was full of magic. By the time fall hit, I'd sleep with my windows open and let the cool breeze in.

Soy Conejo from the western days
When the sun goes down,
I show my wicked ways
Have you ever been so panicked in this
paranoid dimension
The tensions runnin' high, a critical situation.

—*Conejo*

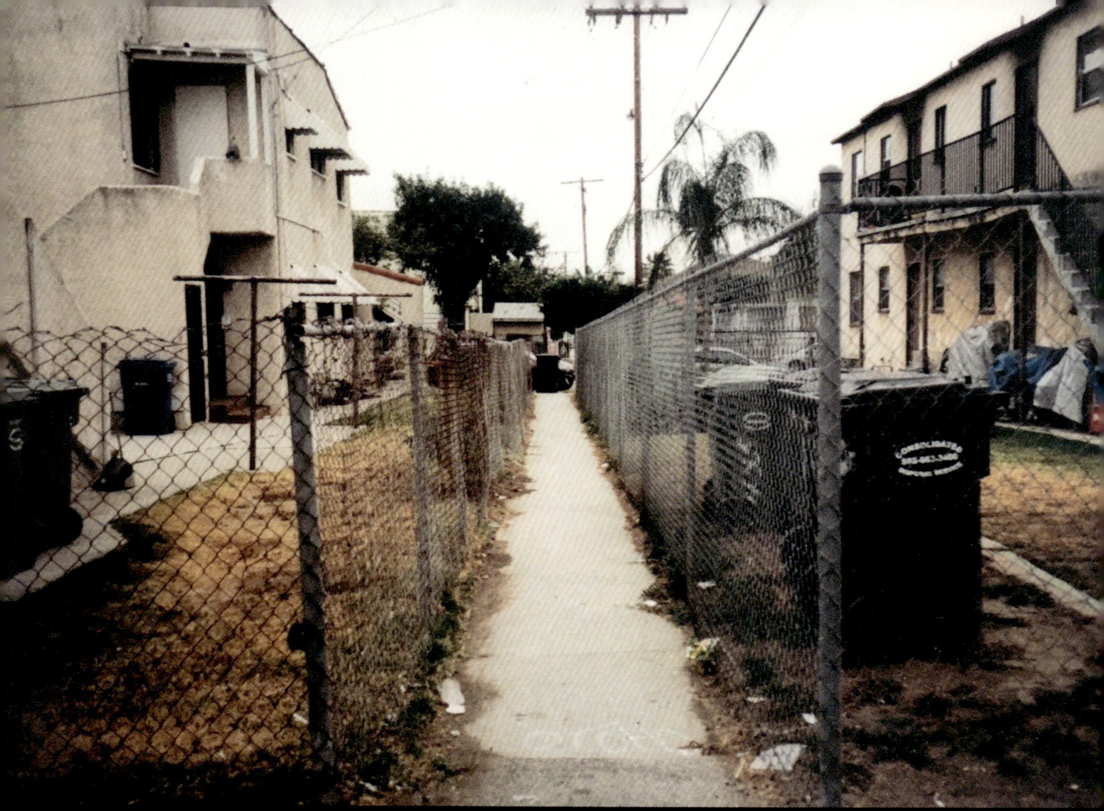
CONSOLIDATED

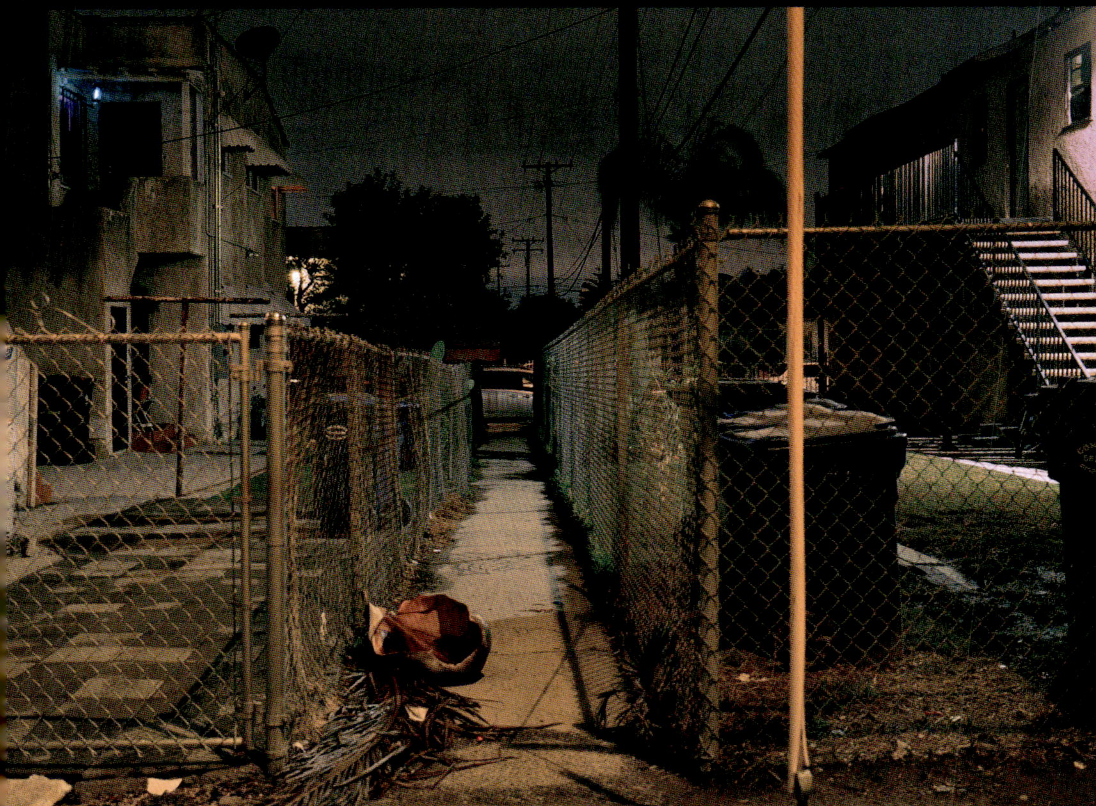

Photo of a neighborhood shortcut at night, near Leonard Ave.

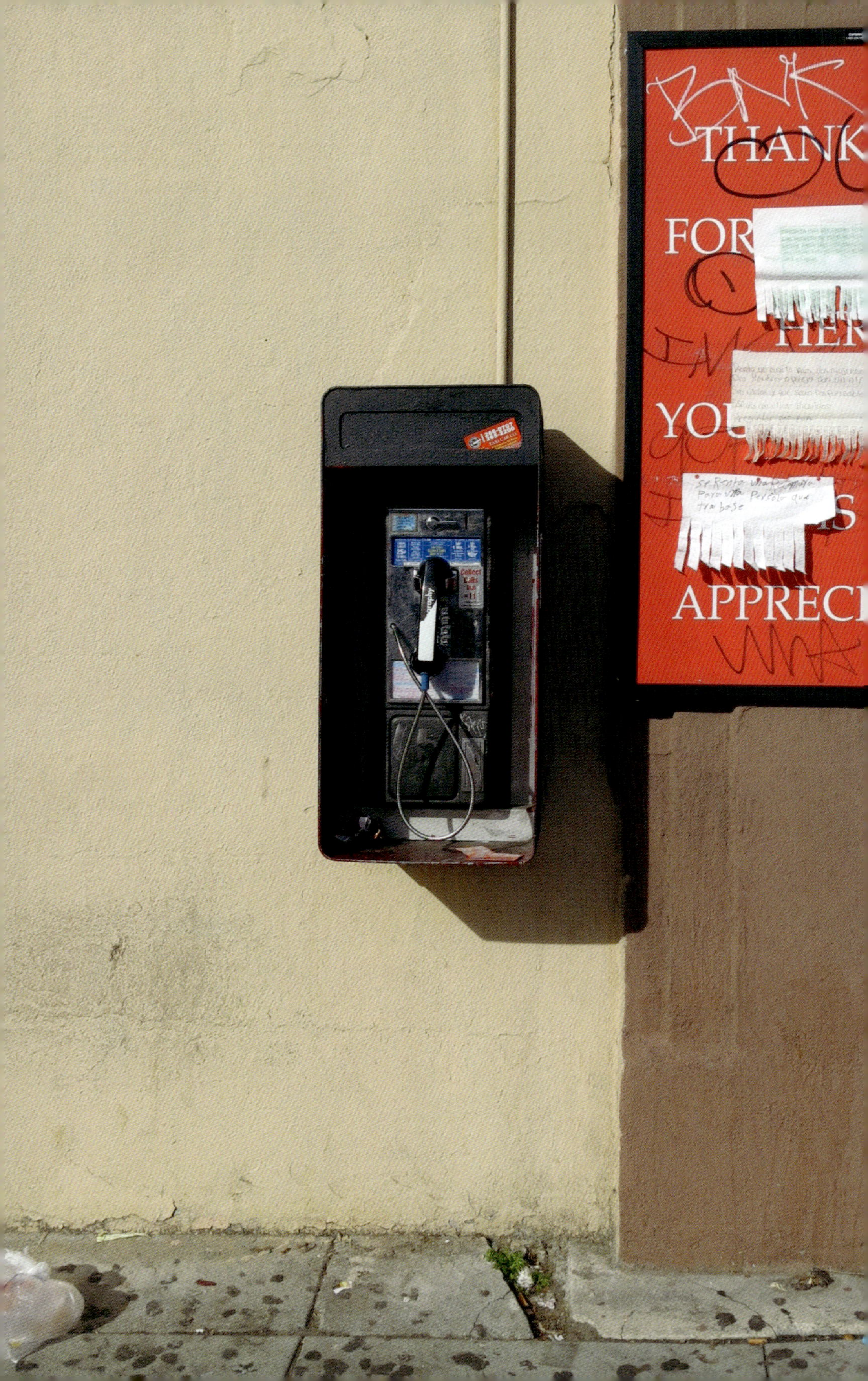
THANK
FOR
YOU

THE PAY PHONE

AS WE GOT OLDER AND OUR MOM'S PATIENCE grew thinner, our new hangout spot soon became the pay phone directly across the street from our home. There, we received and returned calls from friends and lovers, any time of the day or night. We claimed the pay phone as ours, even though the corner it was on was dangerous. One night, my sister Maria ran back to the house gasping for air, saying, "This fuckin' pervert came up to me at the pay phone and pulled a gun on me!" She had gone out to call a friend and a man had approached her, pointing a gun at her with one hand and pulling out his dick with the other.

When he came closer, she hit him on the head with the phone and ran back to the house, and he ran in the opposite direction, startled.

My younger brothers never belonged to a gang, but they were still treated as if they were. They often got hit up by rival gangs driving by. Things were scary; it was hard to rest and relax because we had to stay vigilant. My younger stepbrother, Junior, also had his share of pay phone stories. He was a couple years younger than me and had blond hair and light eyes like his Czech mother but thick, straight untamable hair like his Mexican father.

OPPOSITE: Pay phone on Leonard Avenue and Whittier Boulevard

Growing up with us in East L.A., he developed the vocabulary and rhythmic accent of the local kids—and that really fucked with me and everyone in the neighborhood because his appearance was so mixed. If you didn't know him, you really didn't know what to expect to hear coming out of his mouth.

Junior was more of a tagger and was from a tagging crew. But back then, if you were a teenage boy, everyone assumed you were part of a gang. It was common for gangs to drive through rival territory, looking for someone to jump or shoot.

The Maravilla Gang would often cruise through our neighborhood, always looking for trouble. They were rivals in our area.

One time, the Maravillas drove through the area in the dead of night and one of them pulled a shotgun on my brother and his friend when they were by the pay phone. They got hit up—"Where you from?"—and when my brother said "Nowhere," the guy pulled the trigger. The bullet missed him by a few inches. He told me he could hear it hit the wall behind him. Luckily they got away: "I ran like a bitch, fuck that."

I used this pay phone to call my ride to come pick me up or a friend, boyfriend, or crush—as a collect call. If we didn't have a coin on us, we made a collect call like this:

AUTOMATED OPERATOR: "You have a collect call from . . ."
ME: "Heycanyoupickmeupfromthemall?" or "Meetmeatnicks-burgers!"
OPERATOR: "Do you accept?"

Then we hung up. Sometimes we kept calling until our message was clear and complete.

When we had access to our house phone—and my mom hadn't hidden it—sometimes we'd connect calls from jail through three-way. They called us and we called their girlfriends or homeboys for them. I'd set my phone on the counter and check in now and then to hear if they were still talking.

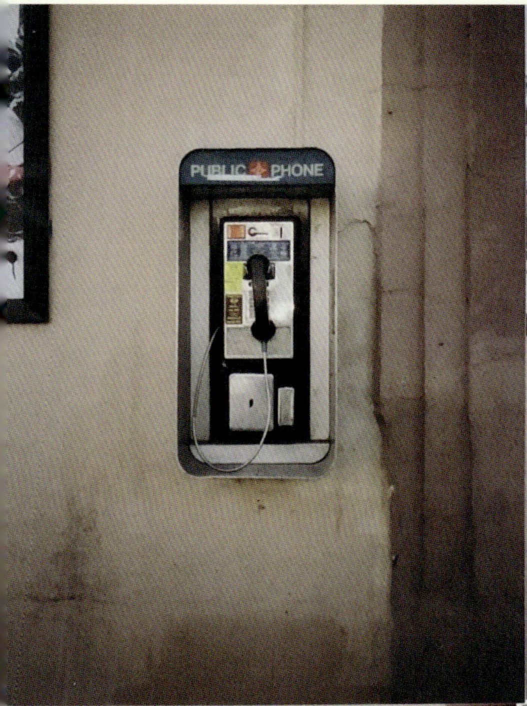
PUBLIC PHONE

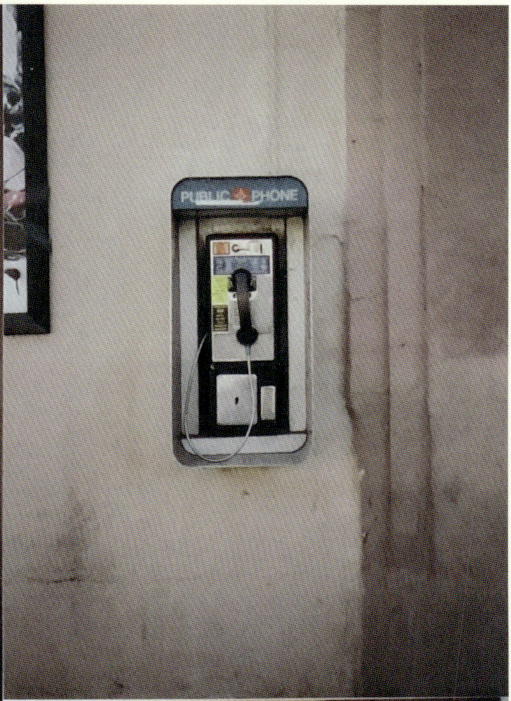
PUBLIC PHONE

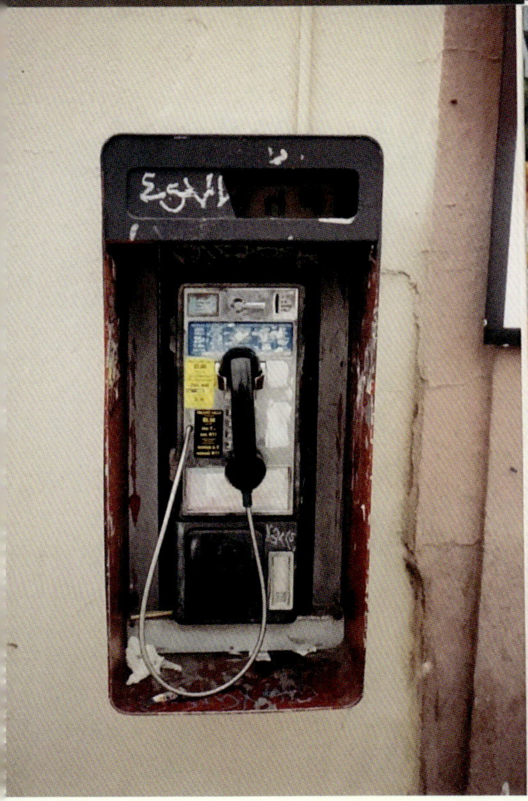

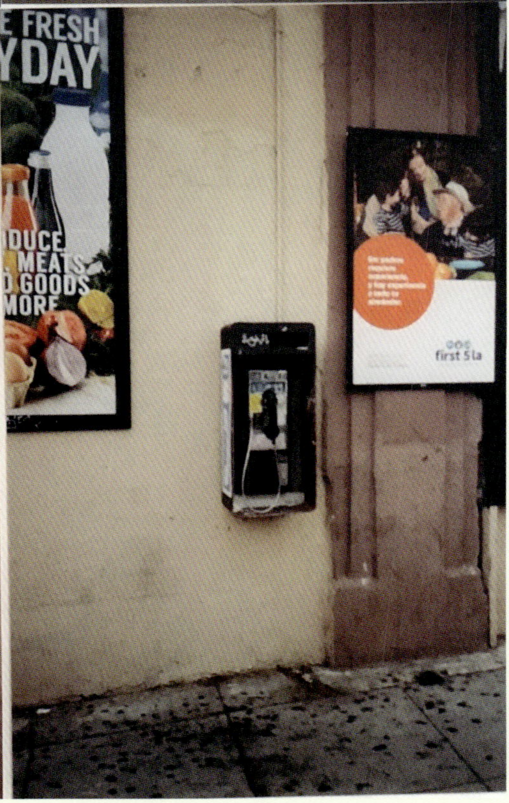
E FRESH
YDAY
DUCE
MEATS
D GOODS
MORE
first 5la

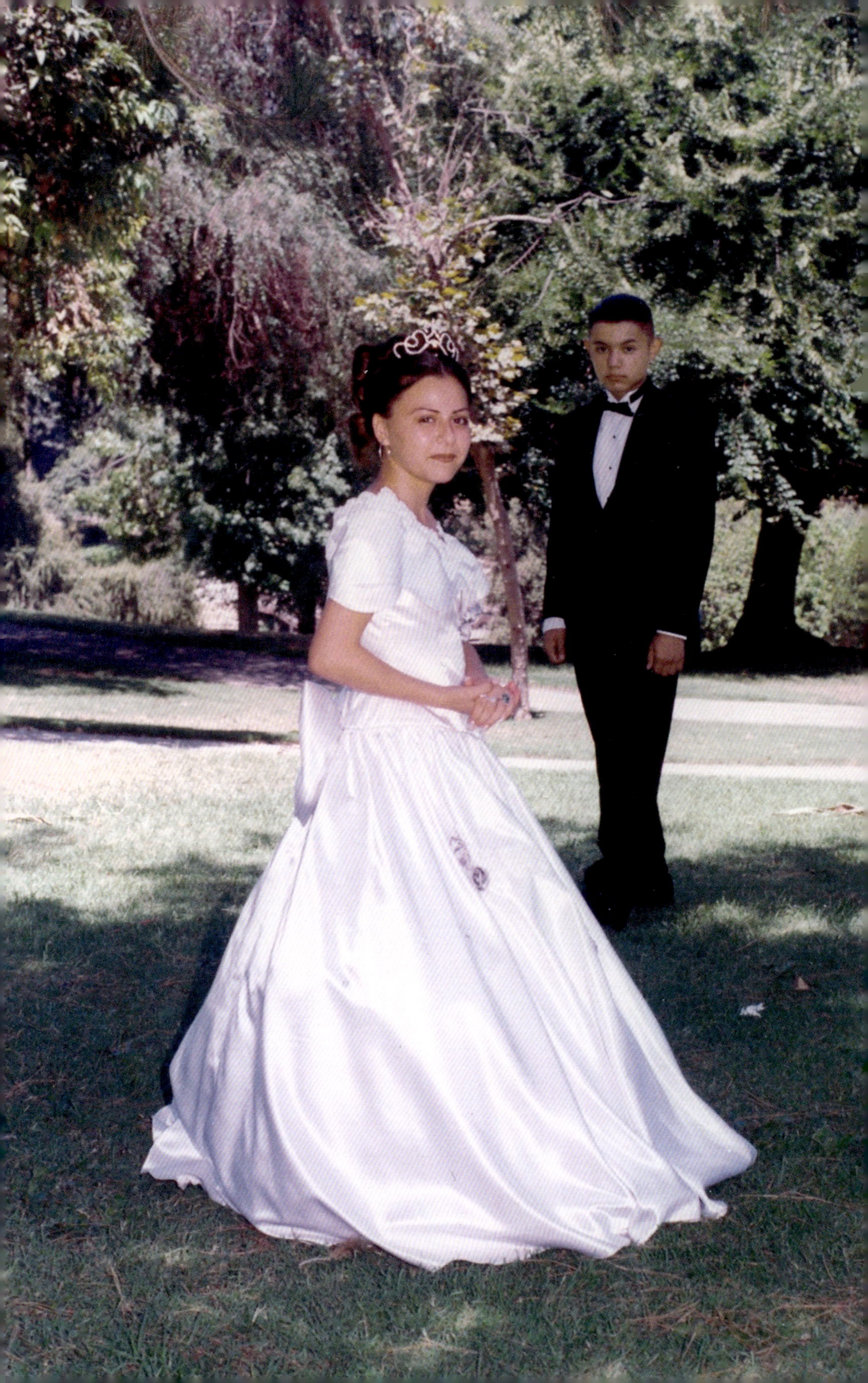

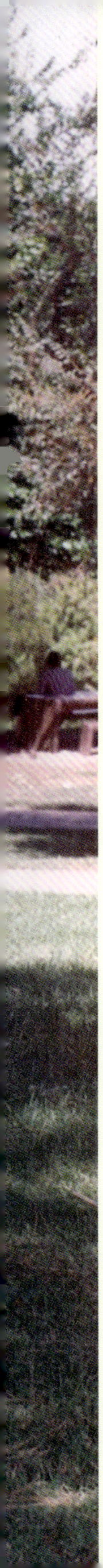

QUINCE

THE CONFLICTS IN MY HOUSE HAD BEEN BUBbling for years, and sometimes even with gang violence around us, the streets felt safer than home. Still, my mom wanted us to do traditional things. When it came to quinceañeras, though, she usually wouldn't have agreed. They were too expensive, we were broke, and I had mixed feelings about having one in the first place, but my mom insisted. But this time, it felt like a cover-up, maybe even subconsciously—a way to hide what was really happening. Maybe we were all blinded by the abuse in the house.

My quinceañera took place under a cloud of pain, and in some ways I can't even believe it happened at all. I was the last of all my sisters anyone would've expected to have one. I dreaded every moment of it: the dress, the invitations, the thought of asking people to be part of it. Underneath it all, I was carrying so much anger and resentment toward my mom. Having my stepdad still around after everything he had done—and the way she still tried to bring him around as if nothing had happened—made our relationship almost unbearable.

I never felt comfortable alone with him. After years of leering and inappropriate behavior against me and my sisters (I later learned the extent of his abuse), he had come into my room when I was alone in the middle of the night,

OPPOSITE: My quinceañera in 1995, shot at Hollenbeck Park

me feeling him sit on my bed while I was fighting off a bad cold, and his weight on the edge of my bed waking me up. I moved my leg like a spasm so he knew I was awake and aware. He got off my bed and walked fast to the bathroom, and I got up and walked to my mom's bedroom and told her what had happened: I said, "He was in my room on my bed and I must've scared him off because he went to the bathroom to pretend he was showering." She banged on the bathroom door and then she called the police. He was arrested, and she filed a restraining order against him.

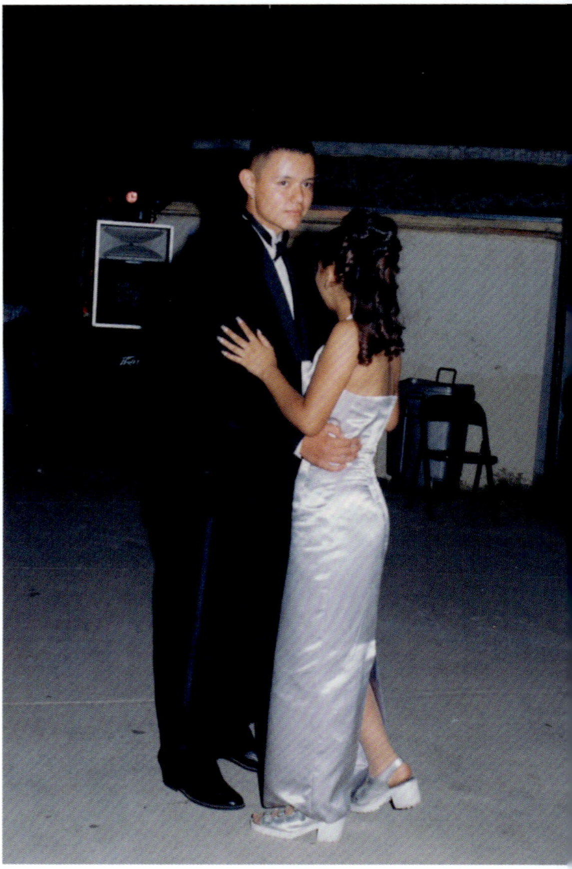

Maria and José dancing in our backyard on my quinceañera, 1995

But that didn't mean I felt safe. Weeks later, he started showing up again at strange hours, slipping in and out like a secret, and I couldn't help but wonder if my mom was hiding him. The betrayal of that silence, of having to pretend nothing happened, cut deeper than the abuse itself. It left me questioning whether I could ever trust her, or if I'd ever truly be protected.

In the middle of all this, the quinceañera was already being planned out, unstoppable. I felt guilty for not wanting it, for not being grateful. For so many girls it's a privilege, a blessing, something you dream about. But for me, it felt like a performance I couldn't escape. Everything moved so fast. Too fast to even plan it right. When I think of that day, it only brings back traumatic memories. It was too late to rent a banquet hall, so we had it in our backyard. Too late to spend weekends searching for dresses, so my mom asked her comadre Margarita to sew one for me.

On the outside it might have looked like a celebration, but inside I felt fractured—dressed up in a costume that wasn't mine, trying to carry a tradition that felt heavier than the dress itself. It was too late to turn back and cancel, so I decided to make it the best party I could.

What I had full control over was inviting my friends to the dance party. I lasted maybe an hour in the dress after my church ceremony and photos. As soon as that hour passed, I went inside and changed into something more comfortable—and more *me:* a silver satin skirt, a black top, and some platform shoes. A couple hours later, my neighborhood friends started showing up. We changed the music to house and hip-hop, and that's when it finally felt like my party. Even though I was a sad, insecure, and depressed teenager, the quinceañera, like many other fun parties, gave me power and agency to dance to the music I wanted to dance to and invite anyone I wanted to invite. Once again, on the dance floor I felt free.

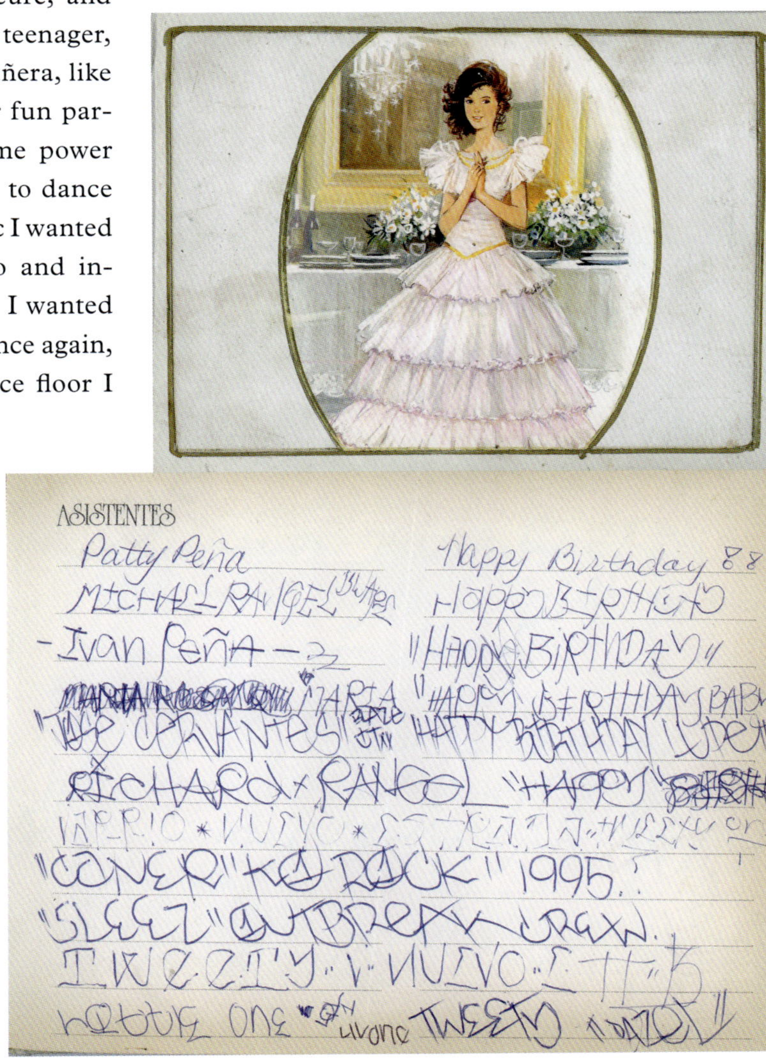

My quince book. Once my friends showed up to my quince, they tagged up the guest book.

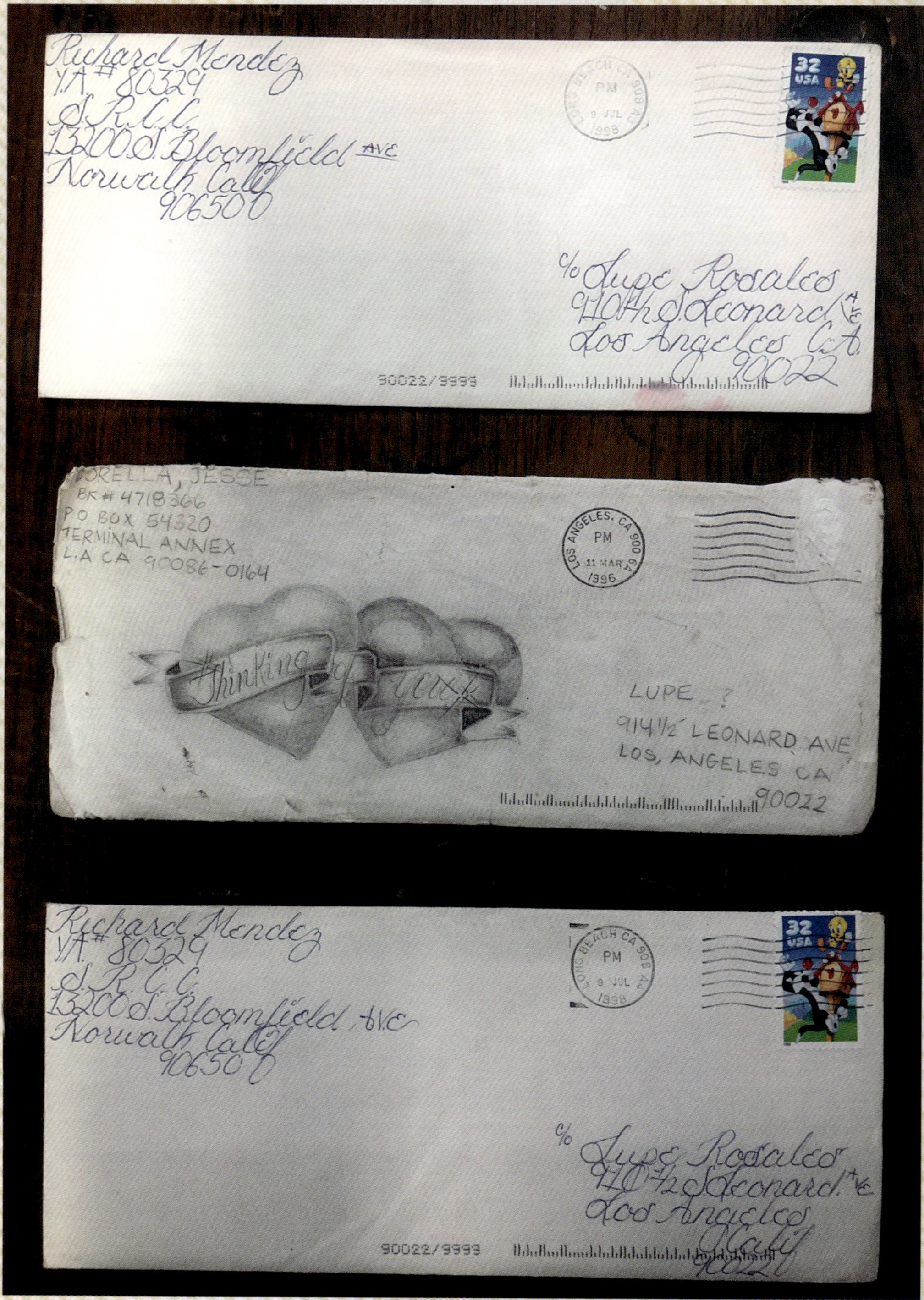

Prison letters

YOUNG LOVE

RICHARD, MY FIRST SERIOUS BOYFRIEND, WAS in juvenile hall when I had my quince, so he couldn't be in it. Instead I asked my friend José to be my chambelán. Months after the quince, Richard was released from juvi, and I wanted to spend as much time with him as possible. One Sunday morning, Richard—aka Chuckles from Marijuanos Locos—invited me to spend Easter Sunday with him and his family in South Whittier. I thought it'd be a good idea to bring Yesi along—around this time I was hanging out with her a lot more than with Maria—so she came with us. When we got to his family's house, his aunt asked if we could go to the nearest store to grab some ice for the party. As Yesi, Richard, and I were stepping outside the local liquor store after buying the ice, things took a sharp turn. Out of nowhere, Richard got hit up by a rival gang. I remember feeling my heart race. Richard froze, but didn't flinch. With his head held high, he proudly said, "Marijuanos Locos." Most gang members would've lied or backed down when confronted in rival territory, especially when outnumbered, but that wasn't Richard.

Then, in a flash, someone threw a hard punch. It landed right on the side of his face, his eye swelling almost instantly. The punches kept coming. He dropped to the ground, and when he turned around, his face was almost unrecognizable. A kick followed, and stomps on his head, while my sister and I yelled at them to stop.

They finally did, and Richard got up, dusted himself

off, picked up the bag of ice he had just bought, put the ice on his face, and walked back to the party. It was too much for me to handle at fifteen, but in that moment, I learned what it meant to date a cholo. I understood the unspoken loyalty and the danger that came with it. After that day, I knew how to be by his side—even when shit went down. From then on it would become part of life.

EVEN AS A fifteen-year-old girl, in some ways I was his protector: I took on the responsibility of taking care of him and begging the rival gang to stop hurting him. We tried to pull him away from the gang. If things had gotten worse, I probably would have even jumped in. His family was already familiar with this because he came from a long line of old gangsters and veteranos/veteranas from East L.A. When we walked back to the house, people at the party were upset, but not surprised. When everyone saw his busted face, they said, "What the fuck happened, mijo? Who the fuck did that to you?" And then they went back to the party.

Another day, I was hanging out with Richard on my stoop when a cop pulled up on us and began to question my boyfriend. The details of that day are blurry, but I do remember the police throwing him against the wall and searching him and then handcuffing him. They took him away. I didn't know what would come next. I didn't hear from him for a few days. Then he wrote me from Eastlake Juvenile Facility. From there on he was "in the system," in and out of juvi then jail. Our relationship turned into months of not seeing each other and writing letters back and forth. I saved all the letters he sent me. Luckily I have never been to jail, only arrested. But almost every man in my life has done time in jail or prison.

FAMILY TIES

Rangel brothers and Rosales sisters (with our friend Silvia) hanging out in the neighborhood. This was our daily ritual and the most memorable times of my life.

I MET RICHARD THROUGH THE RANGELS, WHO lived in the neighborhood. Richard lived in East L.A., closer to Arizona Avenue and Whittier Boulevard, and his family was from Maravilla Gang, a different and rival territory, but he was always at the Rangels' house in the Varrio Nuevo Estrada (VNE), Tik Toks, and Tiny Winos click territory. Richard and the Rangel brothers had all been in the party crew East LA Madness and the tagging crew STK (Shoot to Kill) before ever getting involved with gangs. There were six Rangel brothers and one sister. Four of the oldest brothers were all close in age, the same age as my sisters and me. That family moved around a lot from block to block to avoid paying rent, and their parents ne-

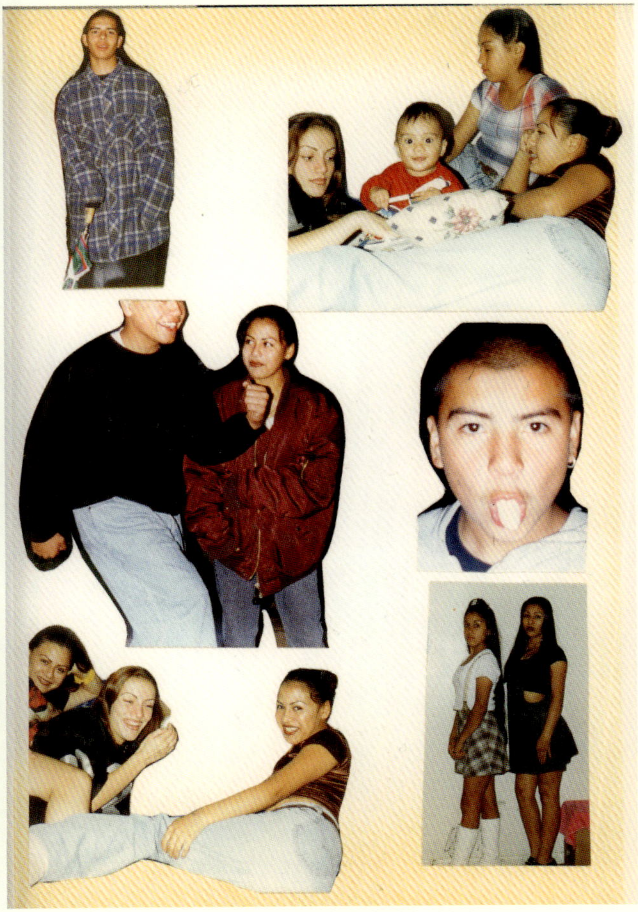

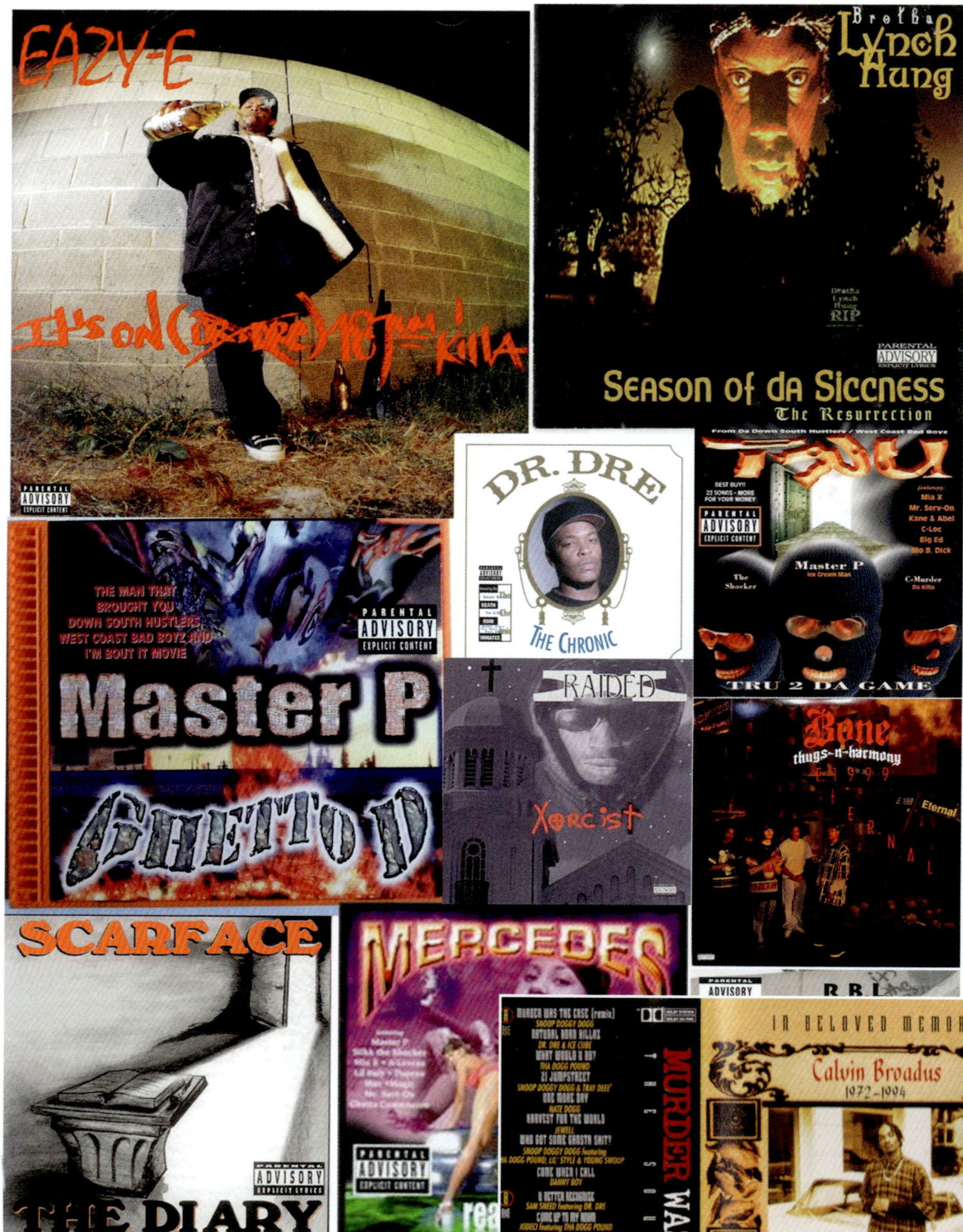

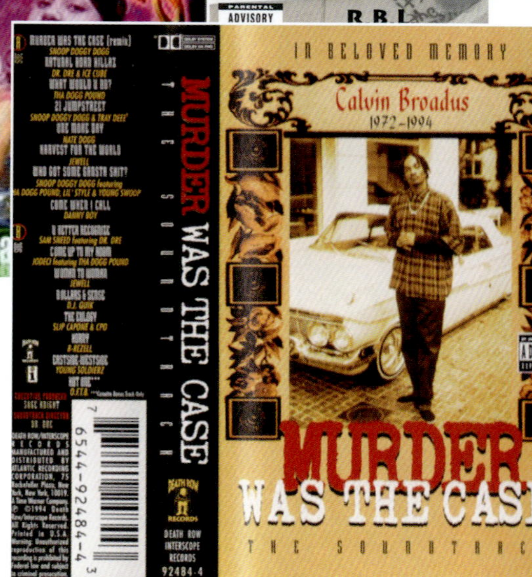

Music that the Rangel brothers and I listened to when we hung out, circa mid-1990s glected them. Finally they moved into an apartment building across the street from us and stayed there for a few years.

We quickly became close friends, and my sisters and I often hooked up with the brothers because we were the same age and shared similar interests. Together we'd listen to Bone Thugs-n-Harmony, Eazy-E, and RBL Posse, especially their song "Don't Give Me No Bammer Weed." My two sisters would run off with two of the brothers and I would scam (as in make out) with Michael, aka B-ware. Many times we smoked a lot of weed and ran around the streets together like little traviesos. My mother also became close with them, so they came around a lot, like relatives would do. They'd knock on the door looking for us and to show respect to Mom. Sometimes they'd sit on the porch to wait for us if we weren't around and take a breath of air like it was their second home.

On many nights, while everyone in our house was in bed, Maria and I waited until around midnight to sneak out of the house. Since the landline was the only way to communicate, and the phone was unplugged and hidden somewhere in Mom's bedroom, everything had to be planned to the minute. The first thing we would do was make sure everyone was asleep. Then Maria and I would craft our pillow silhouettes: We'd make our pillows into body shapes and cover them up with blankets to make it look like we were sleeping soundly.

Our bedroom was on the street level, but our bedroom window was a bit high, which made it difficult to jump out of. There was also a small tree (or large bush) that blocked our window. When the tree was trimmed, it was easier to sneak out because we used it as a ladder to climb down. Eventually, my stepdad caught on. He told Mom he had a feeling Maria and I were sneaking out through the window by using that tree. Then he cut it down.

We developed another strategy: One of us would go to the bathroom and flush the toilet to cancel out the noise of the other unlocking the door. I was usually the toilet-flusher; Maria gave me the "easy" job and took on the riskier one, which was unlocking the door. We did this once we got a signal from our ride waiting outside. They usually gave a distinctive whistle or played a song we'd recognize—that was the code to let us know they were waiting for us in the alleyway. Once we were in the car, it was on.

We also went to visit the Rangels. Many nights Maria and I snuck out of the house and walked over to their place across the way. Their parents had lost control of them years ago. Perhaps that gave my mom some com-

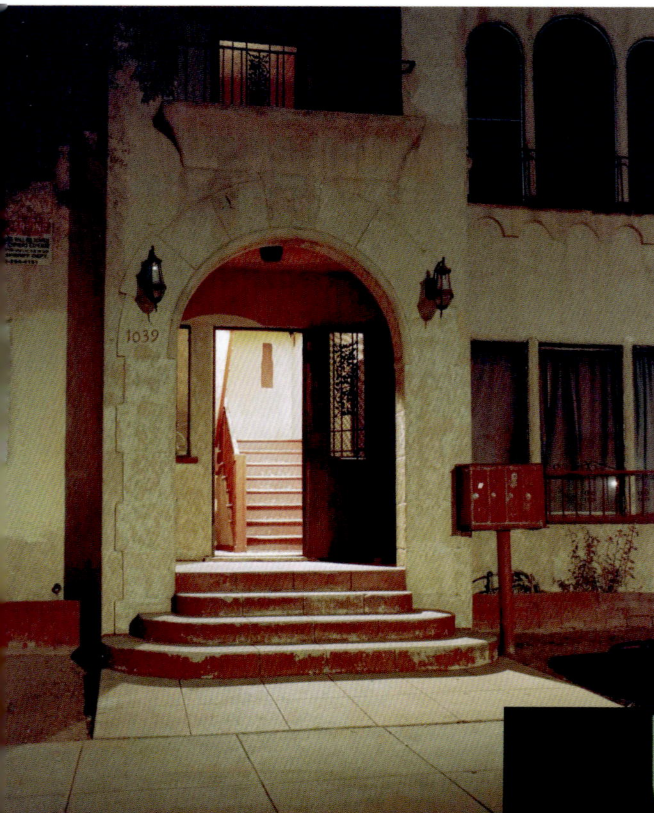

The entrance to the Rangel brothers' apartment building at night

passion for them. Because they were from the party crew East LA Madness, they always had flyer parties in their backyard. Their apartment was small—a one-bedroom in a big Art Deco building. The living room was the biggest space, so they turned it into their bedroom; their parents had the only real bedroom, in the back. When you walked in, the television was the first thing you saw. It was one of those big wood-finish consoles that sit on the floor. There were some bunk beds and a futon against the wall by the window. The apartment was narrow, with two big windows facing the park.

. . .

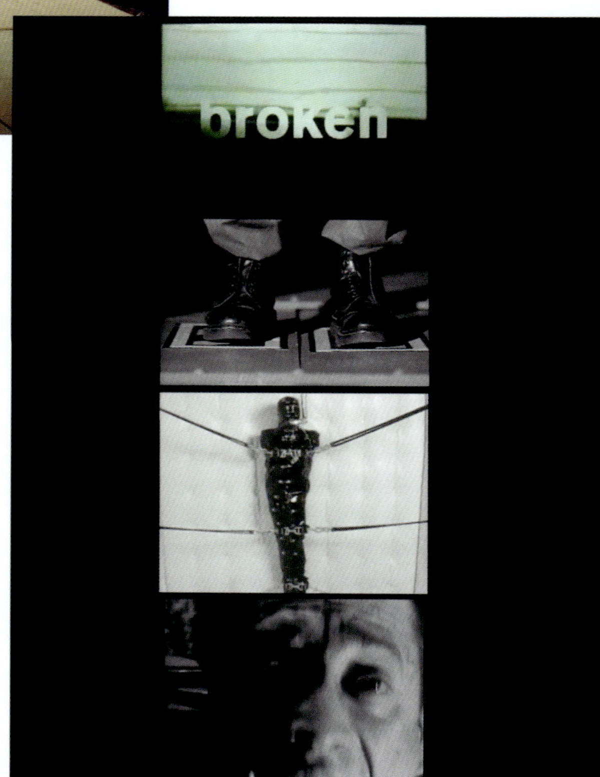

NIN screen stills from *Broken* on VHS

ONE NIGHT WHEN I was about fourteen, Maria and I snuck out around 3 A.M. We were hanging out with the Rangels when we heard loud music blasting from an upstairs apartment—Ramiro, aka Lion, had a brother who lived up there. He was a goth kid with long black hair.

In the summer, the Rangels and Lion's brother had this habit of leaving their doors wide open, no matter the hour. Anyone could just walk in. Drawn by the music and flickering light, we followed the sound up the stairs. The door was halfway open, and a television inside was playing music videos—loud, heavy industrial music. On the screen, a man was being tortured by a machine. Ramiro's brother told us it was a Nine Inch Nails video called "Happiness in Slavery."

It turned out Nine Inch Nails had released a VHS box set of music videos and had included a short film called *Broken*, which had been leaked as a bootleg because of its extreme graphic violence. The band had made it in 1993, and it was banned almost everywhere. It was part of a limited-edition video box set, but *Broken* was different—underground, disturbing, and passed around like contraband. It had scenes of graphic violence that felt more like horror cinema than a music video. Watching it felt like crossing into a darker, hidden world that most people weren't supposed to see. Just like the video compilations called *Traces/Faces of Death*.

VHS tapes of *Faces of Death*

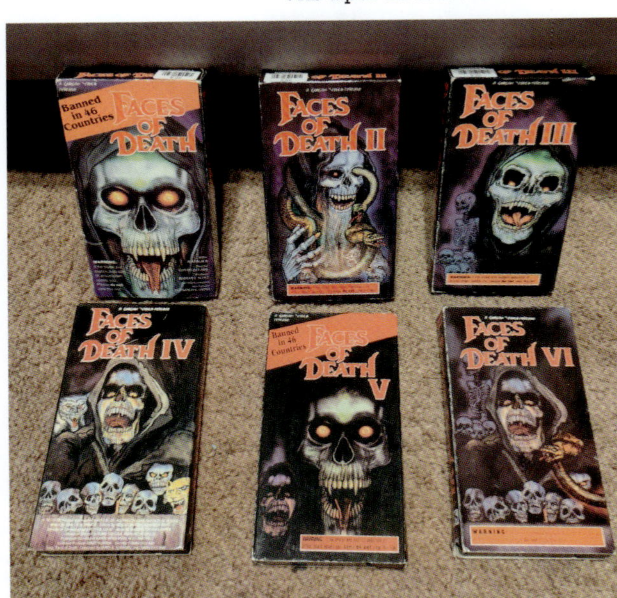

WE SAT DOWN on the floor and joined him. From that night on, we kept going back because we wanted more of that newness and images we weren't supposed to be looking at. Every night we would watch something gory. There were other times when we walked around the neighborhood with the Rangels late at night telling jokes and vandalizing the streets—all the brothers were in a tagging crew called STK. Once I even brought us hot chocolate in Styrofoam cups to drink while we hung out in the middle of the night tagging. Part of it was because the Rangels and my sisters and I could relate to being poor and not caring too much about rules, so even drinking hot chocolate felt like a luxury. It felt special.

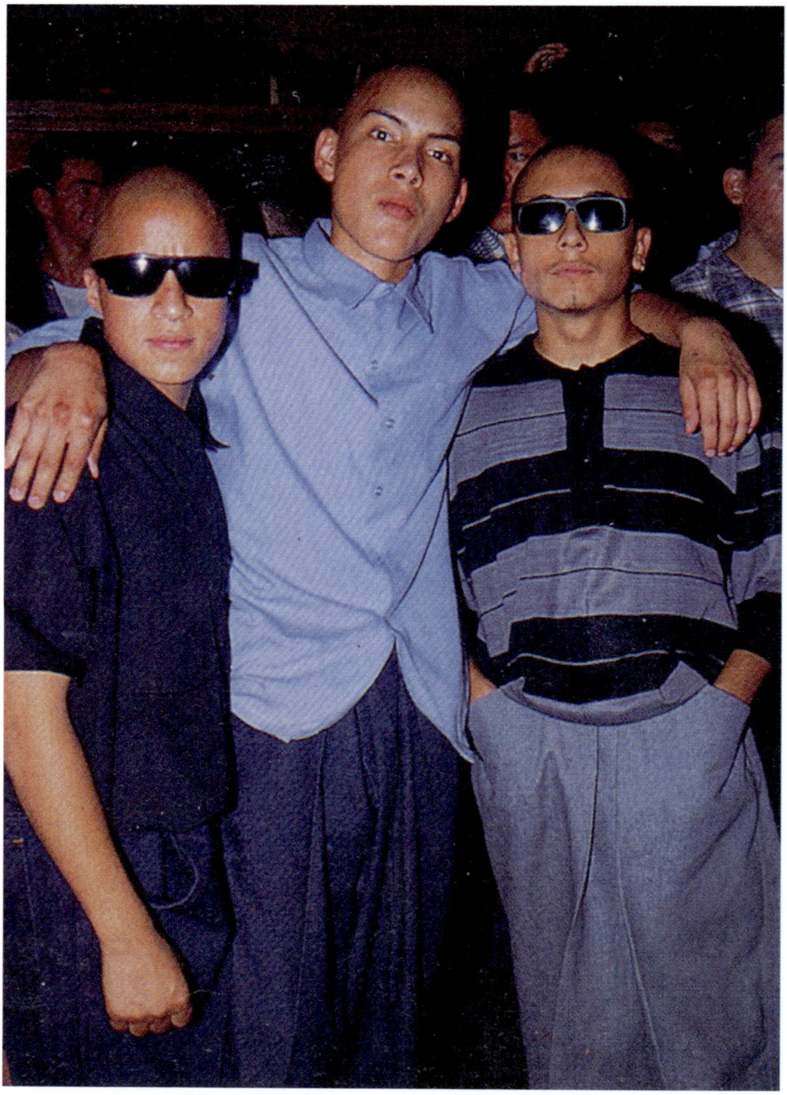

Cholos at an all-ages club called Baby Doe's in Monterey Park, sourced from *Street Beat Magazine*

. . .

ANOTHER TIME WE got caught red-handed when we stupidly decided to take Mom's car and drive to Venice Beach to visit Maria's boyfriend. Maria had smoked a huge amount of weed that night and was still faded. I didn't know how to drive yet, so Maria did the driving. On our way back, she was paranoid and thought she'd hit the freeway median's divider fence. Luckily she hadn't—she was actually driving extra-careful. When we finally made it back at around 2 A.M., we sat in the car for a few minutes. It was so quiet out. We parked the car in the garage and walked back to our house—and saw Mom standing outside waiting for us. Who knows how long she'd been standing there and how long she knew we'd taken the car?

My stepdad had probably heard us and told Mom. My stomach dropped when I saw her small silhouette by the door. I told my sister she needed to take the rap this time because this was on her. Did I want to go to her boyfriend's house and watch them make out all night? Absolutely not. But did I enjoy that rush of sneaking out, of doing something "bad"? Yes, I did.

You'd think that getting caught would stop us. Instead, we rebelled in different ways.

My mom would follow us around the house yelling at us and calling us names, but at this point the yelling went in through one ear and out the other. "Aquí no es hotel para que salgan y lleguen cuando les da la chingada gana," she would yell with frustration. If we did leave, she'd lock the door behind us to punish us. So many times we'd come home to a locked door. But by this point, we didn't care. If we got locked out, we'd just crash at a friend's house. Sometimes we'd end up stranded far from home in Fontana or the San Gabriel Valley and have no way of getting home for a day or two.

MY SISTERS AND I ran the streets with other kids from the neighborhood like a pack of wolves, day and night, and the streets quickly became our home. My mother still had a glimmer of hope, but not much. She had already lost her children to the block.

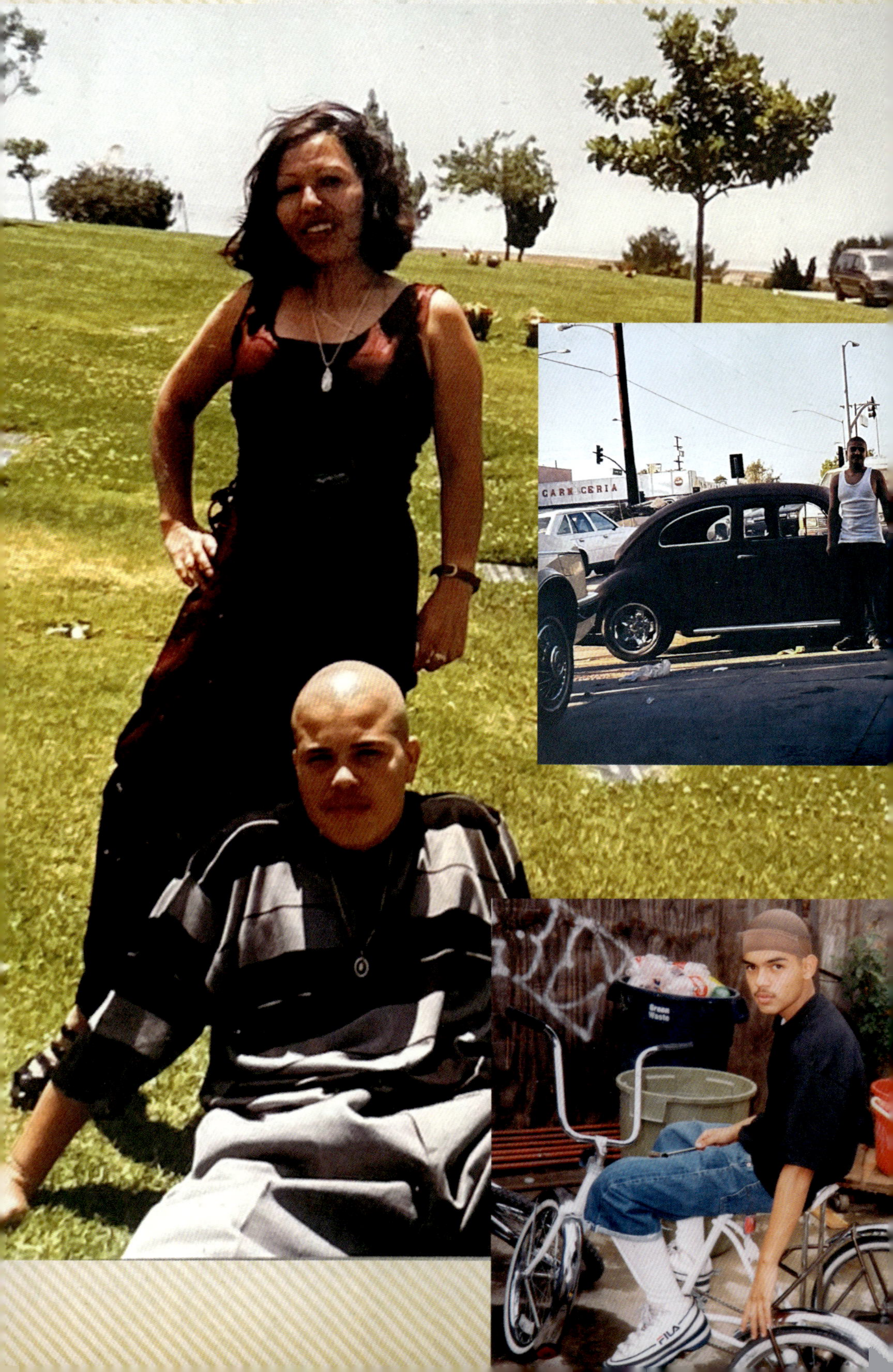

RIDE OR DIE

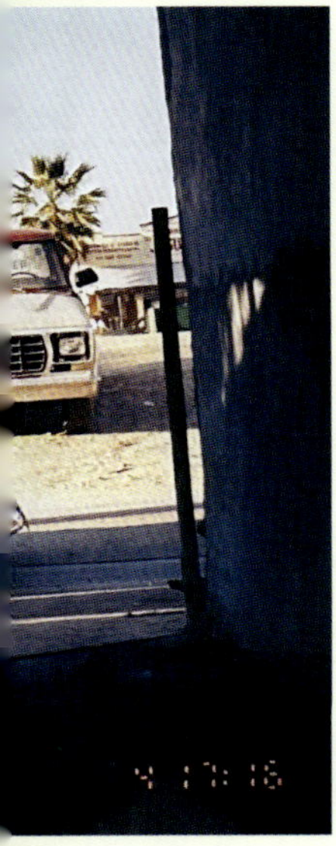

ABOVE: Chili Bean and his VW bug. He always came to visit us.

OPPOSITE: Danny and Mom at the cemetery visiting Ever in 1997. We all went there after baptizing one of Ever's kids.

LEFT: Our neighborhood friend Nelio on his bike and wearing Fila sneakers

MY MOTHER KNEW THAT MOST OF OUR friends were in gangs, but I think that the level of respect they had toward her won her over. If any of our friends came knocking on our door looking for us, they knew they had to ask for us very politely, sometimes playfully. Even though Mom could be very strict and intimidating, on a good day she was welcoming to our friends and was able to build friendships with them. She understood them and sympathized with them. Sometimes she'd make fun of their baggy pants—she'd crack jokes with them and say things like "Ese pantalón parece falda" (Those pants look like a skirt).

There were also times when she didn't want our guy friends near us and guarded us. She stood her ground and wasn't intimidated by them. If they came looking for us, she responded with "Vayanse a la chingada y no vengan a molestar, pinche bola de huevones" or "Pinches pandilleros!"

But when Mom was gone for even an hour, it was party time. She spent most of her time at church. That was her hangout spot—she went to church every Sunday and usually stayed there all day, volunteering after the service and catching up with her friends. We grew up going to a Catholic church in Boyle Heights called Resurrection Church, and even after we moved to Leonard and Whittier we continued to go.

We stopped going when Maria, at sixteen years old,

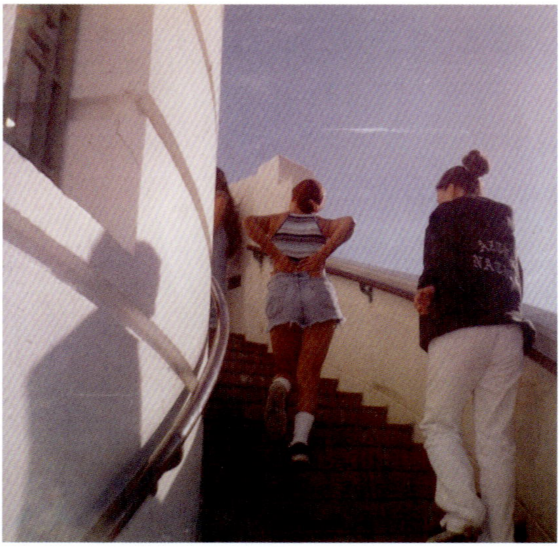

Maria and me in Griffith Park. I love this photo because Maria is hiding her back tattoo from Mom (lol).

was caught with a new tattoo on the back of her waist. This gave us a sense of relief and freedom—we detached ourselves from the weekly routine, and Mom stayed longer than she ever used to—and she also found new freedom she didn't know she needed. On the days we didn't have Mom yelling at us, we lounged around the house and talked on the phone for as long as we wanted or invited our friends over and listened to music. The streets would get busier as the sun went down. The boulevard was where we went to see new and familiar faces; where we connected with our friends and made new ones, and encountered some enemies, too.

The only time I dealt with a cheating boyfriend happened on Whittier Boulevard behind a taco truck. Richard and I first got together when we were fifteen. I was sixteen when I found him with a girl I had never seen before, hiding behind a taco truck parked close to a chain-link fence on the boulevard. When he saw me, I startled him and he pretended they were hiding from the cops. But I kept walking past them, with my heart shattered and sunken in.

The next day, I went over to his cousin's house on Allston and Hendricks, where he was staying for a while. I had a bad feeling about the night before—something in me already knew he wouldn't tell the truth. I can't remember exactly how I confronted him, just that he barely looked at me. He kept busy, pretending to organize his closet, avoiding eye contact. He only gave me a view of his profile the whole time, and that's when I saw it: On the right side of his neck, half-hidden in the shadows, was a hickey. He never acknowledged it. I didn't say anything. I just turned around and left. On the walk back home, I cut through the alley and cried in silence. Heartbreaks like this were so common that we began to normalize them, even if they hurt.

An envelope and letter from a pen pal guy I met through my sister's boyfriend at the time

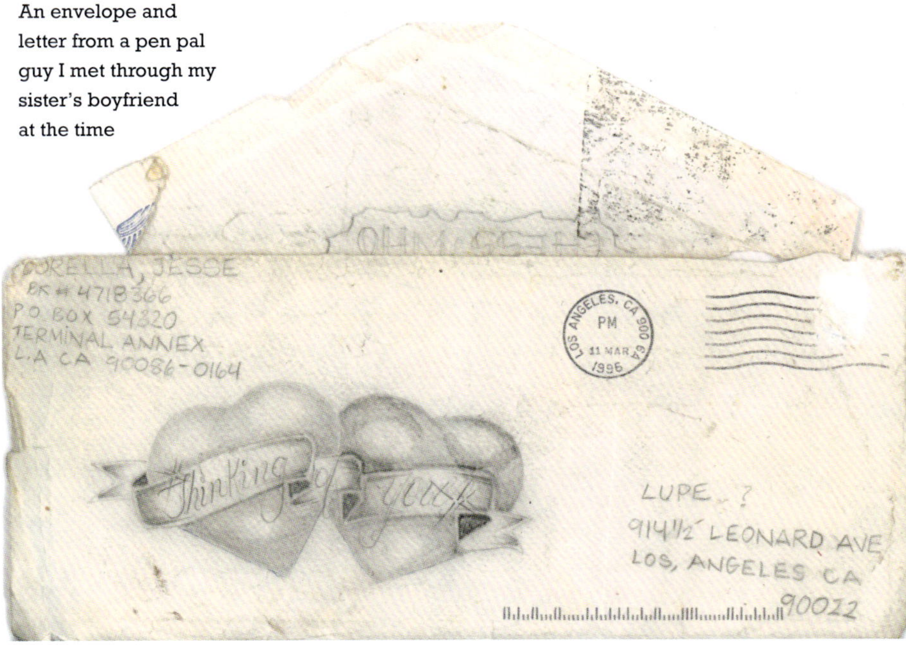

. . .

A FEW WEEKS later, I saw the same girl who I'd seen with Richard. She was walking down the alleyway alone.

I was with two friends and my younger sister, Yesi, who doesn't hold back when it comes to fighting. She told me, "This is your chance, Lupe." As we got closer to the girl, I recognized her and realized what my sister meant. Yesi confronted her, yelling and cursing her out. We circled around her like hungry wolves. Part of me was angry at her, and part of me didn't like fighting, but not fighting or not being confrontational was a sign of weakness or, as we'd call it, being a ranker.

The pressure of others was always there, and specifically with Yesi. She had a reputation for being a good fighter. She fought dirty and there were no rules with her. I felt bad for anyone who fought her. She'd been involved in so many fights at school that I don't know why she hadn't been expelled. She was the type of girl who would fight like her life depended on it, and in some ways, it did.

She was a Tasmanian devil who would tear your shirt and bra apart. She would make you lose sight of things. It was almost degrading, if you ask me. I know this because I've seen it happen before and have seen the fear on the other girls' faces. She once fought a girl after school and left her beaten up and practically naked in front of school, with tangled-up hair and a red face full of scratches. My sister is tiny, but she's a beast when it comes to fighting. She and I are very different. I've never initiated a fight in my life, just like I've never been able to break up with a person

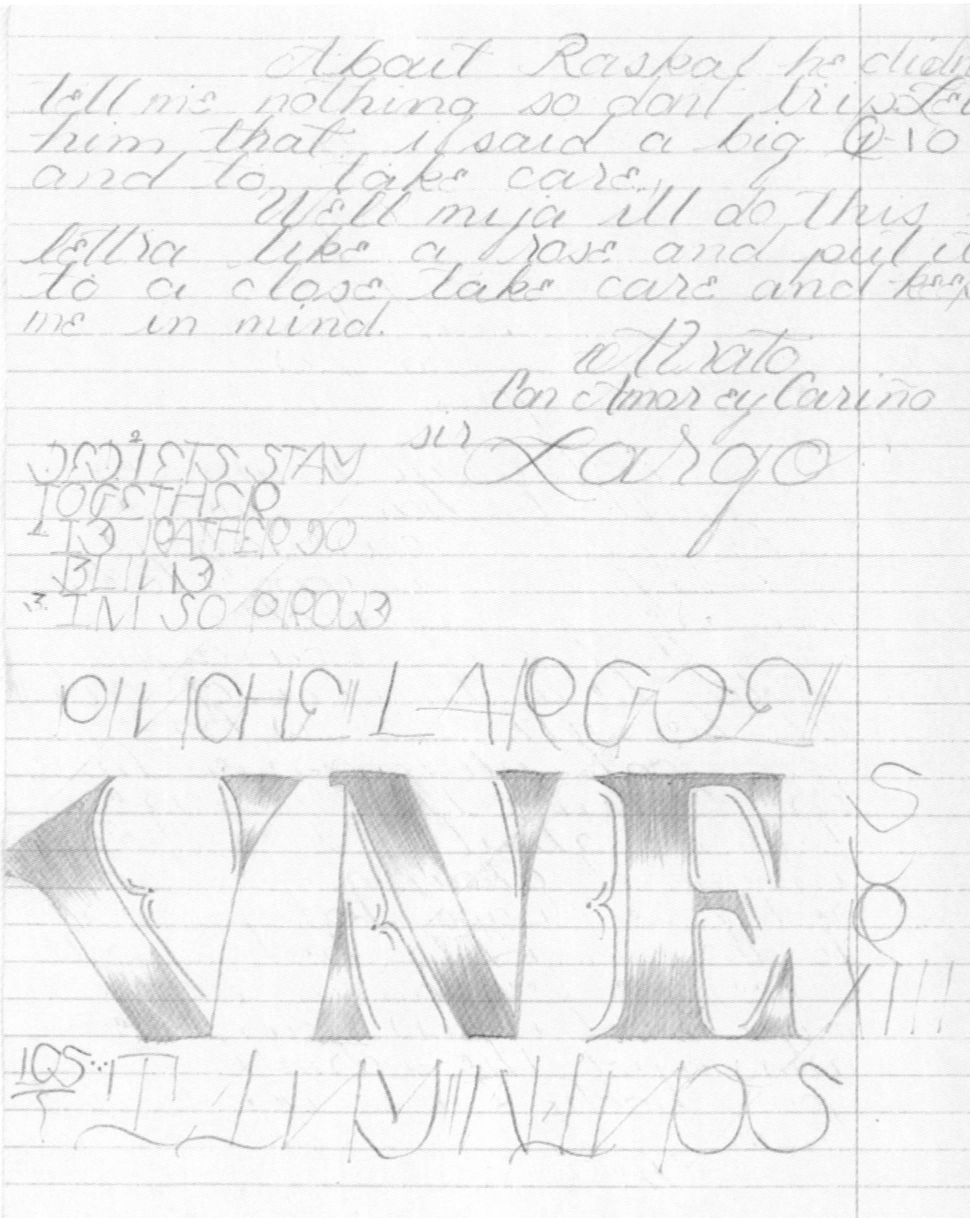
About Raspal he didn tell me nothing so don't trip tell him that i said a big Q-10 and to take care.
Well mija ill do this letter like a rose and put it to a close take care and keep me in mind.
el Vato
Con Amor y Cariño
sir Largo

STAY TOGETHER
2. I'D RATHER GO BLIND
3. I'M SO PROUD

LARGO

VNE

because I always think about their feelings before mine. Maybe those two are related.

Luckily, I've never been jumped. The times I have gotten into a fight or had to jump someone were because I got caught up in the mix. This was bound to happen on the streets, especially on Whittier Boulevard. We were there for one another. No matter the circumstances, we always stuck together. We learned to remove earrings and necklaces so they wouldn't get ripped off, but we'd keep our rings on every finger. Sharp pointy ones. We learned to put our hair in a bun and swing and punch with our eyes closed. We learned not to let our guard down. To fight dirty and do whatever it took to win—punch, pull, bite. Scraped-up elbows and knees. Red faces and smeared makeup. Busted lips, and maybe a broken nose.

My sisters got frustrated with me when I didn't want to fight the girl Richard had been cheating on me with. "Fuckin' Lupe, why don't you hit her?! You're such a ranker." All of a sudden I felt a firm shove from behind. It was Yesi, pushing me against the girl. We started fighting in the dirty alleyway. My sister and two friends jumped in and beat her up with me. As the girl fell to the ground, I kicked her and punched her in the face. It was a quick but dirty fight. We ran off laughing, leaving her on the ground. I held my head high that morning even though I was pushed from behind to instigate the fight. After catching Richard with that girl, things were on and off between us—partly because he was locked up for months at a time. After that, I couldn't take him as seriously anymore.

THE SAME WAY we learned how to survive the streets, we also learned how to heal from heartbreaks. Like my sister told me that night, "Fuck it, just find another boyfriend," and by the end of the night I had several telephone numbers from different guys I'd met. From then on I began to date, flirt, kiss different boys. I had a few serious relationships and wrote to boys who I knew from the neighborhood and were locked up, like my new boyfriend Largo from VNE and my friend Wolfy, or guys I would meet through my sister's boyfriend who were in the Navy or juvenile hall and wanted pen pals. I was a bad girl again.

OPPOSITE: A prison letter from my boyfriend Victor (aka Largo), who I dated shortly after Richard

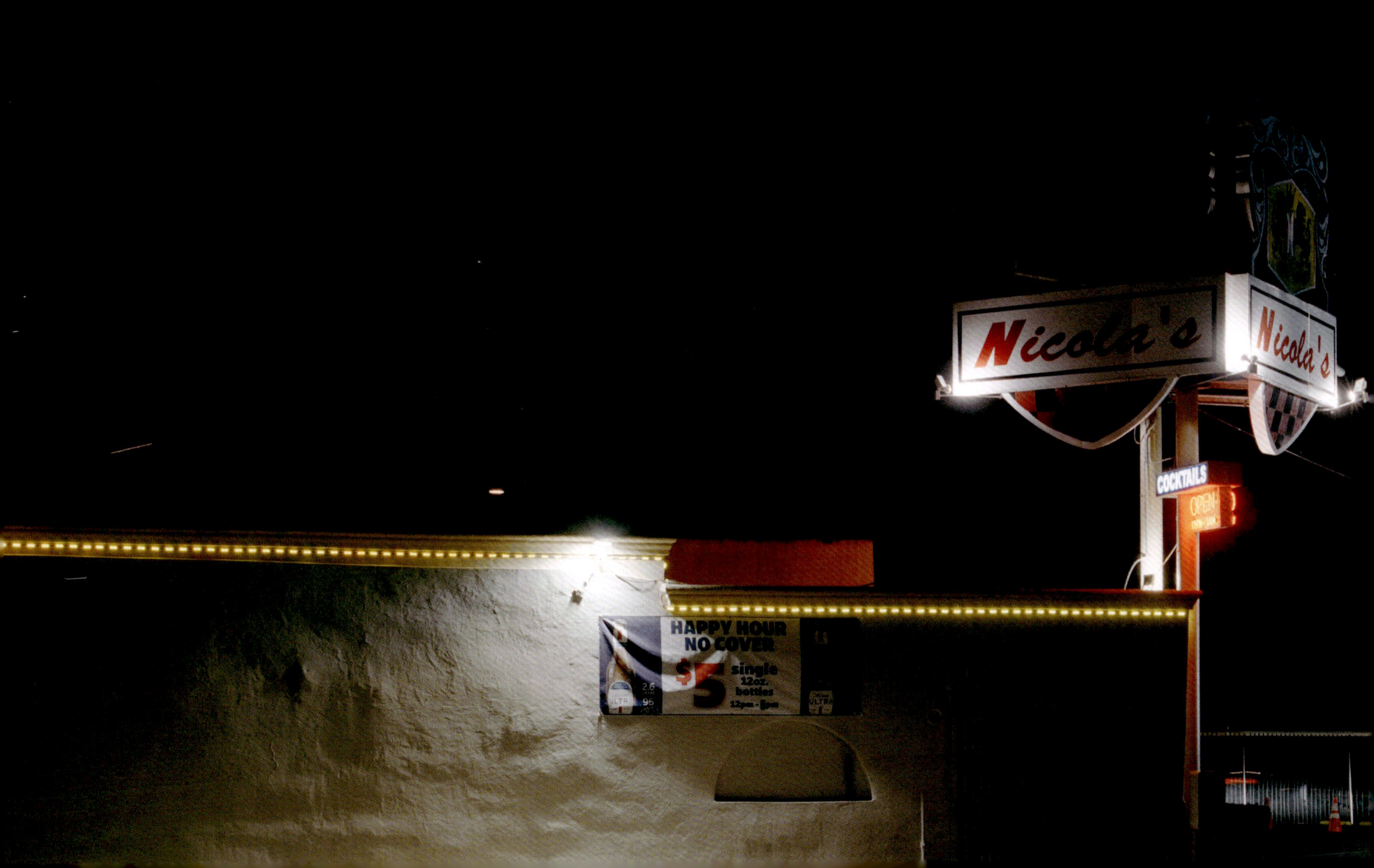
Nicola's
Nicola's
COCKTAILS
OPEN
HAPPY HOUR
NO COVER
$5 single
12oz.
bottles

FIVE-FINGER DISCOUNT

ALMOST EVERY DAY, YOU'D FIND ME, MY TWO sisters, and our friends either walking down Whittier Boulevard or at the Commerce Shopping Center or Montebello Town Center. The Commerce Shopping Center is an outdoor shopping mall on Whittier Boulevard, between Gerhart and Goodrich—walking distance from our house. Even though Mom was strict with us, she let us go to Commerce and hang out with friends. Most kids in the neighborhood went there.

Maria, Yesi, and I would get a little dressed up—501 Levi's, sneakers—just in case we saw a cute guy or a crush. We'd walk to our friend Silvia's house on Simmons Street, pick her up, and keep walking. First grab a bite at Rick's Burgers, which sits across from A & G Customs on Gerhart and Whittier Boulevard, where they usually had a two-for-one deal. After that we'd cut through an alley that led us by the neighborhood's infamous strip club, Nicola's Gentlemen's Club, but known as Nicola's Strip Club. That's where wives went looking for their husbands at all hours. We heard those stories through friends—especially the guys—who spent time there. Nicola's sat just across the street from where the world of the Commerce Shopping Center began. Most of my friends either worked there or hung out there so often that it felt like an extension of home.

OPPOSITE: Simply known as Nicola's by the locals. Still in business, on Gerhart Ave. in City of Commerce.

This was where we got most of our clothes and makeup. We purchased our Jordana lipliners (cocoa, auburn, natural, and cherry) and eyebrow pencils from the dollar store

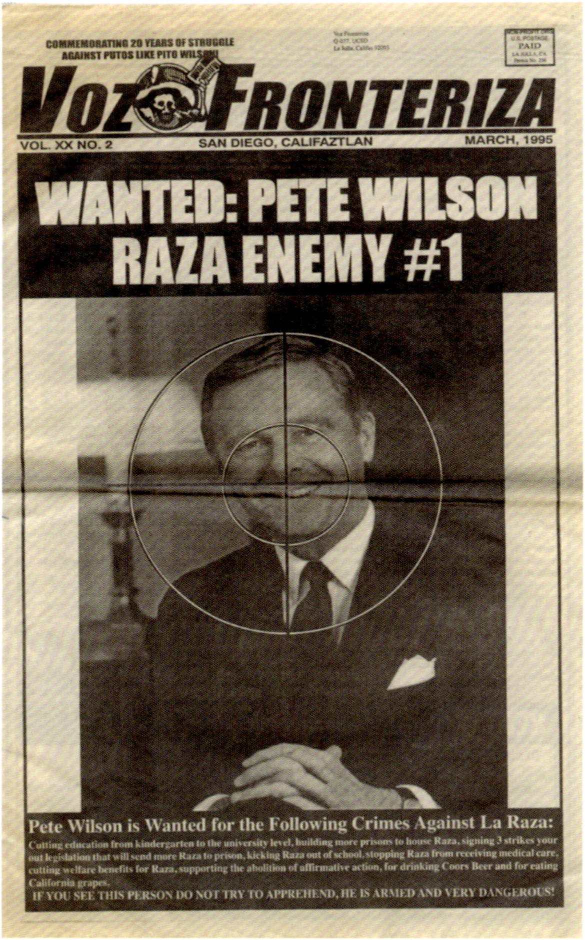

COMMEMORATING 20 YEARS OF STRUGGLE AGAINST PUTOS LIKE PITO WILSON!

U.S. POSTAGE PAID

VOZ FRONTERIZA

VOL. XX NO. 2 SAN DIEGO, CALIFAZTLAN MARCH, 1995

WANTED: PETE WILSON RAZA ENEMY #1

Pete Wilson is Wanted for the Following Crimes Against La Raza:

Cutting education from kindergarten to the university level, building more prisons to house Raza, signing 3 strikes your out legislation that will send more Raza to prison, kicking Raza out of school, stopping Raza from receiving medical care, cutting welfare benefits for Raza, supporting the abolition of affirmative action, for drinking Coors Beer and for eating California grapes.

IF YOU SEE THIS PERSON DO NOT TRY TO APPREHEND, HE IS ARMED AND VERY DANGEROUS!

Newspaper with Pete Wilson on the front cover

across from where Dearden's used to be. We stole CoverGirl compacts and Maybelline mascara from Kmart, because it was easier there than at a dollar store, where the employees were constantly watching us the minute we walked in. Kmart was bigger and easier, and no one really cared if you stole some makeup. Sometimes, friends of ours would shoplift shoes, clothes, and even VCRs, but it was harder for the boys, who were being watched. Like when my friend Michael walked right out with a VCR strapped with his belt under his oversized pants and hooded sweatshirt. He got caught, of course, but the security guard just grabbed him by the arm and yanked the VCR from his waist, and Michael just kept walking out like he could care less.

The fashion stores were smaller than stores like Kmart or Target. And most were run by Asian families. I don't know when they opened, but I know they are the heartbeat of the strip. The store names say it all: 97 and Up, Fashion Area, T-Shirt Wholesale Outlet (but we called it Five-by-Ten)—all offering the kind of clothes that fit our vibe, and that we could afford: cheap and bold.

We were regulars, picking up bootleg brands, Raiders gear, Ben Davis, and baggy Solo pants we all loved to wear. We also bought our sexy 'fits there. Whatever look we were going for, we found it at those stores.

Commerce Shopping Center wasn't always fun; we also experienced heavy policing and criminalization—especially from security guards patrolling the area and from the Korean families who owned most of the stores. Prejudice and discrimination between African American, Asian, and Latino communities were on the rise, especially after the Los Angeles Riots in 1992 and during the debate over Proposition 187 in 1994.

The divide between us was subtle but undeniable, colored by years of mistrust and prejudice on all sides. The wounds of the Riots, which targeted Asian-owned businesses, still stung; Korean Americans suffered heavy losses, with 2,280 stores damaged, looted, or burned. Many Korean Americans even considered leaving Los Angeles. There was an invisible line that got drawn when conversations about race and power came up, one that no one wanted to cross, but that everyone could feel. My friends and family were all caught in the midst of it, but we had one another. It was like a haze that hovered over us—something we carried without knowing how heavy it really was.

BUT MOST OF the time, the shopping center was a microcosm of life in our neighborhood. It's where we met, laughed, grabbed a quick bite, or just killed time walking from store to store. We were like family there, sharing stories, talking shit, and always looking out for one another. We navigated those tensions as well as we could. We learned how to show up for one another when it felt like the world was pushing us down. We found strength in friendships, in our families, and in one another's resilience. The weight of the world pressed on us at times, but we held on—because we had no other choice. Our lives were entwined in this place, in this struggle, in this story, and no matter how many times we got knocked down, we kept showing up. Together.

The Regency movie theater and arcades on Goodrich and Whittier Boulevard were our favorite hangout spots. I almost always snuck into the theater unless I was with my parents and they were buying the tickets. I went with the whole family; we'd watch movies like *La jaula de oro, La puerta negra,* or any movie by Mario Almada. Sometimes, by accident we'd end up in a theater playing one of those mañoso (comedy) films with Alfonso Zayas and "El Caballo."

But when I was with friends, we saw movies like *Dead Presidents* (the year that movie came out, all the kids in the neighborhood dressed up like its characters for Halloween), *Tales from the Hood,* and *Friday.* We

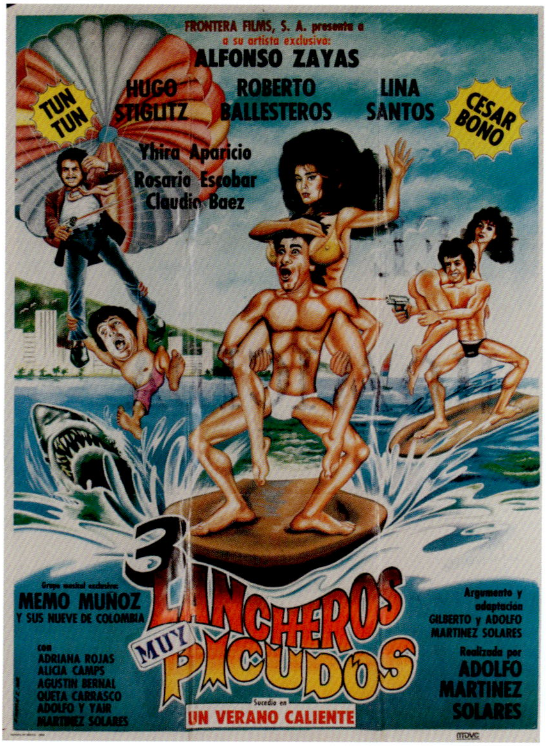

always snuck in through the back door. This was a trick that had been passed on to us by older friends.

Each theater room had its own emergency exit behind the movie screen. The trick was to have a friend pay for one movie ticket and go inside. Once they were inside, that friend would find a seat closest to the screen, preferably in the first row, and wait for the lights to turn off right before the previews began. They would then run to the back of the movie screen and crack open the door for us.

This worked best when we were a big group of girls. I was more excited than afraid of getting caught. And the security guards usually profiled the boys. Adrenaline pumping, we'd rush inside in total darkness and grab any seat we could find. Seconds later, security guards would walk in with their flashlights, pointing them at any kid who looked suspicious to them—teenagers in baggy clothes, in groups. We'd pretend we didn't know what was happening and keep our eyes on the screen. If we got caught, it could be a bit embarrassing. We would do the walk of shame—everyone in the theater would stare as we were escorted out.

We never gave up, though. The movie theater was a bit run-down, like

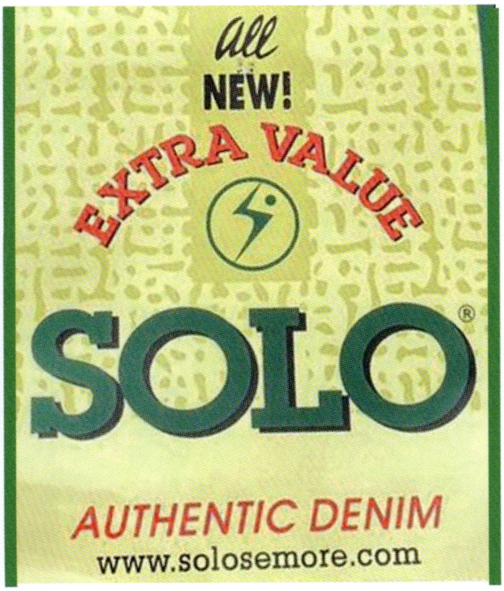

most of the buildings in the area. Inside, the walls were rugged, worn from years of use. The exterior of the building was painted in warm tones—brown, tan, and cream stripes, with patches of paint covering graffiti. This color palette gave it a vintage look, something it had always had. Some movies even required 3D glasses to complete the experience.

SOMETIMES OUR FRIEND Silvia would meet us at the house around noon, and together we'd take two short bus rides to Montebello Town Center. It wasn't far, but it felt like a whole other universe. It wasn't just the stores that drew us in—it was the journey itself: the sense of freedom from getting on the Montebello bus to walking in circles at the mall without any guidance.

We didn't really buy clothes there, since they were out of our price range, but we loved hanging out. I was also scared of stealing there after getting caught once shoplifting a *The Doors in Concert* DVD from Spencer's. But Montebello Town Center wasn't about shopping—it was about being there. The mall was the place to walk

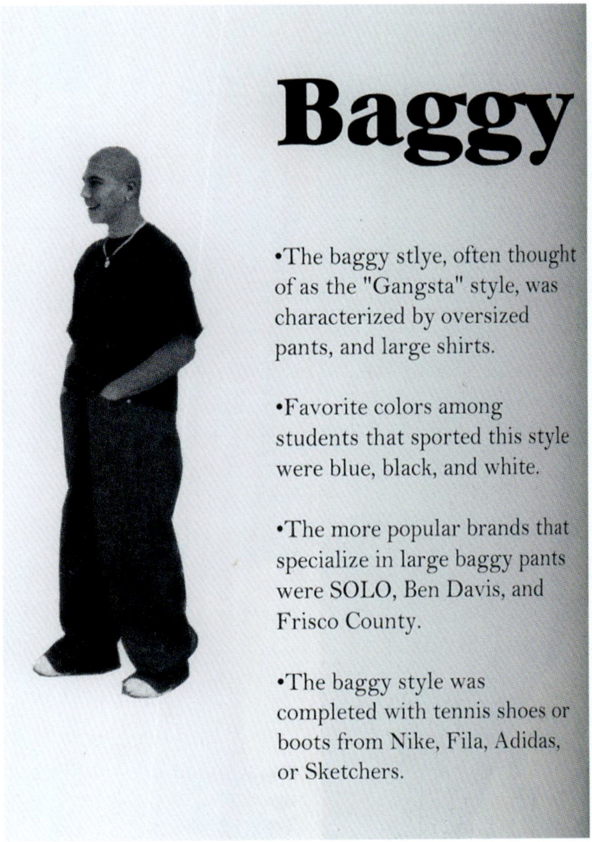

A description of fashion in 1996, mentioned in our Schurr High School yearbook

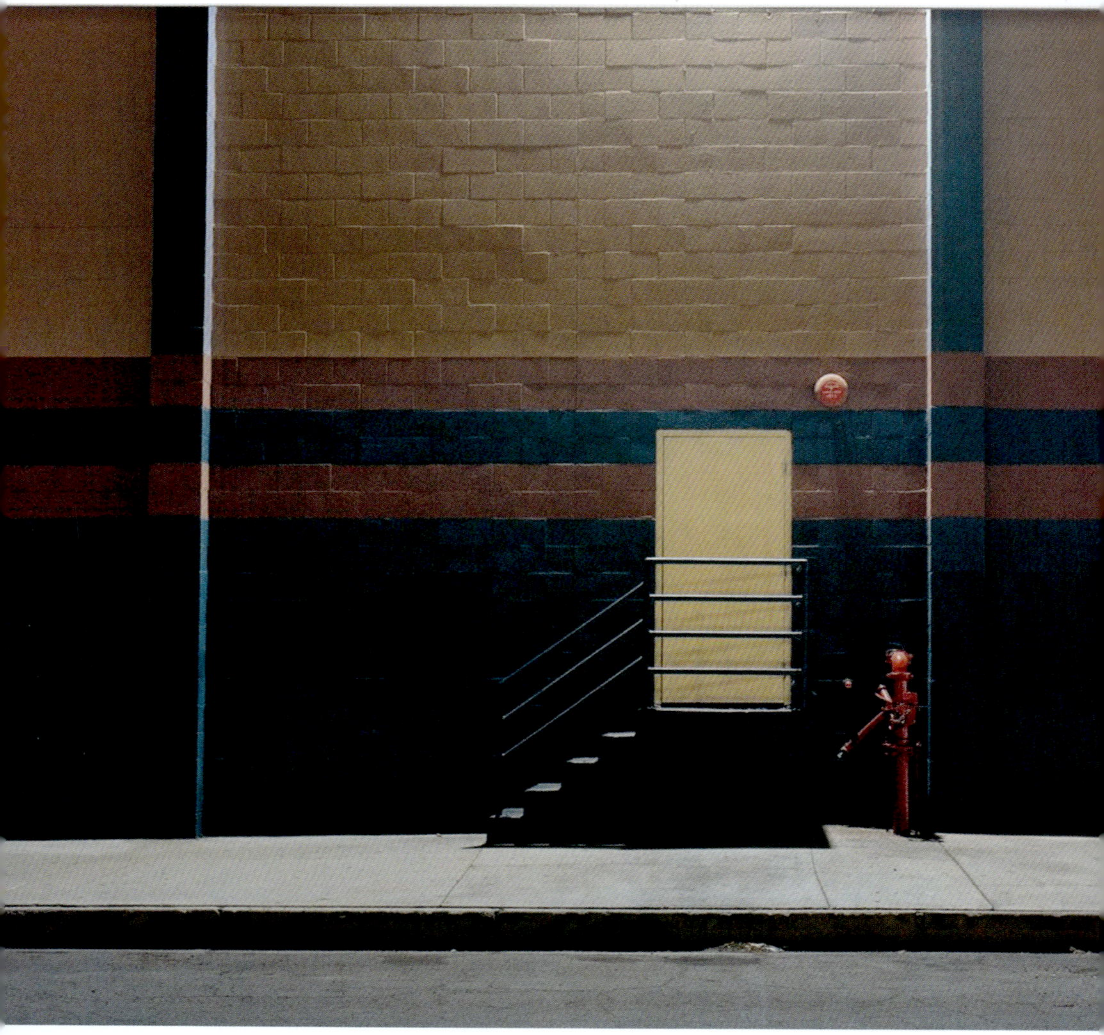

The back of the movie theater in Commerce Shopping Center

in circles, ride the escalators up and down, and flirt with random boys who were there for the same reason.

This was also where we took those wallet-size Starshot photos that I've carried with me for decades since. The little photo studio was tucked in a corner on the upper level of the mall, and for that we always wore our favorite 'fits with good makeup and hair. Sometimes it was three of us in a picture, sometimes five. Once we'd picked up our printed photos, we'd write notes on the backs and pass them around school and among neighborhood friends.

The mall was the perfect place to meet up with friends, wander aimlessly, and make out with our crushes or meet new ones. You didn't need a reason to be there—just showing up was enough. We'd hang out for hours, walking around, eating Jolly Ranchers or lollipops, and flirting. And sometimes, if the stars aligned, you'd catch

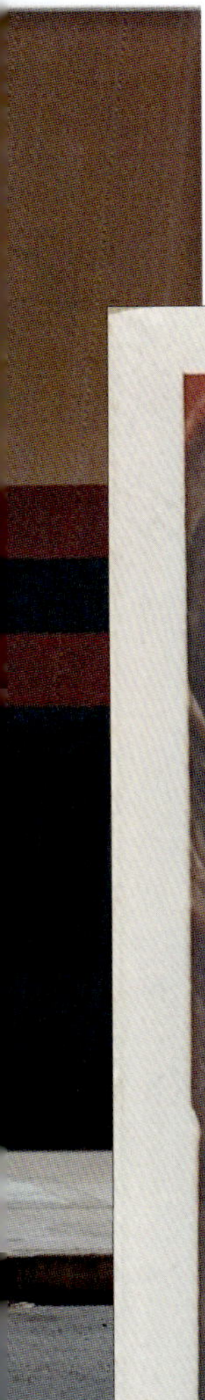

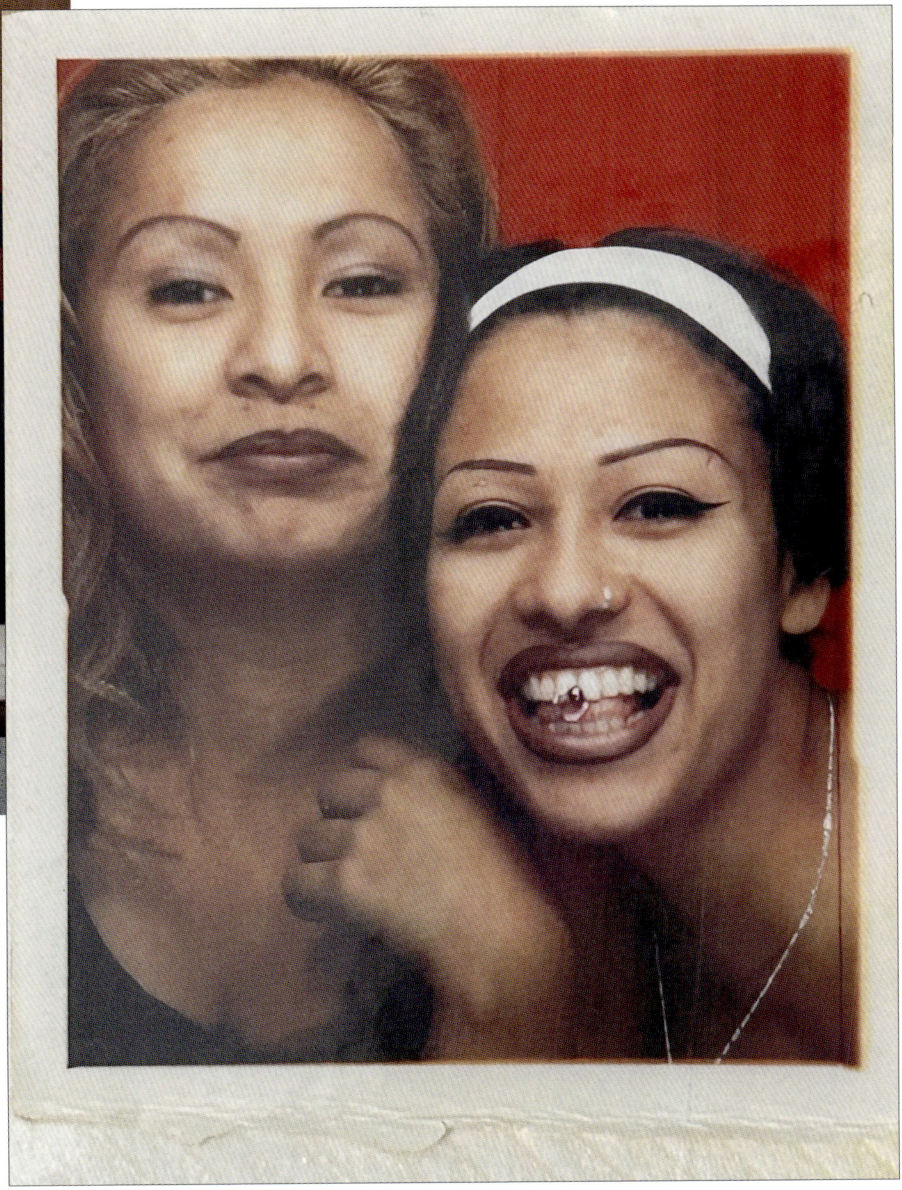

Our friend Sandra and my sister Maria. Taken in a photo booth in the Commerce Shopping Center, circa 1996. Maybe this was at Kmart or the movie theater.

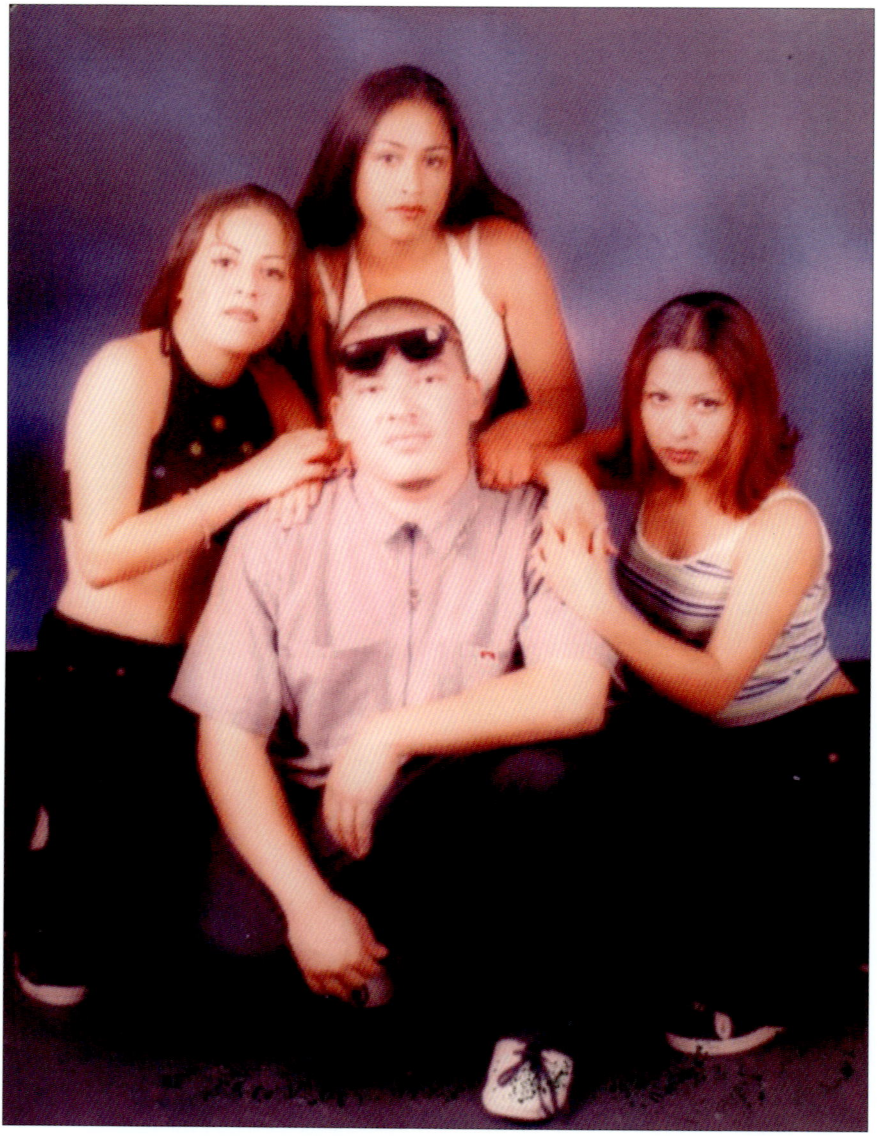

A Starshot photo of Maria, me, Emilio, and Yesi taken at the Montebello Town Center in 1996

OPPOSITE: The backs of personal Starshot photos with notes from friends

To: 10-23-96
Lupe.
Well here is a picture of me and gose, I hope you like it I would want a picture of you, alright? I know he looks funny cuz his eyes, but oh well.
Laters
Take care. always
Jose Rosa Hernandez

To: Lupe
well here is a picture of me and my Baby I hope you like it. call me to go out.
Love you
Natalie Ab.
(213) 887-8136

To: Lupe
hello! Well here's a picture of me and chris and I said I'd give you a picture so here it is I hope you like it.
your friend
Kit [illegible]
991-5062
flower power

6-11-96
To Lupita,
You've been cool with me since I've known you, Except for that one time coming from the mall (remember) Sorry!
Take care.
your friend,
[illegible]
1996 Olympic Trials

To: Lupe
Hope you like this pic. of me and my baby albert take care of it k! and take care of yourself
love love
albert Nancy

[illegible] 27 9[illegible]
"Lupe"
Here's a picture of my baby & me hope you like it
"Class of 98"
Love
Berenice & Lorette 4

TO: LUPE
HELLO :) HERE IS A PICTURE OF ME AND MY BOYFRIEND HOPE YOU LIKE IT AND STAY THE SAME DON'T CHANGE O.K.
YOUR FRIEND,
ARACELY A.
I ♥ LUIS!
(213) 887-4163 K*I*T

5.10.97
"Lupe"
What's up. Hope you like this picture of my friend Arlene and me.
yourfriend
Berenice
class "of 98"
I ♥ FABIAN

To: Lupe (Babe)
Heres a picture of me in baseball. I ho[pe] you like it and keep it forever.
From your good fri[end]
Valentin

the eye of someone new. Then maybe you'd take a walk around the mall with them, trying to figure out if this was just another fleeting high school crush or something more.

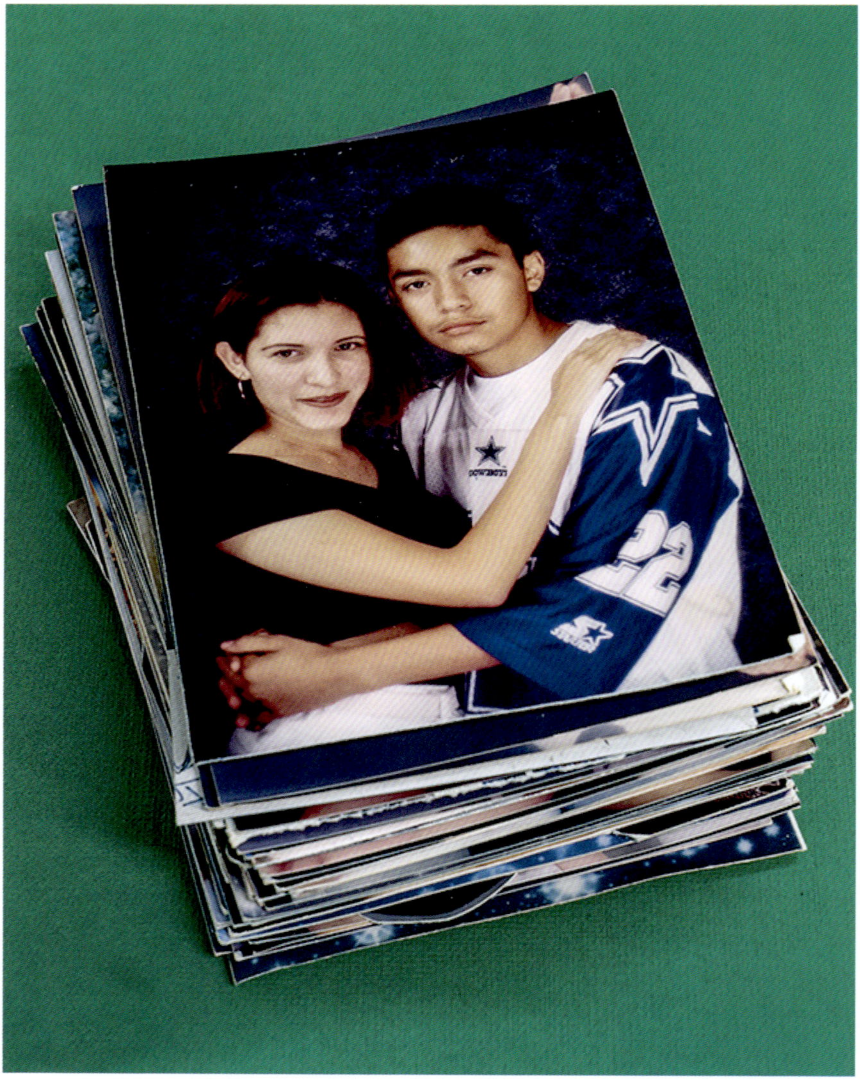

Starshot photos from my personal collection

STREETWISE

WE SPENT WEEKEND NIGHTS PARTYING OR HANGING OUT with friends, risking Mom locking us out of the house. Sundays meant that the weekend was coming to an end, so we made the best of it. We got up early because Mom never let us sleep in. We ate whatever we had in the fridge—bolillo or sandwich bread con frijoles y queso or quesadillas with corn tortillas and any type of cheese. During the day, we loved to be sun-kissed, be lazy lying on the couch, listening to Art Laboe and R&B.

As the sun set, the boulevard seemed fun and inviting. Getting ready, I would turn on Power 106, dig through my closet, and pick out clothes that would keep me warm and yet still look cute. My sisters and friends didn't mind any weather and would wear hoochie clothes year-round—maybe a black Lycra crop tee and a black silk-type miniskirt.

Maria would take out her liquid eyeliner and start with her right eye. The eyeliner was almost always black, but occasionally she used brown and white. Slow and steady, holding her breath to make sure her hands didn't shake, her eyes slightly closed to avoid creases. Then she'd move to the left eye and repeat. She'd add thick mascara, separating every eyelash one by one—she had a special needle for this. Then she'd carefully pencil her eyebrows very thinly. She'd step back from the mirror to take a better look at her makeup. She wasn't satisfied until everything was exactly aligned and symmetrical.

MARIA AND I had the same shoes—black patent-leather platforms. The white ones were all scuffed up. The night often had a cool breeze and was a bit chilly, so I often dressed casual—pants, windbreaker, and comfort-

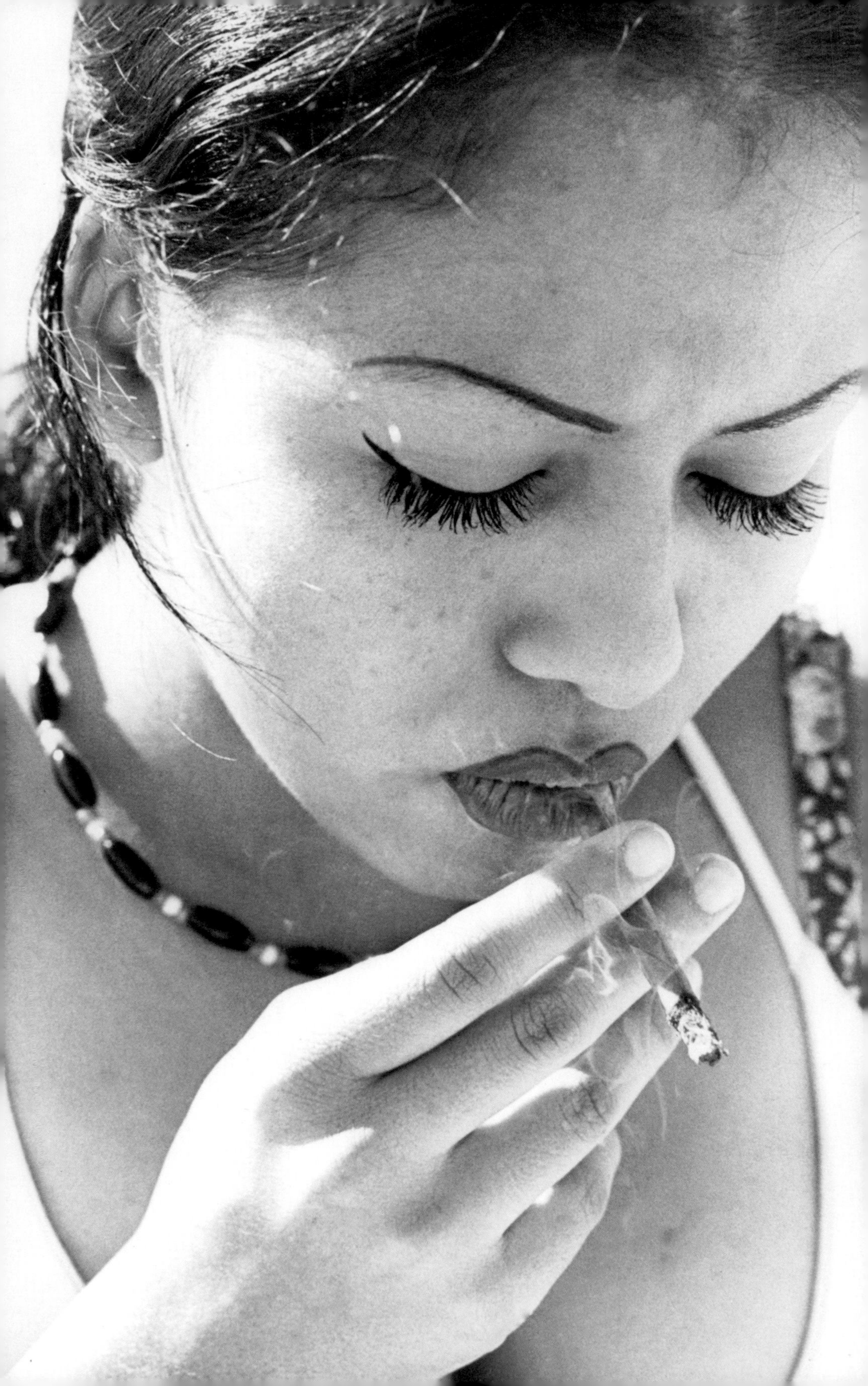

able but cute sneakers. Once I was ready, I'd walk up and down Whittier Boulevard with my sisters.

The streets were complex, just like my home—we could feel safe and confronted by danger all at once. Nights in Los Angeles are not good or bad or how they're depicted on television and in movies. L.A. is not flat like a movie screen. There is dimension. One thing I know for sure is that I rarely walked the streets alone at night unless I really had to. When I was alone, so many things happened, like gangs hitting me up (meaning asking if I bang, meaning if I am from a gang). Where I lived, most of those who asked were either rivals or new in the neighborhood. Or perverts of all ages who'd come out looking for a perfect victim.

Maria taught me one of the most valuable lessons I still carry with me today: how to walk with confidence and power. In many ways, I looked up to Maria—as she got older, she became influenced by friends and grew confidence (she was always on the go-go box dancing at the house parties and clubs). She was a daredevil, rebellious and social. I was timid, uncomfortable with wearing tight little outfits. She showed me how to carry myself with my head held high, walking tough, like I owned the streets.

She never handed me a manual or sat me down for a lecture. Instead, she taught me by example, and I learned by watching her every move. She could be feminine, walk with grace, but if she sensed danger, her whole demeanor shifted. It was like a switch flipped—her posture changed, and suddenly it was clear: She didn't give a damn. Her presence was commanding, like she owned the space, and that's what I tried to emulate. I think some people would describe this as "bitch face." If I was alone, I'd walk with a bit of a tough edge—just enough to intimidate people. It was all about walking without fear, shoulders back, energy strong, because people—especially predators—can sense that.

That's why I always preferred to roll deep when I could—not just for protection, but for vanity, too. Femininity is power, and no one can take that away from us. A group of strong, confident women—hot women, at that—always commands attention. But more important, it's a shield. A pack is safer, and no one messed with us when we were together. We stayed alert with pride. There were people, including the cops, with only one purpose: to disrupt and cause panic. We grew up knowing that if you looked at someone the wrong way or for too long, it was good enough

OPPOSITE: Maria smoking a joint in Venice Beach, 1998

NICOLE
4547602
SATURDAY MARCH 1st 1997
POINTLESS EVENTS
BRINGS TO YOU
REN & PIMPY
To be on our mailing list or if you want the name of your crew hit flyer please call:
(213) 715-3663 - (213) 205-4468 - (213) 470 7623
JUST A TEEZER
7940463
728-0698
Sat Oct 4, 1997
Come Join
PRIORITY
Motorsports
&
Main Line
Prod.
As They Bring U
Bounce That Booty
Ladies in free
B-4 9:30pm
JANUARY 28, 1995

reason to throw down or possibly get jumped. We learned not to make eye contact and stay in our lane. The city was quiet no matter where we went, but once the sun went down, it came alive again.

On nights when we didn't have any plans and stayed home, Maria and I stepped outside, settling on the porch or leaning against the doorframe. The smell of fresh watermelon and carne asada lingered in the air. In those moments we knew the night could take us anywhere. Nights like these were unpredictable—full of both wonder and risk. We might become easy targets for predators or creeps, but we could also share magical moments with friends or crushes we were getting to know. We shared stories and flirted, as we tried to hide our shyness under the silvery glow of the full moon with the city noise all around us.

We didn't keep track of time; we lived in the moment, lost in the city lights, the sky, and everything in between. Inside, the house remained calm. My mom was watching TV in her bedroom. She usually left her door open to keep an eye on us, and I could see the soft flicker of the screen painting her face in quiet light. She cherished nights like this, knowing that when we were home, we were safe. This is a side of L.A. that few understand—the beauty and quiet magic that night breathes into East Los Angeles. The city was synchronized, from barbecues with friends and family, lying in the sun and feeling the heat on our beautiful brown skin.

Most nights ended with making out with boys. When we came home, I emptied out my pockets filled with crumpled pieces of paper. Sometimes the numbers were hard to read, but the paper scraps had little notes describing what the boys were wearing or driving—"Robert from Canta Ranas gang (Cowboys jersey)," "Eddie from Pico Rivera," "Green Eyes from Monte Flores (in a red Mustang)."

Boys usually asked for our numbers, and if we thought they were cute, we asked for theirs as well, a bold move for a girl. If they asked for a kiss, we also agreed. If we didn't like them and they were persistent, we gave them a fake number. One night I came back with five different telephone numbers scribbled on pieces of paper, each one tucked in my pockets like a small, passing moment. My lipliner was smudged from kissing, leaving a faint red tint behind. Most of the time, boys were sweet, polite, even a little charming. They would compliment you, ask you out, and maybe they really meant it. It was nice, really. Most of the time.

OPPOSITE: A collection of scraps of papers with telephone numbers of people we met at parties or on the boulevard

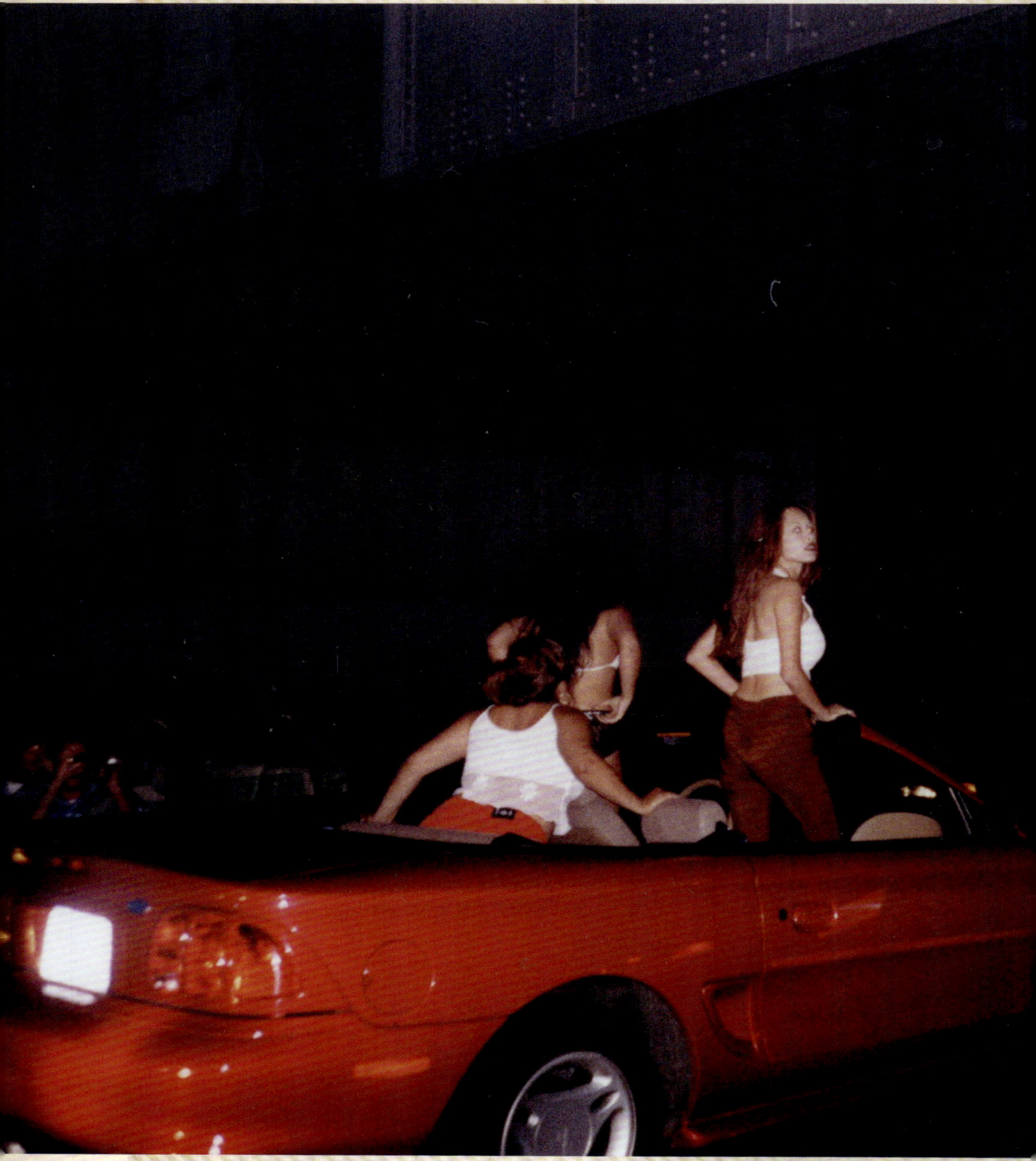

A group of girls cruising
on Whittier Boulevard in
Montebello, 1995

CRUISING

WALKING OR DRIVING A BUSTED CAR (WE called that a "bucket") or stealing Mom's four-door Chrysler sedan for the night was just as good as a 1964 Impala to us. Six to eight girls crushed like sardines in a Honda Accord or walking down Whittier Boulevard with our heads held high, wearing cut-off Levi's shorts or L.E.I. (Life, Energy, and Intelligence) shorts and a tank top or bra top, with platform shoes or Nike or Fila sneakers if I wanted to be more comfortable.

We put our heads out the car window, sometimes almost our entire bodies, like a newborn baby taking its first breath of air, with our arms wide open embracing the L.A. breeze at night. We yelled out "Chaau!!!" We felt free.

We drove slowly, through parking lots to check out the boys hanging out. My friend Miros was the one with a car, a red '91 hatchback Honda Civic, and she always drove us around. The usual suspects were our friend Christina, my sister Yesi, and me. We had to sit closest to the left side, because if we put too much weight on the right, the tire would rub against the wheel well. She'd stop when we asked her to or when she saw a cute boy. We'd make quick U-turns to take a closer look.

We cruised Whittier Boulevard, back and forth, from Arizona Avenue in East L.A. to Durfee Avenue in Pico Rivera. The whole night, we'd be collecting phone numbers scribbled on scraps of paper or crumpled gum wrappers, stuffing them in our pockets to deal with later. We made pit stops at gas stations, parking lots, shopping centers, and burger joints like Arry's, John's Burgers, Tommy's, and In-N-Out. At each stop, we caught glimpses of hot boys and girls, flirting, laughing, some sneaking off to dimly lit corners.

One night, as Miros was driving down Whittier Boulevard crossing Rosemead, Yesi and I in the backseat, we spotted him—a cholito, looking too good for his own good. He was wearing creased gray Ben Davis pants, a crisp white Cowboys jersey, and probably a spritz of Cool Water or Polo. His head was shaved smooth, and the way he stood there, so full of pride, so full of himself, we found it hot. He had this whole presence, like

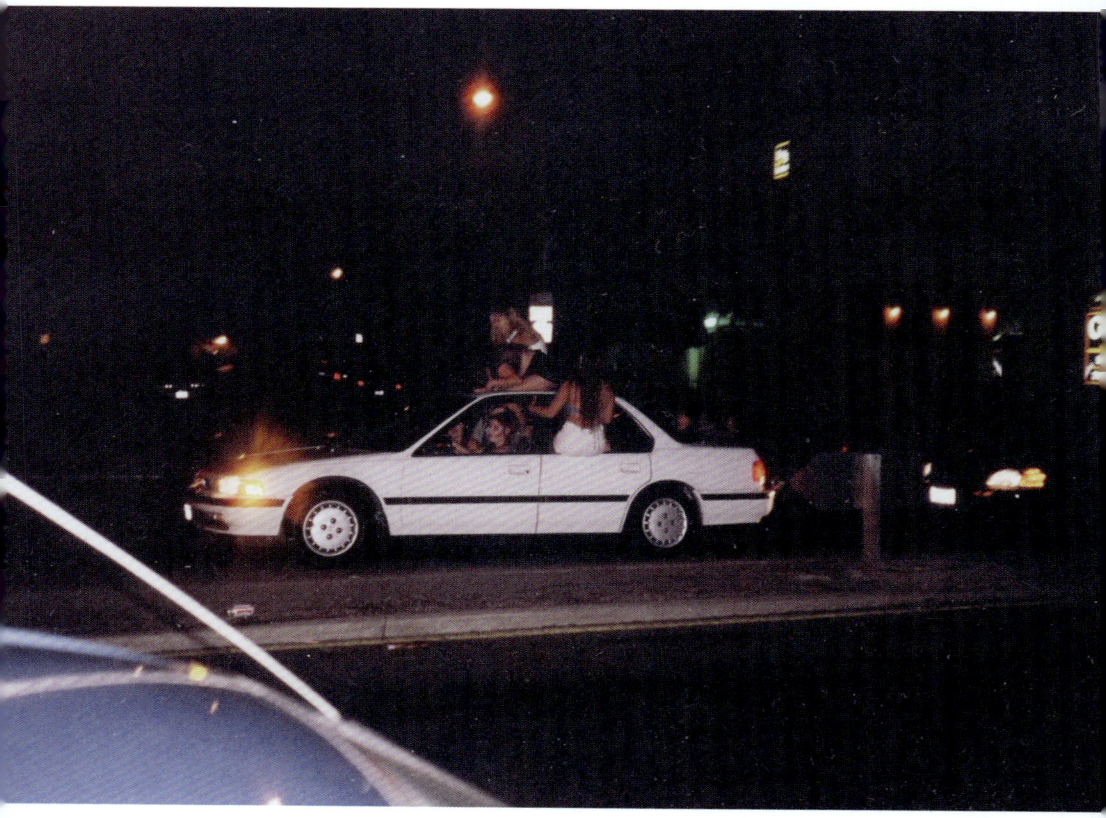

he owned the corner, like he was performing for us. He was singing "Reasons" aloud by Earth, Wind & Fire. With every note, his voice cut through the night air—loud, confident, full of swagger, like he was serenading every girl cruising down the boulevard. He sang from the depths of his chest. For a moment, he was untouchable, bold, maybe a little reckless—but no one dared mess with him. Not tonight.

"Reasons" by Earth, Wind & Fire
The reasons that we're here,
The reasons that we fear
Our feelings won't disappear
Ooh, and after the love game

The police often detoured us onto the 605 freeway to get all the cars off Whittier Boulevard. This was a common tactic they used to herd us like cattle onto the freeway. We always had a backup plan, though. We took a left on Rosemead Boulevard to look for the next spot. I looked back and saw a row of cars waiting to make a left with us. I realized that the car I was in was leading the way to the unknown. No GPS, no maps in hand, and only memory to guide us through the streets. We remembered that there was a gas station with a big open parking lot on the corner of Rosemead and Beverly headed toward Montebello, so we led the way there and started a party in the parking lot.

L.A. curfew started at 10 P.M., and being sixteen years old, I wasn't supposed to be out on the streets after that time. But I'd been breaking that rule for years. On more than one occasion my sisters and I had been picked up by the cops for being out late, and each time, we were handed community service.

But community service wasn't that bad for us. We'd just head to Eddie Heredia Boxing Club, where we already hung out after school anyway. We loved it there. Chuck, one of the trainers, would sign our papers, no questions asked, as if we'd actually put in hours doing something like sweeping the place and maintaining it. Instead we were there flirting and training on the punching bags and boxing in the ring.

We weren't just hanging around to kill time—we boxed. We loved the sport, and everyone in that gym took it seriously. Of course, we also had our crushes there, and it was where we built friendships—Robert, Adan Reyes, and so many others who became more than just friends. Adan stood out: a rising pro-boxing kid training for the Olympics, already a Southern California Silver Gloves champion.

Being surrounded by kids our age with that kind of drive gave us a sense of purpose, too. It also made working out exciting and communal. It connected us with people who had our backs. The people at the gym

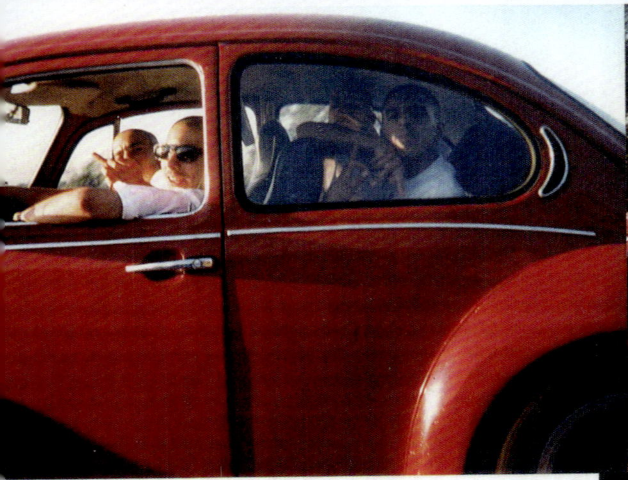
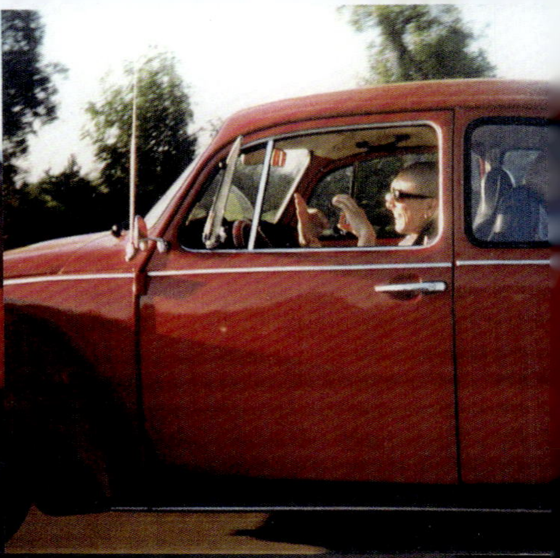
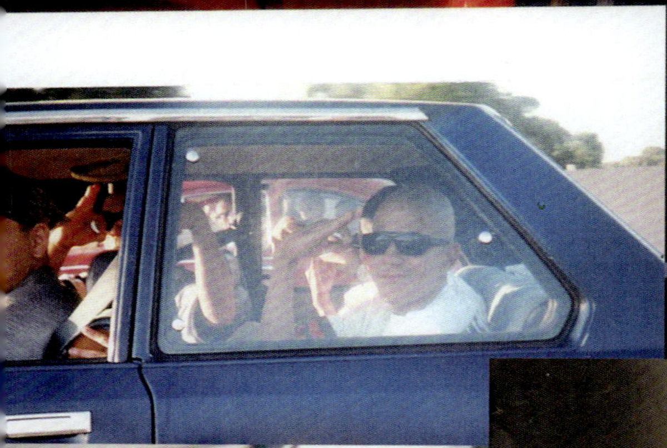
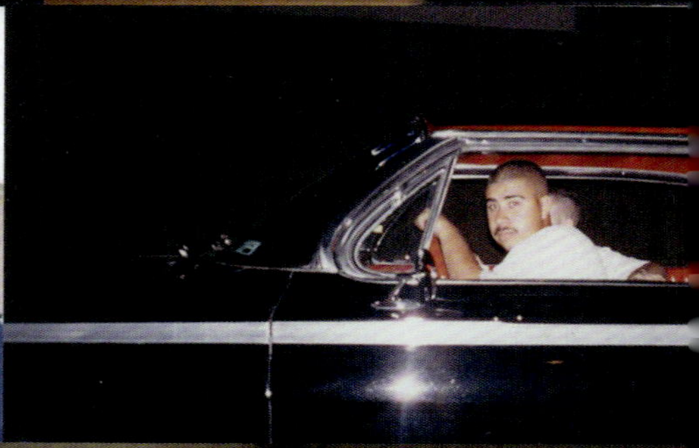
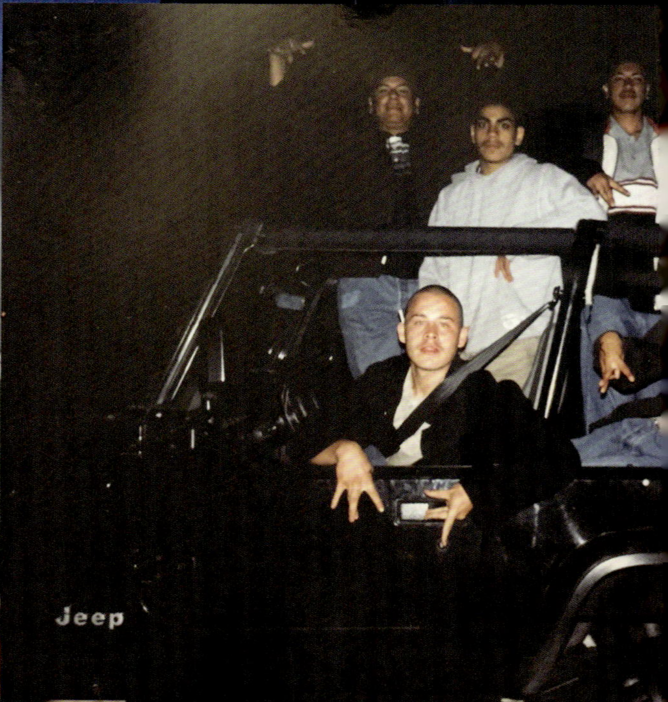
Jeep
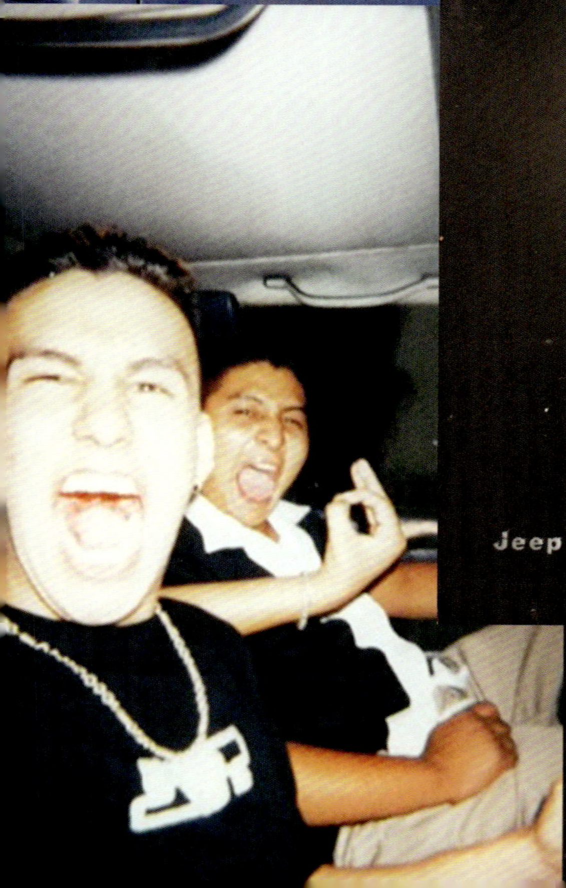
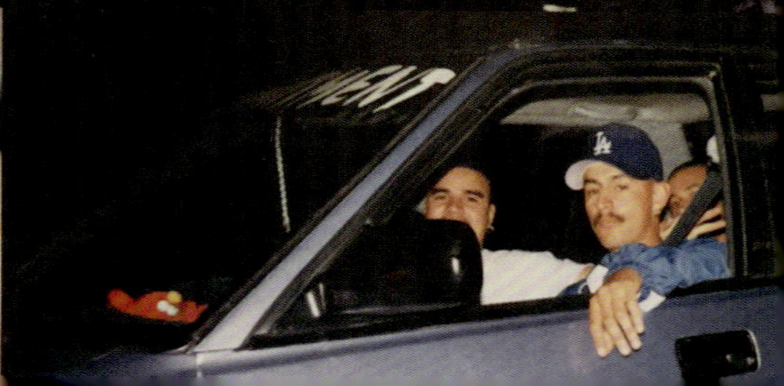

became like family, and when trouble with the law came around, they helped us cover our tracks.

But that didn't mean the police didn't make our lives difficult. They used the curfew law to their advantage, and often, their interactions with us crossed the line. Sometimes it wasn't just about authority; it was about intimidation and harassment. And if it wasn't the cops, it was the boys. On the streets, dodging bullets from police or gangs wasn't as much of a concern for us as the threats we faced from young men who couldn't take "No" for an answer.

If we weren't interested, the response was always the same—"She's just playing hard to get" or "She's stuck-up." As the quiet one in the group, I often became the target. More times than I can count, I was cornered into dark backyards, forced into situations I didn't want. There were times when I was kissed against my will, but luckily, that's all it ever turned into. Still, just because it didn't escalate doesn't mean it wasn't wrong. Consent was something those boys never seemed to understand. This is something I've learned as I've gotten older. There were so many times that I couldn't speak up and say "NO."

I kept this to myself most of the time because all the girls I knew experienced this, so we spoke with no words. Sometimes, though, we were casual about it and spoke about it as if it was gossip. We loved expressing our sexuality and our femininity with our clothes, but men would see this as an invitation or opportunity to grope or corner a girl who said "No" multiple times. We loved dressing up sexy, because it was a way to reclaim our bodies and freedom. We wanted to explore our sexual liberation, our beautiful brown bodies. We were always being told that before our time, women were decent. That if a woman dresses sexy, she is a hoodrat or a ho. Knowingly and unknowingly, we were now changing these narratives.

I was about sixteen when I got my first job, working at a McDonald's on Beverly Boulevard in Montebello, about a thirty-minute walk from home. Walking to work at night always had a sketchy vibe, like something was always lurking just beneath the surface. But I practiced what I had learned from other girls—walk with a bit of a tough edge. If I got lucky, a friend from work would pick me up, but many nights I had to walk alone in the dark. This was when I put into practice everything my sister had taught me.

OPPOSITE: Young boys cruising on Whittier Boulevard, circa mid- or late '90s

TEAM MEMBER PERFORMANCE UPDATE

Employee's Name Guadalpe, Rosales Review Date 1-17-00

Your contribution to Team Performance counts. . . At McDonald's, your performance is the key ingredient in our "pay for per mance" philosophy which will deliver *Total Customer Satisfaction.* Our Performance Management System provides us the opportunity identify your developmental needs. It also helps us discuss opportunities for continuous improvement, determine where you stand and m importantly, how you can achieve greater success in the future. This process enables us to clearly recognize individual and team contributi and see that employees receive fair compensation.

McDonald's is. . . First and foremost a company dedicated to *Total Customer Satisfaction!* No matter what position you work, y primary responsibility is to satisfy our customers. We would appreciate your comments on how we can improve our customer satisfacti Customer satisfaction is directly related to *Employee Satisfaction.* Your comments count! We encourage you to provide comments on how can improve both *Total Customer Satisfaction* as well as your job satisfaction.

PERFORMANCE BEHAVIOR	OUTSTANDING	EXCELLENT	GOOD	NEEDS IMPROVEME
TOTAL CUSTOMER SATISFACTION - ***anticipating customer needs; demonstrating sensitivity to the customer's perspective; giving high priority to customer satisfaction.***				
Delivers hot, fresh product.			✓	
Achieves 100% accuracy in customer orders.			✓	
Handles complaints quickly and effectively.			✓	
Personal interaction treats each customer like a valued guest.		✓		
Delivers quick service.			✓	
Delivers impressive service.			✓	
TEAMWORK - ***actively working with others to achieve goals; taking actions that demonstrate consideration for the feelings and needs of others; being aware of the effect of one's behavior on others.***				
Makes contributions and participates as a member of the team.		✓		
Supports co-workers in responding to and meeting customer needs.		✓		
Helps other team members with tasks as needed.		✓		
Follows Management directions and observes store policies.		✓		
WORK STANDARDS - ***setting high goals or standards of performance for self and others; accomplishing tasks through concern for all areas of the job, being dissatisfied with average performance.***				
Follows all restaurant procedures carefully and correctly (i.e. cash, grill, food safety/sanitation procedures).			✓	
Strives for continuous improvement on every station worked.		✓		
Consistently shows up on time.	✓			
Stays busy without direct supervision.			✓	
Wears a complete, neat and clean uniform.		✓		
Displays good personal hygiene.		✓		
JOB FIT - ***the extent to which the individual can adapt to the job's activities, hours and responsibilities.***				
Works well in a fast-paced environment.		✓		
Takes pride in accomplishing tasks under time pressure.		✓		
Willing to offer assistance to customers without being asked.		✓		

OVERALL PERFORMANCE ☐ **OUTSTANDING** ☐ **EXCELLENT** ☒ **GOOD** ☐ **NEEDS IMPROVEMENT**

DEVELOPMENTAL NEEDS	**By when?**	**Manager Responsib**
Stay bussy At All times / treat Each Customer With High Expectations / Be Quick in DT Au		

PROGRESS SINCE LAST REVIEW:

EMPLOYEE FEEDBACK:

PAY INCREASE .10

CURRENT RATE: 6.00 **NEW RATE:** 6.10 **NEXT PAY REVIEW:**

On Monday, ______________, your Manager will be available to go over your review with you. Please see him/her schedule a time.

EMPLOYEE SIGNATURE/DATE ______________ **MANAGER'S SIGNATURE** [illegible signature]

McDonald's wasn't just about the work; our friends would visit us, we'd hook them up with free food, and they'd just hang outside in the parking lot. As a twisted kind of revenge, sometimes we'd spit in the cops' orders when they came through.

It was also a way to get the clothes we actually wanted. Getting new stuff was rare. Our mom always bought us clothes as birthday or Christmas presents, but it was what she wanted us to wear, or things like socks and underwear. Once we had cash in our pockets, we bought whatever we felt like wearing—when we weren't relying on hand-me-downs from our older siblings. I preferred my brother Gus's old clothes—baggy 501 jeans and Cypress Hill T-shirts—over my sister's hoochie outfits, though I couldn't resist sneaking her Jordana makeup now and then.

I barely lasted two months at the McDonald's before getting fired for always being late. The hours were brutal. I'd sometimes walk to work at 4:30 A.M. on Sundays.

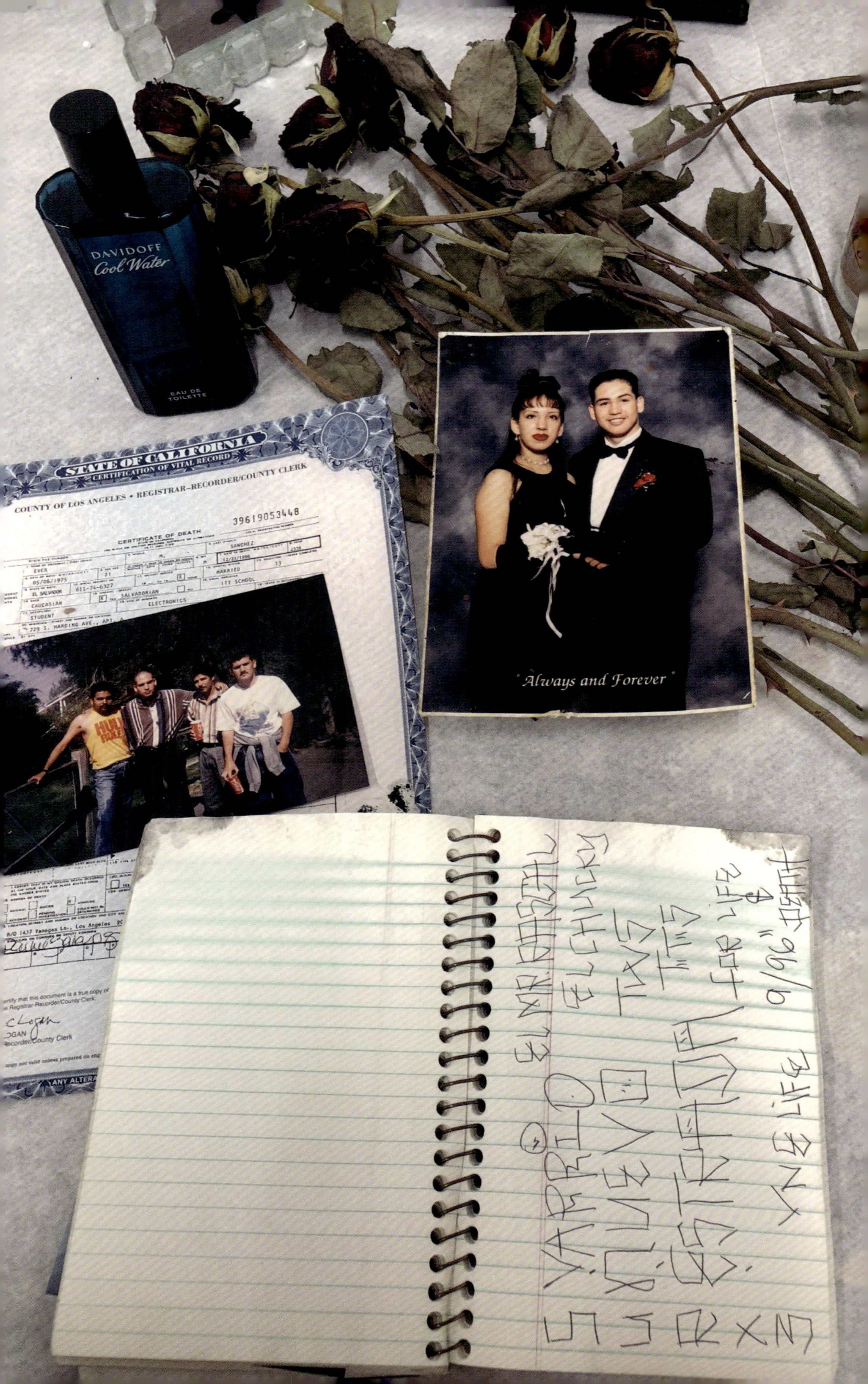
DAVIDOFF
Cool Water
EAU DE TOILETTE
STATE OF CALIFORNIA
CERTIFICATION OF VITAL RECORD
COUNTY OF LOS ANGELES • REGISTRAR–RECORDER/COUNTY CLERK
3961905344 8
CERTIFICATE OF DEATH
"Always and Forever"

FOR (EVER)

WHEN MY COUSIN EVER WAS LOOKING FOR A place to rent after he lost his apartment, my mother cleared out the living room for him and his younger brother Danny, who loved orange soda. My mom was the kind of person who always wanted to help; she had also welcomed my stepdad's son Junior to live with us when his mother died. When my mom took in Ever and Danny, Ever became Danny's legal guardian. They didn't have a relationship with their mother, and none of us really knew anything about her.

When Ever moved in with us he was around nineteen, four years older than me, and he quickly became a brother figure to me and like a son to my mother. Ever did not party as much as we did. When he was still at Montebello High, he never missed a day of school. He got straight A's and loved mathematics. After graduating, he went on to study electronics and physics at ITT Technical Institute while working at Burger King.

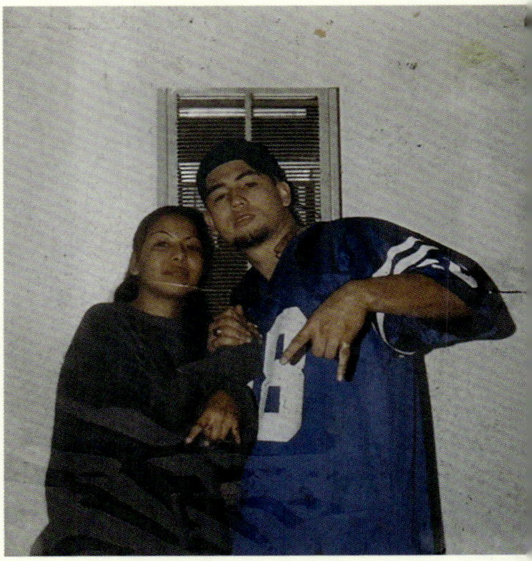

OPPOSITE: Photo altar for Ever

RIGHT: Maria and Ever at our house on Leonard Avenue in 1995

Living in East L.A. with us, Ever was exposed to party

crews and gang life for the first time. For that year, he became part of the pack. He was also friends with the Rangels and was from the same party crew as they were, East LA Madness, before he joined a gang. Ever also started dating my sister's best friend, Silvia, and they fell madly in love with each other.

My sister, Ever, Silvia, and I were always together. He drove a clean '92 Honda Accord—lowered, rosewood color, tinted windows, a sound system that made the whole block vibrate, and just enough shine to catch the sun, but not too flashy. His friend Art, better known as Night Owl, rolled in a similar ride—a '93 Honda Accord in metallic opal green. Even with the tint, he loved driving with all the windows down, music blasting, seat leaned all the way back. He loved that car, and like us, he loved long drives at night.

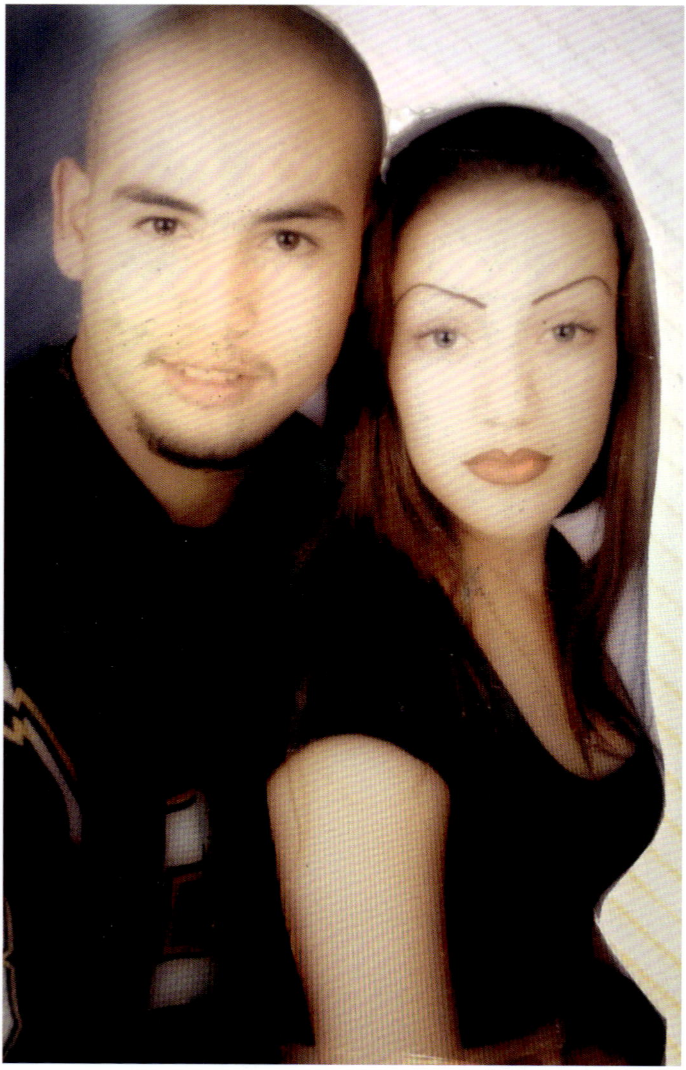

Art would pack the car with a bunch of pelones and cruise the boulevard, windows down, bumping all kinds of music, until the cops showed up. He would sometimes caravan with us, with a friend or two in his car. The tracks that were always in heavy rotation were "My Forbidden Lover"

Silvia and Ever at the Montebello Town Center in 1996

by Tapps, "Crazy Over You" by Desire and Rae Flores, and "Spin It" by Sunbelt. One night the cops pulled us over because the music was blasting too loud. Ever got nervous, and when the officer leaned in and asked if he knew why he was being pulled over, he blurted out, "I was just booming it." We all choked up laughing, even the cop, who let us go.

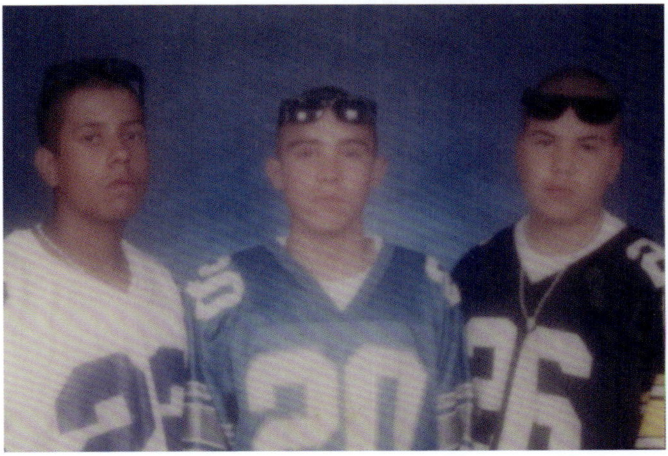

My cousin Danny on the right with school friends who attended Schurr High

Ever was our ride for everything—parties, school, anywhere we needed to be. At our place, friends would come through to hang out, and we'd lace up borrowed boxing gloves and play-fight in the front yard.

Sometimes Mom would ask him to pick us up from school. When he felt like messing with Maria and me, he'd roll up in Mom's beat-up station wagon. The paint was peeling, the seats were cracked, and the horn sounded like a dying donkey. He'd roll down all the windows, and drive it like he was driving his 1992 Honda Accord, blast the horn in front of the school, and wave like we were celebrities. We were mortified, but it was either get in so he could stop, or walk that mile and a half home in the heat. Maria and Ever and I also partied together, and when he was around we felt protected and safe. It was something we hadn't experienced before.

AFTER EVER AND Silvia broke up, he started going out more, hooking up with random women. We all knew that Ever was heartbroken—he was doing whatever it took to move on. Around that time, he got jumped into a gang. His brother Danny had already been jumped in a few months earlier, which made it easier for Ever to follow. Both of them joined Varrio Nuevo Estrada (VNE), one of the neighborhood gangs that was active in the '90s.

During the early 1990s, youths couldn't walk out on the street feeling safe, but that didn't keep us off the streets. If anyone was caught wearing the wrong football jersey—like the Dallas Cowboys or the Oakland/Los Angeles Raiders—they could get robbed, hit up, or jumped, even if they weren't in a gang. At that time, almost every boy and girl in our neighborhood was initiated into a gang by getting jumped. Some were born into it or were looking for protection and a family. Others didn't necessarily want to join a gang, but they didn't have a choice.

My cousin Danny, for example, kept getting attacked on his way back from buying his favorite soda at the corner store or just riding his bike around the neighborhood. It became one of the reasons he joined a gang. In his words, "I might as well get jumped for a reason every time I walk outside."

My brothers never joined because they were always running from the cholos who kept trying to recruit young boys from the neighborhood. My brother Junior constantly had to hide whenever his friends in gangs tried to jump him in—that's how he dodged it.

Although I never got jumped into a gang, I was always surrounded by them. I would be lying if I told you that roaming the streets and hanging with cholos wasn't fun and dangerous. But this was also normal for us and what we knew. We learned how to navigate this world.

On December 21, 1996, the winter solstice, just four days before Christmas, Ever, Maria, and a few friends went out to a "truce party" in East L.A. With gang violence at its peak in the 1990s, these organized parties were common—a way for gangs to take initiative to halt the violence among their own people.

Ever joined a gang relatively late, at nineteen years old. His brother had gotten in for protection; Ever joined to heal a broken heart, to party with his friends and meet girls, because gangsters did know how to party. Ever was older and tougher than Danny. If he had to throw down with someone he would do it, no questions asked. If he ever got jumped, he fought back 'til he couldn't. If someone needed defending, he stepped in. This is what happened the night he was killed.

Ever, a few of his friends, and my sister Maria had gone to a baby shower that night. At the party, Ever was the only one who wanted to head to a truce party afterward. No one else wanted to risk it—especially not in rival territory. One of the guys at the baby shower even called it "the belly of the beast." There was something about that night that felt risky from the start. Maria was too tired to keep going, but she'd go with him anyway. Ever was excited, single, and heartbroken, but he was determined to keep the night going. It was all mapped out for him: baby shower first, then a gangster party.

Earlier that day, he'd seen Danny. Ever was upset with him: Danny kept messing up in school, and since Ever was his guardian, the school would call him about Danny's attendance and grades. Ever cared about school; he believed in it. He had grounded Danny: Danny couldn't go out with him again until he got his grades up. Danny had been getting ready to climb into Ever's car when Ever stopped him. Pissed off, Danny turned around and went back inside. As he walked away, Ever called out, "I love you."

Those ended up being the last words he ever said to his brother.

I hadn't gone out with Ever and Maria that night. Earlier that day, we had argued, Ever and me. Living together often led to such clashes, like with siblings.

That night, I went to a holiday-themed party with Aztek Nation at Kennedy Hall. I wasn't feeling it, so I left early. I got home and lay in bed for a few hours, just staring at the ceiling. I was annoyed at the party but also bored in bed. It was quiet and cold and my sisters were still out partying somewhere in L.A.

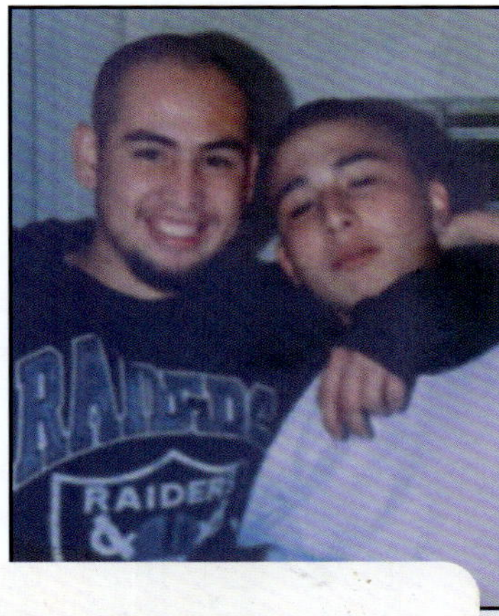

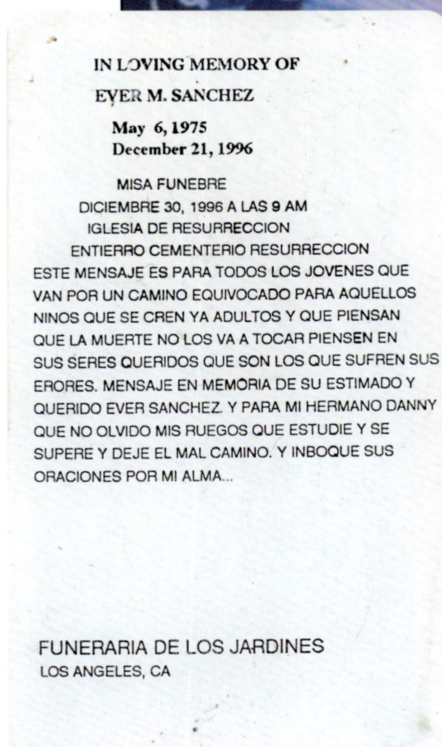

IN LOVING MEMORY OF

EVER M. SANCHEZ

May 6, 1975
December 21, 1996

MISA FUNEBRE
DICIEMBRE 30, 1996 A LAS 9 AM
IGLESIA DE RESURRECCION
ENTIERRO CEMENTERIO RESURRECCION

ESTE MENSAJE ES PARA TODOS LOS JOVENES QUE VAN POR UN CAMINO EQUIVOCADO PARA AQUELLOS NINOS QUE SE CREN YA ADULTOS Y QUE PIENSAN QUE LA MUERTE NO LOS VA A TOCAR PIENSEN EN SUS SERES QUERIDOS QUE SON LOS QUE SUFREN SUS ERORES. MENSAJE EN MEMORIA DE SU ESTIMADO Y QUERIDO EVER SANCHEZ. Y PARA MI HERMANO DANNY QUE NO OLVIDO MIS RUEGOS QUE ESTUDIE Y SE SUPERE Y DEJE EL MAL CAMINO. Y INBOQUE SUS ORACIONES POR MI ALMA...

FUNERARIA DE LOS JARDINES
LOS ANGELES, CA

TOP: Ever on the left with my brother Gus

BOTTOM: Ever's funeral card

What stood out to me was the weather that night and the days after. I will never forget that cold morning, when my sister Maria called me drunk out of her mind, slurring words I could not comprehend, but her drunken slur wasn't the problem. "What did you say?" I asked as if I had misunderstood her because I was half asleep when I picked up the phone. "Ever died last night," she responded, and I could smell the tequila and pain in her words.

I waited for weeks that turned into months for someone to tell me it was all a lie or a joke, or one of Ever's silly pranks, because in everyone's eyes he seemed immortal. I did not get out of bed for days except to smoke almost a pack of cigarettes a day on an empty stomach. I wasn't a smoker, but around this time, I was full of pain, anxiety, and sadness, and cigarettes calmed me for a few minutes.

At Ever's viewing I was afraid to look at his body in the casket and I did not want to touch him for the last time. Instead, I looked closely at his hands, his fingernails, and his skin. I noticed a couple of punctures on his hands, leaned closer, and noticed a bruise on his right cheekbone that the funeral home had covered with makeup. His girlfriend walked over to the casket and kissed him on the lips and placed a wallet-size photo on his chest with a rosario wrapped around it. A photo they had taken together that same year.

A few moments later, gunshots rang out from a car outside. The shooter was firing through the open doorway of the funeral home, the sharp sound of the shots piercing the calm. Women and children screamed in fear, panic spreading through the air. I felt as though I had just awakened from a nightmare, only to find myself trapped in another one. People hit the floor, and then the shooting stopped. The car sped off, tires screeching.

For a moment, no one moved. We just sat or lay there, frozen. And then, the crying started. I could recognize the voices—neighborhood friends', my mom's and siblings'—each one layered with worry and pain. Their wailing filled the space, echoing off the walls like a second kind of gunfire.

The next morning, I somehow made it to school. I was still in so much pain—emotionally—but I went anyway. I carried this rawness in my chest, and perhaps I was able to go to school because I felt numb.

Word about the shooting had already spread. Friends who had been at the wake were talking about it, piecing together what happened. One of them had been shot in the leg, but he was going to be okay. It all felt surreal, like we had lived through something impossible, and now we were back in classrooms like nothing had happened. I still don't know how I got myself to school that day.

The tears we shed when a loved one dies are very particular. They are intimate, and the pain is a kind that feels like no one can understand.

I read the *Los Angeles Times* article the day after Ever's murder. It was a short article describing his death as gang-related. There was no humanization, nothing tender or sweet said about him in the article. He was an immigrant who loved mathematics and philosophy, and in all four years of high school he'd never missed a day. A prankster, a lover, a father, and a brother. Unfortunately, his appearance also fit the 1990s gang member stereotype/aesthetic: shaved head, baggy clothes. This is how the system would like us to remember those we love.

I have read so many articles that are two sentences long with "gang-related shooting/murder" in them. Sometimes this type of violence is so common that it goes unnoticed, but for me and my family, losing Ever was devastating. When someone we love dies so tragically, those who grieve become numb from the pain. That pain makes us want to retaliate and grow thick skin. Some are even willing to kill in retaliation.

When my cousin died, family and friends gathered in my home every day. We sat together quietly in the living room or on my porch at night under the moon until the sun came out. We reminisced and shared stories about my cousin.

It took me years to forgive those who took his life, but eventually I was able to turn the pain and grief into altars and memorials and storytelling. When we lose someone close to us, traditionally we come together to grieve. We turn pain into something beautiful. I will elaborate about grief in these communities and collective healing.

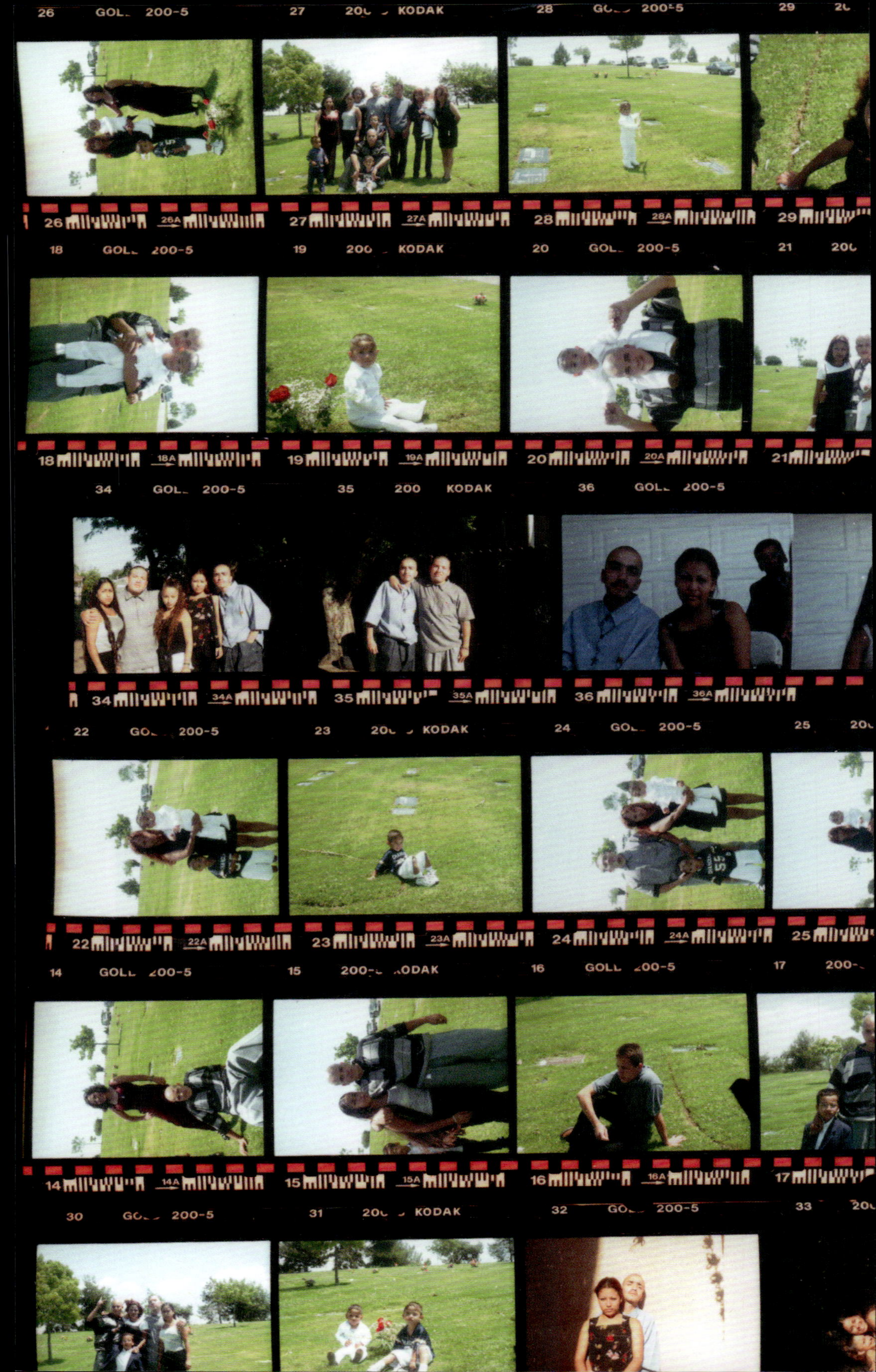
35 200 KODAK

OPPOSITE: Visiting Resurrection Cemetery, where Ever was laid to rest. This was in 1997, months after he'd been killed. We all went to visit him after his kids were baptized. We decided to go for a little hang at the cemetery.

1 Killed, 4 Wounded as Gang Truce Party Erupts in Violence

A truce party between two rival gangs erupted into violence late Saturday night at the Ramona Gardens housing project in East Los Angeles, leaving one man fatally stabbed and four others wounded.

A get-together among about 150 gang members in the recreational room of the housing project came to an abrupt end when someone started flashing gang signs, sparking a knife fight that killed Ever Sanchez, 20, said Los Angeles police spokesman Eduardo Funes.

Sanchez died at the scene. Two others were critically injured and taken to County-USC Medical Center.

ABOVE: *Los Angeles Times* article

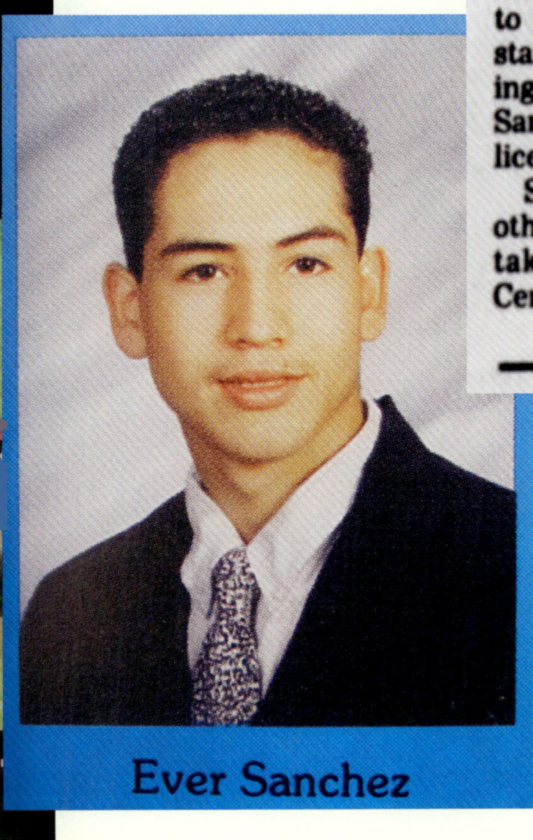

LEFT: Ever's senior-year photo, Montebello High, class of 1994

AFTER EVER

WHEN MY COUSIN PASSED AWAY, WE ALL MOVED AGAIN TO a smaller place, back to a one-bedroom apartment on the same property. One of the hardest things we had to do was clean up his room—the living room he used as his space. I could still smell the Aspen cologne lingering in the air from the night before, the night he got ready for the party. We were all quiet, not saying a word, just putting his things into boxes.

As we got older, the dynamics in the house began to shift. The once-lively home grew quieter, emptier. When we needed a private place to hang out, we turned the garage into our own little space. We ran electricity to the garage with a long extension cord, through the window and under the garage door. But our mom always found ways to keep control over us. When she wanted to punish us, she'd take things away—shutting off the power to the garage or disconnecting the cordless phone and locking it in her closet. She did this many times. It was her way of holding control, but it only made us more desperate for freedom, pushing us further into the streets.

I was still going to school, but barely. My mind was too distracted, too foggy from drinking and dabbling with drugs to help me cope with the pain. But even during this time, there was one class that kept me engaged—it was photography. Even though I got a C, I enjoyed it a lot—the first time I felt like something lit up inside me at school. It was the same feeling I'd had in middle school when I took choir with my friends. Those moments were rare, but they mattered. They reminded me that school didn't always have to feel like survival. I loved taking photos of my family and friends, my sisters and their friends. There was also a class assignment to do a studio shoot, and I invited Maria and her friend Paula to be photographed.

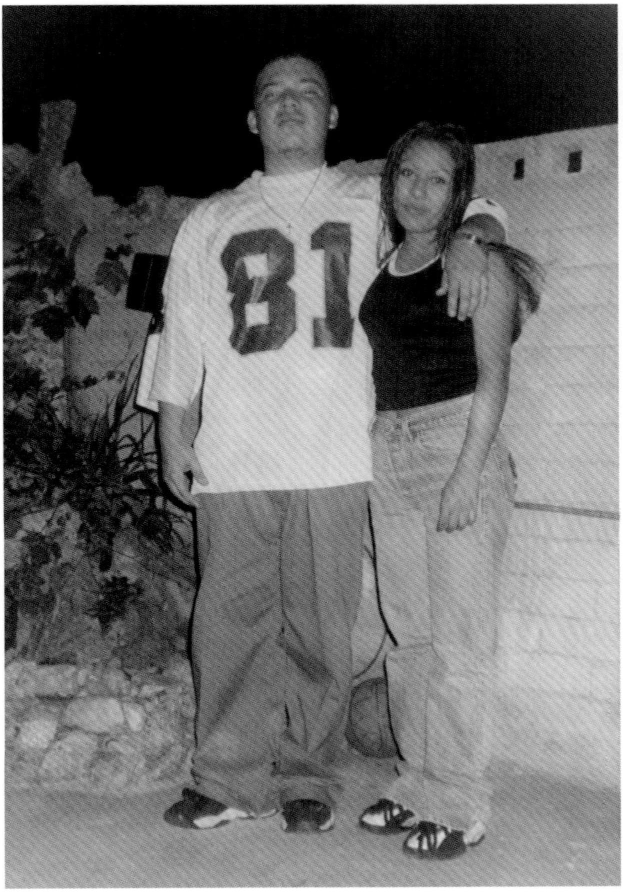

But that class wasn't enough to keep me focused on school, especially after my photo class teacher almost failed me because my photos were underexposed or overexposed or had bad composition. I spent four years in high school, but I didn't have enough credits to graduate and I just stopped going to most classes. By 1997 I was slipping away from school and home. I started to carry the camera I got from school everywhere I went: I took photos of my friends at parties, of my sisters, and of my mom. I was doing this for me, not to get a good grade. This also meant that I was spending more time on the streets with friends and rarely coming home.

Emilio and Maria at a kickback, circa 1997, taken with my photo class camera

Mom still wanted to have some control, after years of us disobeying. She continued to lock us out if we left without her permission. But by this time, it didn't matter because most of us didn't even come home anymore. My sister Maria and I were spending more time in the streets with friends or boyfriends. Every time she got kicked out of the house, I left with her—we already knew what to do. Nothing mattered more to me then than being by her side.

The last time Mom kicked Maria out, it was final—and I left with her. This time, our cousin Cee, Ever's sister, took us in. After Ever passed away, she came around—we hadn't really known her before that. But we quickly grew close. She introduced us to a different scene, one we hadn't seen before—exciting and unfamiliar. When Mom kicked us out, Cee welcomed us into her home.

She lived in La Puente, across from Avocado Heights Park, and was deep in the Riot Grrrl and San Gabriel Valley punk scene. She listened to bands like Bikini Kill, L7, and Minor Threat. Her taste in music shifted mine—more political, more punk, more ska, more underground hip-hop. I traded in our party-crew days for backyard punk shows. I started buying punk CDs from Warehouse Records and ordering others through the

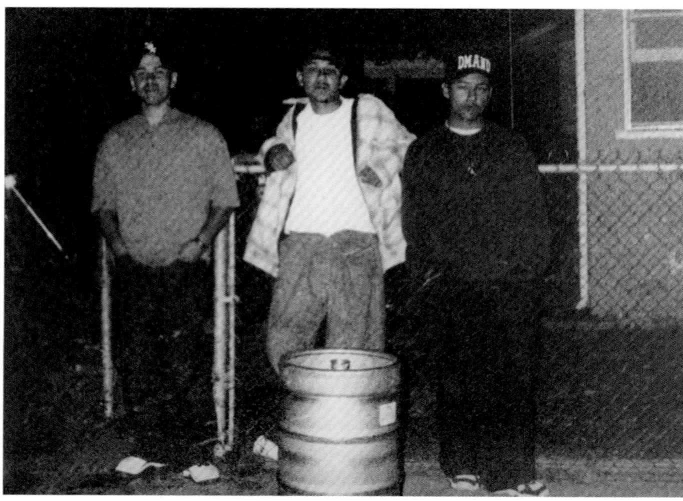

Art, Burt, and D-mad standing outside my house after one of our house parties

mail—Kill Rock Stars catalogs you'd find tucked inside records or zines. Maria, Cee, and I started going to punk shows in South L.A. and hip-hop nights at spots like Club Elements, Dub Night at the Echo, and Luna Sol Café.

This was around '98, '99. For a brief time, I got involved with the Mexica Movement and followed bands like Aztlan Underground and Quinto Sol, Chencha Berrinches and hip-hop groups like Freestyle Fellowship, Aceyalone. I even got to meet Jaguares after a concert in 1999. I moved on to another scene and genre. I bought my first Nine Inch Nails CD, along with Siouxsie and the Banshees, Depeche Mode, and KMFDM at the Wherehouse Music store.

CEE AND I, along with four friends we knew from the scene, started a punk band. We called ourselves Todos Vuelven—Everyone Returns.

Cee's boyfriend, Louie, who was in a band called 7 Gatos Negros, taught me the basics of playing guitar. We all went to Guitar Center and bought instruments. I bought a guitar, an amp, cables, and guitar strings.

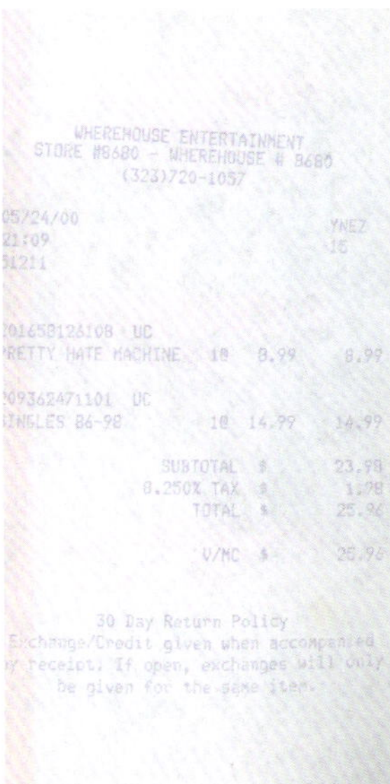

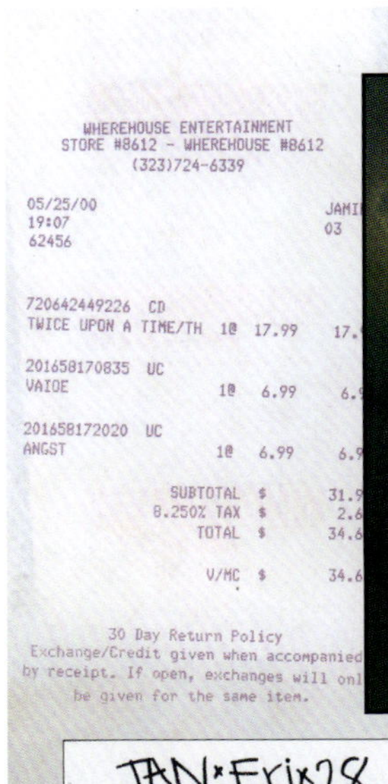

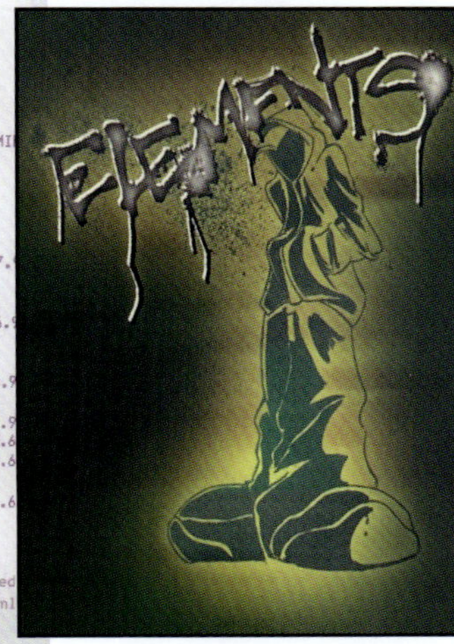

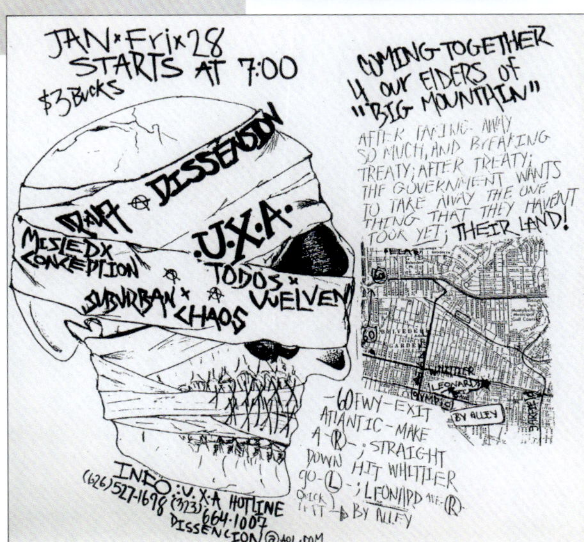

RIGHT: Receipts, flyer from club Elements, and a flyer I drew for a punk show that my band, Todos Vuelven, organized

I was an anxious, nervous kid but determined to learn how to play guitar. We didn't last long, maybe a year, but we played many shows in L.A. We played in MacArthur Park, ELAC, Cal State.

Around 1998, I began to experience Los Angeles in a different way. The city wasn't just noise and concrete anymore—I was drawn to the land itself. I became more in tune with nature and the beach, with rhythm and ritual. I was introduced to traditional practices and ceremonies that rooted me spiritually but also opened me up politically. I was seeing

$ 25.0
SECTION/AISLE
GA
ROW SEAT
GA5
HOB105
A 2NOV
STANDING ONLY +FCSUR1
HOUSE OF BLUES-LA PRESE
() CAFE TACUBA ()
GEN ADM STANDING ONLY
HOUSE OF BLUES L.A.
8430 SUNSET BLVD/ALL AGE
MON NOV 8 1999 7:30PM

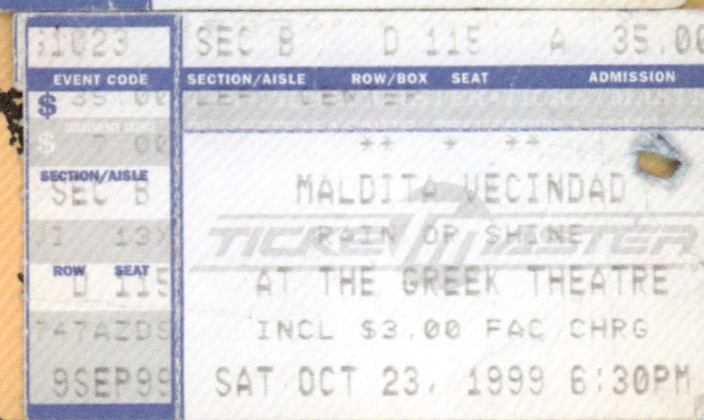
SEC B D 115 A 35.00
EVENT CODE
SECTION/AISLE
ROW/BOX
SEAT
ADMISSION
SECTION/AISLE
SEC B
ROW SEAT
D 115
9SEP99
MALDITA VECINDAD
RAIN OR SHINE
AT THE GREEK THEATRE
INCL $3.00 FAC CHRG
SAT OCT 23, 1999 6:30PM

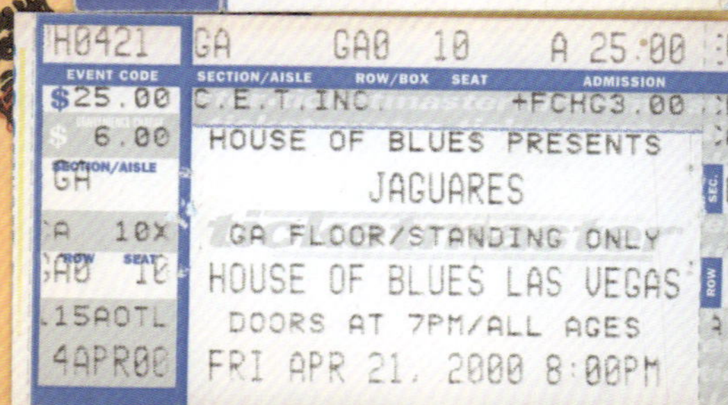
H0421 GA GA0 10 A 25.00
EVENT CODE
SECTION/AISLE
ROW/BOX
SEAT
ADMISSION
$25.00
$ 6.00
SECTION/AISLE
GA
ROW SEAT
GA0 10
4APR00
C.E.T. INC +FCHG3.00
HOUSE OF BLUES PRESENTS
JAGUARES
GA FLOOR/STANDING ONLY
HOUSE OF BLUES LAS VEGAS
DOORS AT 7PM/ALL AGES
FRI APR 21, 2000 8:00PM

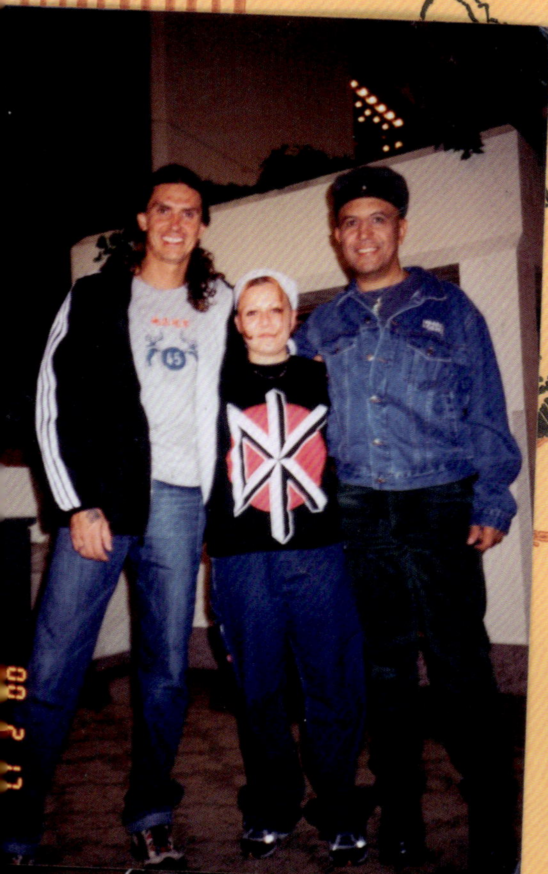

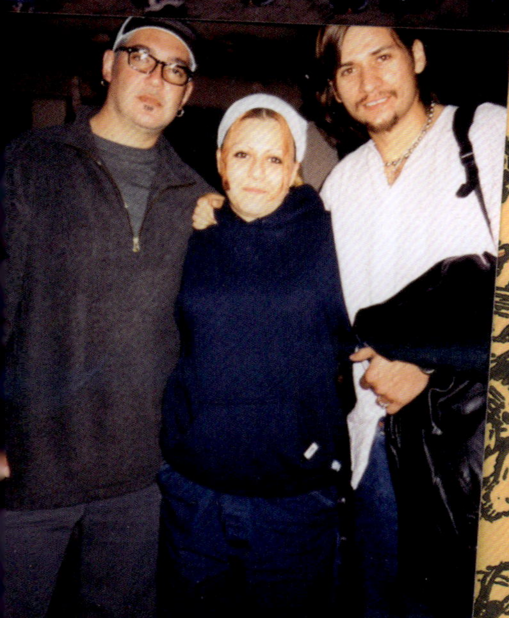

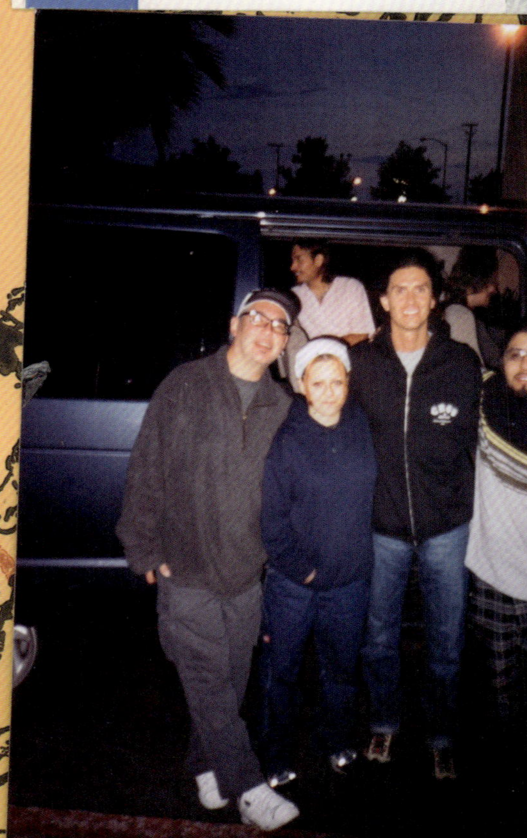

connections between ancestral knowledge and collective resistance. I was also more in tune with myself and understanding my own sexuality. It all collided in that moment: punk rage, brown pride, political fire.

Punk wasn't my first language of rebellion—I had already lived it through run-ins with the police, school walkouts, and protesting alongside my family and friends. But it was a bridge to deeper resistance and queerness—it cracked open a space where that part of me could surface, raw and unapologetic. I grew up in a very heteronormative and traditional environment—and the party-crew scene reflected that. I didn't know any openly gay people.

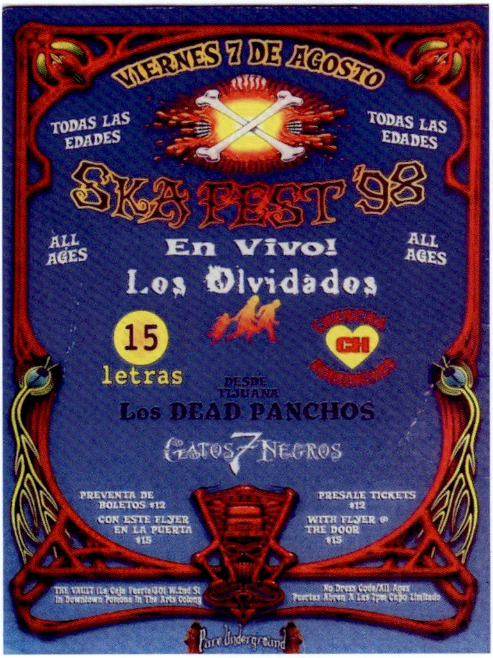

ABOVE: Flyer of Ska Fest '98

It was the era of Rage Against the Machine playing outside the Democratic National Convention, of protests that shut down streets and made the city feel electric and on edge. Cee and I went, but we missed the Rage Against the Machine show. She and I got caught in the chaos when the police started trampling people and shooting rubber bullets at us, but we weren't afraid. It enraged us more. Just like many people in the 1960s, particularly students, we were creating groups and collectives like Mecha and Chicano Studies, and finding other ways to educate one another about politics and chicanismo in institutions. In the 1990s, during the debate around Proposition 187, many students began to organize against racism once again. In the late 1990s/early 2000s, there was a new wave of activism through music and rage.

But despite this new political and spiritual awareness, I was still lost—struggling through the hardest time of my life. The more I immersed myself in movements and music, the more overwhelmed and confused I

OPPOSITE: After a concert, my friend Joel and I followed the Jaguares tour bus because Joel was a big fan. We followed them to their hotel and got to meet them and take pictures with them.

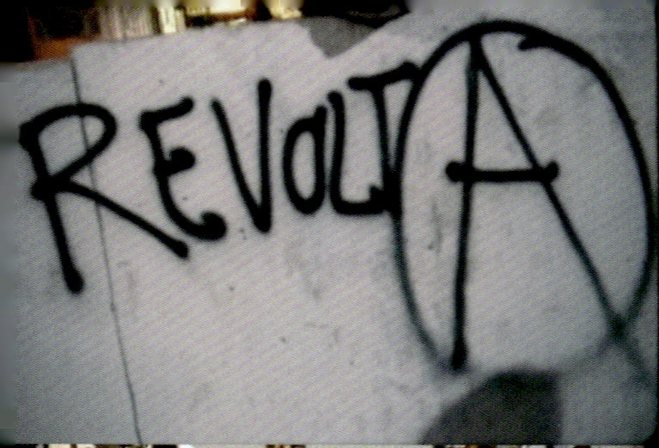
REVOLTA

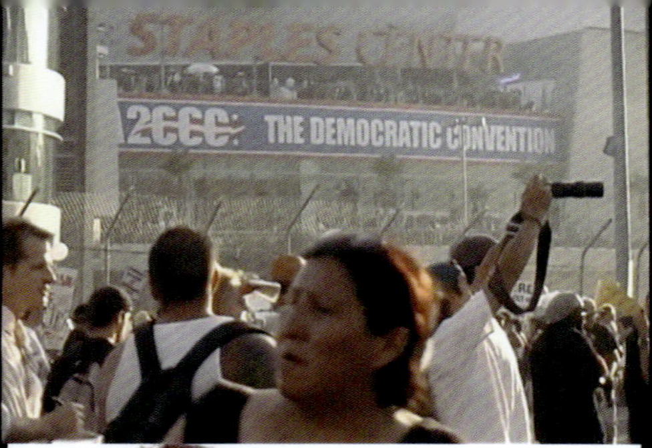
STAPLES CENTER
2000: THE DEMOCRATIC CONVENTION

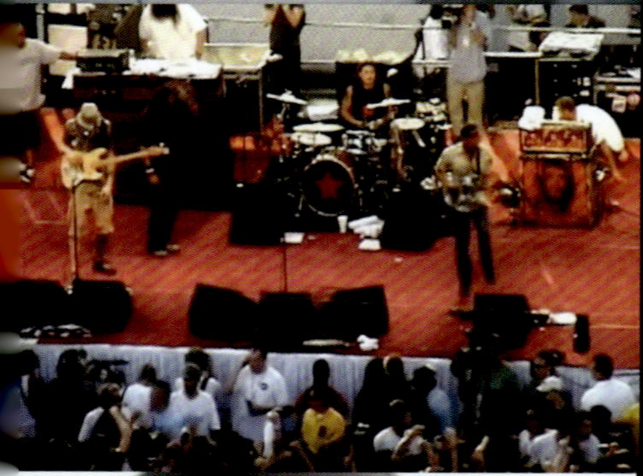

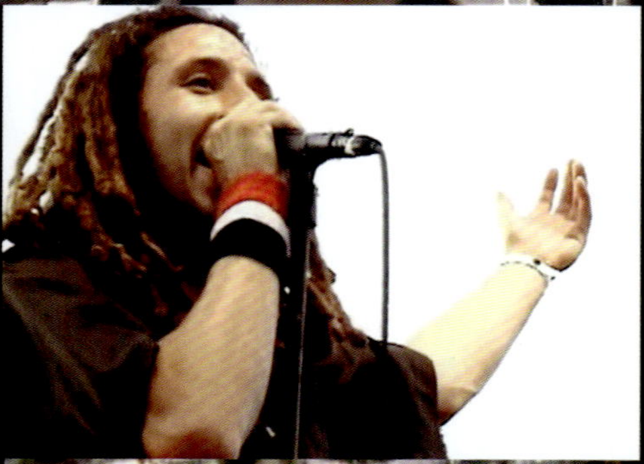

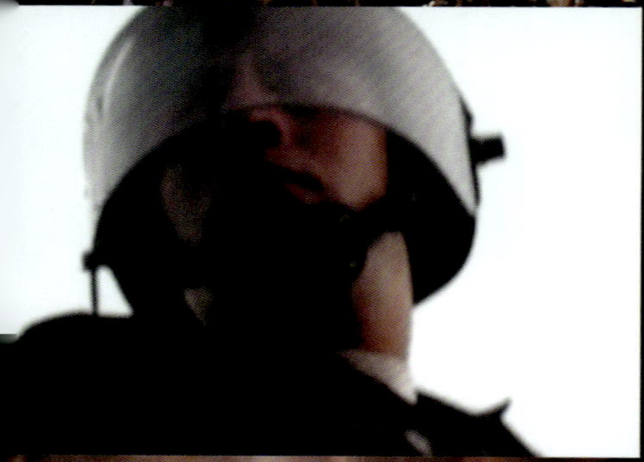

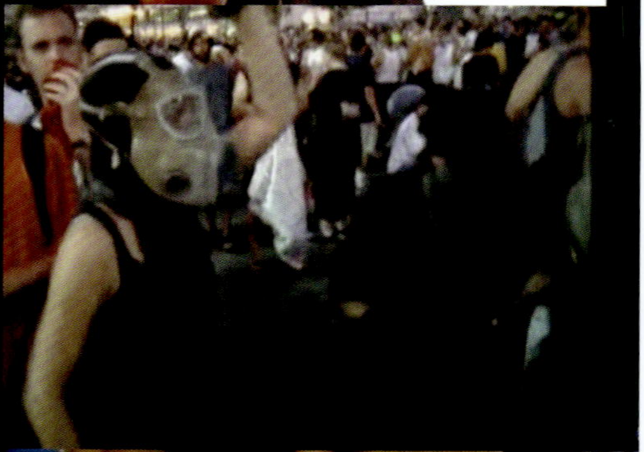

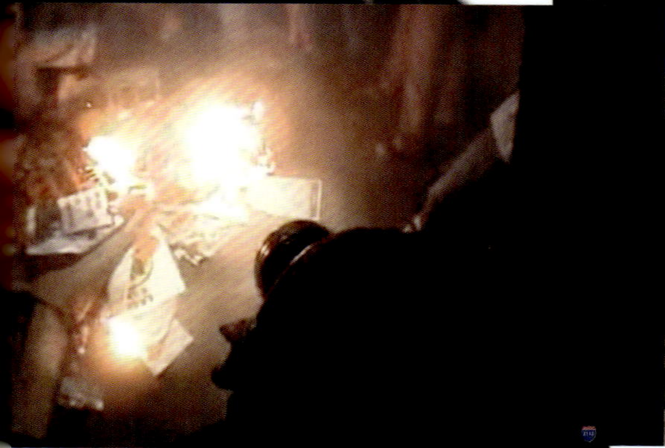

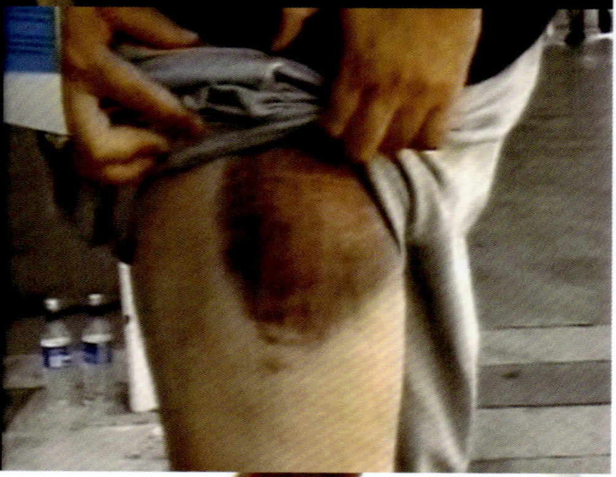

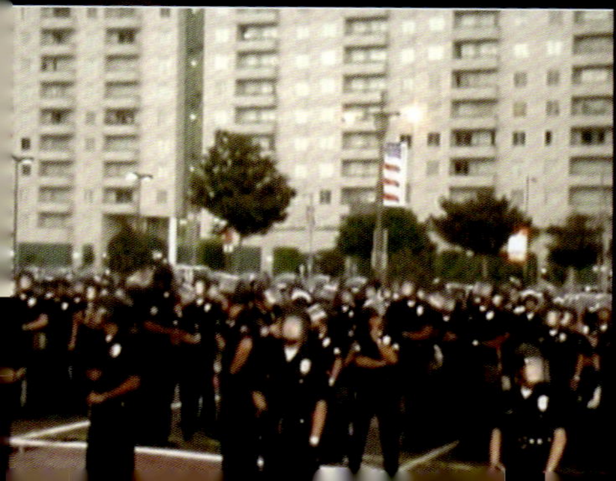

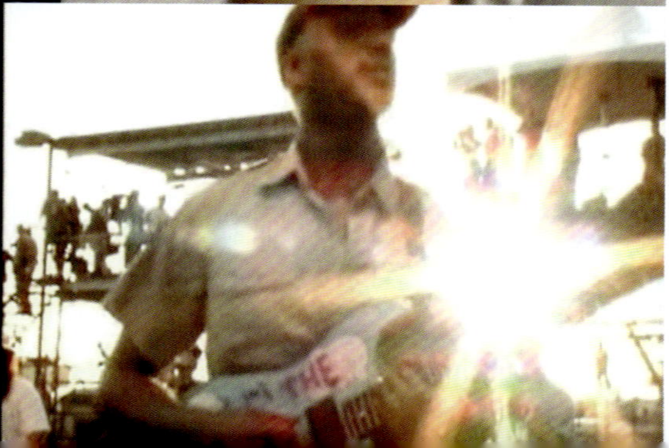

became. I started turning to drugs, self-medicating just to escape the weight of those feelings, though I never really knew where to turn. I felt like I was being pulled from every direction—I wanted to be focused on the band and in rehearsals, but depression and drugs made that hard for me.

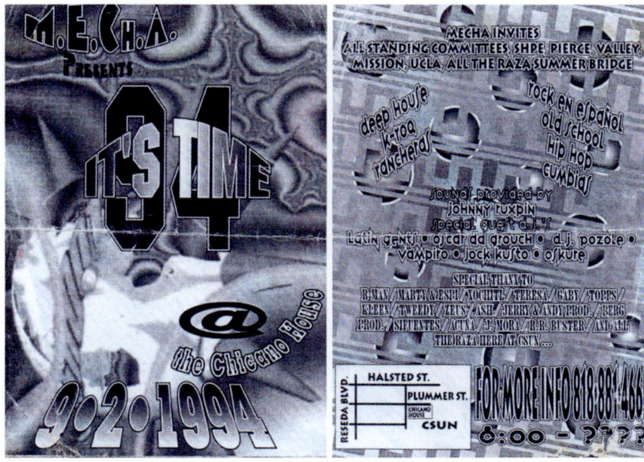

Mecha party flyer

Maria was right there beside me again, but we were both still trying to piece ourselves back together after Ever's death. With Cee and the new scene, we threw ourselves into small projects—at one point even selling random things at Venice Beach. Around that time, Maria had also started dating Phillip, who she would later go on to build a beautiful family with.

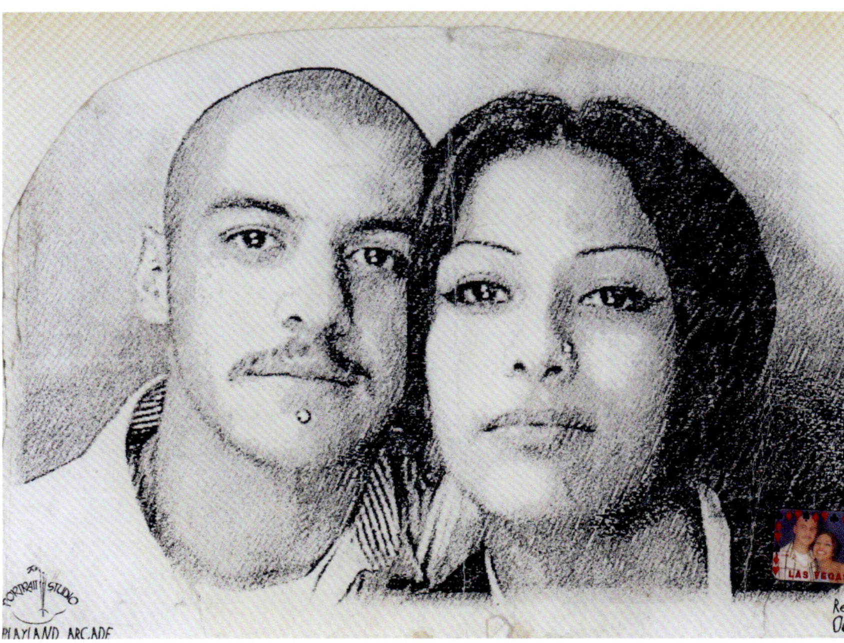

Photo of Phillip and Maria taken at the arcades

OPPOSITE: Protest and Rage Against the Machine playing outside of the DNC

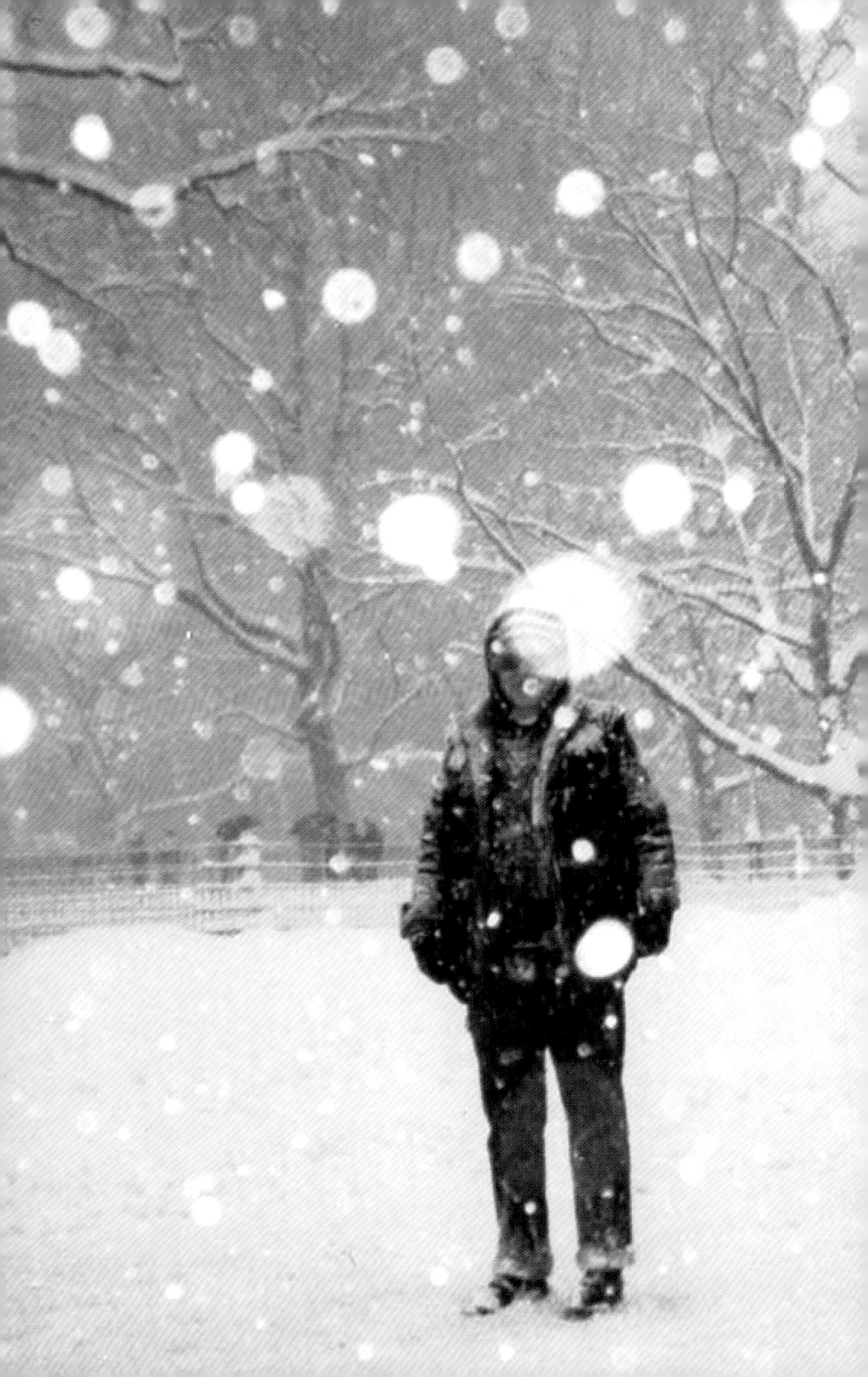

SECTION II

Away

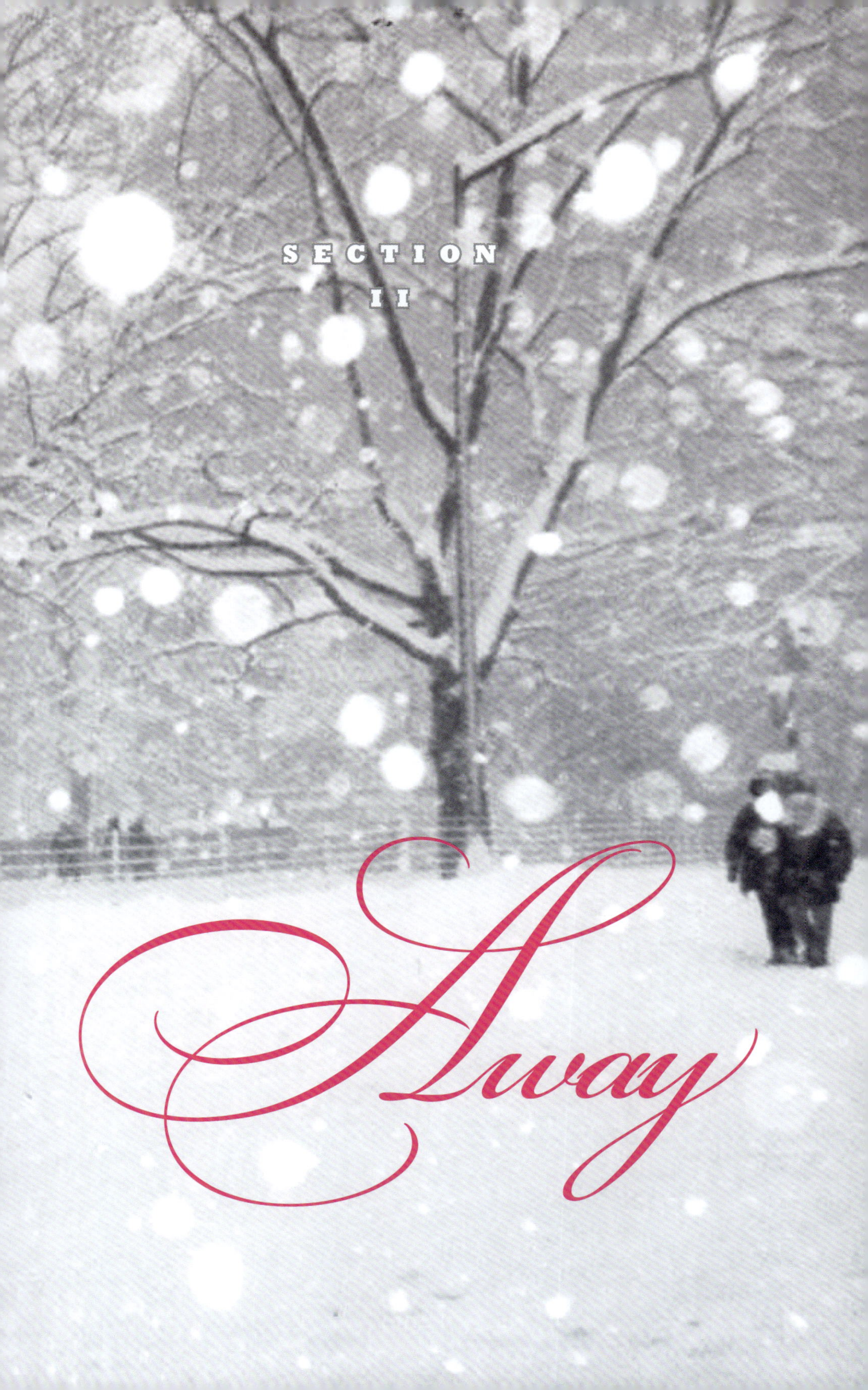

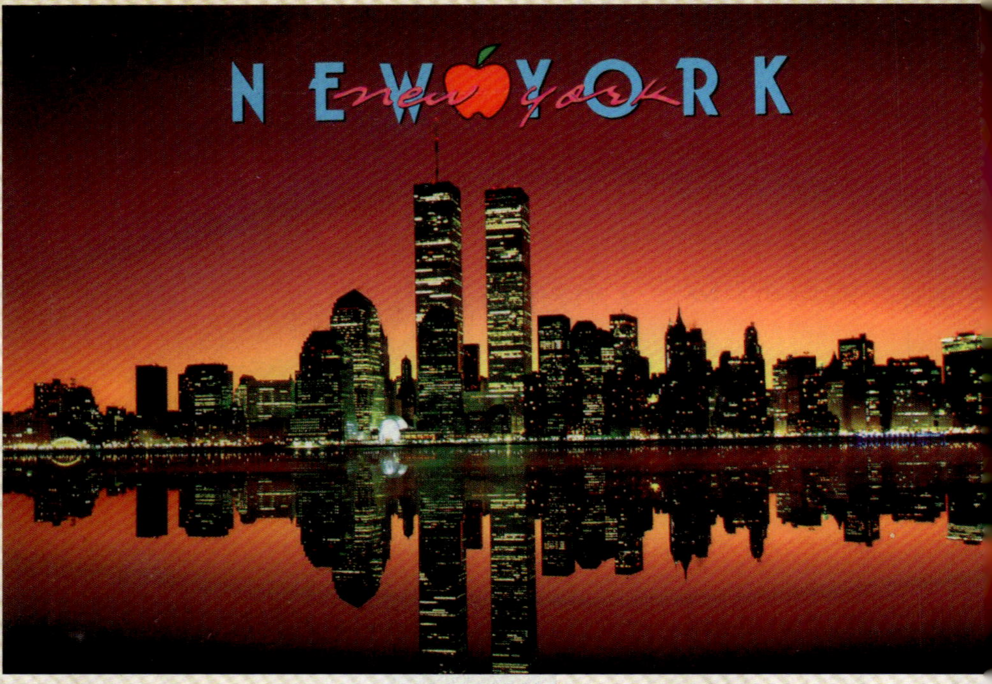

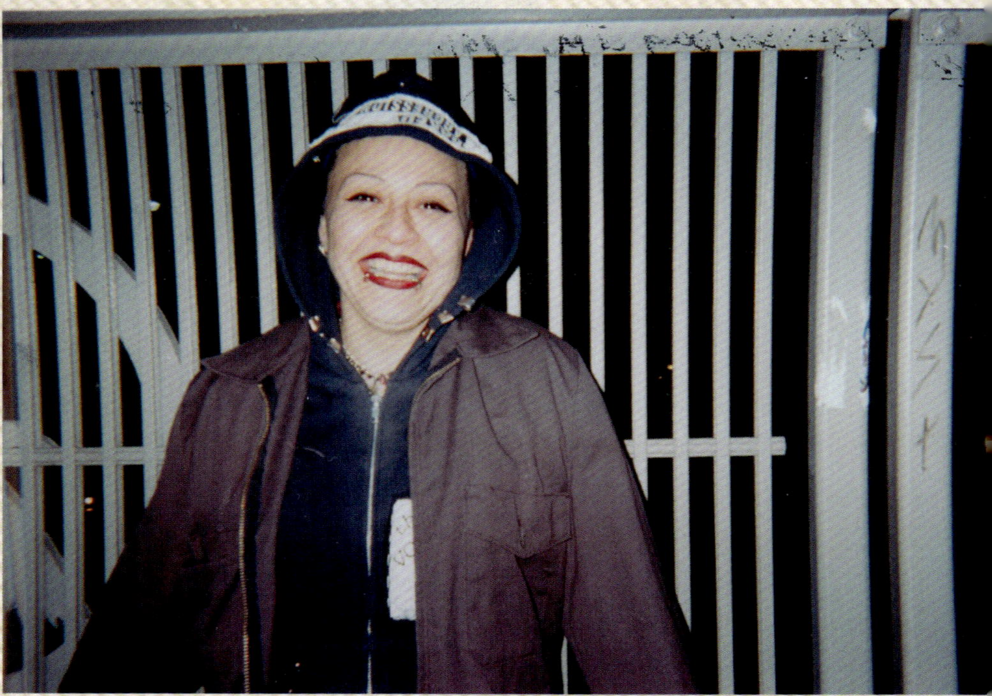

ABOVE: First winter in New York, 2000

NUEVA YORK

I BOUGHT A ONE-WAY RED-EYE TICKET TO NEW York because that's all I could afford. Instead of packing luggage, I layered on two pairs of baggy pants, some shirts, a hooded pullover, a leather jacket, and a punk belt lined with metal studs and rings—just a chaotic pile of fabric, thrown together in a blur of impulse and indecision. I didn't have a suitcase; I had never traveled before. Instead, I crammed a couple pairs of shoes into a cardboard box. But the most important things I packed weren't clothes—they were a handful of Starshot photos, a copy of *Street Beat Magazine,* and my guitar.

My mother drove me to LAX, just us two in the car, at 11 P.M., the air thick with unspoken words. Mom seemed hurt, shocked, confused, upset—a version of her I'd never seen before toward me. She sat there, hands on the steering wheel, face shadowed by the dim streetlights. She said, "No sabes lo que estás haciendo, Lupe," and maybe I didn't know what I was doing. TSA was a disaster, the metal detector going off from all the studs I had on, but I managed to get on the plane.

In my mind, there was no sense of time—how long I'd stay in New York, or how I'd get back to L.A. if I ever came back. When I left Los Angeles, everything felt dark. The party-crew scene had shifted to harder drugs, and my sometimes doing drugs with friends then escalated to my doing drugs behind people's backs. People around me were deep into meth and speed, and I got caught up in it, too. Those drugs made you feel unstoppable, wired, awake for days and not eating, like you were in control of everything.

But underneath that rush was chaos and confusion. Maybe that's why I was so lost—doing things on a whim, chasing something I couldn't name. Even though I was in a band and felt connected to nature and activism during the late '90s and early 2000s, I was also depressed and searching for a sense of belonging, some kind of healing. It was a constant struggle.

I fell asleep on the plane and woke up in New York City, groggy and sore from the kind of sleep that leaves your body aching. The scent of the city hit me as soon as I walked out of the airport—humid, metallic, with a sharp undertone of gasoline. A black car-service car was waiting for me, sent by Marialex, a woman I had met online in a chatroom only a few months prior. We met through a shared love of industrial, goth, and punk music. I didn't know her well, nor was I attracted to her—but I knew her just enough to trust her to host me in her Hell's Kitchen pre-war apartment for a few days.

Marialex was ten years older than I was and working for MTV/Viacom, a world far removed from mine, and she was able to help me out by getting me a car to her apartment through her work. She knew I had never traveled this far to a big city I wasn't familiar with. She was my only contact in New York, and I had no clue what I was doing. There was a methadone clinic down the street from her apartment, and for a moment I wondered why all these people on the block looked like zombies and made New York look dull.

Then there was the other side of New York—the bright, colorful, and exciting side. I remember taking the subway to Times Square with Marialex at night for the first time, stepping out of the station and being hit with a flood of neon signs and giant LED monitors, lights bouncing across my face. It felt surreal, like I had stepped into another universe. Marialex gave me access to MTV in IRL and with cable, where I could finally watch *TRL,* where the newest videos premiered live from Times Square, not far from where I was living. Sometimes I walked over to meet Marialex at the Viacom building where she worked, and I'd catch a glimpse of the crowd gathered and screaming outside during the filming of *TRL*. I remember watching Avril Lavigne's "Complicated," Britney Spears in her glittering pop era, and nu-metal bands like Linkin Park and Limp Bizkit coming up as a new genre. I even got a free VIP staff pass to the 2001 VMA awards, where I saw Sum 41 pull up to the red carpet in a glittery green Ford Pinto.

But despite those glamorous moments, moving to New York didn't make things easier. I was still grieving my cousin's violent death, distracted by drugs, and drifting through that confusion. I got caught up with the wrong scene. I was so young and naïve, hanging with people who had been using drugs longer than me. It was depressing and made me question what I was doing—probably the only time I questioned my impulsive decision to come to New York, and yet going back to L.A. wasn't my first choice. Mostly because I couldn't afford a ticket back.

I gave myself a week there, telling myself it was just a trip to clear my head. I found myself critiquing the city, unable to understand how people could live in such a dirty place with its crumbling buildings, peeling paint, the grime that clung to everything, and clumps of dog and cat hair and dust tucked in the corners of the walk-up apartment buildings. It was chaotic, noisy, and disorienting.

I didn't grow up rich, but my mother was obsessed with cleanliness—always making sure we scrubbed every corner, wiped down every surface. If we didn't clean up after ourselves, there were consequences like disconnecting our telephone, or throwing a chancla at us from across the room. So this unrelenting dirt, disorder, and noise felt like a shock to my system.

But two weeks passed. I stopped counting the days and started appreciating the beauty of the city, its imperfections and noise that cradled me to sleep. I found myself caught in the rush of the streets, the constant movement that defined New York. The city's energy was inescapable, alive in a way that was almost suffocating and yet exhilarating. There was a constant rhythm that seemed to dictate everything. I also realized that the grime was part of NYC character.

Somehow, I began to feel it—this pulse, this frantic energy that didn't let up. The city became something that wasn't easy to dismiss. I appreciated the chaos because it shaped my new lifestyle. A month went by, and still I didn't know what to do—leave or stay? But somehow, I was beginning to feel rooted. I realized that L.A. and New York aren't perfect but that each has its own unique beauty.

NONSTOP

IN 2001, I GOT MY FIRST JOB AT CANAL JEAN CO. ON BROAD-way in SoHo, next to Yellow Rat Bastard. It was a three-story building that carried streetwear, work clothes, camping equipment, army-surplus clothing, jeans, UFO pants, sneakers, jackets, and New York souvenirs. The vibe inside mirrored the life of the streets of New York. The entrance welcomed you with speakers blaring loud music as two security guys stood in the front entrance like you were walking into a club.

I spent about six months there doing retail and making friends. We grieved Aaliyah's death together in the staff room. I was off work the day 9/11 happened. If I had gone in, I would've been just blocks from the towers. Somewhere in the chaos, I managed to call my mom's house, back home—the first time I'd been in touch since leaving. I needed them to know I was okay. I was on the phone with my family in L.A. when the second plane struck. The fear wasn't just in New York—it rippled through the country and all the way back home; I could hear the worry in Mom's voice.

That day, I gave my sister Maria my Hell's Kitchen address—something I'd never thought to do before because part of me hadn't been ready for full contact. But I did this time, in case something happened and they needed to reach me. Even with the tragedy unfolding around me, life kept moving—because that's just how New York is, and I was already used to this. Tragedy happens and you just keep moving on, even in tough moments.

Situations like that would repeat themselves throughout my life in New York. There was always distance between my family and me. I'd go for long stretches with little or no contact, sneaking in quick calls here

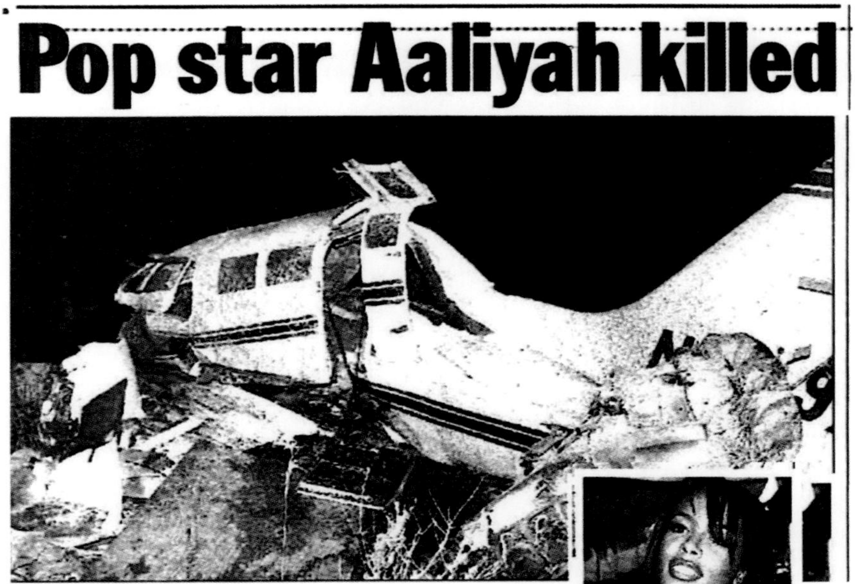

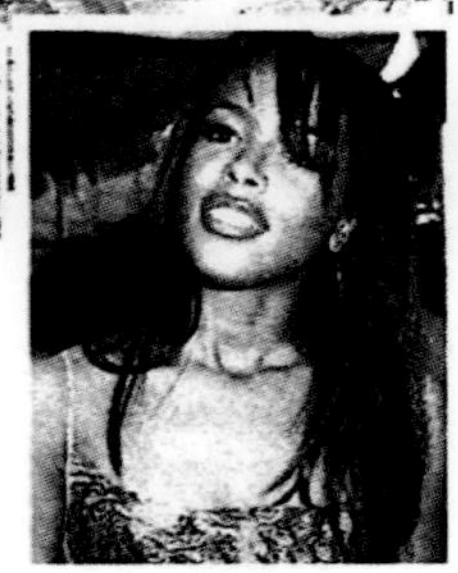

and there, as if staying too close would make things harder—for me, and for them. In some sense I needed to get to know myself through new experiences while taking a break from the past, the people, and the landscape. Knowing how confused and depressed I was when I left Los Angeles, I felt that I needed time on my own to get myself together.

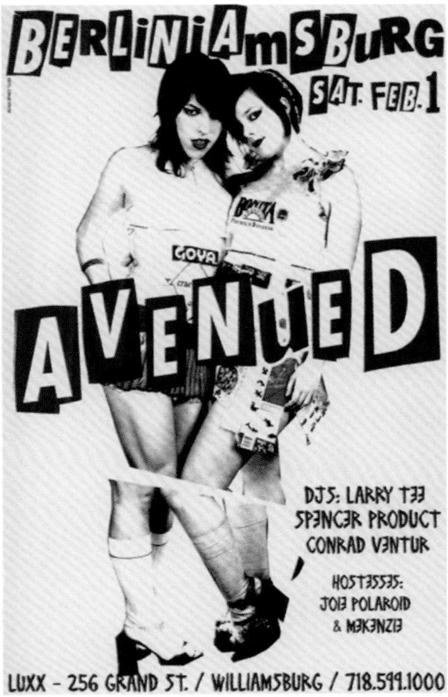

Even when my sister Maria called me to tell me Dad wasn't doing well, I hesitated to go back. She said he was sick and who knows how long he would be alive. I asked her to keep me updated on his health and I stayed put in New York. Some months passed and I continued to work at Canal Jean until I got caught stealing in 2002 along with a group of peers; I quickly got another job at Tower Records.

For the next two years, I lived and

LEFT: Flyer for LUXX w/Avenue D, early 2000s

breathed music in that store, moving up to the art department, where I created backdrop displays for the store and artist "meet and greets"—bizarre, beautiful backdrops for Moby, Madonna, and Le Tigre, and Peter Murphy of Bauhaus. It was there where I met artists, musicians, and unique people who felt like family.

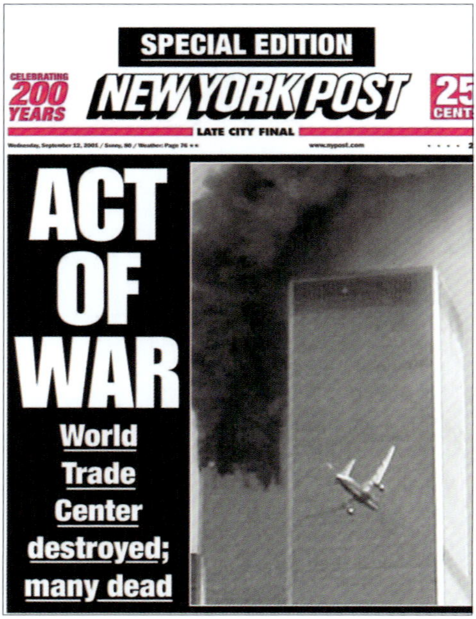
SPECIAL EDITION

CELEBRATING 200 YEARS

NEW YORK POST

25 CENTS

LATE CITY FINAL

www.nypost.com

ACT OF WAR

World Trade Center destroyed; many dead

I had a chance to hang with Peter Murphy, score free passes to shows by bands like Siouxsie and the Banshees, Fischerspooner, Madonna, and many others. The nightlife was my other life. The tail end of the '90s club-kid era, full of strange energy that blurred the line between euphoria and danger. I was just twenty-one, twenty-two, full of energy. I could party somewhere in the Meatpacking District 'til 8 A.M. the next day and go straight to work from the party. It was clubs like LUXX in Williamsburg and Opaline, Mars Bar, The Cock, and The Hole in the East Village where the weirdos and queers hung out. DJs played Peaches, Avenue D, Le Tigre, The Rapture, and The Faint at every club and bar.

Most people around me were strung out on booze, heroin, and cocaine, but in that mix, I found artists, queers, and freaks—who for that moment were my nightlife family. In those dark rooms or descending rickety stairs to a grimy bathroom stall to do drugs, I found a version of myself I didn't know I was searching for. I was out as queer, I was with other queers, and being a young adult in my early twenties gave me a new type of independence. I was allowed to be complicated and messy—raw, unfiltered, and untamed—but this time with a new kind of consciousness. I was more aware of my decisions, no longer stumbling blindly like I had in my teenage years.

BELONGING

GROWING UP, I NEVER HAD ANYONE IN THE CREATIVE FIELD who I could look up to, so being an artist wasn't on my radar. But the neighborhood I grew up in had art everywhere: on the walls, in my mother's cooking, in how we decorated our home—and in the cinematic night sky. The housing projects in Boyle Heights are covered in historic murals that date back to the 1960s. That was art for me. None of this mattered until I was in New York.

Before moving there, I had never visited a gallery or museum. It wasn't until my early twenties that I had my first experience—when I accidentally stumbled upon LTTR, a queer feminist collective focused on creating flexible, self-defined spaces where community and dialogue could happen on their own terms. LTTR was a shifting acronym; it started in 2001 as "Lesbians to the Rescue" and has since stood for everything from "Lacan Teaches to Repeat" to "Let's Take the Role."

One winter night in 2002, after it had snowed all week, I was walking around Williamsburg after a late dinner with a friend when I came across a crowd pouring out of a gallery. Curious, I went to see what was going on. I entered the space, and it was all queer. Then this guy stood on a chair and said, "I don't know why I was invited to be here—maybe because I'm feminist and a fag!" When he said that, I looked over and locked eyes with the person standing next to me. We both smiled. I was twenty-two, and at that moment, I felt like I belonged, because I felt safe, and maybe it was the first time I was in a space where I didn't feel the energy of aggressive men that I had experienced most of my life at that point. The show was put on by LTTR, a collective that would become critical to my development as an artist. I later learned who they were, and I would eventually become friends with them. The guy standing on the chair was artist and filmmaker Matt Wolf. The person I had locked eyes with was artist Ulrike Müller.

New York gave me a new type of freedom. I didn't worry about the police harassing me like they did in L.A., but I did worry about getting mugged. Thankfully I never got mugged, but many of my friends did. New York was raw and unpredictable, which could be magic.

I was home, because everyone seemed to know one another, was friendly, and reminded me of the people I'd met in that last year or so living in L.A.—the ones my cousin Ceci had introduced me to. The Riot Grrrls and punks. They were loud, emotional, political, and messy all at once. There was something about the way they held space for one another that reminded me of backyard parties and punk shows in L.A.—but in a gallery space.

At the time, although I was identifying as queer, I didn't feel well-versed or confident in it. I was just learning how to express that part of myself. Maybe this was a turning point for me: Whatever I had felt before about my sexuality was now reflected back through others. I was still scared to say it out loud, even to people I trusted. I was also too scared to be affectionate or hold hands with a girl in public. I didn't know how to date women—or really how to date at all, as an adult. With my family back home, I kept that secret except with my sister Maria. But even with her, I still felt like I wasn't good at expressing myself; I would mention that I was dating a woman, but I kept it brief. It was like I didn't have the correct language to talk about it with my family, especially with Mom and in Spanish.

When I left L.A., I left with punk and feminism in mind. In New York, I was finally able to fully embrace that part of me and hang out with the people I had looked up to. It was my first real step toward queerness and coming out. From there on, I followed everything this scene was doing.

I started shifting my social scene and traded nightclubs for something more intellectual but that kept that same social energy and partying with people like A.L. Steiner, Matt Wolf, Leidy Churchman, and K8 Hardy. Around this time, I met my first serious girlfriend. She had just graduated from SUNY Purchase and had taken creative writing. She was different: She'd never done drugs, so it felt necessary for me to stop, too. When I think back on this, it feels like angels were watching over me, keeping me from falling through the cracks of the city and subconsciously pulling me away from the chaotic New York nightlife I'd landed in when

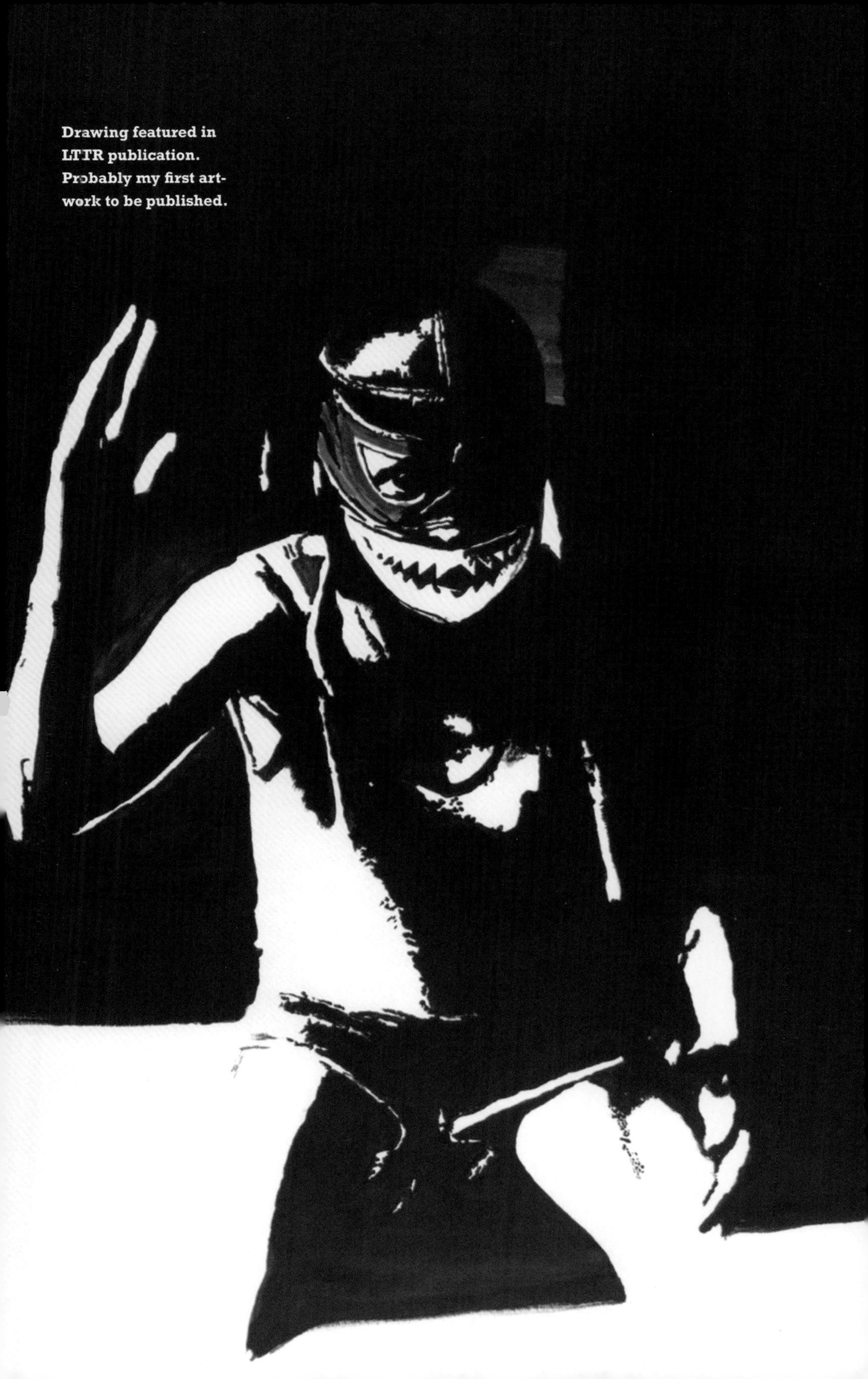

Drawing featured in LTTR publication. Probably my first artwork to be published.

I first moved there—the drugs, the club kids—and guiding me toward a more focused and creative environment.

With the new friends I was making in New York, many nights I'd walk over the Williamsburg Bridge or Manhattan Bridge to Brooklyn after a long night out. The new people I met taught me so much of what I know now—like what books to read, how to look at art, and how to be comfortable with my queerness. In New York, sometimes you came across magical nights unexpectedly. It wasn't always at a club that you met the most interesting people; it was at galleries, someone's house party, or an art opening.

With this new creative scene, I wanted to be a part of everything they were doing. I was drawn in because they were putting on powerful, radical shows about queers and trans folks that challenged fixed ideas about art and art spaces. LTTR was founded by Ginger Brooks Takahashi, Every Ocean Hughes (fka Emily Roysdon), K8 Hardy, and Ulrike Müller; they changed my life.

Rather than pushing a fixed political agenda, LTTR emphasized asking questions like "What can we do for each other now?" They were about building power through mutual support, embracing contradictions, and learning how to exist together—imperfectly but intentionally—in ways that reflected feminist ethics and care. Once I became friends with the collective, I was invited to participate in their show. A few years later, I even had one of my early drawings featured in their fifth and final zine, *Positively Nasty,* in 2007.

At first, it felt like I had finally found a place where I belonged—a community that shared my politics, my love for DIY art, and a hunger to create outside the mainstream. We partied together almost every weekend, got drunk, and had barbecues in other queer folks' backyards and rooftops in Brooklyn—Williamsburg, Bed-Stuy, and Greenpoint. Afterward, we rode our bikes home together through the streets, still buzzing from the night. We were all looking for a chosen family, and for a while, it felt like I had found mine.

But over time, I started to notice the differences, too. One of the biggest was educational privilege. They had all gone to art school, and even though many of my friends from that time were awkward and weird in ways I thought were cool, they carried themselves with a kind of confidence I didn't have. They were mostly white queers. They were the cool art-school kids, and all they talked about was art, what they were reading, and what they were making in their studios. They had developed a language around their work, and I was just getting started.

Me? I was a high school dropout from East L.A.—poor, brown, and still trying to figure out where I fit. My insecurities began to creep in. What had started as a feeling of belonging—of finding community and chosen family among people I looked up to—slowly shifted into something more complicated: a quiet sense of shame. Like I didn't really belong. Like I was different in ways I couldn't ignore. It felt like I was so different from them. I did everything I could to avoid having these two worlds come together.

I felt like that fly on the wall, observing. I was often the quiet one at parties while my friends got drunk and danced together, singing along to songs by Ani DiFranco or Tracy Chapman—lyrics and artists I wasn't familiar with. I felt the difference. I grew up listening to Juan Gabriel, Alejandra Guzmán, and Ana Gabriel—not Ani DiFranco.

I wanted to talk to someone who was like me or shared similar interests and experiences—a friend, a family member who spoke with slang words I knew and used. In L.A., people knew or assumed I was Mexican/Mexican American. But in New York I often felt unseen except in rare moments. In 2003, I went to a concert that took me back to Los Angeles. I remember how happy I was when I found out that some of my favorite bands—bands I grew up with and had seen back home—were playing in New York. Seeing Nortec Collective, Los Rabanes, El Gran Silencio, Molotov, and Maldita Vecindad play the Hammerstein Ballroom in Manhattan felt like finding a small piece of home.

Being there, surrounded by so many brown people of all ages, filled me with pride. In the mosh pit, people raised Mexican flags high, moving with the music, unapologetic and loud.

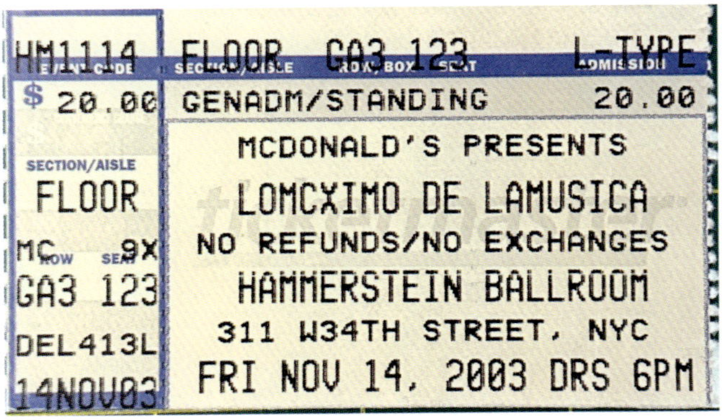

Ticket stub for the concert of Lo Maximo de La Musica

RIDE THE WAVE

THEN TRAGEDY HIT AGAIN. I GOT A FRANTIC CALL FROM MY sister Maria to tell me that our father was very sick from liver failure caused by alcoholism. She had saved my number, and I hadn't spoken to her since 9/11, almost two years—until this call. I realized then that for those first years in New York, it was tragedy that had bound us together. First, it was 9/11 in 2001, then when she called me to tell me our father was not going to make it and it was urgent that I come home to see him one last time. Somehow, that was enough to keep our relationship going from a distance. She became the only person I spoke to on and off while I was living in New York. During this time, when I felt disconnected from the people I considered family, Maria showed up in the most urgent times.

I never expected that this would be what took me back to L.A., even for just a short visit. I landed only minutes after he passed away. It felt like he had waited for me—held on—just long enough to let go. Even though I missed him by moments, I still felt like I had been there. I stayed in L.A. for a couple of weeks. That time now feels like a blur. Part of me had already made peace with my father. After that violent fight my parents had when I was a child that ripped us apart as a family (Mom going to jail and us kids to foster homes), knowing that his alcoholism ran so deep that he couldn't keep a job, it felt like death was the only place he might finally find rest. I knew that for a long time he tried to get sober; he went to AA and to rehab for alcohol, but that wasn't enough to save him. After my mother was released from jail and we were all back home, except Dad, the court granted us visitation with him. It wasn't often, but sometimes he'd take us to Chronis on Whittier Boulevard for lunch, or to Chuck E. Cheese in Bell, or we'd meet him at Hollenbeck Park.

Dad didn't have much money, but at Chuck E. Cheese he knew the people who worked there, and they'd hook us up with games and food. I saw how he tried to be a dad the best he could. Those small gestures went a long way. We knew that he was trying, even if he struggled. I always think about these moments with him.

He never drank in front of us, but we knew by the smell of alcohol. And if he was wearing sunglasses, we knew that he was either drunk or hungover. This was the only time he wore sunglasses.

My father passed away in February of 2003. Soon after, I was back in New York; I had no intentions of staying in L.A. When I returned to Brooklyn, I didn't know what direction to take—should I keep hustling and moving forward, or slow down and allow myself to grieve? For a while I tried to do both, but eventually my energy shifted toward hustling, keeping my mind busy. I was also excited about my new relationship with my first girlfriend, and part of me couldn't wait to be back in New York to see her. New York was becoming my home.

Then, in the summer of 2003, a massive blackout hit—one of those endless widespread outages that dragged on for around thirty hours. It was blazing hot. With no A/C, no lights, and no traffic signals, everything felt surreal but weirdly exciting. So instead of worrying, many of us spilled out of our apartments and onto the street and rooftops. We drank forty-ounce beers and watched the skyline disappear into the night. Like after 9/11, the city came together as if it was a big family looking out for one another. The bodegas gave away melting ice cream before it could go bad. It felt like a party in the midst of the city's chaos.

Those moments made me feel more connected to the city, like a true New Yorker. The blackout and 9/11 showed me that New York could be brutal, chaotic, and communal all at once, and I had already lived and experienced that so early in my time there. That's when I started to piece things together in my own way. I pulled from what I'd learned while working in Tower Records' art department, and I signed up for a figurative painting class. I wanted to create my world through art—not just because I was starting to question my place in New York's queer community, but because I wasn't even sure I could call myself an artist without a formal background or solid experience. I didn't last long in the painting class. Most of the people there were much older than me—or they treated it like a casual hobby. Even if I was inexperienced, I was serious about art. I had never taken a painting class before, and some of the

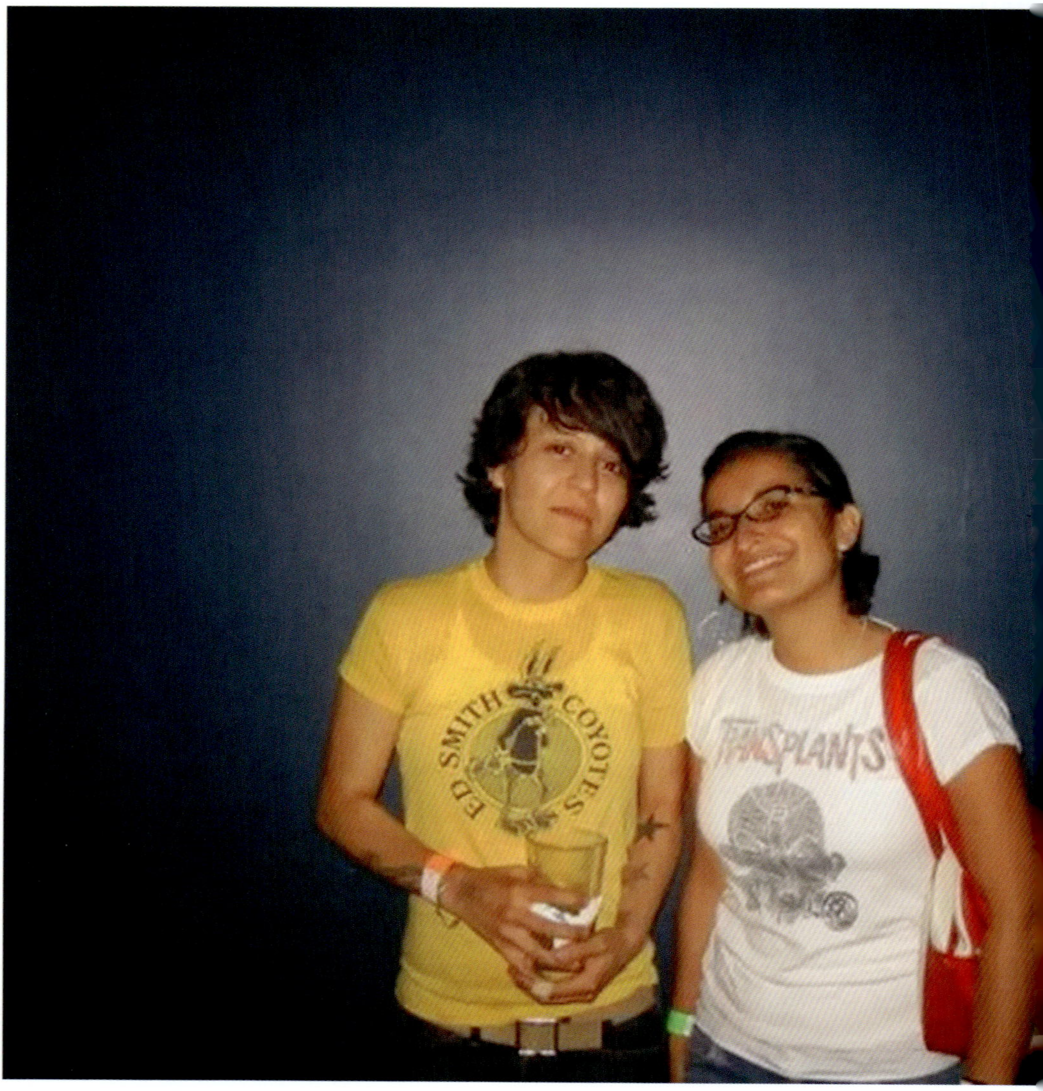

My friend Michelle and me in 2004 or 2005. We were in Todos Vuelven together before I moved to NYC, and then she became part of Go Betty Go. This is when they were touring and I went to see them in Maryland.

material felt too advanced. Still, I picked up a few basics—how to mix oil paints, which brushes to use. But after a while, I dropped the class.

I was feeling frustrated with myself, not knowing what would come next or what my future plan would be. That frustration deepened—and maybe even turned to fear—when I found out Tower Records was going out of business. From 2003 to 2005, working there had felt like a dream job, especially for the artist I was becoming. But soon, that dream unraveled.

Before the store closed, I got a job at the Park Slope Food Coop in Brooklyn (where I was already a member) and ended up staying there for ten years. I was twenty-five, and I was very annoyed that I got the Sunday-morning shift and couldn't go out anymore. Working there left me with little time to go out to shows, see friends, or go to parties. Instead, I poured myself into learning how to make art on my own.

At the time, I was renting a cheap loft space in Brooklyn, on Spencer Street in South Williamsburg by the Marcy Projects, and I used every free hour to paint. With just the little I'd learned in the class, I started figuring things out myself. I taught myself how to stretch a canvas for the first time, and I mixed paints by instinct and trial.

Somewhere in the process, I pulled out the stack of old photos I'd brought with me from L.A. Tucked in among them was a picture of my father, taken when I was a child living in Boyle Heights. He was wearing a brown suede jacket, a cowboy hat, denim pants, and brown boots to match his jacket. It was such a beautiful surprise to find that image again. I decided to use it as a reference and painted my first—and only—oil portrait. This painting was so large that I just leaned it against the wall to display it. It felt like a relative was there with me in Brooklyn. With so little from home, making art became my way of rebuilding something familiar. It became a way of shaping a space that felt like mine, a material that felt like home.

I didn't think of it this way, but part of me was perhaps seeking a new beginning when I left. Los Angeles had been a very unhappy place later in my teens. The underbelly of L.A. became more apparent as I got older. This is why no matter what happened back home, I needed to keep my distance. But as years went by, I began to miss family and friends. I had experienced loss, grief, and drugs in Los Angeles, and there was always a cloud hovering over me, but with time I was able to see past that again, and I began to find my way home.

2

BLACKOUT!

MILLIONS LEFT

Power failure zaps city & Northeast

By JOEL SIEGEL and CORKY SIEMASZKO
DAILY NEWS STAFF WRITERS

New York City and much of the Northeast were paralyzed by a sudden blackout yesterday that stopped 50 million people in their tracks.

From New Jersey all the way to Toronto, trains stopped, computers crashed, planes were grounded, air conditioners cut off and thousands of homes and businesses were plunged into darkness by the largest power outage in the nation's history.

In the city, rush-hour subway riders were trapped in the tunnels and the streets were gripped by gridlock, forcing thousands to hoof it home through the sweltering evening heat over the crowded bridges.

In the blackout region, 21 power plants shut down, affecting Detroit, Toledo, Cleveland, Newark and Ottawa, Canada.

It was 4:11 p.m. when the lights went out in New York. Four hours later, the city's famed skyline formed an eerie silhouette against a moonlit summer night. Stars could be seen for the first time in recent memory.

By 11 p.m., lights flickered sporadically in some city neighborhoods, and Mayor Bloomberg said there should be power by this morning — but no subway service until later.

His advice for today? "Treat it like a snow day: Get up and listen to the radio," the mayor said.

Still, he added, "It wouldn't be the worst thing to take the day off."

Unlike the 1977 blackout, which was marked by riots and looting, the city was mostly calm. In the most serious incident, a police SWAT team besieged a bank in Harlem after an alarm went off, and some looting was reported in Bedford-Stuyvesant, Brooklyn.

Officials quickly ruled out terrorism. Canadian officials blamed a lightning strike that knocked out a power plant upstate, on the Canadian border. But the cause was far from clear.

Automatic shutdown

"Like most New Yorkers, we were taken by surprise," said Con Edison spokesman Michael Clendenin.

He said computers automatically shut down the system when when the flow of outside electricity into Con Ed's power lines can't keep up with demand.

"The system reacted as it should," he said. "It protected itself, and it shut down."

Shortly after the power went down, Bloomberg tried to allay fears in a city still scarred by the Sept. 11, 2001, terror attack.

"There is no evidence whatsoever of terrorism," he said. "With a lot of luck, later on this evening, we will look back on this and say, 'Where were you when the lights went out?' "

President Bush warned that it could take time before life in the region gets back to normal.

"Slowly, but surely, we're coping with this massive, national problem," he said.

The blackout triggered a set of NYPD security precautions that were put in place after the World Trade Center attack, and within minutes heavily armed teams of special counterterror officers were dispatched to city landmarks and other sensitive locations.

Fighter planes creased the sky as the military sent up an extra air patrol in the East as a precaution. Flights into area airports were diverted.

But there was remarkably little panic as New Yorkers dealt with the latest calamity to befall the city — and carried on.

Relaxing in park

"How often does New York City come to a standstill?" said Phil Gormley as he and two pals stretched out on a blanket in Bryant Park and sipped red wine.

Millions of workers were ordered to evacuate their buildings and forced to flee down flights of stairs because the elevators had stopped working — trapping many for hours.

For those in the subways, it was the start of a harrowing exodus through the steaming darkness of the train tunnels.

Maria Hiller of Madison, N.J., was on the uptown A when the train stopped, stranding her and hundreds of other riders between Canal and W. Fourth Sts. for an hour.

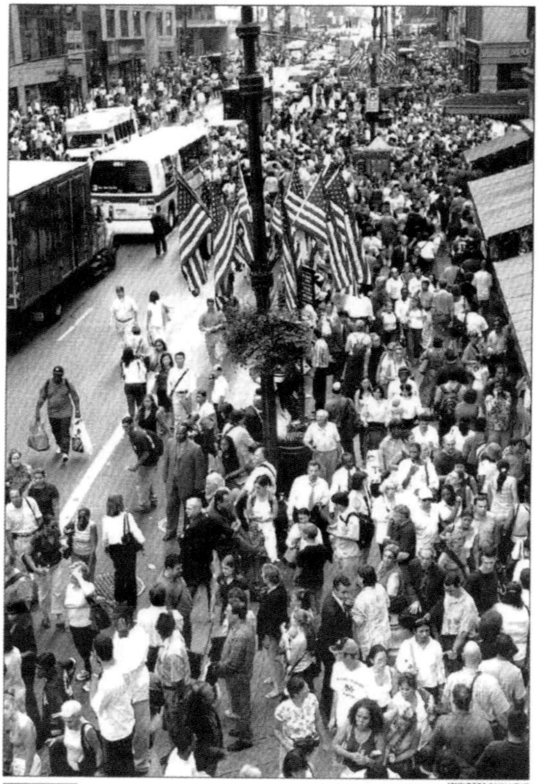

JOHN ROCA DAILY NEWS

NO ESCAPE Throngs of people mill around in front of Grand Central Terminal yesterday and spill out into 42nd St., hoofing it home after traffic lights went out and gridlock set in.

"We sat there for an hour, suffocating," she said. "People started getting out. I jumped off the train with everybody else. . . . It was terrifying."

Trains to Long Island, Westchester and New Jersey also came to a halt as the blackout plunged commuter terminals into darkness, forcing riders to find their way out by the glow of cigarette lighters.

Outside, Red Cross workers handed bottled water to the parched and treated dozens of people who were overcome by the stifling heat.

On the streets, chaos reigned after the lights stopped working, and traffic snarled into knots. As the din of honking cars rose, some drivers tried to helped overwhelmed police officers by directing traffic themselves — often adding to the confusion.

The bridges and tunnels were closed, and the sheer volume of

Friday, August 15, 2003 • DAILY NEWS

BLACKOUT!

IN THE DARK

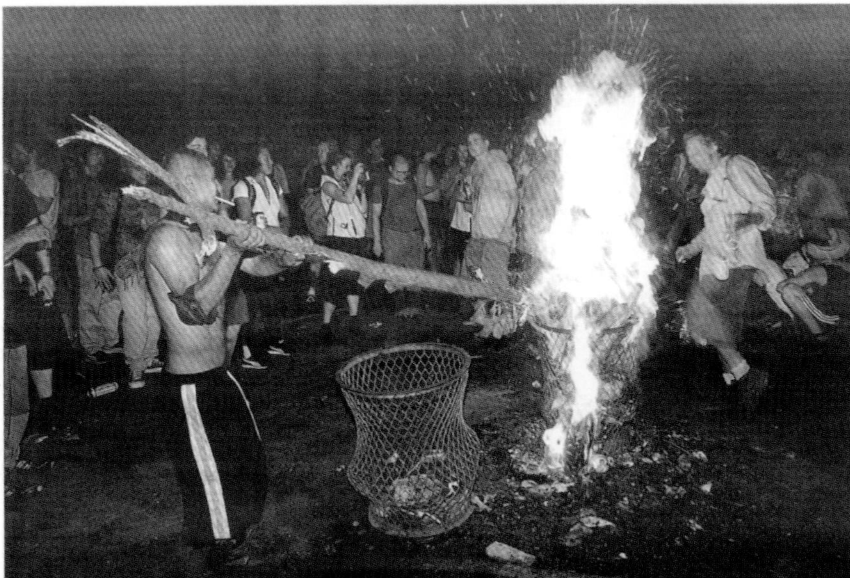

CHET GO[illegible]

MAKING LIGHT OF IT A bonfire drives away the dark last night in Tompkins Square Park, in the East Village.

so many cars trying to get out at once slowed the exodus to a crawl. Many bus riders were trapped when the Port Authority closed its terminal at Eighth Ave. and 42nd St.

"I got to get back to Jersey," said Abbas Muhammad, 45, an accountant from Teaneck. "I'll walk across the George Washington Bridge if I have to. I just can't stand out here in the heat all night."

Some bargains

Thousands of other commuters simply threw up their hands and headed for the nearest bar or restaurant, many of which reduced prices to clear their refrigerators of perishables.

Broadway canceled all shows — to the dismay of tourists — because theaters literally did not have the juice needed to raise the curtains.

In Times Square, no steam rose from the Cup of Noodles billboard and there were no news flashes on the Dow Jones news zipper. But it was business as usual for the postcard sellers, photo vendors and bejeweled men hawking incense to the trapped tourists.

The blackout also forced the evacuation of workers and players from Shea Stadium hours before the Mets were to take on the San Francisco Giants. The game was postponed.

Across the city, lines formed outside bodegas and grocery stores. Some grocers cut the prices on fruit, vegetables and meat for fear they might spoil. But a few tried to profit from adversity by jacking up the prices on bottled water, batteries and other necessities.

Powered by generators, city hospitals continued to provide services, but emergency rooms quickly filled up with people needing treatment for overheating. At Bellevue Hospital, doctors completed four operations that were under way when the power went out, with generators keeping the lights on. "We're confident we can weather this," spokesman James Saunders said.

Stepping out

Most New Yorkers appeared to take the adversity in stride. Instead of sweltering in their apartments, many carried chairs outside and dined al fresco by candlelight.

"We've been through 9/11, we can get through a couple hours without light," said Roger Anderson, as he sipped a glass of wine on a stoop in the West Village.

In midtown, three lawyers sat serenely around the case of beer they had bought for $60 and watched the drama unfold.

"The point is, we don't have a strategy," said Timothy Pfeifer. "Our lives are governed by strategy and plans. Now, with this power outage, you have the luxury of time."

Across the Hudson, New Jersey mobilized 700 National Guard troops and 300 extra state troopers. There were no reported injuries attributed to the blackout, but in Newark at least six people had to be rescued from stuck elevators.

At the height of the blackout, about 1 million PSE&G customers were without power, mostly in Essex, Bergen and Hudson counties, spokeswoman Leslie Cifelli said.

Gov. Pataki, who helicoptered to Albany from his Lake Champlain vacation home when he learned of the blackout, said the apparent breakdown in the power transmission system was troubling.

"It clearly shows the grid s
tem didn't work the way it
supposed to," he told repor
at the state Emergency C
mand Center. "We had
Northeast outage back in
'60s. It wasn't supposed to h
pen again. It did happen ag
We have to ask some tough qu
tions as to why."

At 11:15 p.m., Pataki s
"We're still in a situation wh
probably two-thirds or 60%
New Yorkers don't have pow

In New York, Con Ed's Cler
nin denied reports of a fire
the 14th St. power plant. He
said he could not predict wh
the electricity would be resto
in the city — only that it wou

"We're asking New Yorker
be patient," he said. "It's not j
flipping a switch. It is someth
that has to be done carefully
has to be done methodically."

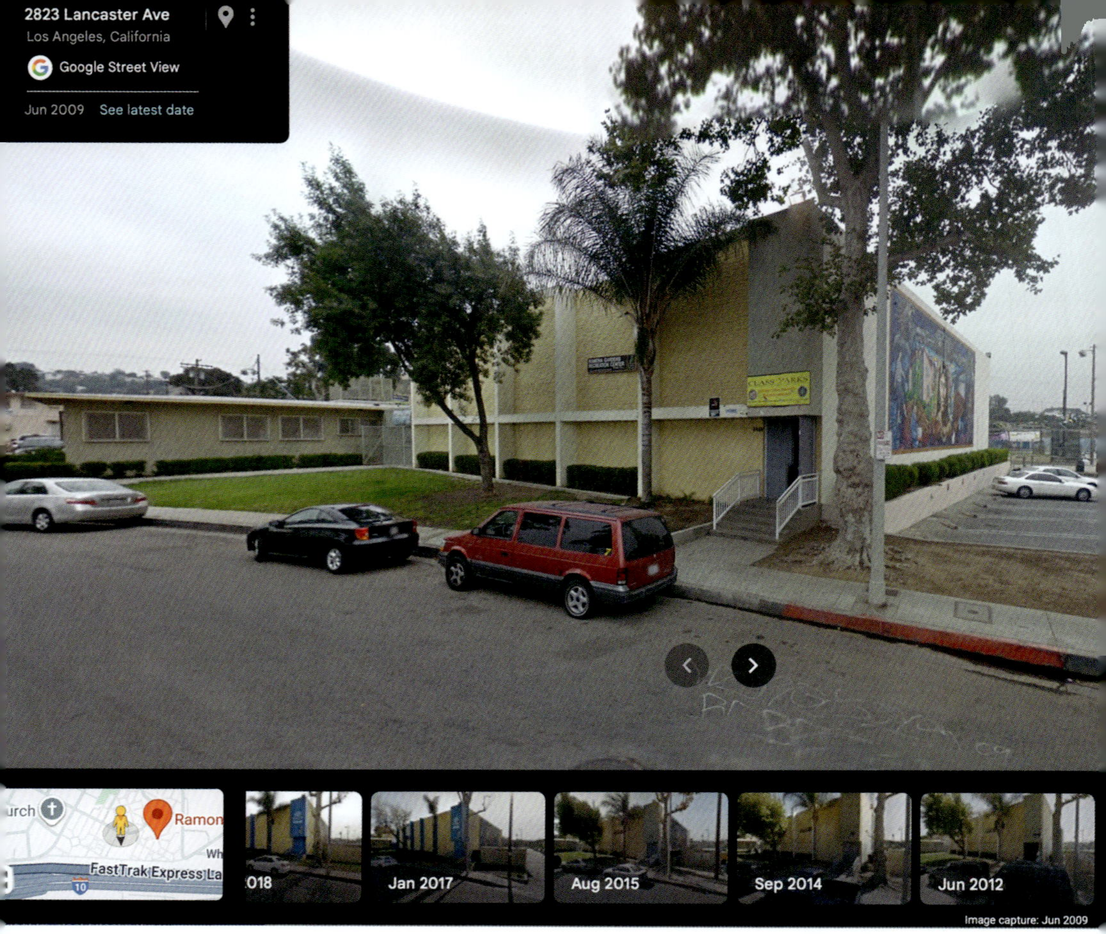
2823 Lancaster Ave
Los Angeles, California
Google Street View
Jun 2009
See latest date
CLASS PARKS
Ramon
FastTrak Express La
018
Jan 2017
Aug 2015
Sep 2014
Jun 2012
Image capture: Jun 2009

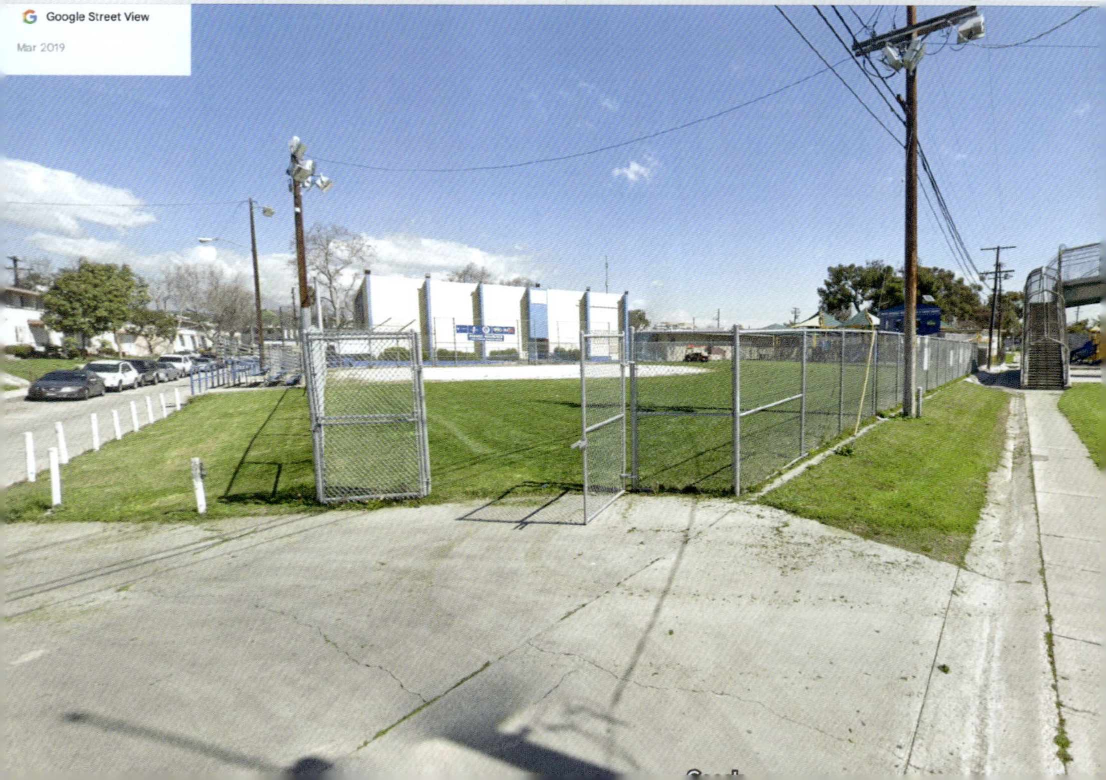
Google Street View
Mar 2019

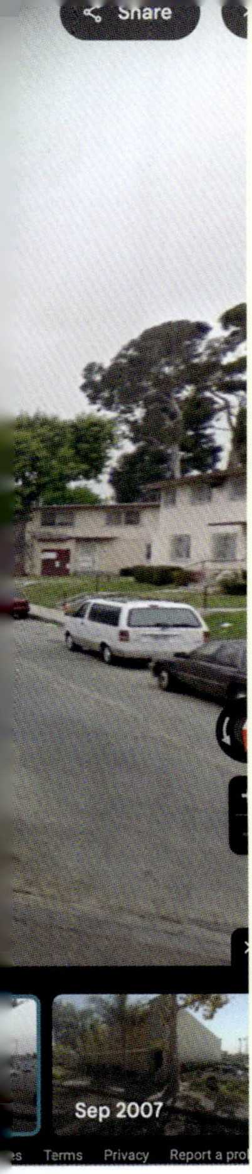

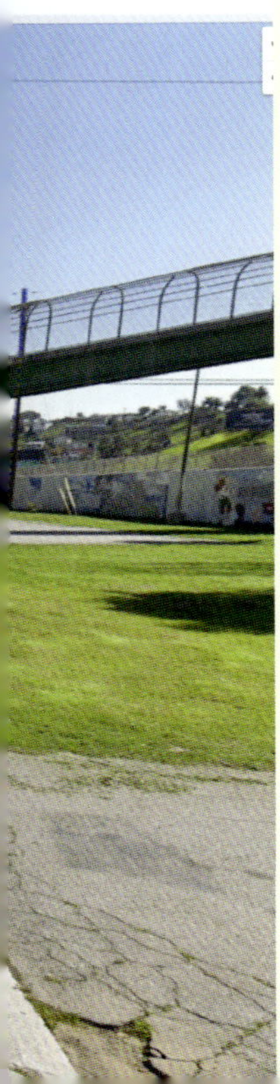

SPIRITUAL PURSUITS

WITH TIME, NOT BRINGING PHOTOS OF MY cousin to New York made me wish I had. When I missed him or my friends and family, the only thing that made me feel close to home and gave me comfort was going online and visiting the Los Angeles landscape remotely. In 2010, I started using Google Maps and Google Street View. I hovered over familiar streets and landmarks—where my cousin was killed, where I went to school, and my home on Leonard Avenue and Whittier Boulevard. Using the internet made me feel close to home from a safe distance. I could visit when I wanted to without anyone knowing. Retracing steps and staying out of sight.

I noticed change at every click. Places began to look different. New buildings and stores that weren't there when I was in L.A. erased the secret corners I once knew, the hangout spots, where we tagged the walls and made out with boys. I felt disoriented, and part of me was again grieving the L.A. I once knew. Not just the people but the places. The images like our local bike shop on Whittier and Hendricks that isn't there anymore, and streets like Allston, Saybrook, Hendricks, and Montebello Park Way that I could trace back with memory but didn't look the same. Our corner store, Beto's, had a new owner and a

OPPOSITE: Screenshot of Google Maps showing Ramona Gardens/Hazards. This is what I was looking at every time I google-searched my neighborhood and other areas that cause so much joy and pain.

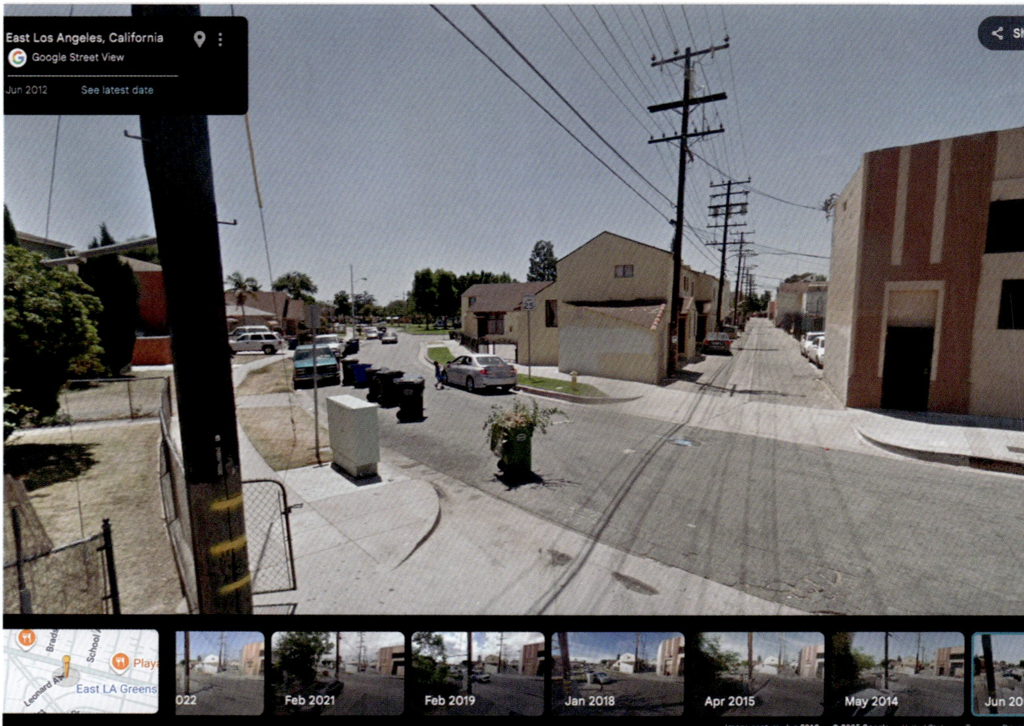

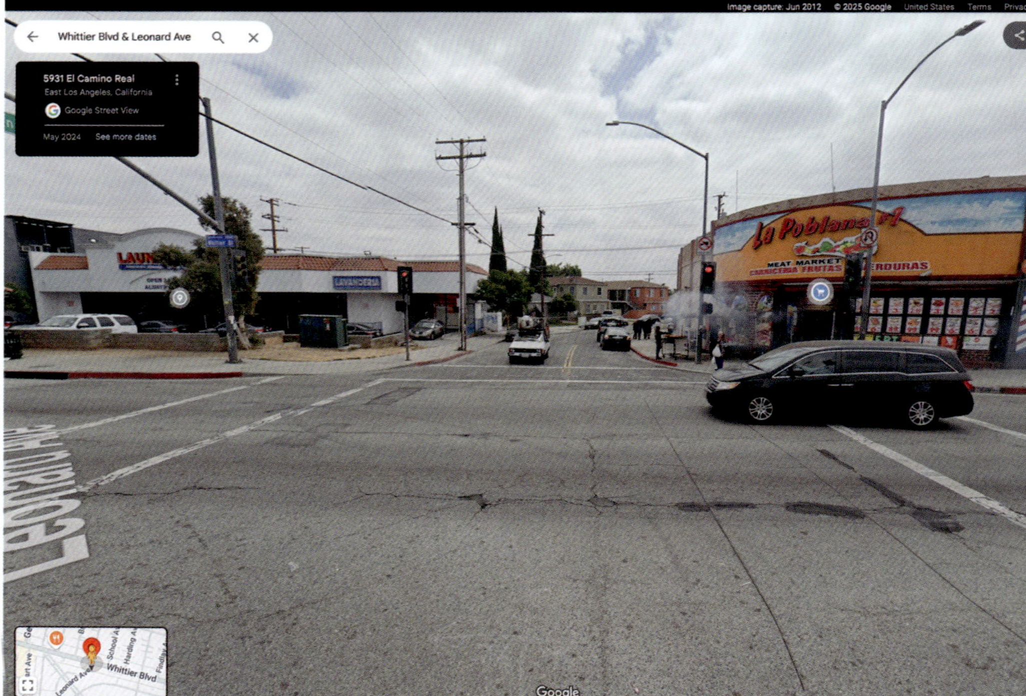

Another screenshot of the
Leonard Avenue block

new name. I saw all of this change unfold on my computer screen, from a few thousand miles away.

When I started calling home and communicating with my family again after years of not speaking, the first thing I wanted was for my sister to share details about our cousin's death—what exactly happened, what time did we lose him, and where was his body found. I was also aware that opening this door again had risks—as a friend once said, don't open a door that has been closed for so long. My friend and Maria were at the party when Ever was killed. The day I called Maria, I had her on the phone while scrolling through Google Maps on my computer. She guided me through the L.A. streets, retracing memories over the line. I asked her, "Tell me, where do you remember his body being found?" She said, "I don't know, but there's a playground behind the Ramona Gardens Recreational Center. Find that. I heard he was found there."

I searched and, sure enough, there was a playground—but it looked new, nothing like the '90s. The whole area had been remodeled, and in that moment, I felt the erasure. The city had changed, and with it, pieces of our story disappeared. These sites suddenly carried a charge, an urgency—to hold on to them before everything shifted, before more was erased.

I thought about how the people I love have deep relationships with places in L.A., whether tender or violent. They've left marks—through touch, through our stories, by walking those streets, and sometimes by dying there. Blood runs through so many corners of L.A. I can think of countless sites where someone took their last breath. Sometimes we built an altar, sometimes we painted a mural—acts of remembrance marking the last place someone stood alive. But when a place is demolished, cleaned up, or torn down, their story is stripped away, too.

I also asked her questions about our past, the fun times and the sad times we both shared. About our childhood friends and all the parties we went to as teenagers. I asked her about our family as well. *How's Mom? Have you heard from Art, aka Night Owl?* I had so many questions, too many to write down, but the answers slowly came to me. There were friends who were doing well (although doing "well" can be subjective), who have become professionals, who now have office jobs, and/or have children and a family. Crazy to think of friends who I'd only known as kids or teenagers now having kids and families. So much time had slipped through my fingers. Some friends were almost unrecognizable, but I realize it's because I had a fixed image of them as teenagers and now they are adults. I'm happy for those who "made it out" but also sad for those who didn't. Those who had been doing time in prison before I left Los Angeles. Like my childhood friend Michael, who was arrested in front of me in front of my house and had never seen freedom since. It's hard to see people I love get swallowed up by the prison system.

I would also go online to obsessively read anything related to Los Angeles. I'd search for hours online for names of friends, starting with people I went to school with, then people from the neighborhood. I googled "Schurr High School 1994–1999." I looked at the *Los Angeles Times* and Homicide Report. I clicked and clicked, and one search led to another. Sometimes no information popped up; sometimes I found a familiar name. I also found the *Los Angeles Times* article about my cousin Ever's death, now in a digital format. I began to see a pattern: Many of the people I knew back then were no longer alive or were locked up like Michael, who was doing life. (His sentence was later reduced, and he's now out of prison.)

Now that I had a bit more experience—and confidence—in the art world, making work in response to my research, obsessions, and longing became my outlet. I was also studying and looking closely at artists like Pauline Boudry and Renate Lorenz, Hilma af Klint, Nan Goldin, ASCO, and Mike Kelley. Each of them opened something up for me—new ways of seeing, of working with archives, performance, photography, spirituality, or subcultures. Art gave me a way to get lost, the same way I do on the internet—wandering, searching, falling into rabbit holes. But this was also different. Here, I was making something tangible, like the painting of my father or drawings inspired by maps and grids. Something I could hold in my hands, like the wallet-size photos I carried with me—images that felt like anchors to another time. First I began to show my work by donating artworks to nonprofits and organizations like the Sylvia Rivera Law Project. Donating work to auctions encouraged me to keep making something that had meaning.

In 2012, when I had some work under my belt, my friend Kate Brewer Ball, then a PhD student, invited me to be part of a project she was curating. It began with an artist talk at NYU that year, and the following year, in 2013, it culminated in an exhibition at the ONE National Gay & Lesbian Archives in Los Angeles titled *Stand Close, It's Shorter Than You*

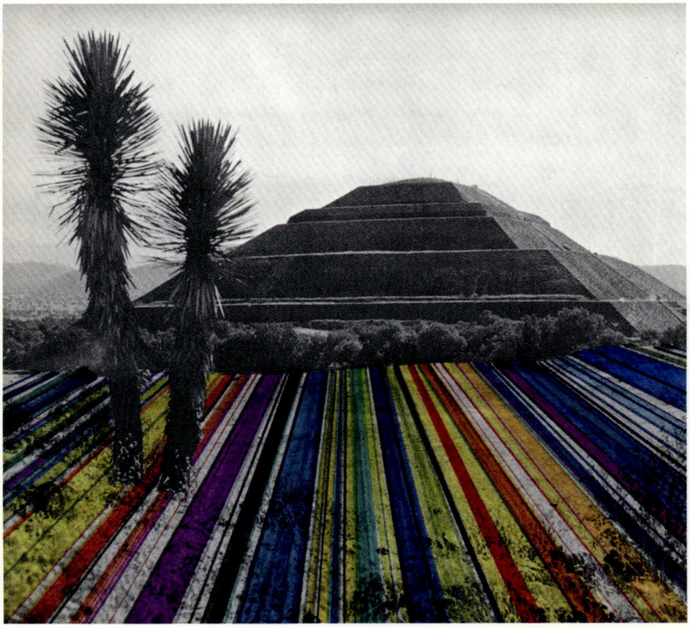

Collage drawings I donated to nonprofits and fundraisers like Sylvia Rivera Law Project

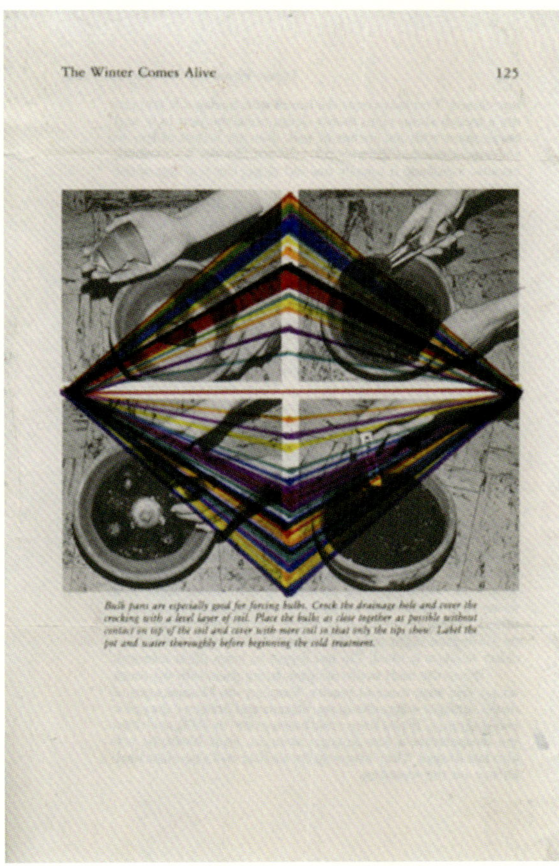

One of my first drawings shown in an exhibition. I think this was in a show curated by Ulrike Müller.

Think: A Show on Feminist Rage. It felt like the perfect opportunity to bring New York and L.A.—two parts of my life that had always lived in separate orbits—into the same frame. For a moment, the distance between who I had been and who I was becoming seemed to collapse into something whole.

It was also the first time I was creating and showing work in direct response to my research. For the first part of the exhibition, there was an artist talk at NYU, after which the poet and writer Corrine Fitzpatrick wrote a beautiful piece about my work. Her words felt like someone seeing me clearly—maybe even for the first time in a while. Her writing gave me a sense of pride I hadn't felt since I left Los Angeles, and a quiet reassurance that it was okay to share this part of my life with the world. That my story, with all its raw edges, was worth telling.

It was also the first time I had to give an artist presentation. I froze—completely. I mostly said nothing, because the words just wouldn't come out of me. The silence was humiliating, but it was real. I wasn't ready to speak out loud about what the work held. I was still learning how to show it, let alone explain it. But somehow, Corrine's response helped carry the weight of what I couldn't say yet. She helped give voice to something I hadn't figured out how to articulate myself.

Excerpt from "The work as a result" by Corrine Fitzpatrick:

Guadalupe Rosales left California for New York City twelve years ago, and this exhibition marks the first showing of her work in Los Angeles. "Almost like having two worlds collide" (Email from Guadalupe Rosales to the author. February 2013.) Incidentally, she has taken to stalking locations, using Google Earth to cruise over, onto, and virtually near the terrain of her upbringing. Alleyways, playgrounds, gymnasiums: some sites are mundane, others resonate with personal trauma and violence. When we look back, what are we looking for? In order to visualize nostalgia, imagine thin beams of light extending from a person—here, the artist in her Brooklyn studio, trying to come to terms with aspects of the past through time, distance, and the Internet. The Internet, meanwhile, is constructing a memory of its own, a public realm for each of us to access and add to; it is an archive that is always

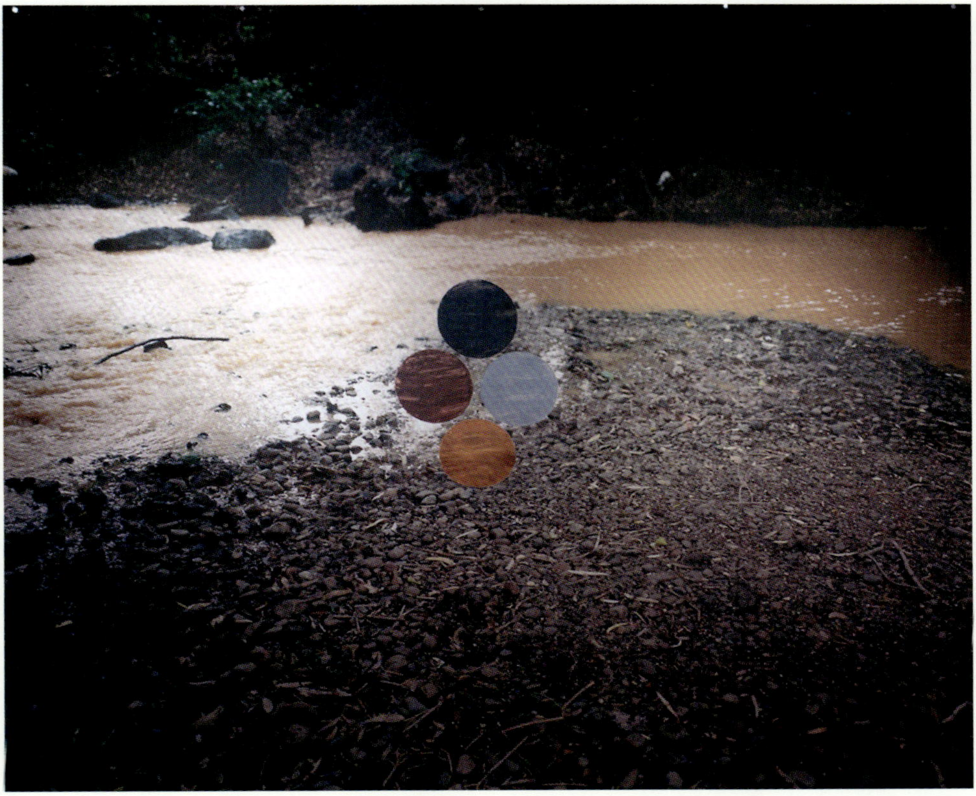

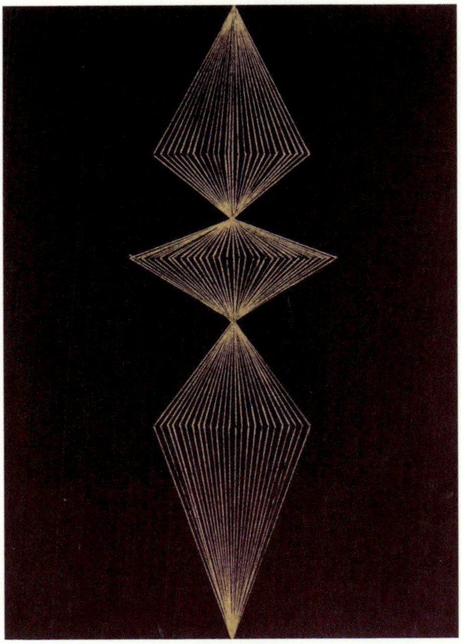

being built just as it sidles up to, borrows from, and affects our memories.

The work that was exhibited in ONE National Gay & Lesbian Archives felt like experiments—tests in form, material, and value. I was drawn to what was considered cheap or disposable and wanted to see how far I could push it. One series consisted of three geometric drawings made with gold ink on black construction paper, turning something fragile and ordinary into an object of precision. I also made drawings on scraps of found leather, treating them like canvas and allowing their imperfections to shape the work.

Alongside these was one of the first photographs I ever took with a medium-format camera: a landscape with a muddy river, layered with four painted circles on translucent Mylar that seemed to float over the water.

Instead of printing it on paper, I chose fabric—another way of refusing the expected of photography and treating an image as something that flowed like soft fabric, like sculpture. It was my first time back in L.A. since my father passed away in 2003. I didn't see my family. It broke my heart not to. But I was still trying to find my place back in New York. Trying to mix both worlds felt like too much—I wasn't ready, but I was getting closer.

EVERYTHING HAPPENS AT THE SAME TIME

I SPENT YEARS BUILDING A STRONG PORTFOLIO, BUT I STILL felt like there was something missing. I felt out of place and like what I was doing wasn't enough. By 2012/2013, I had already been working at the Park Slope Food Coop for about eight years. I wasn't going out as much because the hours at the coop made it hard for me to party or stay out late. I was slowly drifting away from the night life. The work hours were brutal: I had no weekends off, I went in at 5 A.M. and stayed until 1 P.M. A quiet but persistent voice inside me kept saying, *Maybe this is as far as you'll go. This job gives you what you need: stability, health insurance, and healthy food. After all, you're a high school dropout.* That belief may have been why I stayed there for ten years. But the job didn't help me grow, didn't give me time to socialize. My world became small. I couldn't help but wonder: Was this self-doubt rooted in my lack of a formal degree? Or was it something deeper—something shaped by how society defines success and legitimacy?

When I moved to New York, I was able to come out as queer, and I found a new kind of family—friends who understood me in ways I hadn't known I needed. It reminded me of why so many of my friends in L.A. turned to gangs: When the world made us feel like we didn't belong, we found belonging in the people who saw us, who made us feel like we mattered. I was now free in a new way, with other queer artists, teachers, amazing thinkers, and weirdos who were also my mentors.

But I still found it difficult to share my past with my lovers and friends. I felt free, but afraid to share about growing up in L.A. because I feared I would be misunderstood, stereotyped, or put in a box. Living in a city like New York, people like me can start feeling lonely, alienated, and isolated. Getting older also meant becoming more aware of the world around me, and the cultural differences, racism, and injustice. Art is what helped me reclaim and feel empowered by my upbringing and learn to share that part of my life again.

While trying to find my place in NYC, not just as someone from Los Angeles but also as a brown queer artist who had just come out, I began to feel how difficult it would be for someone like me to do anything with the art world, more particularly this specific art world. I also began to miss my family, my friends, and my home in L.A. I began to feel that maybe art wasn't for me. Or I wasn't an artist after all. Then in 2013, I had a revelation when I went with some friends to a group exhibition at the New Museum called *NYC 1993: Experimental Jet Set, Trash and No Star.* I knew some of the artists in the show, but most I wasn't familiar with.

In many ways, this exhibition changed my view and understanding of the art world. I remember making my way to the second floor. I turned to my right and all of a sudden, I felt like I had walked into a telenovela or a movie set or a crime scene or my own home. Or all of the above. This was my first encounter with Pepón Osorio's captivating work. Even though it was highly dramatic, and he is Puerto Rican from the Bronx and I'm Chicana from East Los Angeles, somehow, I was able to see myself in this work. It spoke to me.

There were porcelain saints and candles in the room, and the table was covered with a clear plastic sheet that protected the tablecloth. It reminded me of my mother's taste in furniture, home decorations, and color scheme, and I could smell my mother's cooking. The arc of wrought iron hanging above was like a relic and reminder of the homes I grew up in and my neighborhood in Los Angeles.

Finally, I found a sense of belonging in the art world. Work that reflected me back and reminded me of my own world. This work touched all my senses and took me back to the coziness of my home, regardless of the overly dramatic scene that looked like a telenovela. This is the type of art that made me curious, gave me joy and sadness. This work made me think and ask questions. I got transported to a home that felt familiar.

> When this piece, "Scene of the Crime (Whose Crime?)," was at the Whitney Museum, it almost felt as if I'd taken a piece of the South Bronx and placed it in the middle of Madison Avenue.
>
> —*Pepón Osorio*

After this visit to the museum, I went back home and picked up a pencil again and began to draw. Anything. I was really inspired by maps, grids, and time, but I didn't have the right language or skill to articulate this. I made large-scale geometric paintings using Flashe paints, all inspired by maps I looked at on Google Maps. I pushed myself to find my voice and vision in art. I lay on my apartment floor with large sheets of white paper and brushes, markers, and pencils. I went to as many art shows as I could. All of this while I had a voice reminding me that maybe this was as much as I could do, because I was a high school dropout.

Then, something unexpected happened. In 2014, my mentor, friend, and fellow activist, Gregg Bordowitz, invited me to apply to the MFA program at the School of the Art Institute of Chicago (SAIC). Gregg was a co-founder of ACT UP (AIDS Coalition to Unleash Power), an international, grassroots political group formed in 1987 in response to the AIDS pandemic.

The offer felt surreal—almost impossible. This is when I realized I had been ready for it all along, the only thing standing between me and this dream was not having a degree or even a high school diploma, something that for years made it feel impossible, like I didn't deserve it. *Could a high school dropout really leap straight into an MFA program?* I was upfront with him, saying it seemed out of reach, especially without an undergraduate degree in art. But Gregg didn't hesitate. "I've seen your work," he said with conviction. "You should consider applying." He once said to me, "Poetry and art are forms that can articulate things otherwise unspeakable, that allow us to approach grief, rage, and desire when conventional discourse fails." This made me trust his thinking and that he believed in me.

His belief in me shifted how I viewed myself—it reminded me of how I felt when I first read Corrine Fitzpatrick's text in response to my work back in 2012. That feeling gave me the push I needed to take the leap and apply—and I was accepted to SAIC with a full scholarship. I had applied to two other schools, one of them being Bard College. I got in, but I decided not to go there for a few reasons, most important that I wanted to be far from what was familiar—away from friends, community, and especially far from New York—so I could focus.

I chose Chicago because I wanted that challenge. The idea of moving to a place I didn't know for at least three summers in a row felt intimidating, but in a good way. It meant I would have to focus, make new friends, and push myself in ways I hadn't before.

At that time, I was also developing a new relationship with my personal archives and reflecting deeply on Los Angeles—my home, my history, my culture. L.A. was always in the back of my mind, shaping who I was and what I wanted to make. Using Google Maps and Street View only made this urge stronger. It made sense to use school as an opportunity to finally sit with the thoughts and ideas that had been brewing in me for years. And because I didn't have a high school diploma or a college degree, I knew I had to take full advantage of this rare opportunity. I packed my favorite outfits (my worn-out A.P.C. pants, vintage jerseys, Red Wing boots, and stacks of Oxford button-ups) and the materials I thought could fold into my studies.

Most important was the stack of personal Starshot photos I'd saved since I was a teenager—photos of friends, of my sisters and me. I'd brought them to New York years before, when I left L.A. Now I carried them again as I made my way to Chicago for grad school.

Being in Chicago allowed me to dedicate all my time to my studies. I read all the books and watched all the films that were recommended by visiting artists like Zoe Leonard, Andrea Fraser, Yvonne Rainer, and Glenn Ligon. I read art theory and poetry, and I really enjoyed anything related to philosophy. I fell in love with José Esteban Muñoz's *Cruising Utopia, Citizen* by Claudia Rankine, and Fred Moten's *The Feel Trio*. I was obsessed with Gilles Deleuze.

Over the three years that I was in graduate school (I spent the summers in Chicago studying and then had the rest of the year to work), I immersed myself in developing a thoughtful and experimental art practice. I approached the work with an open mind and a willingness to explore, even when I had no clear idea where it might lead. Art school wasn't just a place to grow creatively—it became a kind of sanctuary, a buffer between my past and future selves. Art articulated all those feelings I'd had since I was a kid: confusion, chaos, beauty, and dreams.

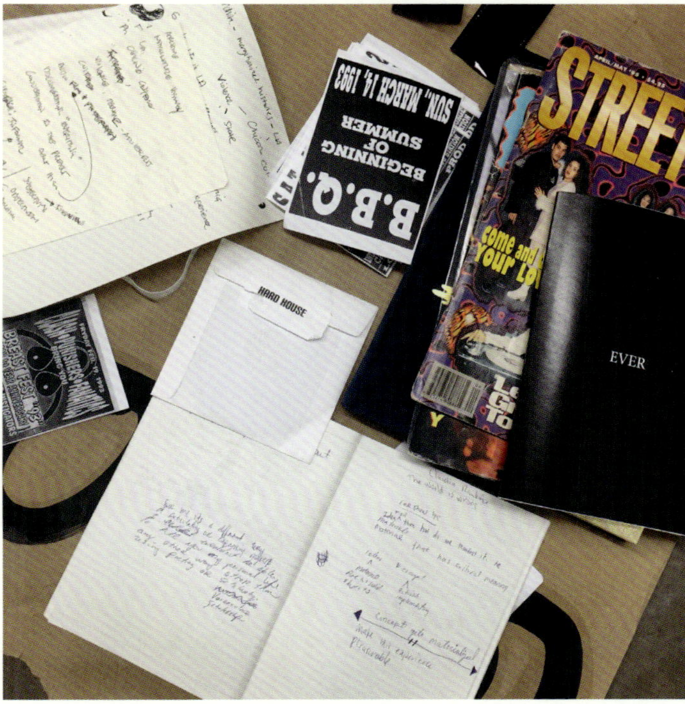

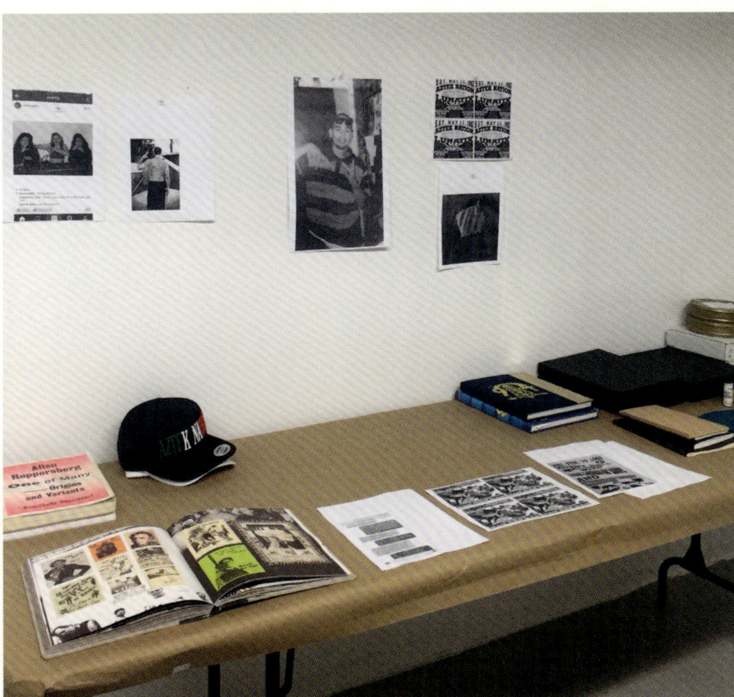

Studio at SAIC in 2015

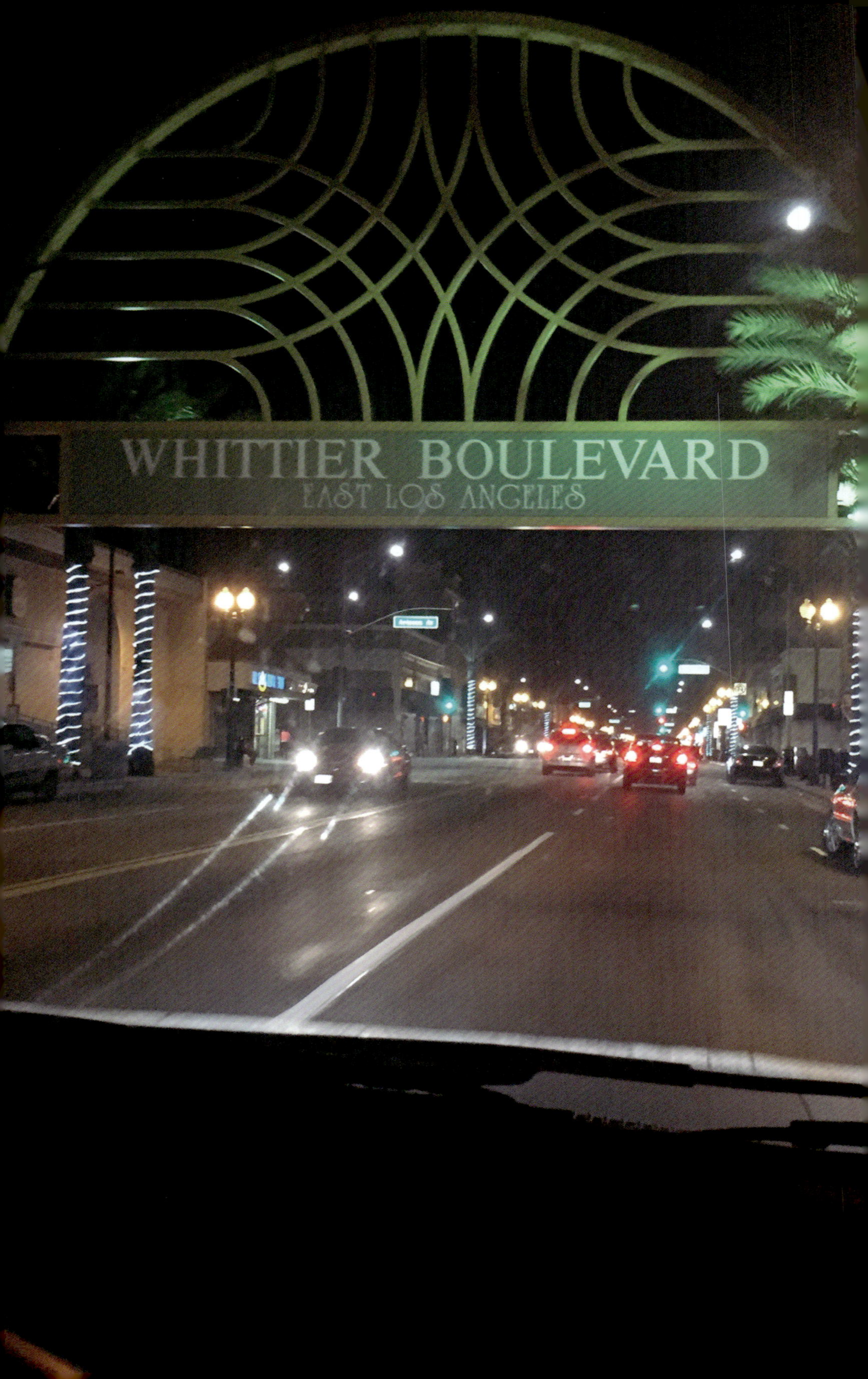
WHITTIER BOULEVARD
EAST LOS ANGELES

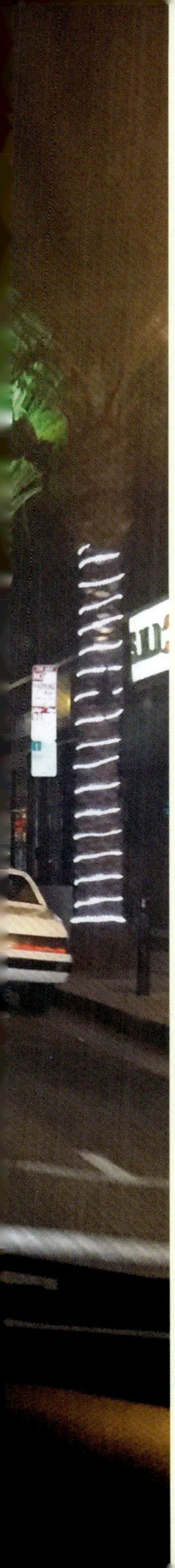

RASCUACHE GARDEN

IN OCTOBER 2014, I WENT HOME, JUST DAYS BE-fore Halloween and Día de los Muertos. Mom pulled out boxes of my things she had been saving for me. We sat at the table, and I opened up the box labeled "cosas personales de lupe" in Mom's writing—letters from Richard, Largo, and my brothers, all written from jail. There were also pay stubs I had saved. This gave me a sense that Mom had known I would come back one day. She was now living in a house in La Puente, which she and my stepdad had purchased sometime around 2010, with a backyard big enough to get lost in.

I had always known she had a green thumb. Even when we didn't have a proper garden, she found a way to grow vegetables and fruit in tin cans and five-gallon buckets and kept it *rascuache* (a term coined by scholar Tomás Ybarra-Frausto that means "an underdog perspective—a view from los de abajo. An attitude rooted in resourcefulness and adaptability yet mindful of stance and style"). Here, with space to spare, she still kept some plants in her improvised pots, stubbornly tending them as if they were treasures. An orange tree stood in the corner of the yard, heavy with fruit. On this trip, it was the first time I felt like I had stepped into one of those families from movies—the kind with a real home, a backyard, fruit trees—and I couldn't quite believe this was ours now.

I appreciated every detail about L.A.—the palm trees, the freeways, the sunsets. My sisters took me back to our old stomping grounds: Whittier Boulevard, City Terrace, East L.A., low-rider cruise nights on the boulevard, car shows at Elysian Park or Legg Lake.

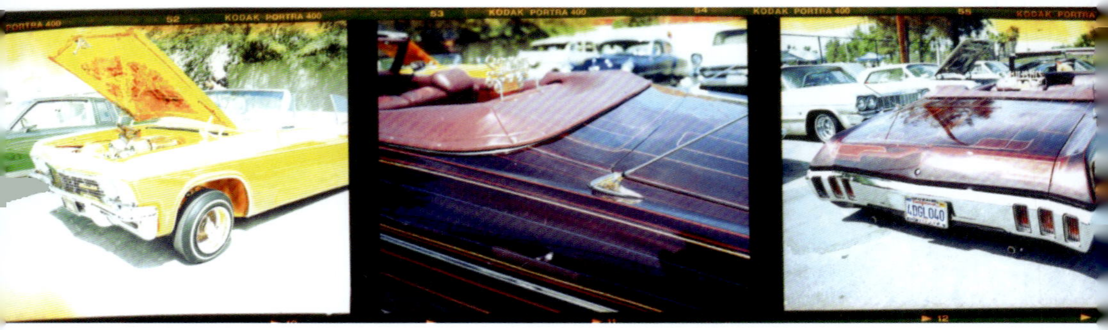

I'd brought with me a 16mm Bolex camera I rented from school and filmed my drives with my sister Yesi, down Whittier Boulevard. I guided her—"Drive slow," "Can you turn around? I didn't catch that"—and she let me guide her.

I also took photos with a new camera I had purchased, and this was the first time I'd gone to the location where my cousin was killed. I didn't get the right shot but promised myself I would continue to go back every year on the anniversary of his death, December 21, as a ritual. Even if the photos weren't great on my first two attempts—too blurry, too under- or overexposed, because I was too uncomfortable to take my camera out at night in a place that carried so much weight, I have continued that tradition.

I photographed everything I could. Mom's door entrance. The streets and events I went to with my sisters. One of my favorite hip-hop groups I had missed while I was in New York was playing during my visit. I mentioned to Maria that I didn't want to miss Psycho Realm's concert, and she responded, "They always play," as if I wouldn't be missing much, so we didn't go. Afterward I wished we had, and I realized that I was appreciating the everyday parts of my city in a way I hadn't before.

A lot had changed, yet some corners remained untouched—like time had folded over itself in the alleyways around Leonard Avenue. I also felt sad because so much time had passed and I hadn't been in L.A. all these years to experience my own culture at home. This feeling also encouraged me to keep making artworks inspired by my visit, the photos I had taken and the energy of the swap meets and everything I'd bought there: bootleg T-shirts, Ben Davis shirts, Chicano rap CDs. I also used these moments to bond with my sisters—getting chucherías for our long drives and catching up on the chisme. With Maria, the conversations sometimes turned more serious, especially when it came to our stepdad. I always knew abuse had happened when we were kids, but not the extent of it.

My stepdad's behavior had always felt creepy. There had been the incident when I was a teenager, when he came into the room where I was sleeping, I told Mom, and the cops were called. We made a report and he was arrested. I felt protected to a certain degree. But then, when he started coming around again when he wasn't supposed to (he had a restraining order against him), that feeling of being protected by my mother went away. I also rebelled. I started stealing money from Mom's purse. Stopped coming home. Maria didn't start rebelling just because she was a teenager; she had her reasons to yell back at Mom, showing no respect toward her. It made sense why she didn't care about Mom's rules.

Maria told me, "I don't care if you write about this. It doesn't bother me at all. What bothers me is that he's still around after everything he's done. It feels like Mom took his side."

Those conversations only made our bond stronger. "You remember how timid I was, right?" she reminded me. "When things happened to me, I didn't know how to communicate it, so I shut down even more. And then I had a reason to be closed off and angry."

Even now when we're adults, I feel protective of her. It hurts to know that someone would take advantage of her, knowing how sweet, gentle, and quiet she was as a child. I've told her that I don't like looking at photos of us when we were little, now that I know what I know.

There are family photos from the day that he first abused her—everyone eating sandwiches and watermelon, our hair and clothes still wet from swimming. Maria was about nine years old. She told me, "The first time he touched me was when we went to Santa Fe Dam. He pulled me into the deep end of the water and said he wanted to teach me how to swim. I felt so powerless. Then he touched me. He seemed awkward, like he knew what he was doing was wrong."

Looking back at those photos from the early '90s—especially ones with our stepdad—it's hard not to feel the weight of what Maria endured. At the same time, I try not to let those memories, that trauma, completely overshadow those moments.

Us talking through these times feels healing, because in those conversations we found moments where we took our power back—ignoring Mom's rules and sometimes not caring if in an argument we made Mom cry. We rebelled for a reason, and as we reflect on that time, it feels good to see ourselves seize agency.

And we also remember the other side of it—the fun we had together, the rebellious nights filled with joy, excitement, and love. We were able to create freedom for ourselves despite the violation and violence we experienced at home and in the streets. That's what we carry with us.

Whittier Boulevard and Commerce Shopping Center were the places we found freedom when we were young together, and even though driving down Whittier Boulevard wasn't quite the same as it had been during my teenage years, it still stirred something familiar in me. Maria told me that cruising was back after years of being criminalized and shut down by police. Cruising happened a lot when I was a teenager but finally got shut down while I was living in New York, sometime around the early 2000s. Now it felt more accepted—almost not as sacred—because Chicano and lowrider culture had become more accessible, more mainstream and trendier and, in some ways, clichéd.

It was a shock to me. This wasn't what it was like before I took that flight to New York fourteen years before. A friend even told me that people (mostly gang members) didn't wear baggy pants anymore. The style had shifted from pelones, Ben Davis and Cascade shirts, and football jerseys to more fitted and casual clothes—something that helped them blend in more easily with the rest of society.

But regardless, when we drove around the neighborhood—whether it was Maria behind the wheel, or Yesi, or sometimes our mom—we'd turn up Tupac or some oldies, and the music would instantly transport me back to those long summer nights filled with possibility, dreams, and the unexpected. School, time in New York, and art, in its own way, helped me see L.A.—and my past—with new eyes.

Through the art I was making and the books I was reading, I began to reflect more deeply on the systems I'd grown up within, the choices I had made, and the ones that had been made for me. Education didn't just open intellectual doors—it softened me, helped me hold space for complexity, for memory, and for grief. Art reassured me that no matter how difficult life got, I would be okay. It gave me a place to sit with my feelings instead of running from them. Through making, I learned that

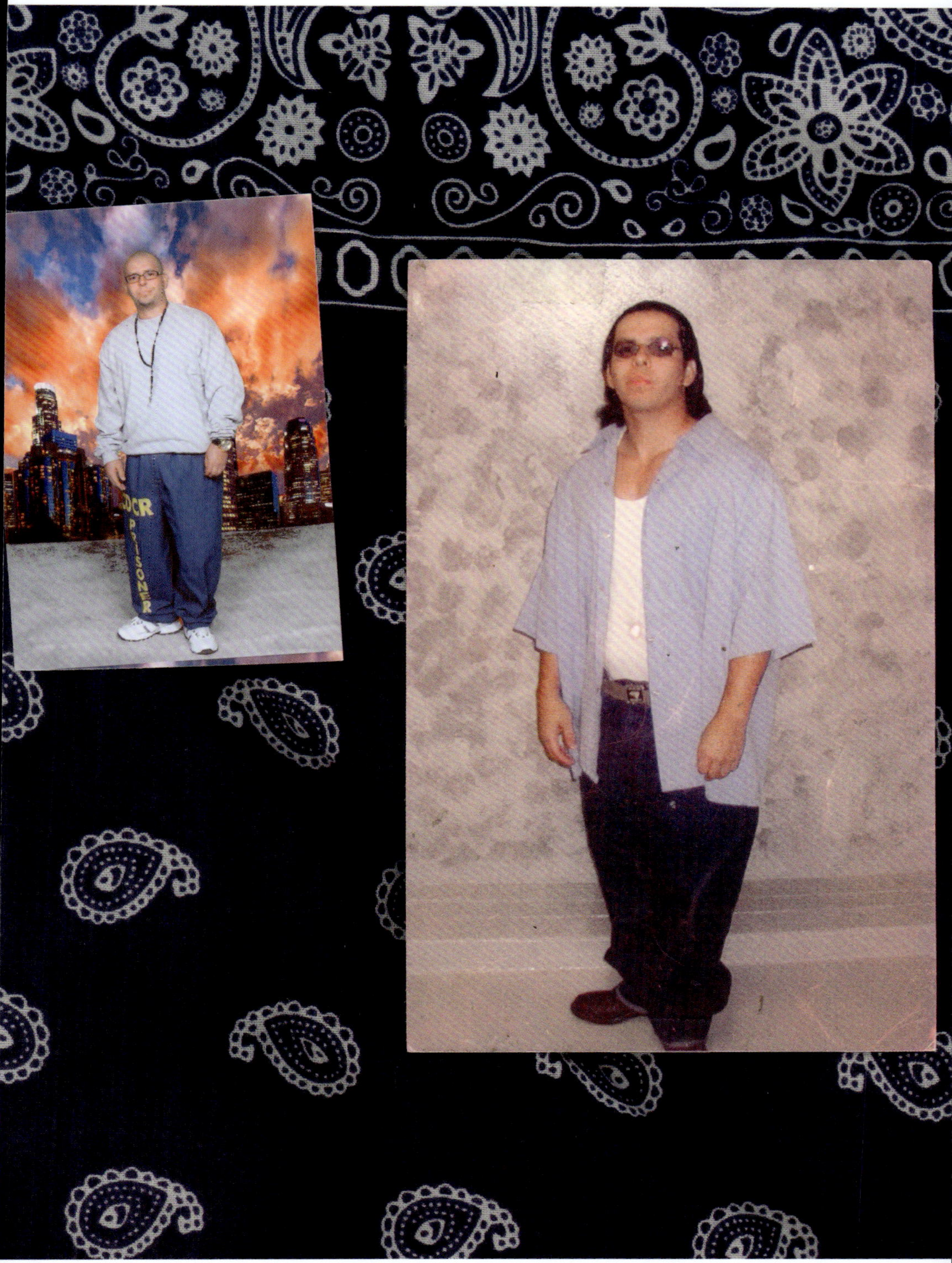

Photos of Michael that he
sent me from prison

it was okay to ask questions I didn't yet have answers for, and to move forward only when I was ready. When I wasn't, art became a way to stay present with what was coming up, to work it out through the process itself. That's how I knew I'd be okay—because art showed me that I could hold both the pain and the possibility of transformation at the same time.

Back in New York that same year in 2014, I became friends with Dean Spade—a lawyer, trans activist, and writer. We bonded over our shared experiences in the foster care system, trading stories that only someone who had lived through it could truly understand. In one of our conversations, Dean encouraged me to start writing to people in prison. He and his partner had been corresponding with incarcerated folks for a while and spoke of how meaningful—even life-saving—those letters could be. So many people inside had been abandoned by family and loved ones who'd lost hope. The idea of offering even a sliver of connection to someone in that kind of isolation struck me deeply.

I followed through. It was during that time that I felt a strong pull to reconnect with people I had known who were incarcerated. I started with my neighborhood friend Michael, who was a member of the Rangel family that my sisters and I had been so close to. I typed his name into a prison locator and tried different combinations, cycling through possible birth months and years, trying to remember the details. The results always came back with more than a dozen files with the same name, but I remembered that Michael was a year older than me, and a little information helped me narrow it down. After several attempts, I finally found his information online. The first letter I wrote to him was a shot in the dark. I didn't know if it would get to him or just get lost in the mail. Luckily it did get to him.

Here's an excerpt:

> *The humidity on the east coast puts me in a bad mood; remember being stuck in bad traffic in LA? The feeling is pretty much identical. The underground subway stations are perhaps the worst, waiting for the A train on west 4th street on a hot summer day makes me feel exhausted and dirty. In California, it's very different for me. The sun feels comfortable on my skin and the air is dry and crisp. Someone once told me that Los Angeles feels like being inside a womb. I'm listening to "The Metro" by Berlin as I write this letter. Listening to*

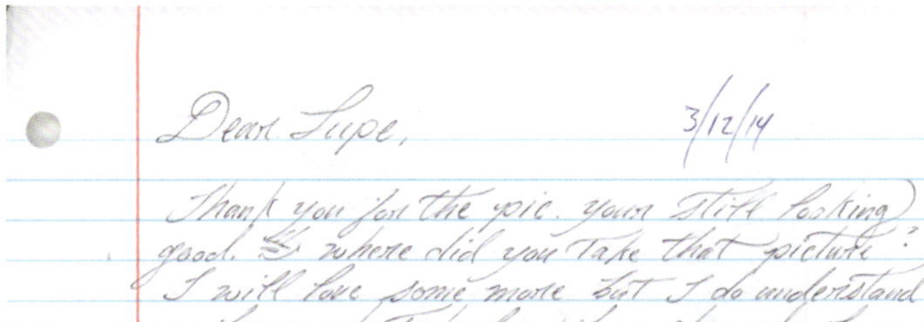

Dear Lupe, 3/12/14

Thank you for the pic. your still looking good. & where did you take that picture? I will love some more but I do understand

A prison letter from Michael

CALIFORNIA

Ever's redacted death certificate

the song takes me back to that winding road that leads us to the Baby Doe's club in Monterey Park.

I will never forget those nights when my sister and I would sneak out of the house and walk over to yours. You lived across the street from us and there were a few oval-shaped parks with four big trees between your house and mine. You, your five brothers and sister slept in the living room and your parents slept in the only bedroom in the apartment. The living room had two big windows facing the street. Your apartment felt narrow but cozy. Your upstairs neighbor was a goth kid and lived alone.

For about a year, I exchanged letters with several incarcerated pen pals I found through online listings. Michael was the only person who I knew in real life. Those dialogues opened me up in new ways. They reminded me how powerful it is simply to be witnessed and to share stories even with strangers. And that stayed with me.

All of these moments—conversations with strangers, reunions with childhood friends like Michael, long drives with my family—began to weave themselves together, and I started developing a desire to explore how art, storytelling, and community could come together.

I also figured out how to get a copy of my cousin's death certificate. Around that time, I was receiving many letters in the mail from Michael. That feeling—holding on to something so ordinary yet so charged—made me seek out my cousin's certificate. Michael's letters inspired me to get hold of my cousin's certificate because I knew that it would be the last documents he'd leave on earth.

The certificate was printed on thick, official-looking paper with a felt-like texture, bordered in patterned pink and blue that looked like printed lace. At the top it read "County of Los Angeles" and "State of California." It listed his full name, the date, the time, and the cause of death. Reading those words—"multiple stab wounds"—and seeing the exact time printed out so plainly was jarring. It was like a printed autopsy. Before this, all I had were memories and stories from friends and family. But the document told me exactly what happened. It made everything feel disturbingly real.

This piece of paper inspired me to actually start looking at physical material and seeing the way it could tell a story—what emotions came up for me just by touching and holding an object or material that was saturated with meaning. Or write a text that could paint a picture. It could humanize a memory, and it pushed me to value and archive material. I kept thinking about "Doubting Thomas," how seeing and touching makes something undeniable. The documents made my memories more physical—something I could actually hold in my hands.

When I received the death certificate, I felt like I came closer to my cousin. Like I was holding a small part of his story that had always felt out of reach. It didn't bring closure, but it brought weight, presence, and a sense of truth that I had been missing. He had been stabbed multiple times with an ice pick and was left to die in a playground in East L.A. These details inspired me to understand the archive (photos, letters, even clothing) as relics because they connected me to a person, place, and time. I began to understand our bodies as vessels that collect memories, trauma, pain. Bodies that scar, feel, and contain. Our bodies are archives of our experiences.

ALL OF THESE experiences, culminating right before and during grad school, as I was increasingly looking at my own experiences as source material, deeply shaped my desire to start engaging in more profound conversations and reflections. I felt an increasing pull to connect with others over shared experiences—stories that went beyond surface-level exchanges. After lengthy discussions with my friend Luke (or Baker), *Veteranas and Rucas* took shape in 2015.

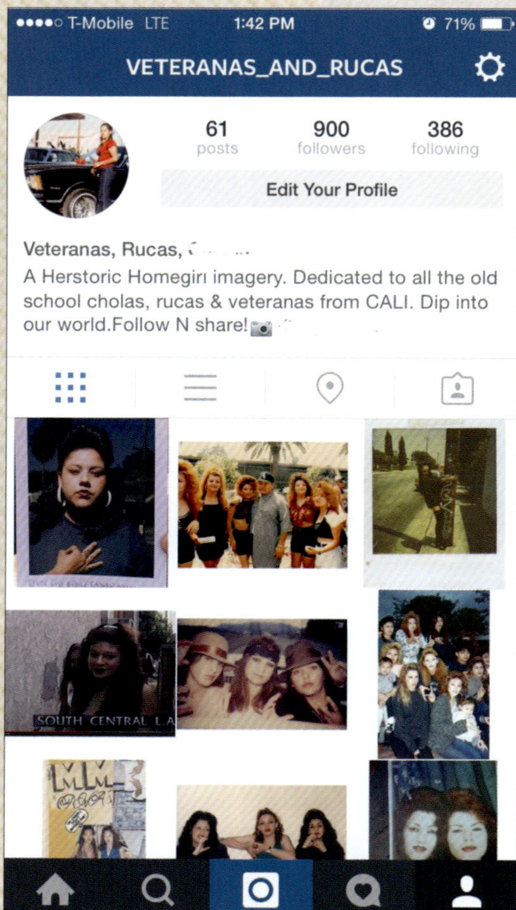

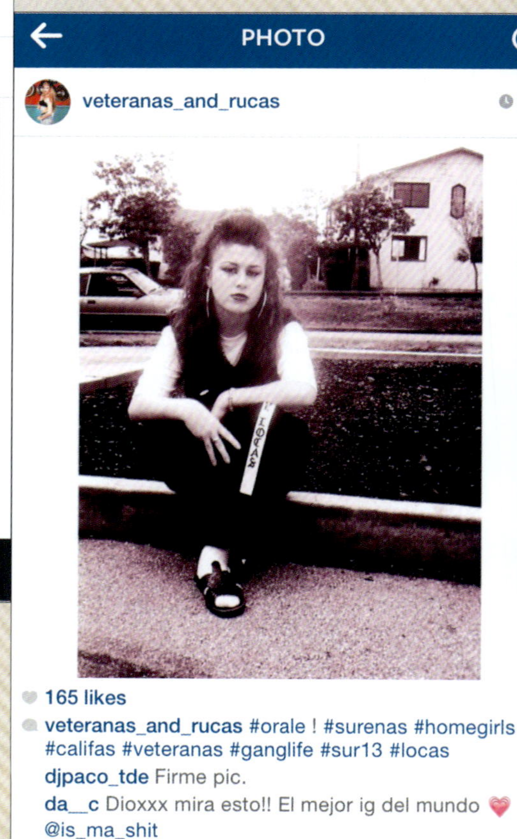

The beginning of
Veteranas and Rucas

VETERANAS AND RUCAS

THERE'S NO LINEAR ANSWER TO WHY I STARTED *VETERANAS and Rucas*. Maybe it's about my cousin—wanting to make sense of his death, I knew the facts but I wanted to put a name and a face back into the world in a humanizing way so he's not forgotten. Maybe it's about me—about trying to understand where I come from, my own upbringing, and why I've carried this feeling of being misrepresented for so long. Or maybe it's because I want a space where women who are like me—brown girls from L.A.—can see ourselves with pride and dignity, instead of as clichés or footnotes in someone else's version of the story.

Men have always had that space. They could tell their stories, show up with pride—good or bad—without anyone questioning their worth. For us, it was different. We were always being erased, misrepresented, shown as props or in the background. But in *Veteranas and Rucas,* the women were at the forefront, centered—our faces, our voices, our memories leading the way.

Growing up in Los Angeles at a time when gang and state violence was at its peak, it was only natural for us to normalize it, and we became desensitized to violence. Although I had been around violence all my life, when my cousin was murdered in 1996 something awakened in me, and I experienced a different type of pain than I had ever felt before.

If we lost someone to violence, the first thing we did was collect ourselves. We came together at someone's house, got drunk, cried. We just spent days together, sometimes weeks. Just telling stories or whatever needed to happen. That's how we healed. When my cousin died, I had family and friends who gathered in my home every day. We sat together quietly in the living room or on my porch at night until the sun came out. We reminisced and shared stories. When I think back on these gatherings, I realize that this was my first collective healing experience and that through that pain we were able to cultivate unforgettable and beautiful memories.

When I moved to New York and came of age away from the violence that had marked my youth, I held on to photographs of my family and friends. They were reminders of unresolved trauma and also important links to my past. I kept looking at these wallet-size photos and wondered how we could tell our own stories and find the agency to do so with a sense of belonging instead of feeling shame, especially we women. In New York, when I came out as queer and embraced my sexuality for the first time, my queerness allowed me to see these photos through a different lens—that identity is not linear, but layered and complex.

My queerness directed me to explore questions and revelations of my intersecting identities: What does intimacy look like under conditions of violence? How can community experience outshine oppressive conditions? Underneath the fashion and makeup, what did it mean to be a woman in this environment? My position, as someone who grew up in and maintains close ties to the Latino communities of East L.A., but who has spent a number of years at a distance, means that I can explore questions and perspectives that might otherwise be too difficult to engage with.

As an artist, my queerness granted me the freedom to look at things differently, to approach subjects and concepts with a more creative, open eye. I stopped viewing identity as something fixed or defined, and instead, I embraced the notion that identity—like art—is constantly evolving, often contradictory, and full of unexpected beauty—the moments that exist just beyond the surface. My queerness allows me to recognize these layers and to seek out the spaces where people's truest selves can emerge. My work is about honoring the contradictions and complexities of who we are, allowing the moments of vulnerability and strength to co-exist.

When I started the digital archives *Veteranas and Rucas* in 2015 and *Map Pointz* in 2016, words like "marginalized" and "underrepresented" were often used by academics to describe the communities and neighborhoods I grew up in. These words were new to me. Growing up, I felt the pride of my brown culture in East Los Angeles, where Latino communities are heavily represented. The pride was in the air, we carried it in our bodies and in our swag. In my home and among my friends, I felt *seen*. My home played mostly Spanish music, the restaurants served Mexican food. The markets catered to Latino families with their fresh tomatillos, chiles, carne from the carnicería. The music on the streets was anything from rap to banda.

The thought of being underrepresented never crossed my mind until I moved three thousand miles away from my Los Angeles neighborhood in 2000 and spent over a decade in New York. I began to notice the ways my community was overlooked and misconstrued by mainstream media. I began to research my own culture and to understand that deeply rooted communities had largely remained unrecognized at best, underrepresented and criminalized at worst.

Over time, I found that I wanted to connect with people who were like me, who understood the complexity and beauty in the communities that raised me, so I created these two community-generated archives where people like me had the agency to represent themselves the way they wanted to be represented. I didn't really know what to call it at first. I wasn't expecting it to go viral or become what it is now. I chose words that people from L.A.—especially Latino communities—would recognize right away. *Veteranas* was a reference to OG cholas, and *rucas* is an old-school term that goes back to the 1940s pachuco era, meaning girl or girlfriend. Over time, *Veteranas and Rucas* has evolved. It's not what it was when I started—it's changed, just like many of us have, but it still carries the same sentiment. It's true and real. I've thought about changing the name many times, but what's stopped me is how iconic it's become worldwide. I began by sharing my own story, in many cases with people whom I'd never met but who had similar stories to mine. I also reconnected with friends I hadn't seen or spoken to since high school. The more involved and serious the archival projects became, the more I discovered. In the years since, the archives have become a thriving site of collaboration and exchange, where images and narratives, memories, and anecdotes have been posted and shared, creating visibility and a sense of history for the participants.

It became a space where people could reflect on their own memories and find common ground in the stories that shaped them. It was about turning these memories into something more tangible, more meaningful. The digital archive has also become a way for lost friends and acquaintances to reconnect. I put up the images people submitted, and people would have a dialogue with one another in the comments section, whether they knew each other or they were strangers.

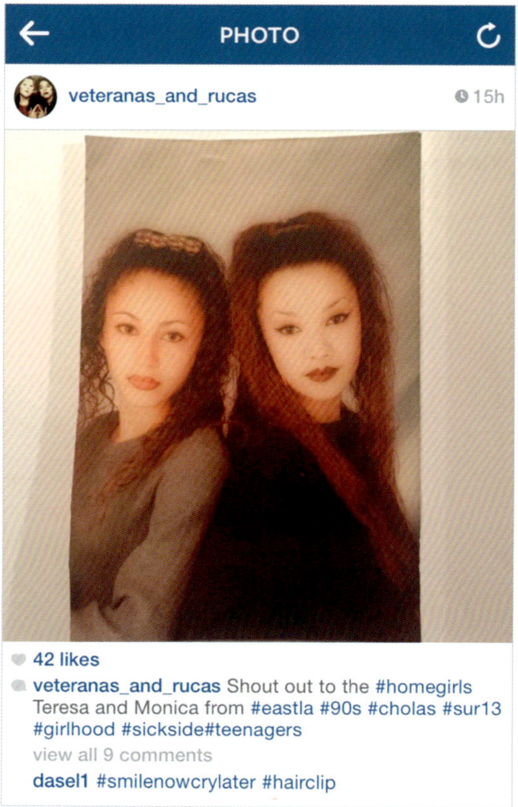

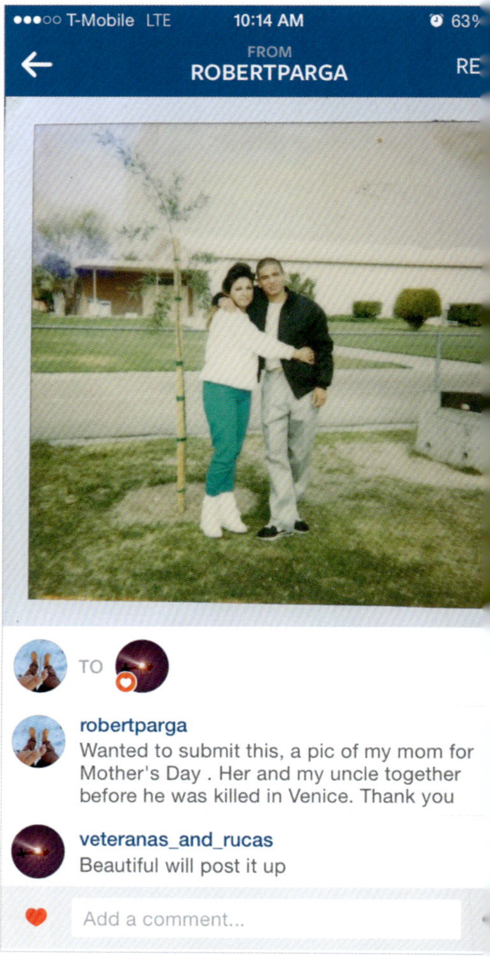

For the first year of *Veteranas and Rucas,* I posted three photo submissions a day. My strategy was to think of a common daily schedule: one in the morning around 8 A.M. right before work, one around noon (lunchtime), and the last one around 6 P.M., the time when people got home from work and could finally catch up with texts and social media. When I first started the page, people wanted to hear about me and my life, and I felt like, "Actually this is not about me." I wanted to offer this platform for the people. I mean, I posted one image of myself, but I don't know. It just felt weird. I'm also shy.

When *Veteranas and Rucas* first started to circulate widely, it wasn't because of just one post going viral. I had started the conversation around something deeply familiar to me and to so many others, yet it had never been spoken about publicly in this way. People who knew nothing about brown L.A. culture were being exposed to something new and different. For the first time, we were naming our culture as part of history, as memory. Mainstream outlets like the BBC, KQED, and others began reaching out, but when they covered the project they almost always used words like "gangs" or "gang lifestyle." No one outside of those who were part of the party-crew scene really knew how to approach this history or how to name it, so "gang" became the easiest description.

That was only a portion of reality. What I was showing was something beyond that: the underground worlds of raves and party crews, the ways sisterhood and friendship took shape, and the complicated realities of our youth. The risks young women took and experienced. The beauty of coming together even in the most tragic moments. It was like putting together a love song and a rap verse—intimate, raw, and honest—showing the beauty and complexity of lives that had always been flattened or erased.

A few months after I launched *Veteranas and Rucas,* people started catching on. The account had gone from 9,003 followers on June 16, 2015, to 12K by July 18, then 12.1K the next day. People began to engage on my platform and tag friends with messages like "Did you see this IG?"

I don't remember which posts got the most attention—there were too many to keep track of—but I do remember when my interview with *LA Weekly* came out on November 6, 2015. That article from a beloved Los Angeles publication ignited a wave of recognition: It felt like my city was seeing me. I woke up that morning in my Brooklyn apartment to find my phone blowing up—notifications, messages, and a flood of new followers. After that, the account reached 33.4K by the end of November. I suddenly felt the project shift into another realm. What had started as a small gesture—an offering to memory, to my community—had become something much larger, something people everywhere were connecting to and wanted to be a part of.

I was still in New York when my relationship to East L.A shifted. It was becoming about connection, memory, and how those stories moved between me and others. I started to recognize my own history inside the stories people shared with me, as if we were building a collective memory together. That's what *Veteranas* did—it opened up a new way of seeing my city and connected strangers who felt like kin because of what we carried.

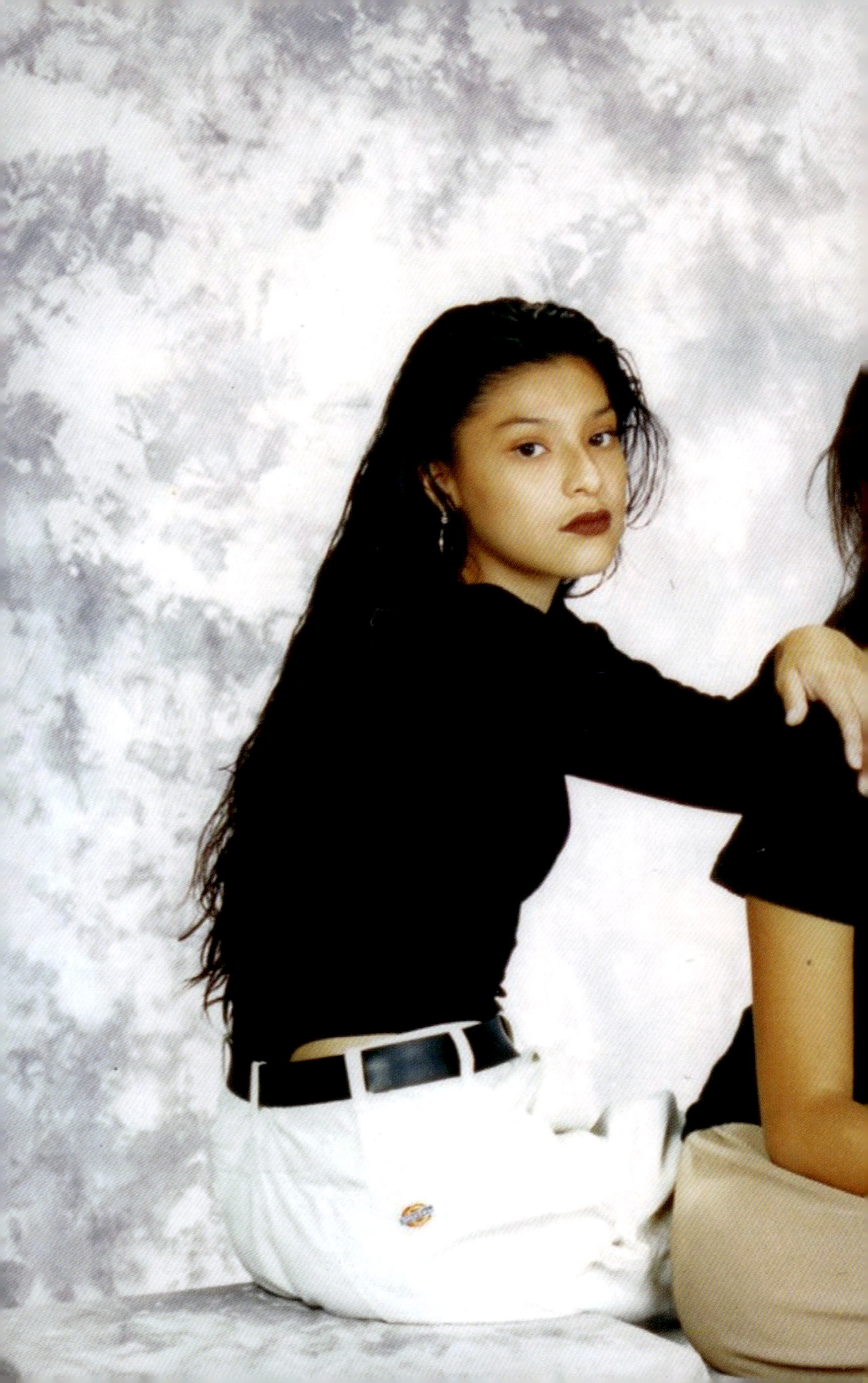

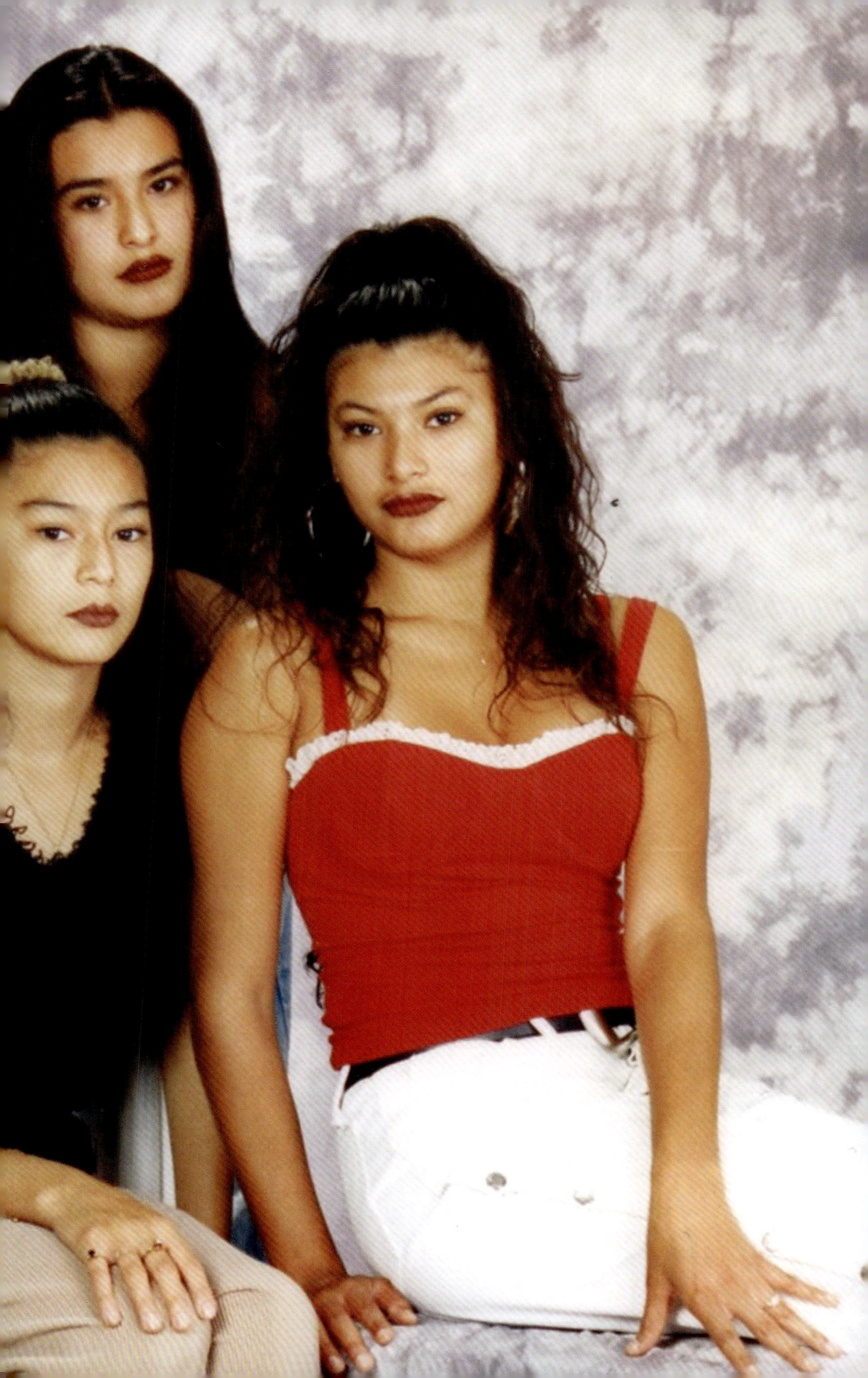

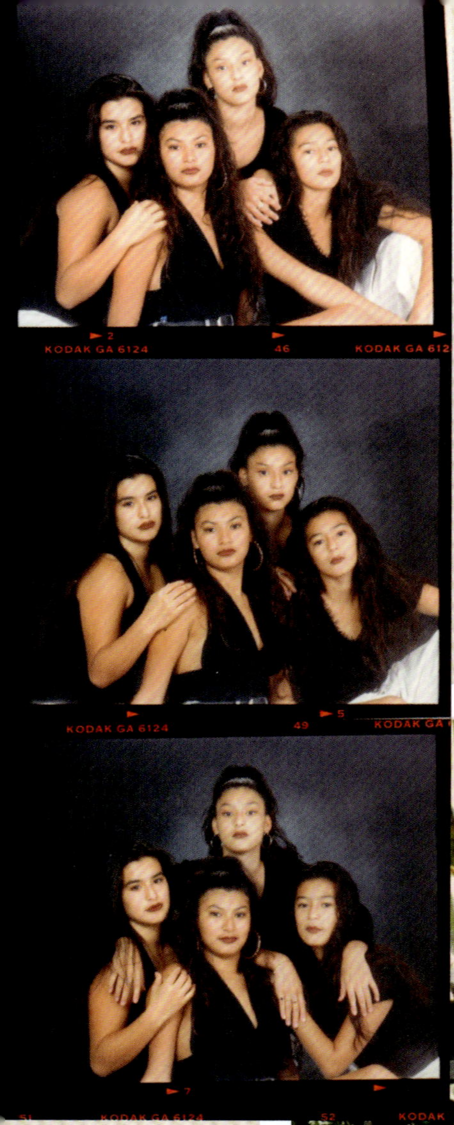

PREVIOUS, LEFT, and BELOW: Firme Hinas/ Cifuentes sisters

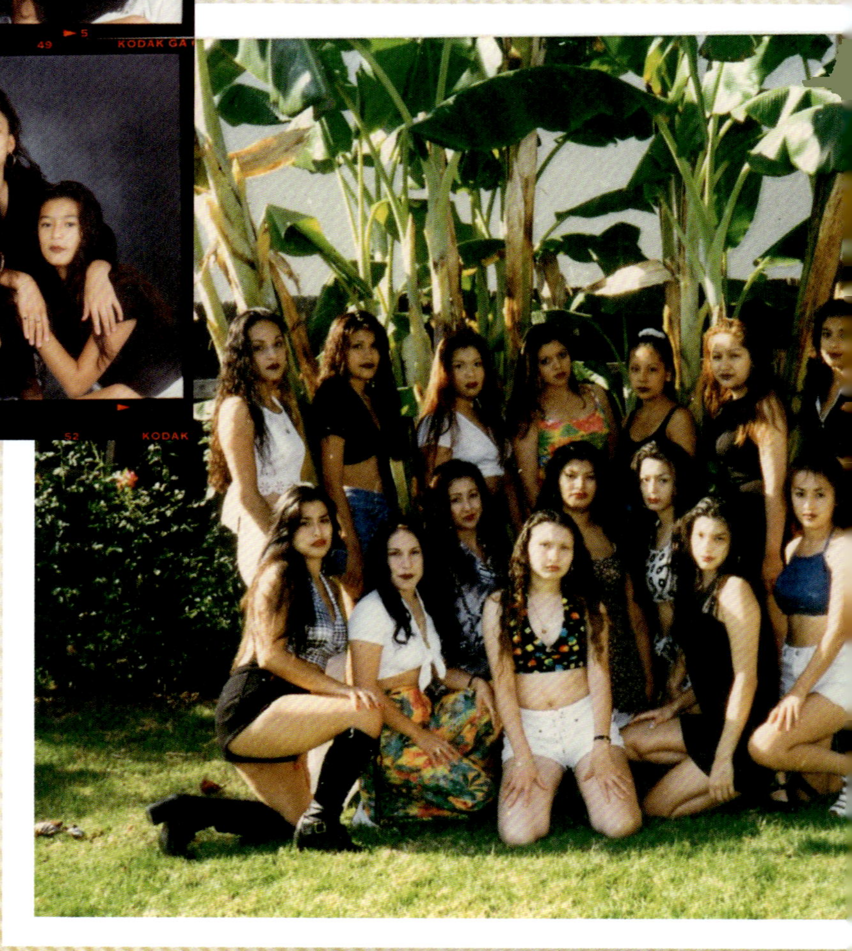

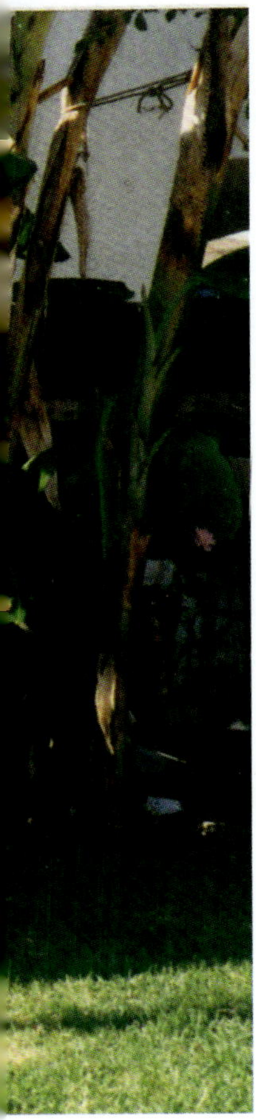

LOOKING FOR A FIRME HINA

FIRME HINAS WAS AN ALL-FEMALE PARTY CREW from the Westside (West L.A.) with thirty-plus members. Their name was inspired by musical rap group Proper Dos's song "Firme Hina." I was still living in New York but beginning to visit Los Angeles to reconnect with my family when I received a message from Nancy. I opened my DMs and saw a message that read:

> Hello my name is Nancy and I used to be from a party crew my sister and I made up called Firme Hinas back in 1994. I'm the one in the middle bottom wearing black shorts and the one on the right is my sister Kim. On the left is my sister Brandy and top is Michelle. We are all sisters. Kim says she texted you once before. She is the one who drew all the flyers. LOL. here is a picture of us back in the party crew days.
>
> —*Nancy*

A few weeks later, Nancy's sister Kim reached out and submitted one of her photos, and we connected immediately. Not long after, Nancy, Kim, their younger sister Brandy, and I started a group chat in our DMs. For weeks straight, we'd stay up talking for hours. I enjoyed talking with all of them, but Kim and I sparked a special bond.

Although she is a couple of years older than me and grew up a few miles away (she moved around a lot but mostly lived in Inglewood), we had so much in common. I love thinking about that—how people can be complete strangers in this world yet live such parallel experiences.

Sometimes Kim and I stayed up 'til three o'clock in the morning sharing stories, sending each other photos, and sharing some of the most beautiful and tragic memories. We spoke openly about boys, gangs, getting into fights and brawls, being part of a party crew, and sneaking out of the house. Many times we hesitated to share details of these memories and of friends we lost to gang violence. We questioned whether it was safe to talk about it now after all these years but never doubted each other.

There was trust the first time we interacted. It all had to do with knowing what we shared. She knew I was real and not someone pretending. I knew exactly what she meant every time she shared a moment with me, and she understood mine as well. We talked about music, about those times on the boulevard, and what it felt like to be out there as young Latinas in this big city of Los Angeles.

Sometimes, though, there were things I had never experienced and were new to me. For example, I have never seen anyone die right in front of me, let alone a lover. But for Kim, that is exactly what she had to witness on one tragic sunny Sun-

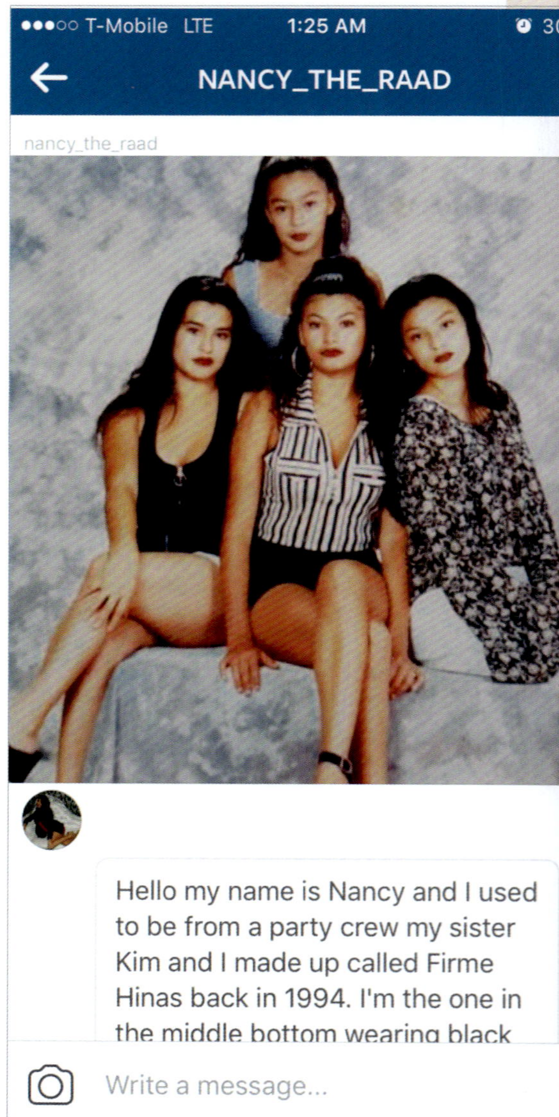

Nancy from Firme Hinas's first DM, circa 2016

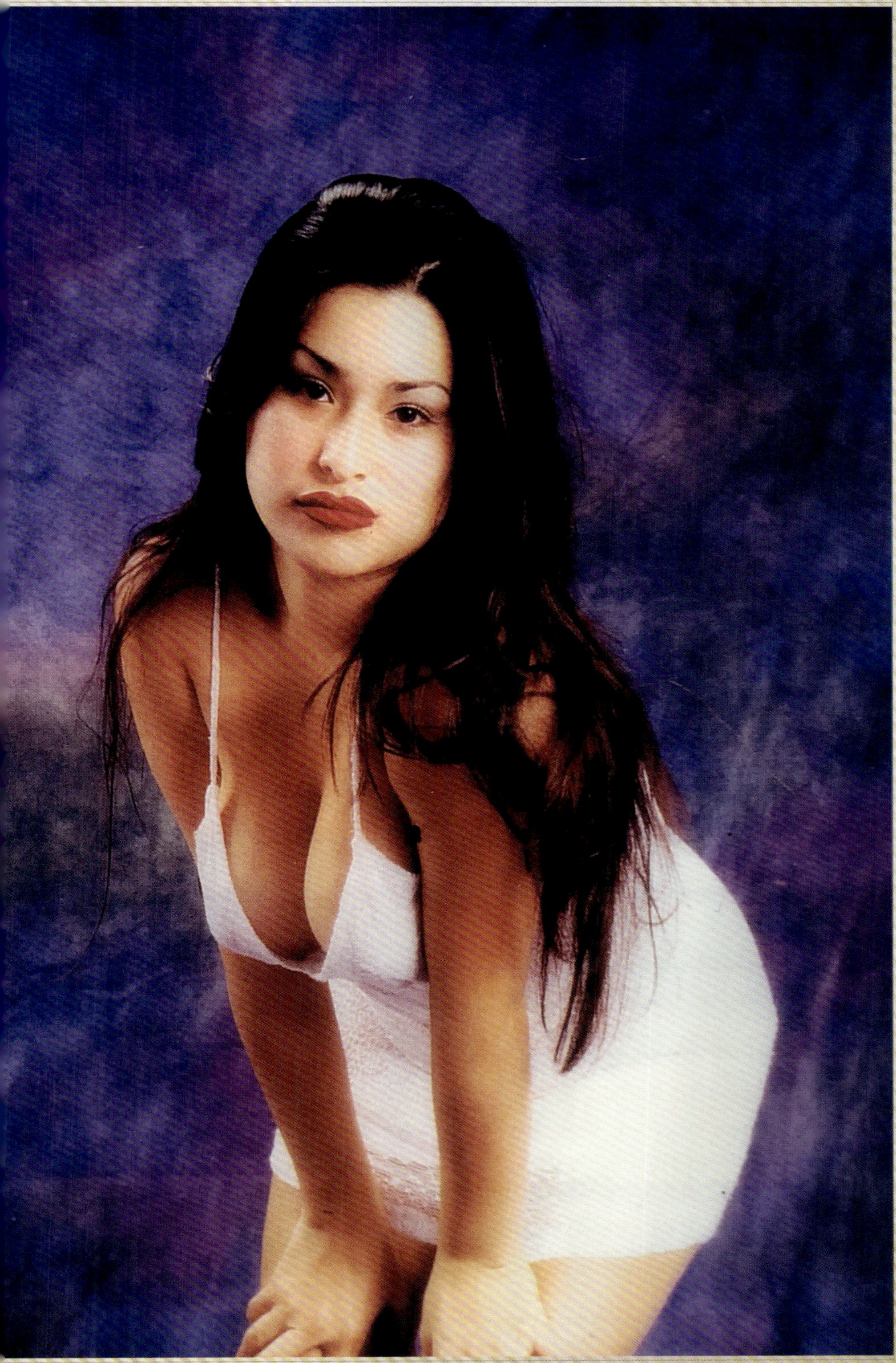

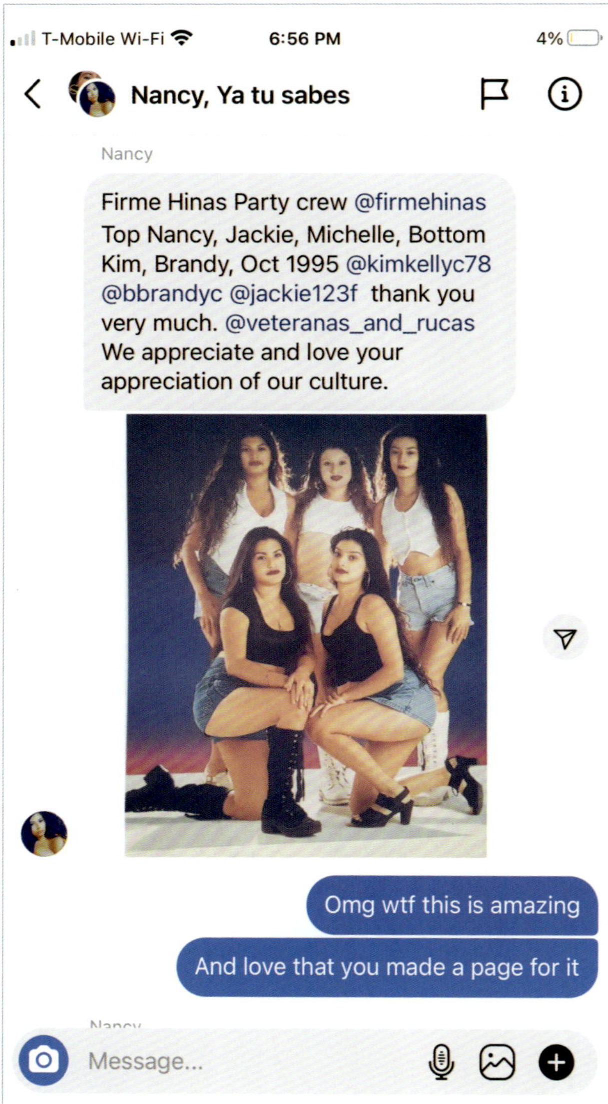

day morning. There was also a sense of relief or recognition and understanding of each other: We wanted to connect and share everything about our past. It was exciting and new, because she and I had never experienced this sense of understanding from a stranger—and most important for me, from a woman who wasn't my sister or my mother or my friend from school. Sometimes I'd fall asleep midsentence because I didn't want to stop engaging. About a week into our DM sessions, we finally decided to exchange phone numbers.

EVERY PHOTO THE sisters shared with me was followed with a story: *This one was at a BBQ in 1994. I think this is a gangster party.* Or *This was at my homegirl's baby shower.*

They showed me images of the most beautiful girls. Five of them were sisters. Their photos reminded me of my own. Sometimes of the girls I wish I could have been. They were tough, gangster, and beautiful. It felt like we had known one another for decades. It was the first time I chose to meet someone face-to-face, guided by the deep connection we had already formed online. We felt like sisters. They opened up to me and I did to them.

We spoke through Instagram for some weeks before connecting in person. Eventually, Kim's youngest sister, Brandy, invited me over for a barbecue at her house in Lynwood.

I arrived and they greeted me like I was one of them, like a sister or a friend they had known since their teenage years. I cracked open a beer and sat outside with them while their boyfriends cooked up a meal on the grill. It was hot that day, but I could feel the ocean breeze in the air. When it got dark out, we went back inside and sat on the couch while a football game played on the television. Kim spoke over the television with excitement, sharing countless stories about her teenage years. The first story was about one of the worst brawls she'd been in with her two sisters and a rival party crew. Recounting the memory, Kim swung in the air with her fists and eyes closed as we all laughed, and I was using my imagination now that I had a face to put into these stories.

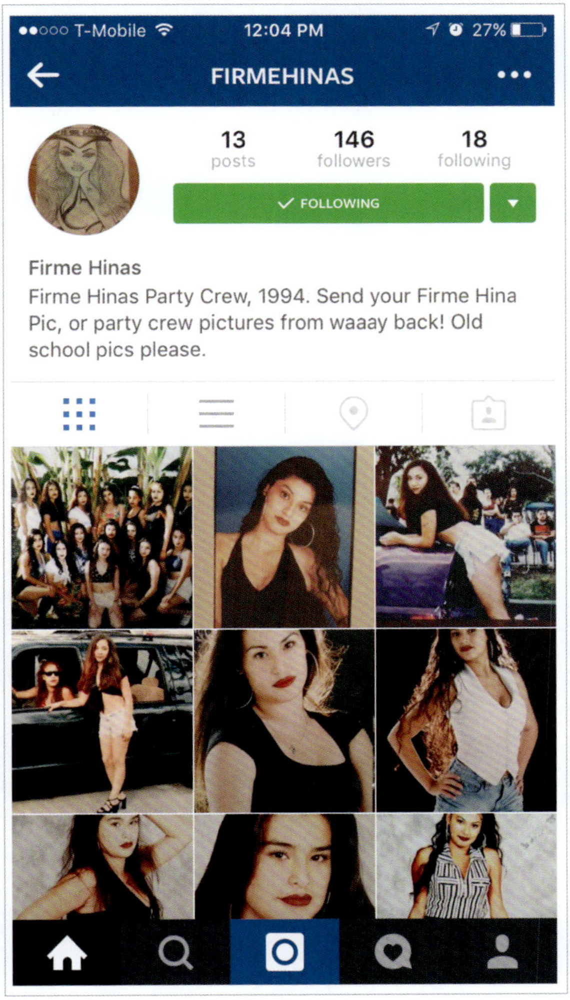

Firme Hinas Instagram

KIM TOLD US she'd jumped into the fight because her sister was getting beaten up. Kim was almost knocked unconscious. She remembered being pulled off the ground by one of her friends. Kim kept telling them to leave her alone because she wanted to go to sleep. She had no clue what had just happened. Her friends had to drag her out.

THIS WAS THE beginning of many hangouts with Firme Hinas. Kim and I quickly became close friends. We both shared stories that made us cry and laugh. Weeks after that first meeting, she sent me a private message. "Lupe, I have trash bags full of photos from back in the day." She invited me over, and together we went through her collection of photos. Many beautiful ones. Some taken at house parties, some taken at funerals. Many Starshot photos of her with friends and lovers, taken at photo studios. Photos friends had given her with notes written on the back.

Kim told me, "Lupe, I was about to throw the bags filled with photos away. But your work inspired me not to. Instead I am holding on to them." Kim put them back in the closet. A week later, I saw a new account on Instagram named "Firme Hinas" with a DM saying "Lupe! It's Kim! I decided to start a page dedicated to Firme Hinas chaaaauu!" Kim began her page in 2017, posting images from her personal archives.

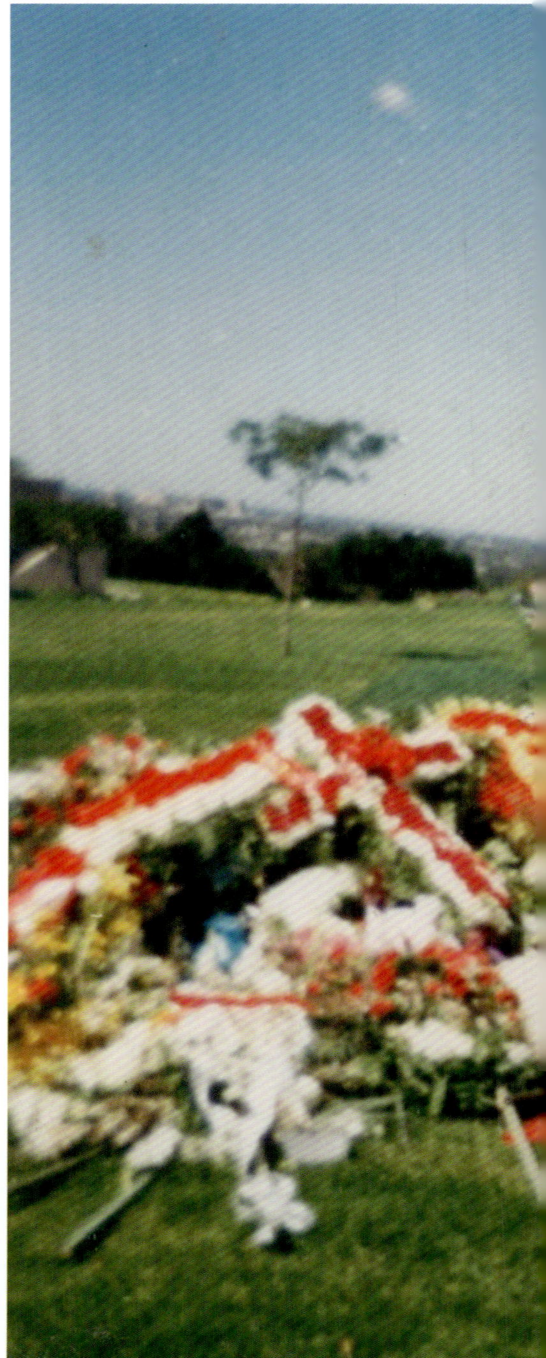

Firme Hinas at a friend's funeral around 1994/1995

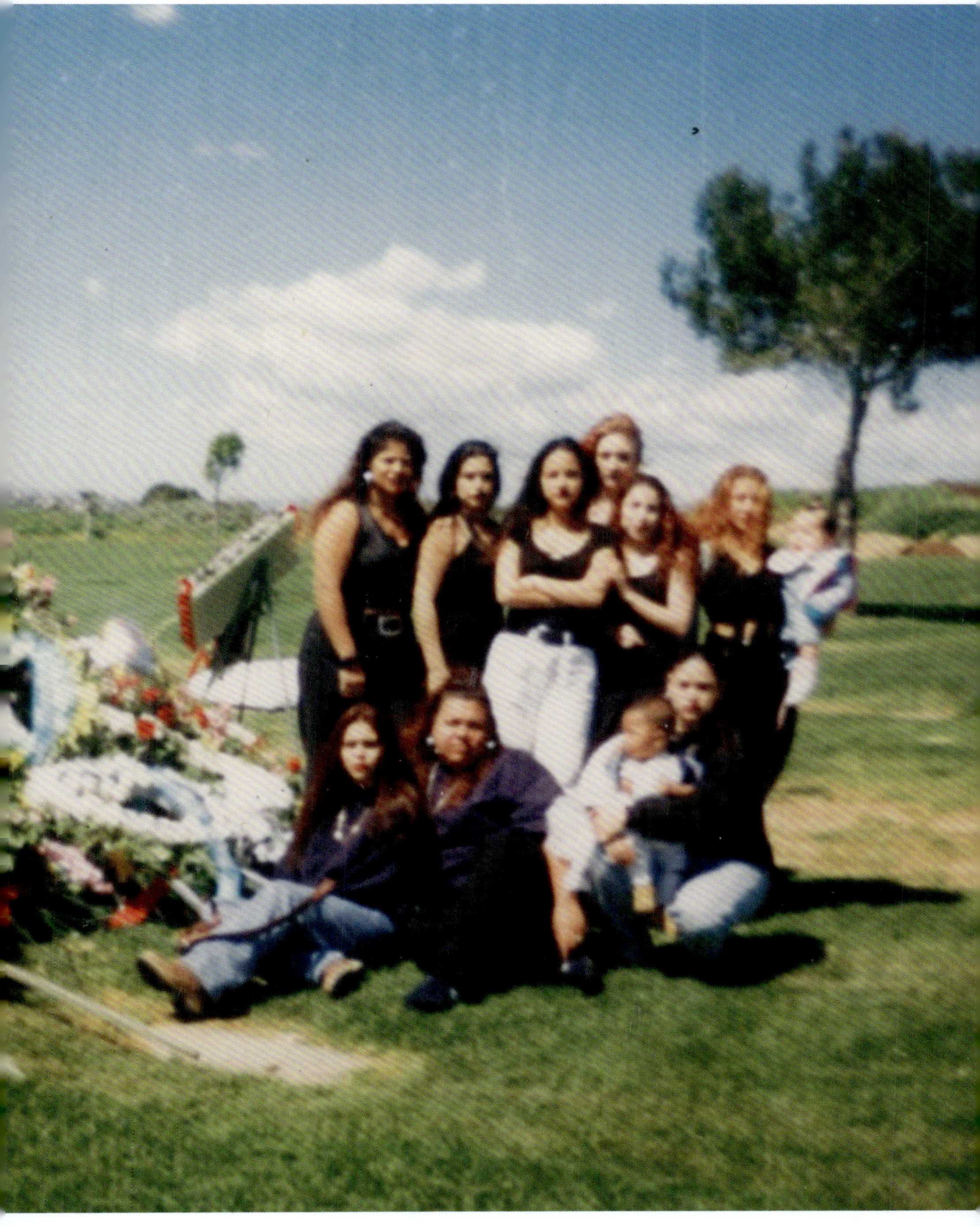

VALLEYWIDE FOCUS

VAN NUYS

Police See Deadly Message in T-Shirt

To the unknowing eye, the T-shirts reading "187 Hudda" may seem harmless. But the shirts are considered anything but to police and school officials who have banned students from wearing them.

While the literal translation of the shirt is the police code for homicide ("187") followed by gang slang for police ("hudda"), many Valley police, school officials and gang experts see it another way: "Murder a Cop."

"We don't like them. Absolutely not," said Sgt. Ed Brayton of the Van Nuys police station.

But Ruben Laguna, owner of the Los Angeles clothing store that created the shirt, disagrees. "It's probably being misinterpreted," said Laguna, who insists that the shirt's logo simply states the police code for homicide. "I'll tell you one thing—if I wanted to say 'Go out and kill cops'—I would do that. Because that's my right."

At least two schools, Taft High School in Woodland Hills and Cleveland High School in Reseda, have made students remove the shirts or turn them inside out.

"We have a rule that says 'appropriate school attire.' That's not 'appropriate school attire,'" said Everett Macy, dean

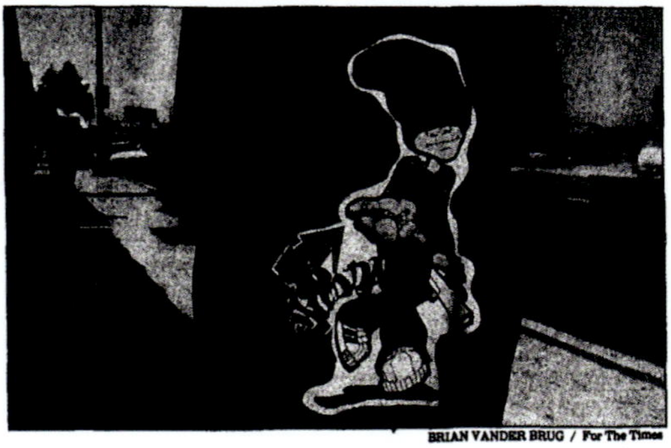

BRIAN VANDER BRUG / For The Times

Some believe that this T-shirt logo means cop killer in street slang.

of students at Cleveland High.

A number of trendy stores in the Valley—Odd Spot 23 in Tarzana and Behind the Groove in San Fernando—have turned down offers to sell the shirts. That does not stop youths from going into Hollywood to buy them, even though some have no idea of the statement that their fashion is making.

Such wa... woman cau... if she knew... she laughed...

no idea."

When told how police interpreted the shirt, the woman's smile faded.

"I don't want to wear it any more. I'm all shocked," said the woman, who asked not to be identified.

Meanwhile, Laguna is expecting to come out with a new shirt that promises to stir up more controversy. It's called

Conference Planned for Latino Students

Catherine Campos, the ninth-grad class president at Sepulveda Junio High School, hopes to beef up he leadership and public speaking skill when she attends a conference for 24 Latino middle school students fror across the San Fernando Valley o Saturday.

"It gives you so much confidence," said Catherine, who learned about par liamentary procedures during a simila conference last year.

The conference at Porter Junior Hig School in Granada Hills is co-sponsore by the San Fernando Valley chapter o Future Leaders of America, a nonprof organization that encourages Latin students to become student leaders volunteer in their communities an finish school. The organization als sponsors a weeklong conference fo about 45 students every summer at Santa Barbara camp, which Catherin attended last year.

Sylvia Guzman, who serves as th chapter's regional director with he husband, Carlos, said the one-day even will feature workshops on assertiveness self-esteem and goal-setting, all aime... ...ntial schoo

...ALENCIA

Newspaper article about 187 Hudda, circa 1993

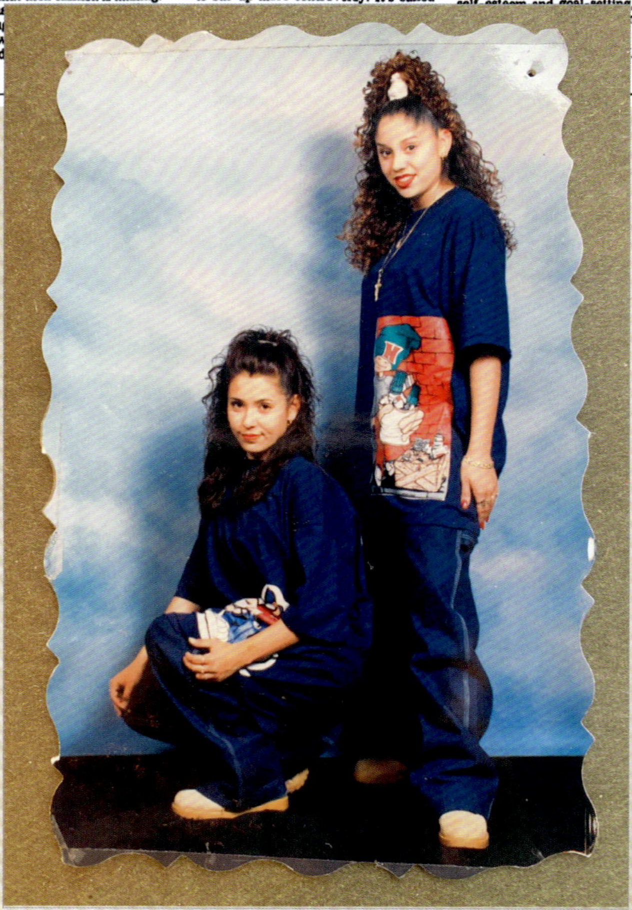

Veronica and Yanira wearing 187 Hudda

STYLE WARS

WHEN I WAS GROWING UP, POLICE HARASSMENT and brutality were ever present, and so was our resentment of the cops; this was the era of the Rampart scandal, when seventy cops were indicted for police brutality and planting evidence. In the 1990s, a street brand called 187 Hudda came out with shirts that eventually got banned from both schools and the streets. 187 Hudda—slang for "kill" (187) the cops (hudda)—made headlines in 1993.

"We don't like them. Absolutely not," said Sergeant Ed Brayton of the Van Nuys police station in 1993. Everett Macy, dean of students at Cleveland High, said, "We have a rule that says 'appropriate school attire.' That's not appropriate school attire."

Brands like 187 Hudda were embraced by youth as a marker of style and counterculture resistance, and hated by others.

From the beginning of *Veteranas and Rucas,* my intention wasn't just to highlight cholos and cholas, but to expand the picture. I didn't know how that would take shape. I wanted to dive into the lesser-known subcultures that shaped us—like the raves and Latino party crews. They were heavily documented in the '90s by partygoers, *Street Beat Magazine, Party-Time! Magazine, URB,* etc., but they're almost never talked about now.

The page started with images of style and everyday life, but as I reflected more on my own upbringing, I began connecting to deeper stories. If I was going to talk about heavier subjects, I wanted to ground them in the world I knew. Style became a way into those conversations. One of the first posts I made along those lines was about 187 Hudda, then called Sucker Brand, a street brand that turned our reality with police harassment into something you could wear. Over time, I kept returning to fashion and subcultures as both a form of memory and a lens to rethink how we were represented. I also used *Map Pointz* to investigate these themes.

Map Pointz captures a generation that came up in the underground party scene, kids in their bedrooms getting ready to go out or posing in front of apartment buildings, alleys, or massive speaker stacks, repping their crews with custom embroidered hats they designed themselves. The style was its own language. Unlike the "candy raver" look people often associate with that era, the Eastside scene had its own vibe, more like taggers than ravers. Baggy jeans, Adidas, white tees, and baseball caps. There was a strong connection between graffiti culture and the rave world; both were built from the streets up.

Aesthetically, *Map Pointz* was nothing like the glossy clubs or stadium raves you'd see in magazines. Everything about it was raw, streetwise, and DIY. The photos and stories on *Map Pointz* document a generation moving through East L.A.—dodging gangs, cops, and everything in between just to carve out their own space. A world that was underground, creative, and completely their own.

There are many subcultures and lifestyles that embraced the baggy look. For the more gangster look it was Ben Davis, Dickies, hoodies, and football jerseys, creased up and paired with clean sneakers. If you were a tagger, a graffiti artist, or a "tagbanger" (a cross between a tagger and a cholo), the look was also baggy, but the pants and shirts weren't creased up. They were smooth and a little less clean-cut. All these lifestyles and looks were beginning to merge and overlap to the point that even the police couldn't differentiate between a cholo and a tagger or a hip-hop head.

For teenage girls, the 1990s was an era of thin eyebrows, dark lipstick with a heavy outline around the lips, big hair, and, of course, oversized clothing. Femininity is not what it used to be, and wearing oversized clothing was the new trend, making many people uncomfortable. The definition of womanhood had a new meaning and look. In many ways it was more about the attitude and how one carried oneself than what one

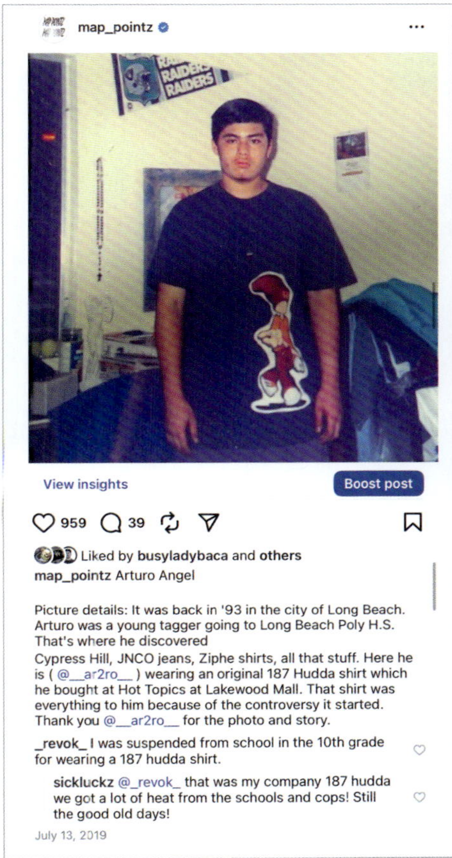

Map Pointz post

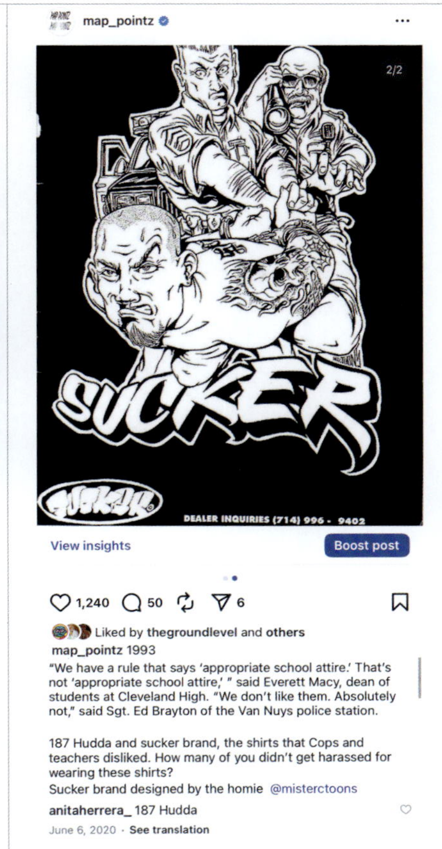

Map Pointz Sucker Brand post

wore. The traditional aesthetics and ideologies were being challenged by brown youth.

A beautiful young woman could choose what to wear and how much or little makeup to wear. We wore baggy clothes, felt sexy in them, and owned it as we walked down the street with pride. This was the time when girls wore baggy pants with a cropped tank top and a dolled-up feminine face. Our pants were big, sometimes size 40, and boys found this attractive. We carried this swag with confidence. Wearing boy clothes doesn't take away the sexiness or femininity of young girls. A young woman can be sexy, feminine, and tough all at once. We were refining what womanhood looks like.

The older generation like our parents, schoolteachers, and police would say that women should not wear pants, especially baggy pants. Women should smile, not show too much skin, and wear dresses and

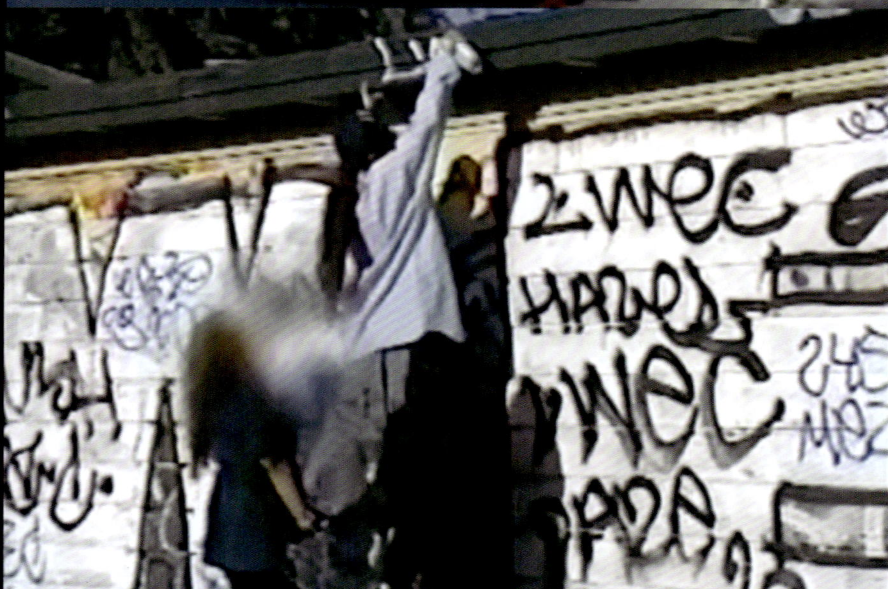

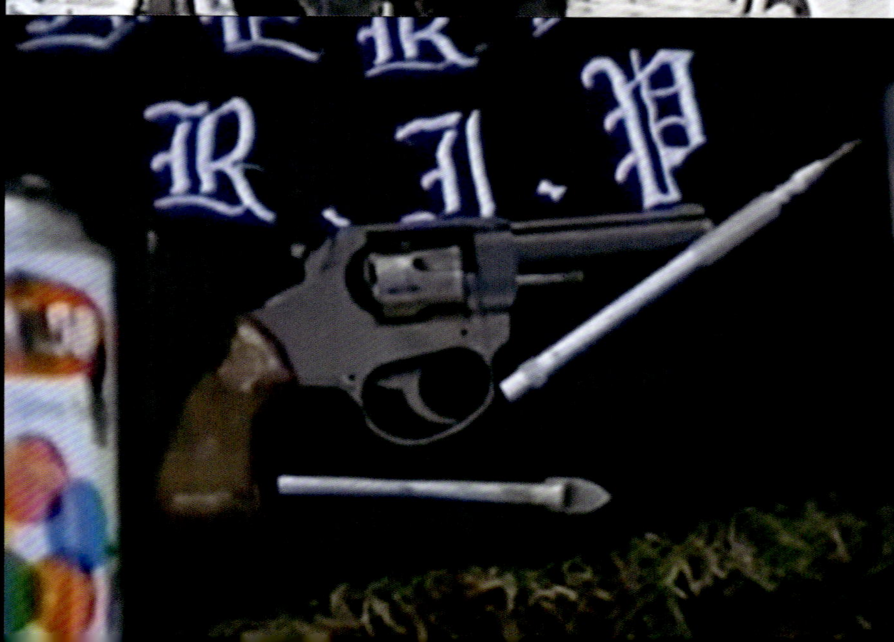
R.I.P

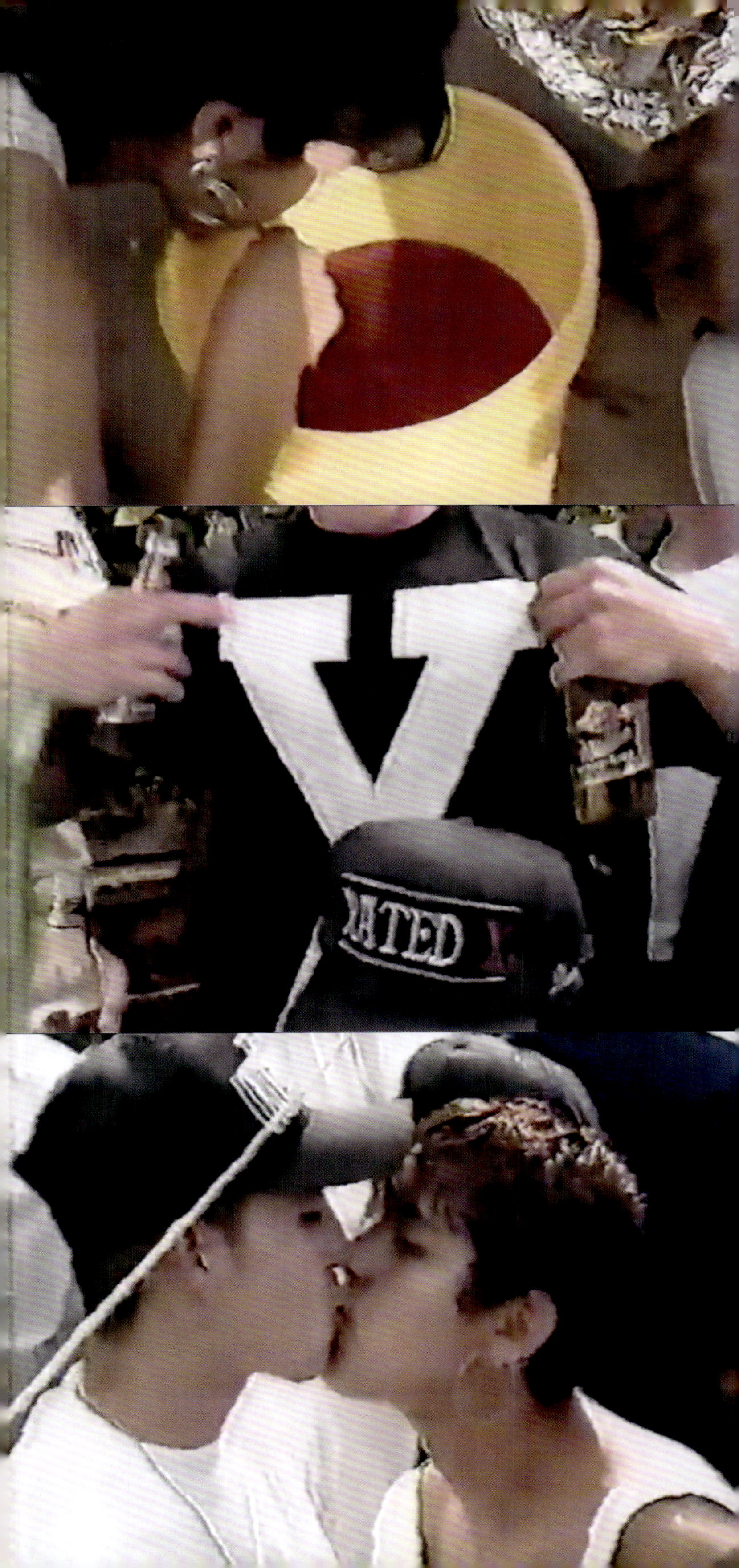

skirts. This is a conventional, old-school mentality that is quickly being left behind.

The clothes were comfortable and (gender) fluid. We could also easily walk into a liquor store and throw a few forty-ounce beers in our pants. Running from the police was a bit complicated, but one could just lift the baggy pants, like pulling up a long, flowy skirt, in order not to trip over them or get caught on a fence.

The baggy look traced back to the pachuco era, which had roots in places like El Paso, Texas, and Harlem, New York. Wearing wide-legged zoot suits was a statement of pride and resistance—a way of standing out and taking up space. Over time, that style evolved into the working-class uniforms of Dickies and Ben Davis—creased, oversized, and carried on through the cholo aesthetic. By the time it reached my generation, that look was still alive, reshaped but never gone. We wore it our own way, without even realizing we were carrying pieces of that same history. My brother Gus once told me that in prison he'd put his pants under his mattress so they had a crease, because the inmates didn't have access to an iron. But now on the streets, the baggy clothes were more about practicality, comfort, and fashion. Nike Cortez sneakers fit perfectly into a chain-link fence, making it easy to jump over. The shoelaces were always tucked between the tongue and woven laces so they didn't touch the ground. We called that bunny ears.

We made something out of nothing, as they say. Being poor made us creative in many ways. We rarely bought new clothes. The first time I ever wore baggy clothes was when my brother let me borrow his Cypress Hill shirt. When I first wore that shirt, I paired it with some raw-denim 501 Levi's that I stole from my brother while he was in school. He was in high school and I was in middle school, so he never got to see me wear his clothes.

I'd rather borrow or take my older brother's hand-me-downs over clothes from my sisters, who are only a year or two apart and for the most part wore little shorts and cute tops. That wasn't my style; I felt more comfortable wearing boys' clothes. There were times when I was called a tomboy, but that didn't stop me from dressing this way. I didn't wear makeup, but I did have long hair down to my ass, which made me seem feminine. For the young women wearing baggy clothes, there always had to be something feminine, whether it was makeup, a top, or a cute hairdo.

It makes me think of the discrimination against pachucos and what sparked the zoot suit—high-waisted pants with baggy, pegged legs and a long coat with wide lapels—popular among young Mexican American and Filipino American men in California during the war years, around 1943. The zoot suit was more than a fashion statement. It was part of an identity that signaled a youthful pride in belonging to a pachuco culture that embraced style and swagger—statements that challenged discriminatory "Juan Crow" laws and practices that often limited the rights of Mexican American men.

For the hundreds of predominantly Mexican American victims of what became known as the Zoot Suit Riots of 1943, a jacket and a pair of pants marked them as criminals for white service members and civilians searching for someone to blame for the city's inability to keep up with its growing population. That violence in Los Angeles was the product of rising racial tensions brought on by a variety of wartime factors, but it was their fashion that marked Mexican Americans as targets, in some of the ways that my generation faced decades later.

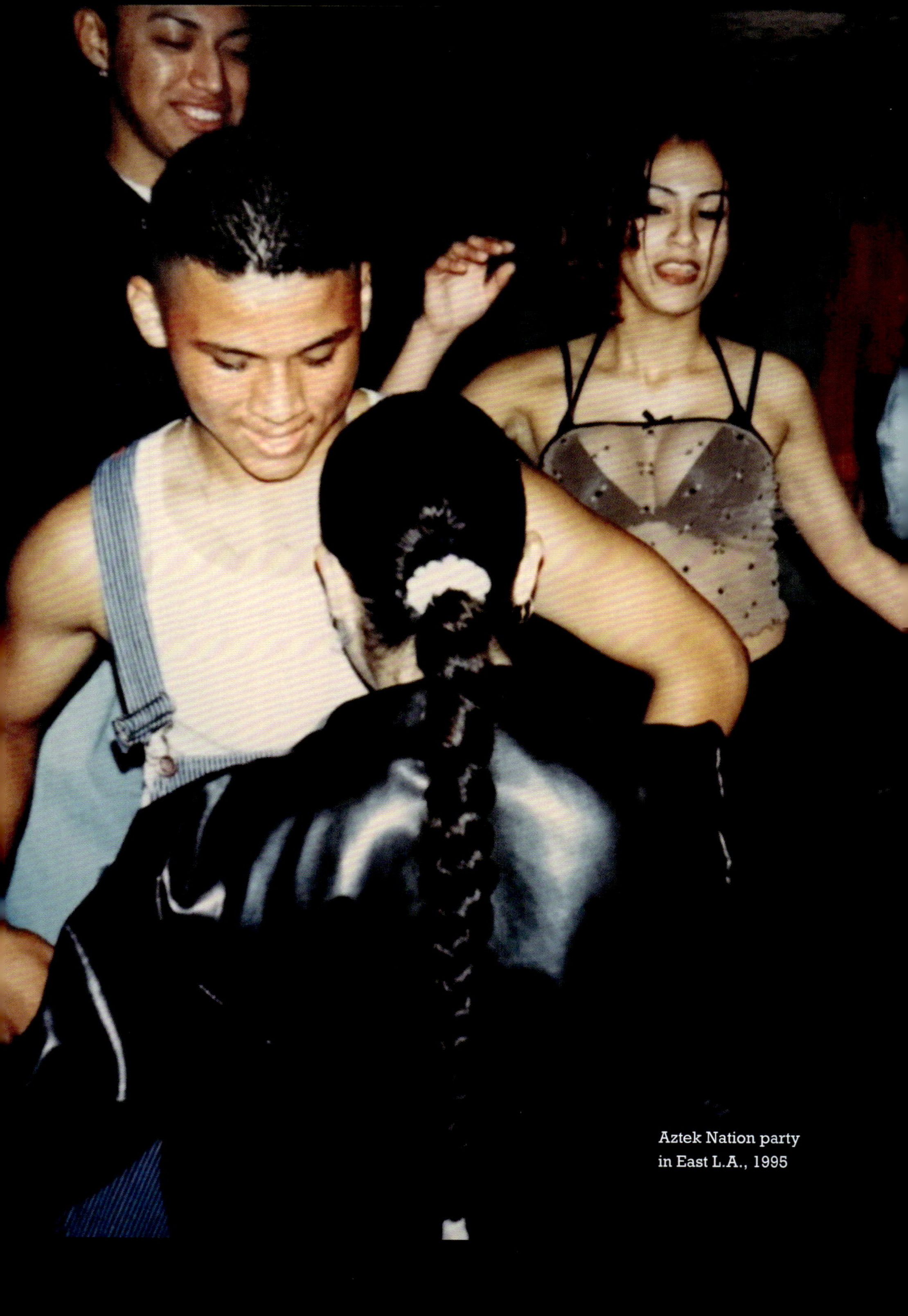

Aztek Nation party
in East L.A., 1995

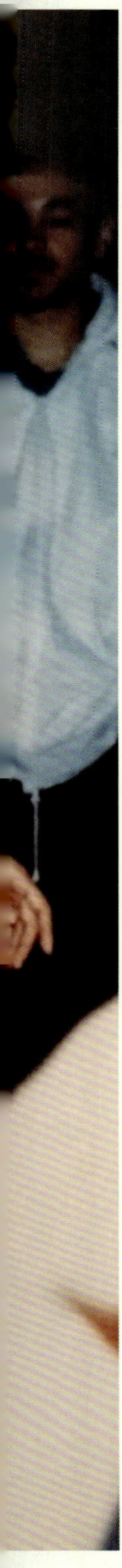

DIY

***VETERANAS* WAS A DO-IT-YOURSELF PROJECT,** and I also learned as this work developed. I'm not a historian or an archivist, but what motivated me was how little our history was being preserved. *Veteranas* was a community-generated archive built from the ground up with our collective memories: People submitted their photographs and stories, and their contributions were the engine for the account. It felt like the preservation of our history had stopped in the 1980s and anything from the 1990s was neglected: the DIY spaces, the music, and the politics besides the 1992 uprising. When I looked up "raves" and "party cultures," the internet was plastered with white teenage kids. This was not my experience.

As I began to collect materials, I was just really interested in preserving the physical flyers, photos, and magazines. When I was visiting L.A., I had already been contacted by strangers who were interested in donating flyers. I would meet them in random places like gas stations and parking lots. In 2016, a woman named Michelle met with me and donated her photo album. I went to UCLA, home to the Chicano Studies Research Center, and shared the magazines, photo albums, and flyers I had been collecting. I told them that the material was all strictly underground L.A. 1990s stuff that I hadn't seen on the internet or in libraries, and that I needed help finding a language to make it accessible.

It's funny, because I went to them for help, but they ended up asking me to help them discuss it. I perceived a gap in their archive, and that pushed me to take the project into my own hands and do the work. Also, looking at how they were making their archive accessible—people had to wear gloves and ask permission to look at things—I felt that there was a great sense of care, but also that it was very sterile and scientific, and limited. I wasn't interested in that. I was interested in having something more engaging, while teaching others how to care for their own materials and perhaps hold workshops and events. Hold space for discussions around the archive and share stories and ephemera. I wanted to make it more accessible to those who had lived it.

As an artist, I use the creative space to put the archive out into the world. But I did have this push-and-pull experience where I questioned myself, wondering: Am I damaging the archive somehow by using it in my practice and therefore making it accessible? Many seemed to have left it in the past. Dusting it off and talking about it twenty years later, I'm glad I was able to bring it back to the surface.

At a certain point, I wanted to move these conversations offline, into a space where people could come together face-to-face. That's why I organized a panel at UCLA's Chicano Studies department with former party-crew members, editors from *Street Beat Magazine,* and DJs who had been part of that world. I started the event with one of Fox News channel's local reports, which painted party crews as promiscuous criminals. I then opened the discussion by sharing my own memories of the party-crew scene—what it meant to us and also how it was portrayed in the media. TV outlets like Fox News had gone undercover to film these spaces, framing us as criminal, dangerous, or simply reckless. The panelists were Rachael Ortiz, aka "Flame" from Aztek Nation, Carlos "Exit" Landeros, Michael Rodriguez from Latin Underground, DJ Manuel Corral, aka "Dose" & "Deluxe," and Eileen "Michele" Torres, editor of *Street Beat Magazine.* The event was moderated by Sandra Ruiz, visiting lecturer in the departments of Chicana/o Studies and Spanish and Portuguese.

RACHAEL: "Absolutely do it yourself, because none of this was authorized. We didn't have permission to go in that backyard. . . . You figure it out, you get it done. It wasn't just you by yourself—it was somebody, and somebody, and somebody—and before you know it, you have a good night."

RACHAEL: "We built our own go-go boxes, did security ourselves, made our flyers, even distressed our own jeans . . . everything was DIY. It was about power in numbers, about showing that we could create these spaces ourselves."

RACHAEL: "We made mistakes, we learned, and it was ours. That hands-on, do-it-yourself approach shaped the culture."

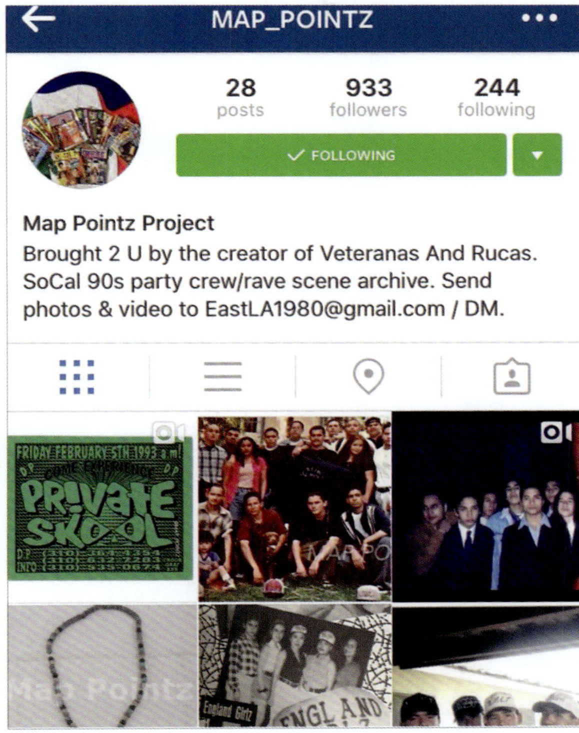

The beginning of *Map Pointz*

What happened in that room was powerful. People spoke about the parties as spaces of innovation and imagination, where young people—many of us dealing with poverty, gang violence, or family struggles—built something beautiful together. We talked about designing flyers, booking DJs, and creating makeshift venues out of backyards, garages, and warehouses.

Michele, the editor at *Street Beat Magazine,* said, "I personally wasn't involved in the party scene . . . but I admired it at the time. Kids would put all the flyers on their notebooks with the clear plastic covers—you were cool if you had them. I probably did it, too, even though I never went to a party. I was just curious.

"Every time I look at the photographs now, I wonder: Where are they now? What are they doing? That excitement, that sense of possibility—it was amazing to see."

The contrast between those memories and the way the media covered us was stark. Where the news saw gangs and danger, we remembered creativity, community, and joy: In a time of extreme violence, we were building an alternative. Sitting in that room, I realized the archive wasn't just about images—it was about opening space for dialogue, about reclaiming how our stories are told.

During that same visit, I reconnected with my friend Miros from Aztek Nation and went to Rachael's house. She brought out her photo albums, journals, and tapes, and we reminisced. People started getting excited to talk about this time; I hadn't realized that that would happen. They were excited to reminisce—public conversation and private reminiscences were feeding each other. The internet was coming alive.

In 2016, I launched *Map Pointz,* another Instagram project focused on rave and party culture from a Latino perspective and rooted in firsthand experiences, just like

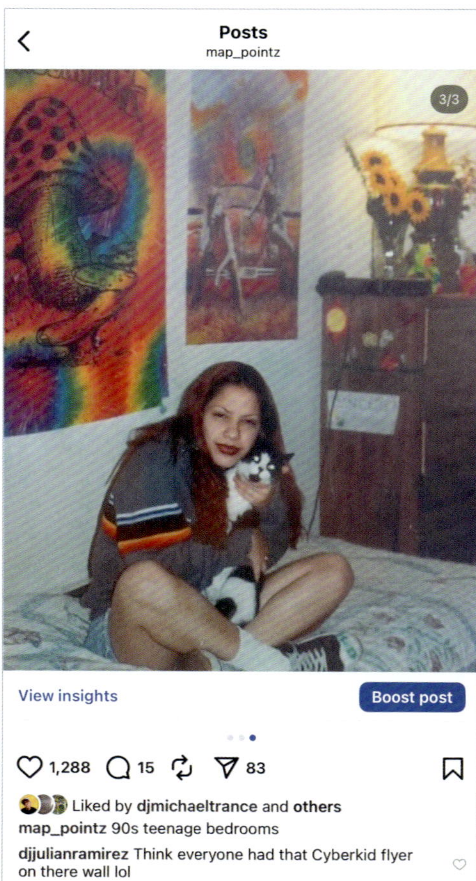

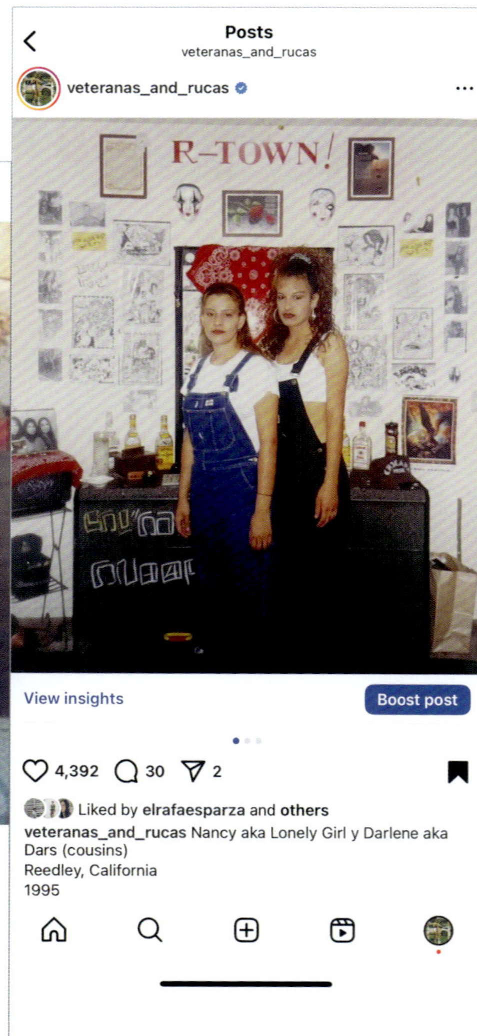

Bedroom posts

Veteranas and Rucas. The name "Map Pointz" came from our location system for parties. Back then, party flyers were often made by teenagers using school computers, but we never put the actual address on the flyer so parties weren't discovered easily. Instead, we used "map points"—essentially a meeting pin where you'd connect with someone who had the directions. It could be a gas station or a grocery store parking lot. You'd meet them, hand over a couple of dollars, and they'd give you a small slip of paper with the real party address. That slip? That was your ticket in. On *Map Pointz,* I post more than just photos. I post freshly scanned flyers from my collection or flyers people have donated to me. I also post video footage of party-crew parties that people generously submit.

All of my work was bringing me back, too—experiences like the one at UCLA, graduate school, *Veteranas and Rucas,* and *Map Pointz* had built my confidence and helped me let go of the shame I'd had about my

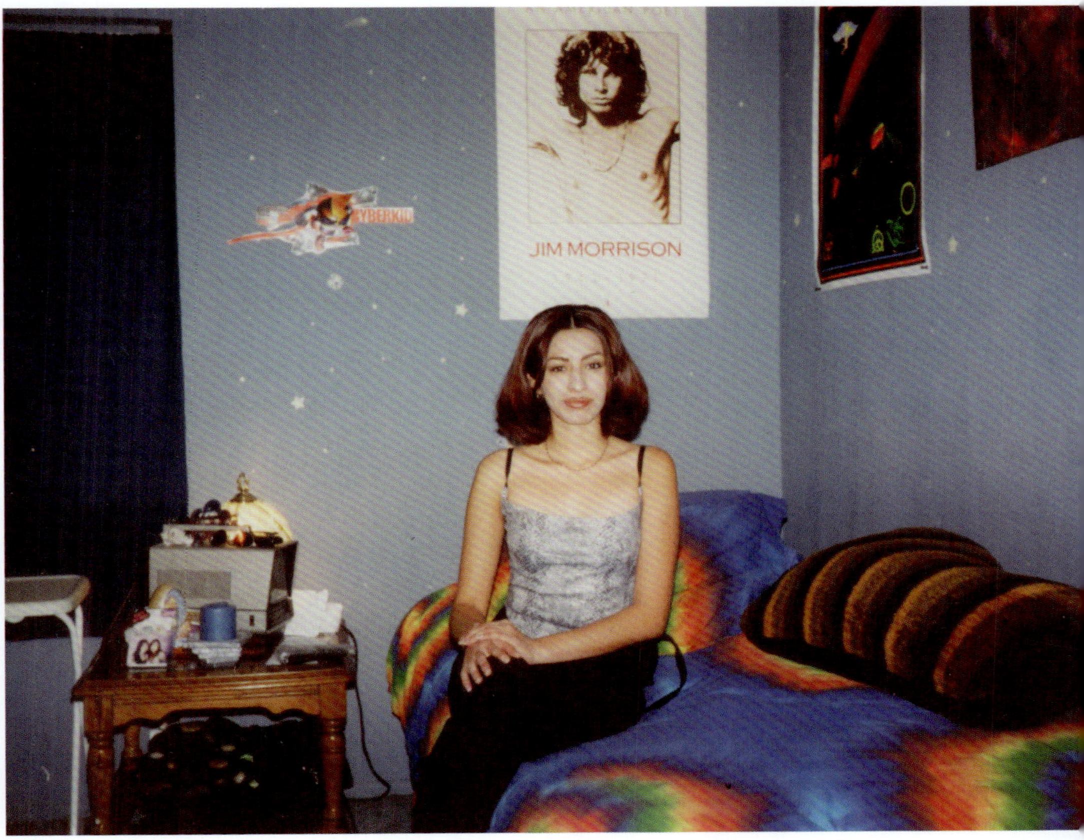

My friend Miros's bedroom in the late '90s

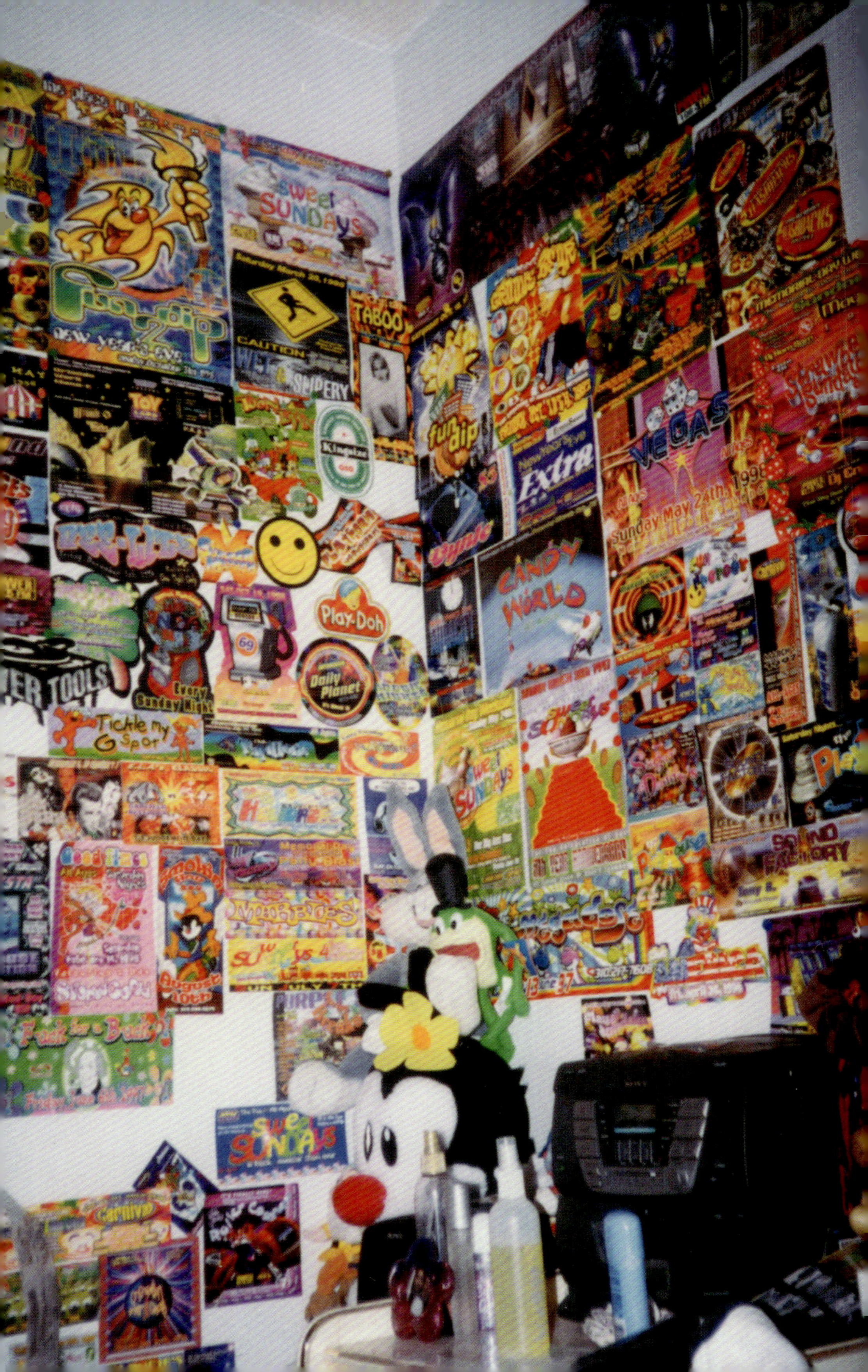

Sweet SUNDAYS
CAUTION
SLIPPERY
TABOO
Kingsize
fun dip
Extra
VEGAS
Sunday May 24th, 1998
CANDY WORLD
Play-Doh
Daily Planet
Every Sunday Night
TOOLS
Tickle my G Spot
SOUND FACTORY
August 10th
Carnival

youth. I was embracing it, and my thesis project embodied that by celebrating a teenage bedroom.

When we were teens, if you wanted to know who we were and what our minds looked like, you only had to step into our bedroom. In the house at Leonard and Whittier, I shared a large room with my sisters, Maria and Yesi, and each of us carved out a corner that reflected our own world. Mine was by the window, Maria's across from me. Yesi, the youngest, technically had no wall space, though sometimes she'd sneak a sticker or photo up, hoping we wouldn't notice. Of course, we always did and took it down.

The room was an overlapping universe of our identities—posters, glow-in-the-dark stars, blacklights, lava lamps we made from Corona bottles and highlighter liquid, ceilings layered with flyers from parties we'd been to, and photos of friends and crushes. Mom once stormed in and ripped our blacklight posters off the wall, shouting, "Esas son cosas del diablo." Days later, we taped the torn pieces back together and returned them to their place, refusing to let them go. With one full-length mirror between the three of us, it was a daily fight for the reflection to redo our hair or adjust an outfit. We thought we had it all figured out; after all, we'd been sharing that mirror for years. But somehow, it was often a battle—elbows bumping, yelling at one another, each of us trying to steal a moment in the mirror. Sometimes it worked, though: One of us would sit on the floor while the others stood behind, adjusting outfits and making last-minute tweaks, like a well-rehearsed routine.

That room, and others like it across East L.A., became the foundation for my thesis work at SAIC. For the project, I re-created a teenager's bedroom—not as a simple replica of my past, but as a curated reflection of identity, memory, and the politics of the world we were navigating. I drew from my own room, from my friend Miros's, and from images shared through *Map Pointz* and *Veteranas and Rucas*. Each bedroom told its own story, shaped by music, fashion, flyers from party crews, and the rituals of adolescence in the '90s.

Teenage bedrooms were never just bedrooms. They were sanctuaries and archives, places where self-expression collided with the larger cultural and political forces around us. They were reflections of who we were becoming and the fleeting moments we wanted to hold on to.

OPPOSITE: Miros's bedroom

To complete the atmosphere, I included a monitor playing videos from YouTube—footage of the 1992 riots, along with recordings of house parties and raves—that spoke to the complex ways violence, resistance, and celebration co-existed in our lives. These clips weren't just background visuals; they tied everything together. They mirrored the duality many of us lived through—where moments of joy and resistance were often intertwined. The energy of the riots and the parties told parallel stories: of survival, of expression, of carving out space to feel alive in a world that often tried to silence us.

They weren't just nostalgic or trapped in another time—they made the past present again, offering a lens to examine how memory, culture, and personal history collide and co-exist. Through this project, I realized how powerful it was to create spaces that invited others to share in that history, to reflect on their own, and to keep those memories alive in a different form.

After I graduated, I finally moved back to L.A. in 2016, sixteen years after I boarded a one-way flight to JFK. After living in New York for over a decade, once again I was nervous to make that big move. Every time I had visited Los Angeles in that period, I'd experienced something that wasn't quite nostalgia; it was more a sadness that I wasn't living there to experience my own lifestyle, culture, and community. That it was happening without me. Knowing how sad I was when I came back to New York from visiting L.A. and seeing how much I was missing out, especially with *Veteranas and Rucas* blowing up, the new relationships it was helping me build, and the old relationships that were being rekindled, the decision became clear. I didn't have a job waiting for me, I didn't have a plan, but I knew I had to be here.

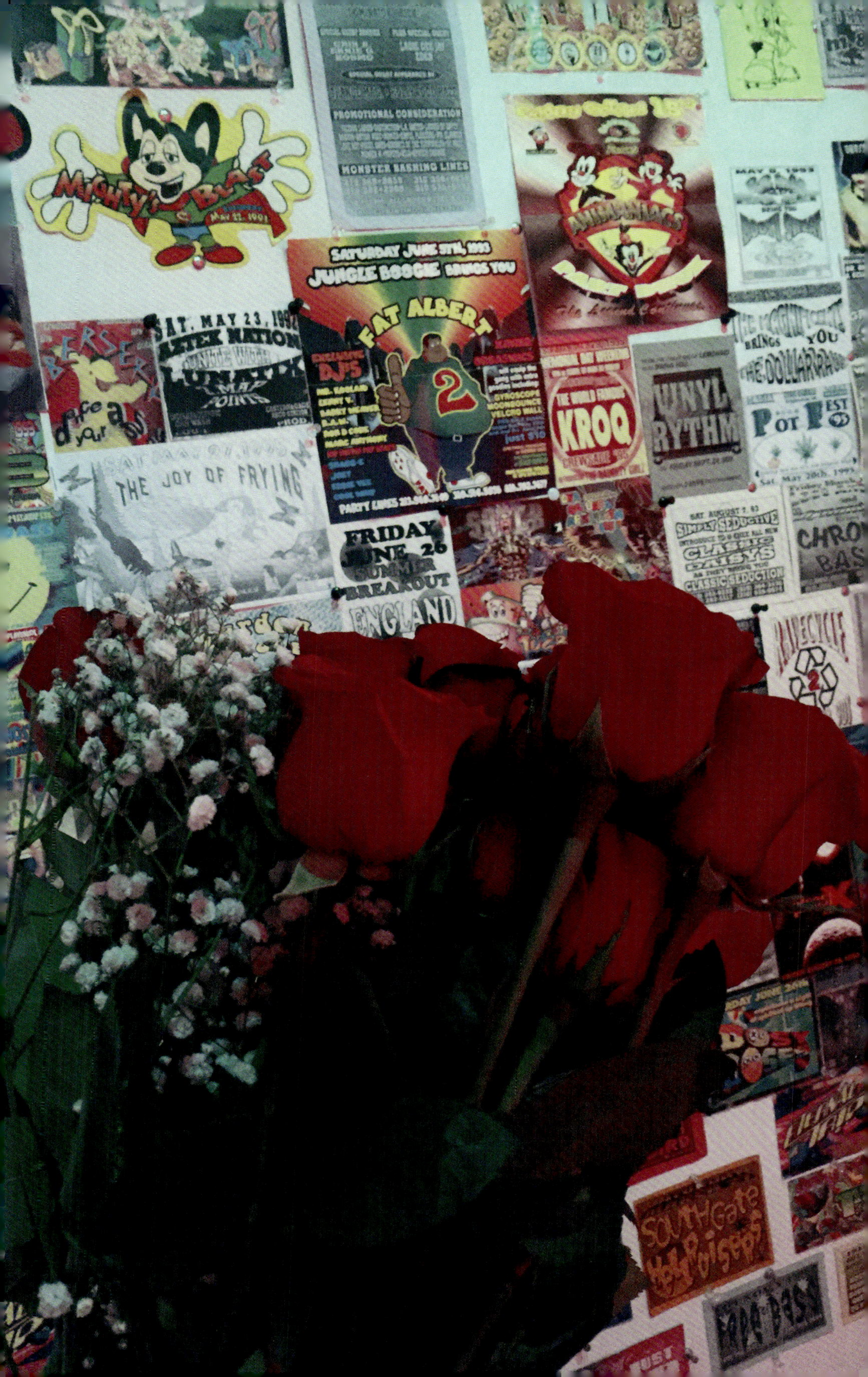

Mighty's Blast
SATURDAY JUNE
JUNGLE BOOGIE BRINGS YOU
FAT ALBERT
2
PROMOTIONAL CONSIDERATION
MONSTER BASHING LINES
SAT. MAY 23, 1992
AZTEK NATION
LUNATIX
THE JOY OF FRYING
FRIDAY
SUMMER
BREAKOUT
ENGLAND
THE WORLD FAMOUS
KROQ
VINYL
RYTHM
BRINGS YOU
POT FEST
SIMPLY SEDUCTIVE
CLASSIC
DAISYS
CLASSIC SEDUCTION
SOUTHGATE

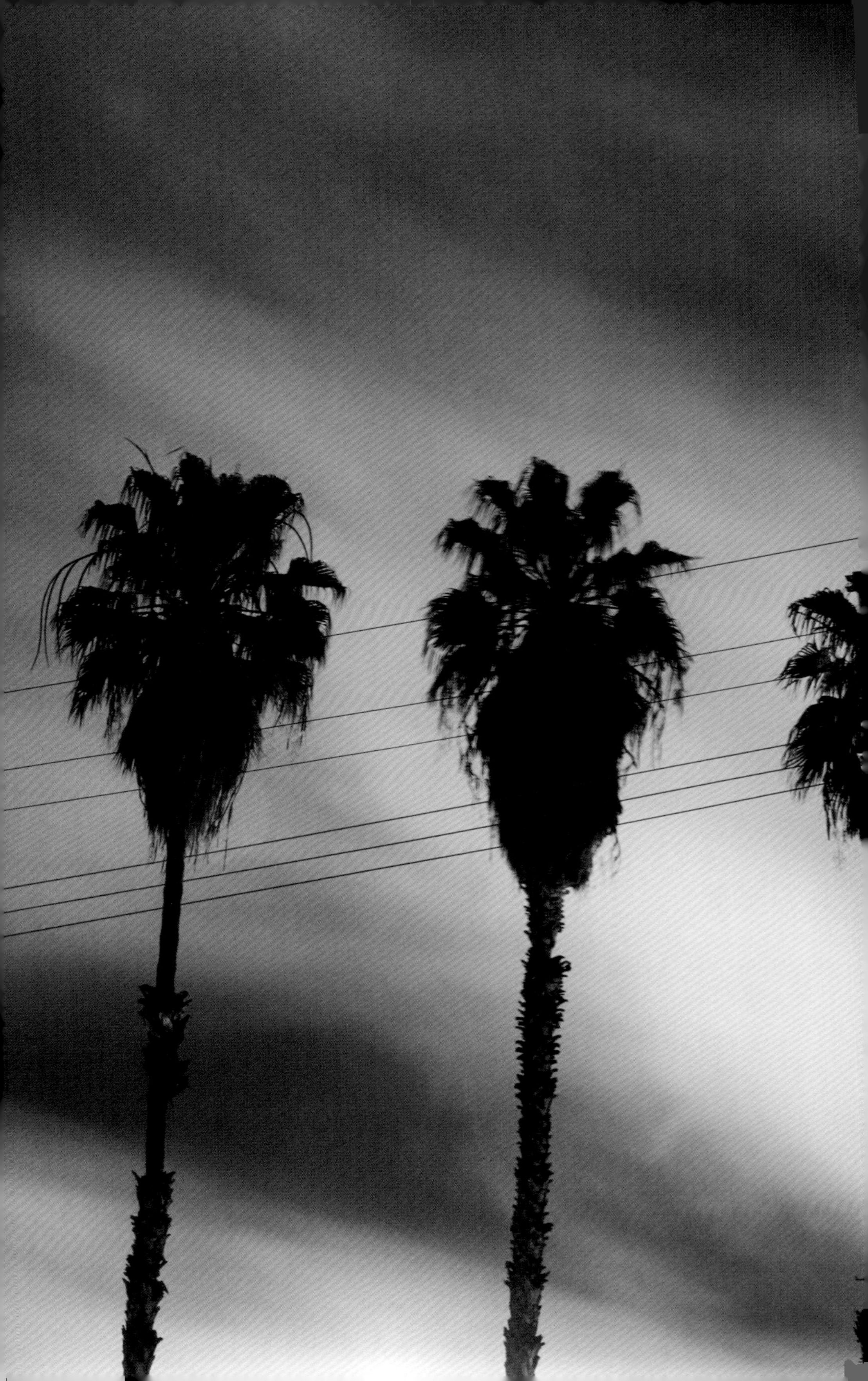

SECTION
III

Coming Home

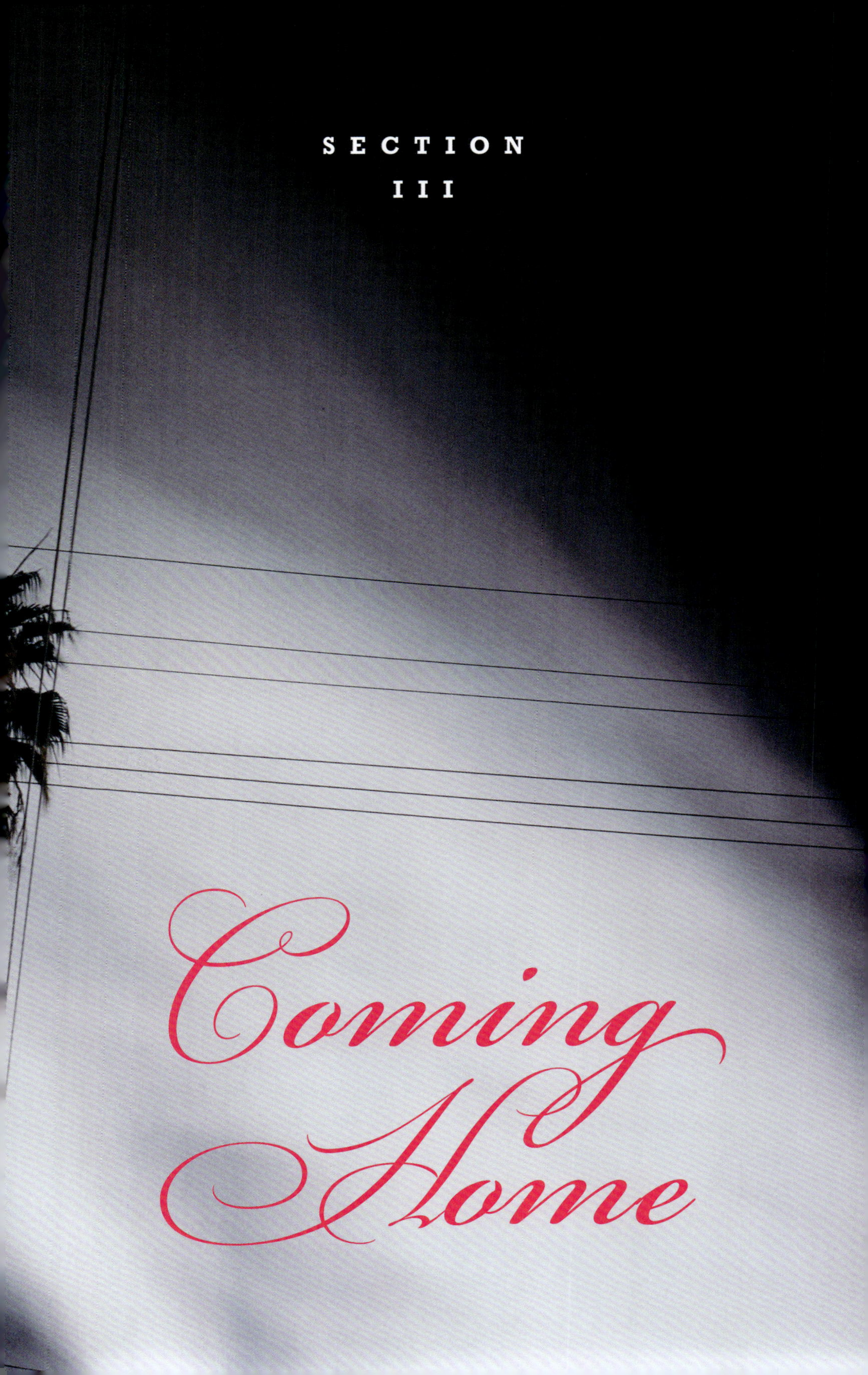

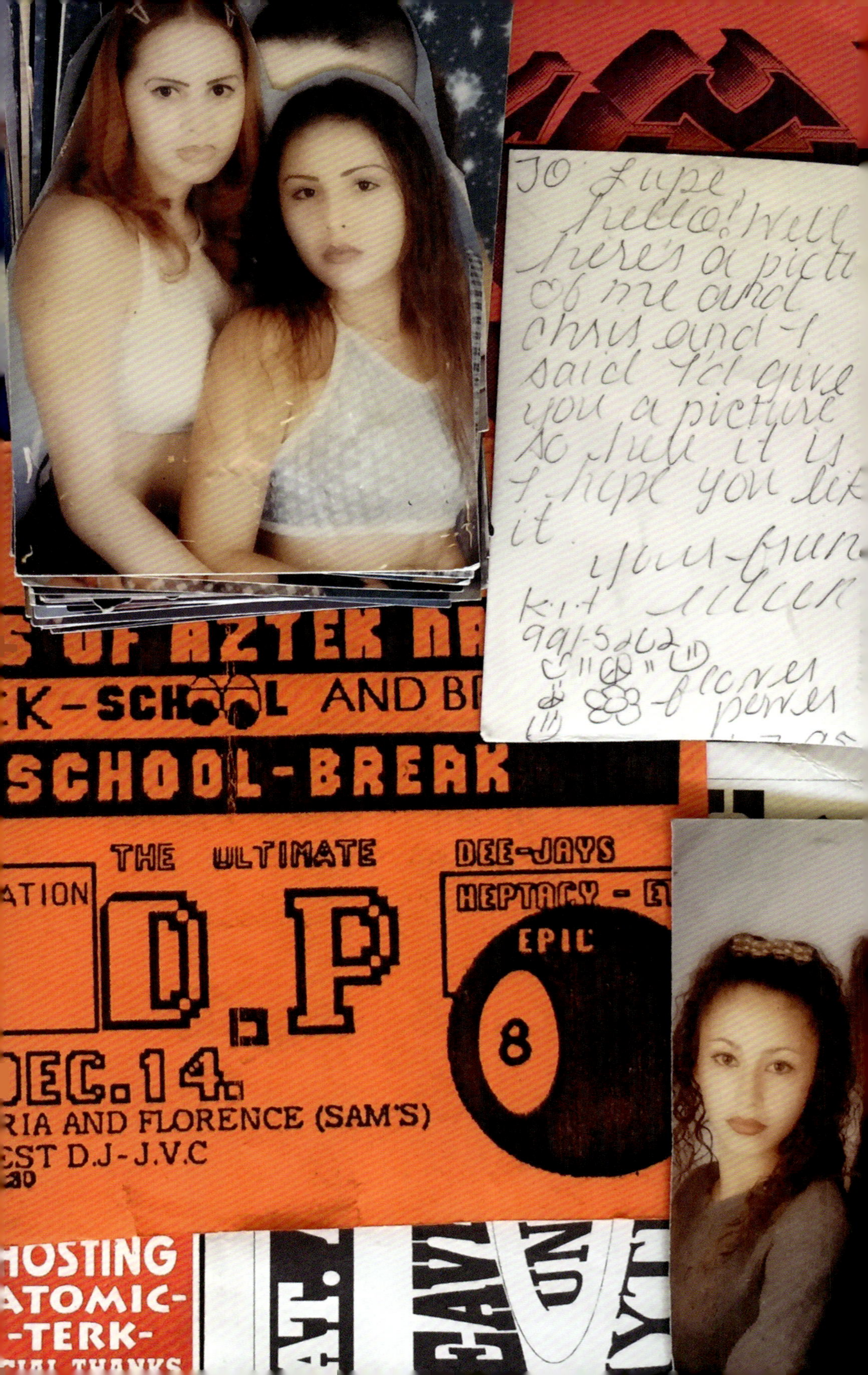
TO: Lupe
hello! well here's a pict
of me and chris and I
said I'd give you a picture
so here it is
I hope you lik
it.
your frien
K.I.T
991-5262
flower power
S OF AZTEK NA
K-SCHOOL AND B
SCHOOL-BREAK
THE ULTIMATE
DEE-JAYS
HEPTACY - E
ATION
D.P
EPIC
8
DEC.14.
RIA AND FLORENCE (SAM'S)
EST D.J - J.V.C
HOSTING
ATOMIC-
-TERK-

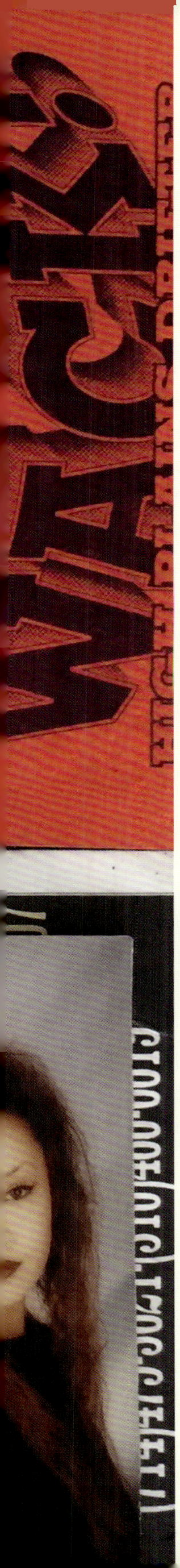

LOS ANGELES TIMES

BY 2016, I KNEW IT WAS TIME TO COME HOME. My sister Maria was getting married to Phillip on August 6, 2016, so it felt good to come back with a celebration on the horizon and a perfect way to spend time with family. Phillip had been part of the party crew Freak Show Tribe in the '90s, and he and Maria first met at a house party. By the time of their wedding, they already had two daughters: Izel, still a toddler, and Kayla, who was a teenager. At first, I stayed with my little sister, Yesi, crashing on her couch for a couple of months.

During that time, I bounced between random jobs to make ends meet. One of my first gigs was making pizza at a place owned by one of Maria's friends in Rosemead, where I earned about $300 a week plus tips. I was saving every penny, learning how to line up the ducks: saving money and pay stubs to secure an apartment, and getting my mom to cosign for a Toyota Tacoma so I could sleep in it as a backup plan in case I couldn't find myself an apartment. The first reliable thing I had since moving back to L.A. was my truck. Luckily I never had to sleep in it, and, months later, I found an apartment.

I also started putting my work out into the world. I gave lectures and talks, sharing the archive, and the history it captured on social media. At that point, I wasn't making art to sell; in fact, I was a little anti–art selling. I didn't want to be a commercial artist. I was a bit inspired by Andrea Fraser's practice, which critiqued and deconstructed the structures of the art world itself, and also by ASCO, the Chicano artist collective active in East Los Angeles during the 1970s and ’80s, who often rejected the “white cube” gallery system by taking their work to the streets. I was focused on the archive itself—developing a language around flyers, clothing, and other ephemera people had started donating to me so I could highlight them on Instagram and lectures, and activating these archives through conversations and storytelling.

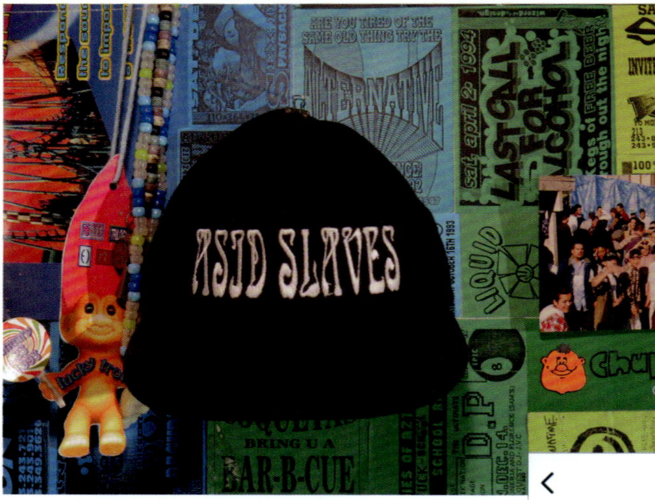

I preferred building context to teach others about this history. I wasn’t a historian, but I was doing a historian’s work. Even though I was broke, I had enough to get by and do something that had meaning and importance—I had faith that things would eventually fall into place, and slowly, my work started gaining attention. People welcomed me and celebrated my work. Michael from Maricón Collective and his partner were among the first people I met who I could really sit with and talk in a conceptual and historical way. They understood the kind of language I was trying to build around the archive. They were a couple years older than me and had also lived it. Those conversations gave

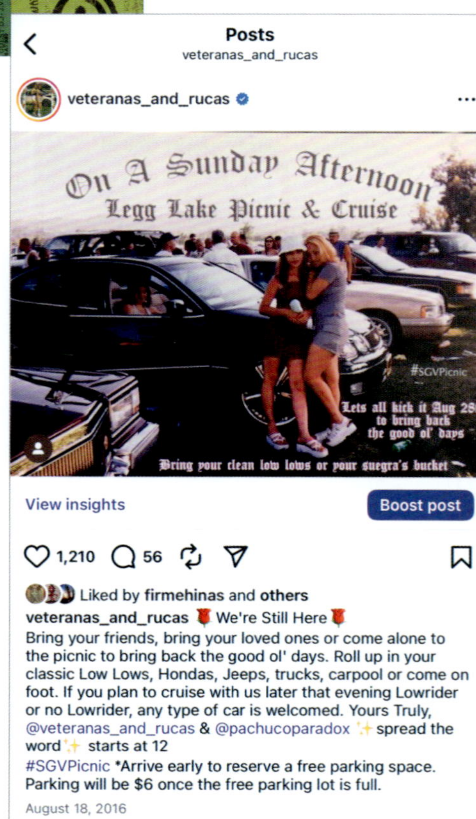

Flyer of our first event

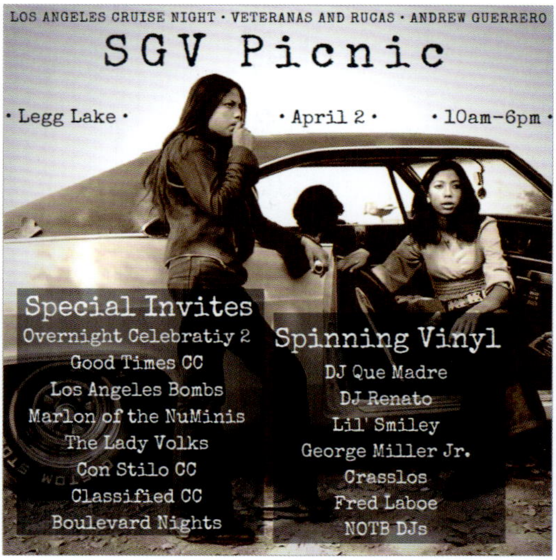

me confidence that what I was doing mattered beyond just collecting—it was about shaping memory, building context, and creating space for others to see themselves in the work.

In the summer of 2016, I began organizing lowrider picnics at Legg Lake, in Whittier Narrows in South El Monte.

My intention was to revive what so many of us remembered from the 1970s—and what I myself experienced in the 1990s. It had long been a tradition to cruise, gather, and hang out at the park. Right before sunset, we'd head out to the boulevard and caravan more than twenty cars from the park.

THE PARK HAD been known for lowrider meetups, but by the early 2000s that scene had faded away. Part of my work was to keep those memories alive by organizing picnics where people from different generations could experience it for themselves. I wanted the younger crowd to see what many of us had grown up doing—something they had only heard about through family stories or seen on my page. Some had been there as kids but were too young to remember. My goal was to revive those feelings and tell our history through action. My friend Andrew and I designed the flyer, invited DJs, and hauled in a generator to power our speakers and other equipment. All car clubs were invited, but we made sure to name specific clubs on our posts so the flyer circulated more widely in order to get people interested and make it legit. I took the same approach as '90s party-crew flyers had done: Everyone was invited, but if you saw your party-crew name on the flyer, it made the invite more special.

We asked the DJs to play a mix of oldies and house, music that carried both nostalgia and energy. Since I'd already built a substantial following—at that point I had almost seventy thousand followers—it was easy for me to promote the events and get people to come out to them.

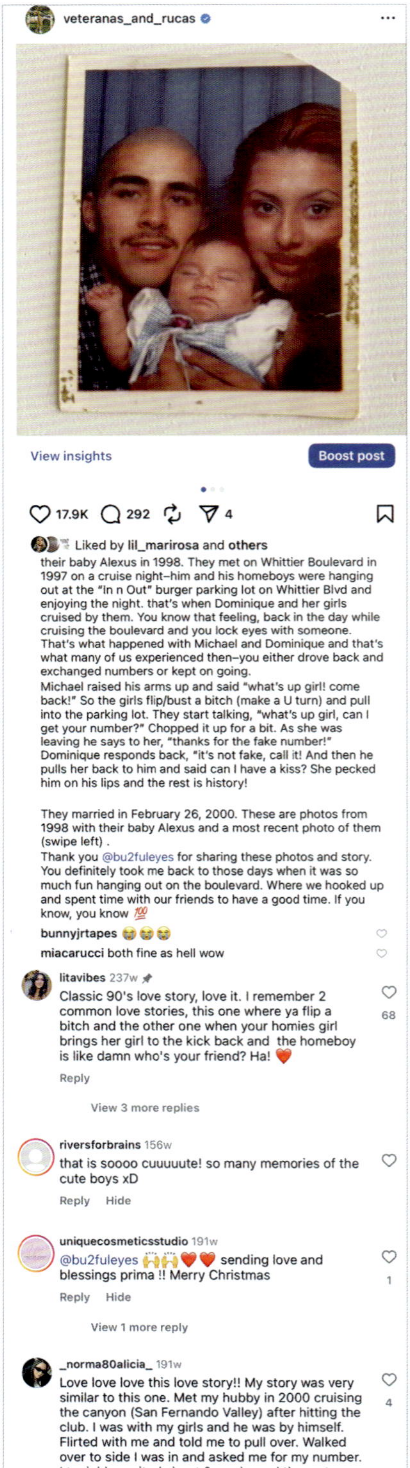

A couple who met cruising on Whittier Boulevard. I love this post because it perfectly captures what L.A. was like in the '90s.

Young admirers of my work were taking note of what I was doing and getting inspired. It's like they wanted to experience what I was showing on Instagram; they wanted to live it. The '90s were back full force, but so were the cops who'd harassed us decades before. They were violent and intimidated people by kicking their grills and coolers. I had also received an email from the city a week before letting me know I had to get a permit to have a picnic. We'd already had four successful events, and I didn't want to put my community at risk with the police so I decided to end the series there.

Like the UCLA panel, these gatherings brought people together and connected the past with the present, blending car culture, music, and community. They became another way for me to connect with the lowrider community, teach younger generations, relive and create new memories, and share a personal experience I had grown up in while sharing history in a tangible, lively way.

In 2018, I had my first show at the Vincent Price Art Museum. Even though the pieces on display weren't for sale and came from the archive, I framed it as an art show—because to me, the flyers, photos, and clothing exhibited were works of art—and the response was overwhelming. For this exhibition, I was also evoking car culture, because in Los

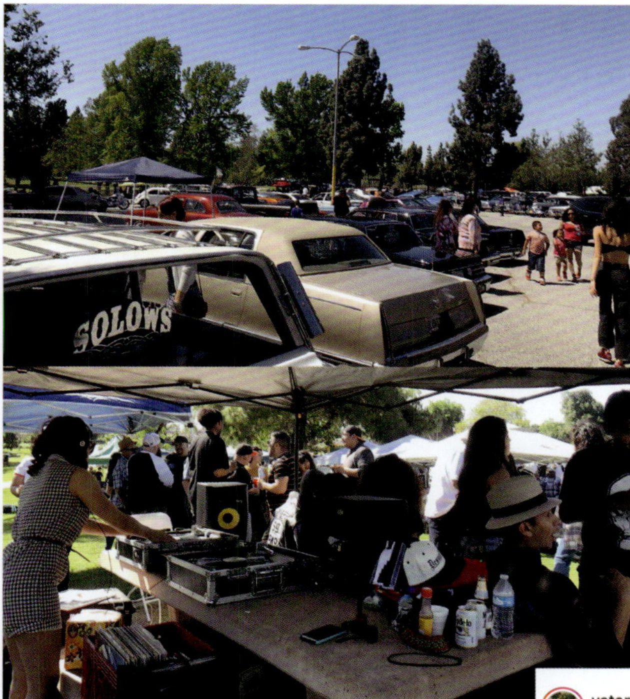

Angeles—especially in East L.A.—car culture is such an important part of who we are. To me, modified vehicles have always been celebrated as works of art in themselves. People were used to seeing classic lowriders at shows and were familiar with them, but not so much with fixed-up motorcycles, Volkswagens, or mini-trucks.

I invited car clubs like Nu Minis, local Volksstyle CC, and East LA Bikers. I wanted to highlight what was less familiar, since people often expected to see only lowriders. People were noticing, and the work was helping me connect with others in the scene. That same year, my work was featured in *Aperture* magazine, with a photograph from *Veteranas and Rucas* on the cover. I had chosen the image with the editor and worked closely with the photo's owner to make sure it was represented with care. Alongside the feature, I organized an exhibition in

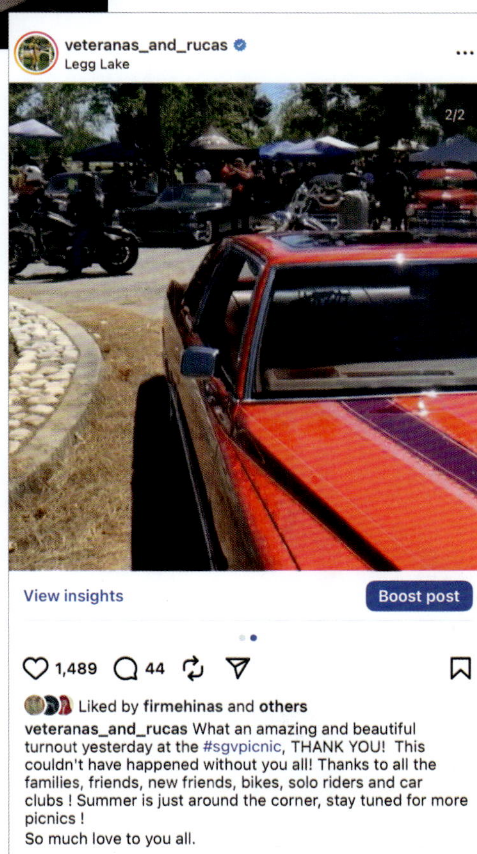

ABOVE: Picnic photo

RIGHT: Thank-you post after our successful picnic at Legg Lake

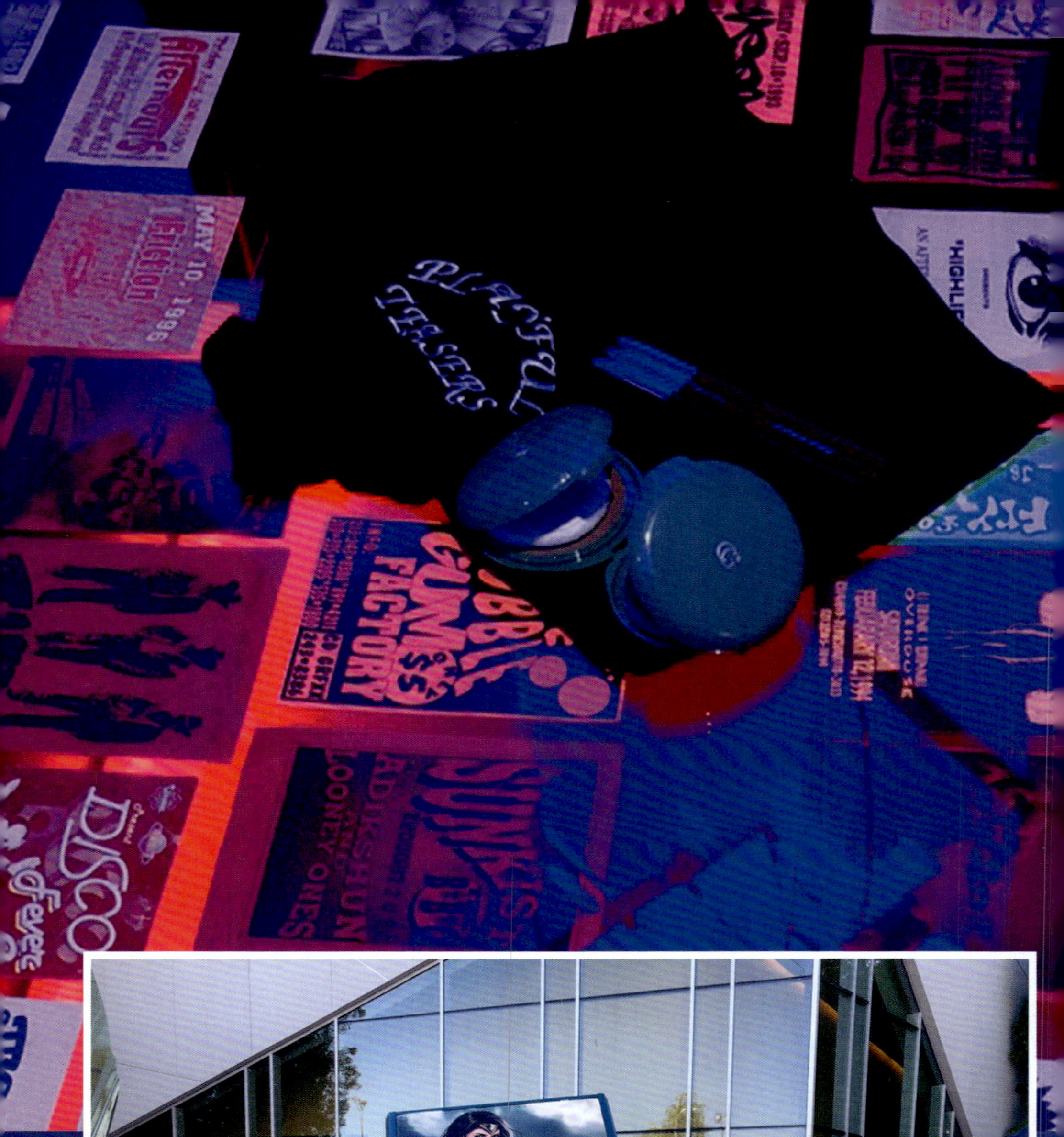

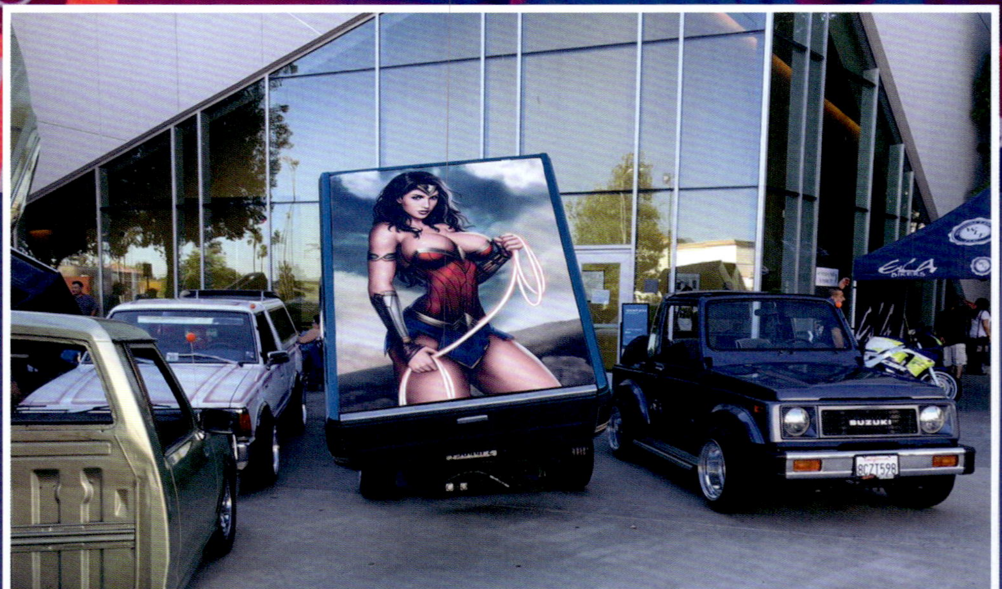

My first exhibition in Los Angeles, at the Vincent Price Art Museum, 2018

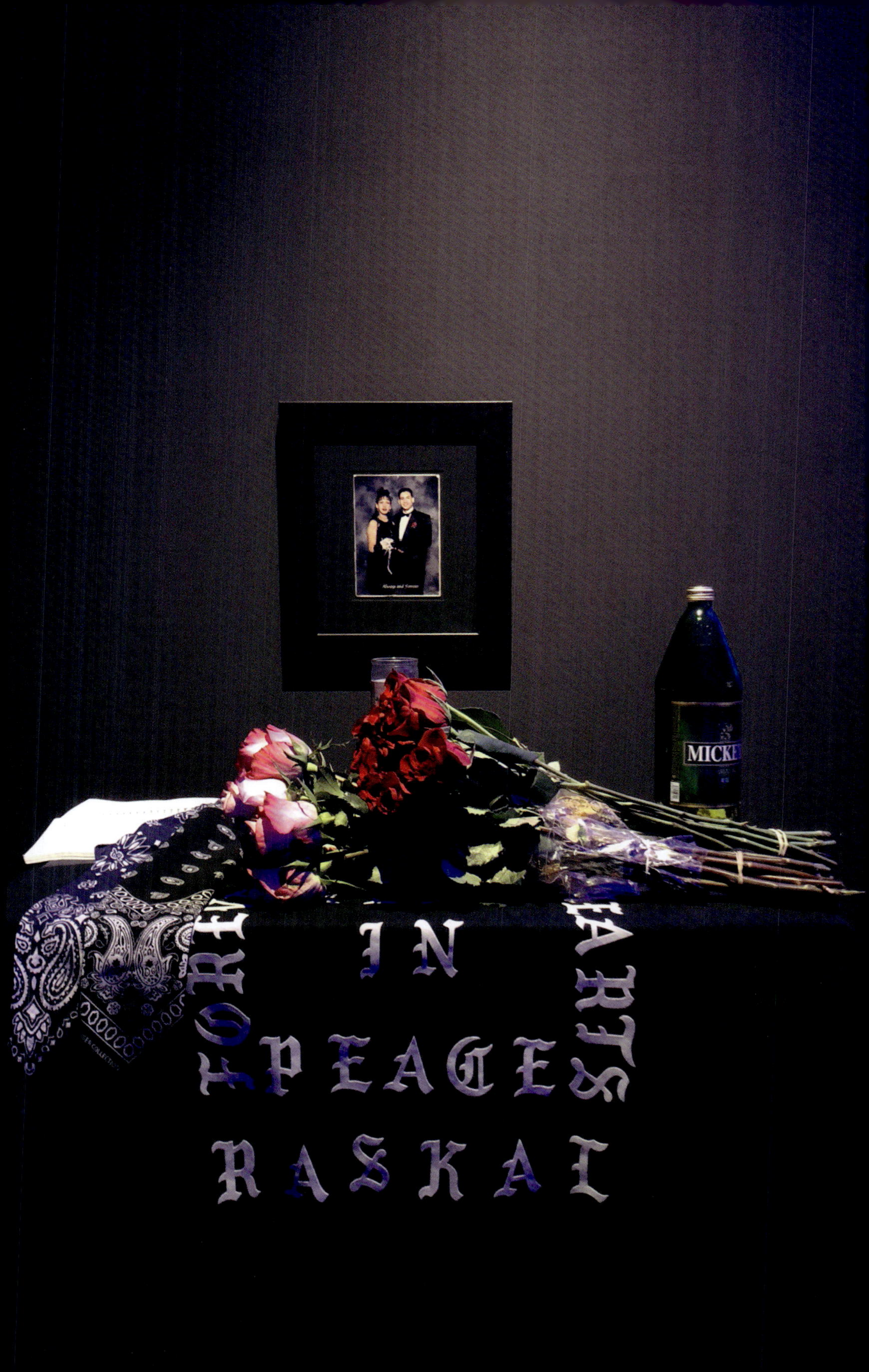
IN
PEACE
RASKAL

Aperture's gallery space, bringing the archive to a wider audience in New York City. For the show, I installed large-scale images as wallpaper across the walls and created an altar for my cousin Ever. I began to realize that a fan base was forming around the work—I hadn't even known people were paying such close attention.

Looking back, it's clear that those months of hustling, working random jobs, organizing picnics, and putting the archive out there were the foundation for everything that has followed. The work itself became a bridge to people, places, and opportunities I hadn't imagined, all while I slowly began saving money and carving out a life in L.A. again.

Outside the Vincent Price Art Museum

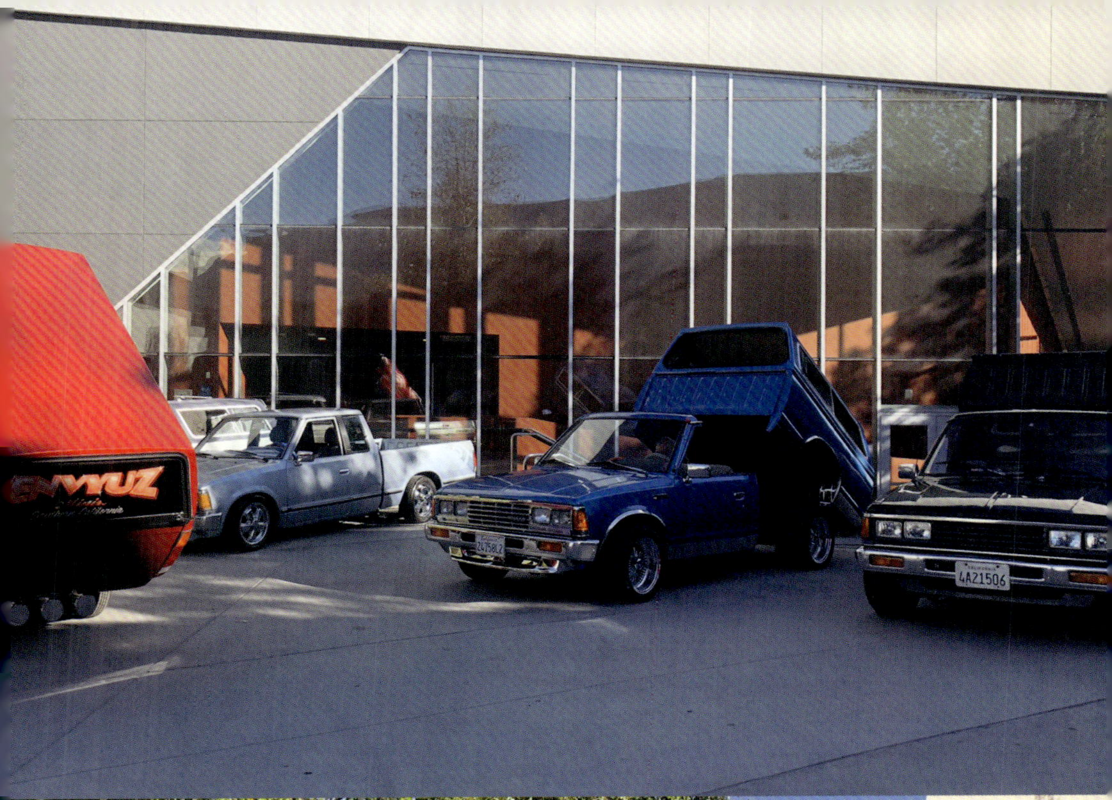
4A21506

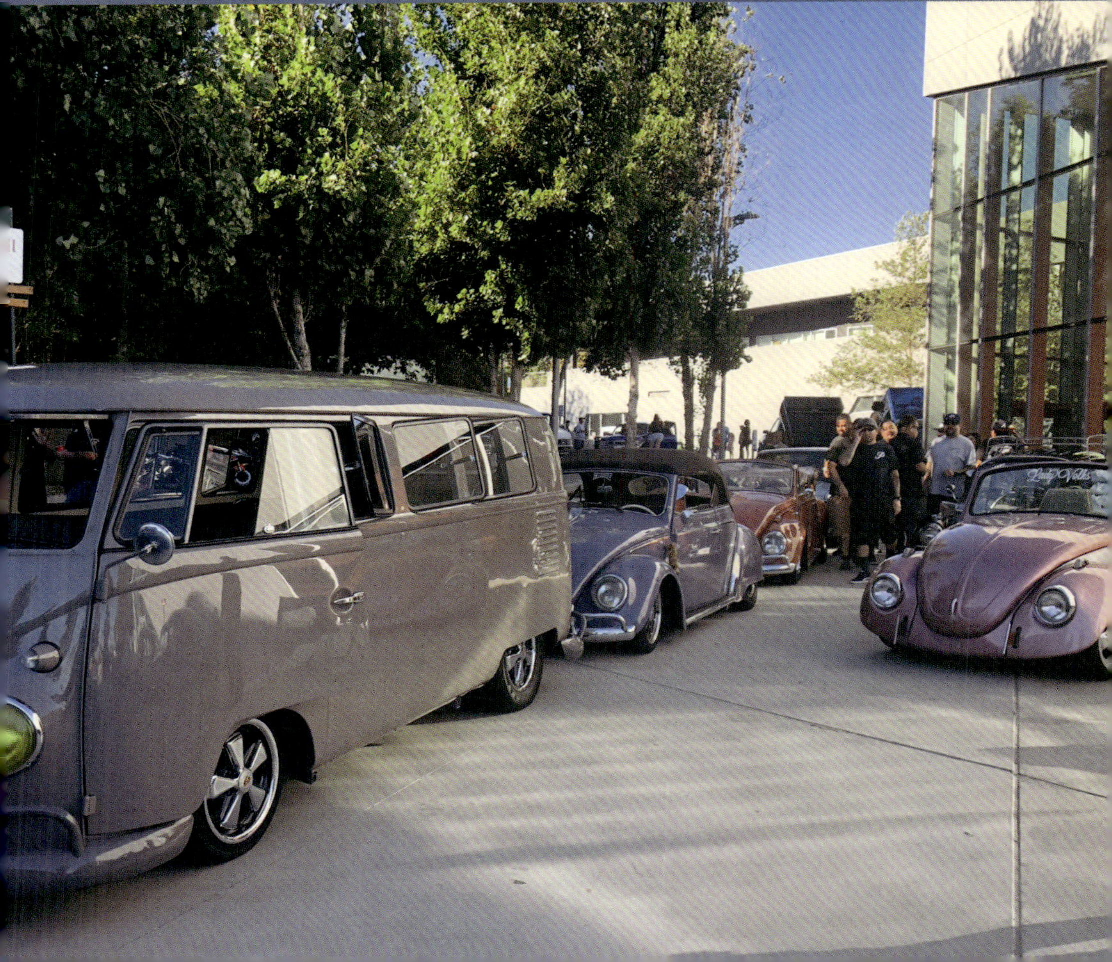

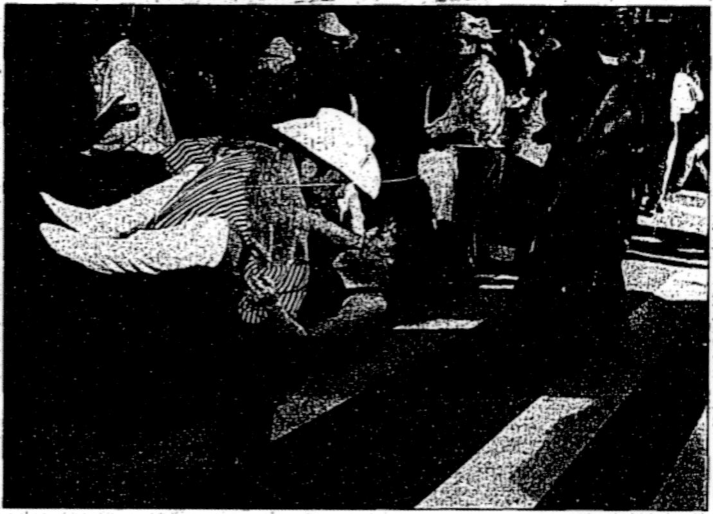

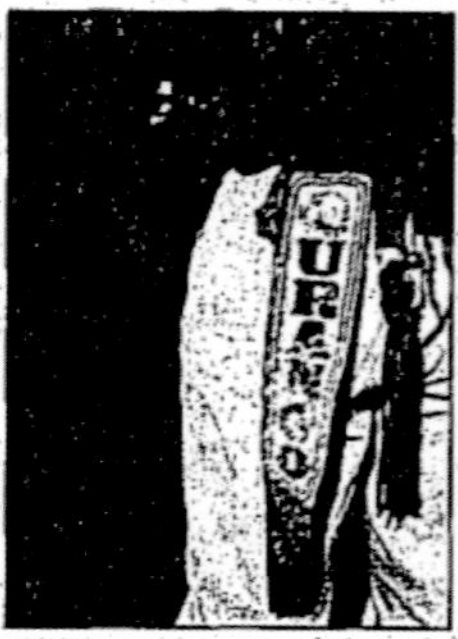

Photos by BRIAN VANDER BRUG / For The Times

Banda dancers Juan Lopez, 18, of Arleta and Maria Rodriguez, 19, of Van Nuys show off moves at La Sierra. *Banda* wear includes leather belt and *cuerda*, left.

Strike Up the *Banda*

■ The popular Mexican dance music is gaining momentum with young and old, who turn out in cowboy gear at local clubs and private parties to do *la quebradita*.

By JOAN EASLEY
SPECIAL TO THE TIMES

It's Friday night at La Sierra in Panorama City, and 300 dancers are stomping and kicking to a tune that takes a moment to recognize: "Under the Boardwalk," with Spanish lyrics and an irresistible beat. So irresistible that one dancer is being paged in Spanish over the loudspeaker because his wife is in labor.

Move over, salsa. Forget *lambada*. The dance of the day is *la quebradita*, and the sound that drives it is *banda*.

"The music comes from the rich tradition of the Mexican state of Sinaloa," said Everto Ruiz, a Cal State Northridge professor of Chicano studies. It's distinguished by having no string instruments. A typical *banda* (band) would have seven to 17 musicians playing mostly trumpet, trombone, clarinet, tuba and percussion.

"It dates back to the military band sound that arose when Europeans first came to Mexico. Folk musicians used that instrument group not only for marches, but also to interpret traditional Mexican music and the popular music of their time. Now *banda* musicians play the past repertoire and have taken it to the popular songs of today," he said.

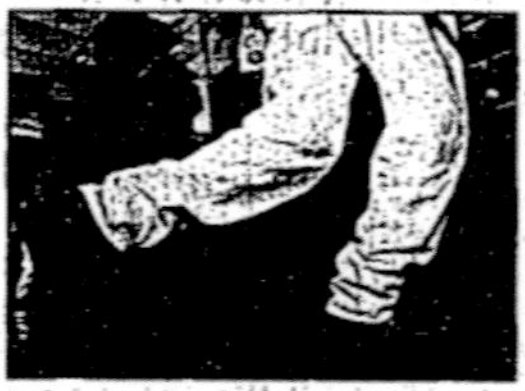

Dancer does *la quebradita*, a cross between Texas two-step and Highland fling.

Sometimes, for reasons of cost and convenience, bass guitar substitutes for the tuba's oom-pah, while keyboard fills in for clarinet.

La Sierra regular Tony Rodriguez, 28, of Van Nuys by way of Durango, Mexico, traces the current *banda* craze to a popular recording five years ago by Mexican singer Antonio Aguilar. "Banda Mobil and other groups followed, and boom! People started dancing in parks, watching others: adults, girls, boys, guys just dancing by themselves." The *banda* craze has been big for about two years, according to the people who run La Sierra.

Rodriguez, dressed *banda*-style in jeans, cowboy hat, boots and hand-tooled belt with dangling leather *cuerda* (cattle whip), is a good enough *quebradora* (dancer) to consider competing for tonight's top prize of $700.

La quebradita, less overtly erotic than other recent Latin dance crazes, looks something like the Texas two-step combined with the fast and furious footwork of a Highland fling. The upper body remains fairly rigid as dancers kick their heels fore, aft and around in circles, occasionally dipping their partners backward into a *quebradita* (break).

Too much salsa-style wiggling can get a couple disqualified, although judges favor acrobatic lifts and sombreros spinning like Hula-Hoops.

"Everybody tries to do something different that looks good," Rodriguez said. "Waltz steps, ballet, country. . . . I learned a step that looks like the Russian *kazatzka* by watching Billy Ray Cyrus. There's only one problem: It's hard on the knees."

Banda has become as popular around-area high schools as in clubs such as La Sierra, Leonardo's in Sun Valley and La Zona Rosa in North Hollywood. The under-21 crowd, and many adults, do their dancing at flyer-advertised parties called *pachangons*, held in rented halls or private homes and organized by *banda* clubs that may have as many as 300 members. Some clubs are all-male, some all-female. The 40-member *14 Kilate de Oro* (14 Karat Gold), started by a group of friends at University High in West Los Angeles, has males and females, adults and teen-agers.

Club President Eric Ramirez, 17, a University High senior, admits that he used to be a

Please see BANDA, 4

Where and When

What: *Banda* dancing to live bands at La Sierra Mexican Restaurant & Nightclub, 8632 Van Nuys Blvd., Panorama City, or 8351 San Fernando Road, Sun Valley.

Hours: 7 p.m. Friday, Saturday and Sunday.

Price: $8 to $25, depending on the band.

Call: (818) 830-1919.

QUEBRADITA

AS I WAS BUILDING A NEW LIFE IN LOS ANGELES— a life that connected my youth, my family, and the person I had become during my years away—I also became more aware of the opportunity the platform I had built offered. Alongside posts about fashion, lifestyles, landmarks, and communities, I began highlighting more specific histories. Sometimes I asked people to submit their prom, Sadie Hawkins, or graduation photos, moments I personally didn't get to experience because I was ditching school—but mostly, I wanted to showcase the unique experiences that existed within our communities. When I was growing up, alongside the house and techno party crews I was part of—which were mostly English-dominant—there were also quebradita crews.

La quebradita hit hard among young people in the early 1990s. Youth organized backyard parties all over Los Angeles—mostly in South and East L.A., where strobe lights cut through fog and DJs played Banda Machos, Chalino Sánchez, Banda Vallarta Show, and Arkángel R-15. This was the sound that echoed through the city day and night, the soundtrack of house parties and weekend nights, especially songs like "La Noche Que Murió Chicago" by Banda Toro or "Un Indio Quiere Llorar" by Banda Machos.

The chalinitos tumbados showed up in custom airbrushed T-shirts repping their crew or club name—Tragos Amargos, Club Falso Orgullo de Guerrero, 4 Espadas—

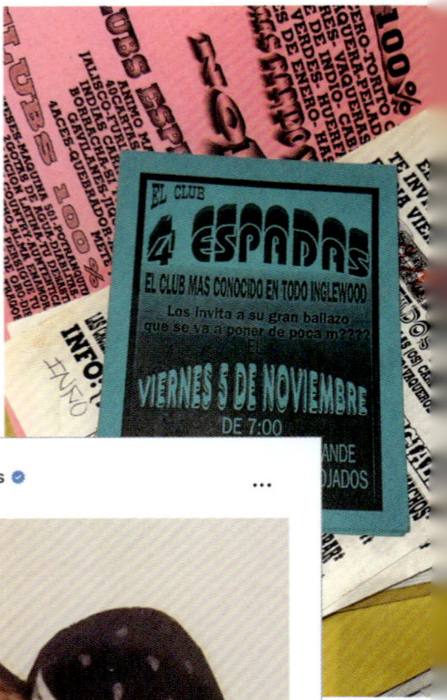

and a bandanna hanging from the back pocket embroidered with the name of their Mexican state. Their hats—or tejanas—were pulled low, sometimes tilted to the side, the brim casting a shadow over their eyes. The dance was wild and acrobatic, couples spun tight, lifted each other, dipped low until their hats nearly touched the floor.

For many of us, la quebradita was the first time we embraced our Mexican roots through music that still connected to what our parents listened to—banda, corridos, and norteñas. This scene, this subculture, became an important milestone in L.A. youth history. Much like the party crews, young people formed their own "clubs" or "crews" united by a love for dancing together to Mexican banda music.

Just as I had been highlighting the house and techno party-crew scene, I wanted to do the same with the quebradita movement. I posted about quebradita because it was an important part of history that had influenced so many—even to this day you can hear "Bailando de Caballito" and people go wild.

The quebradita movement played a big role in shaping youth culture and community identity because it was rooted in our heritage at a time that it was under attack by laws like Proposition 187. In 2017 I made my first post about

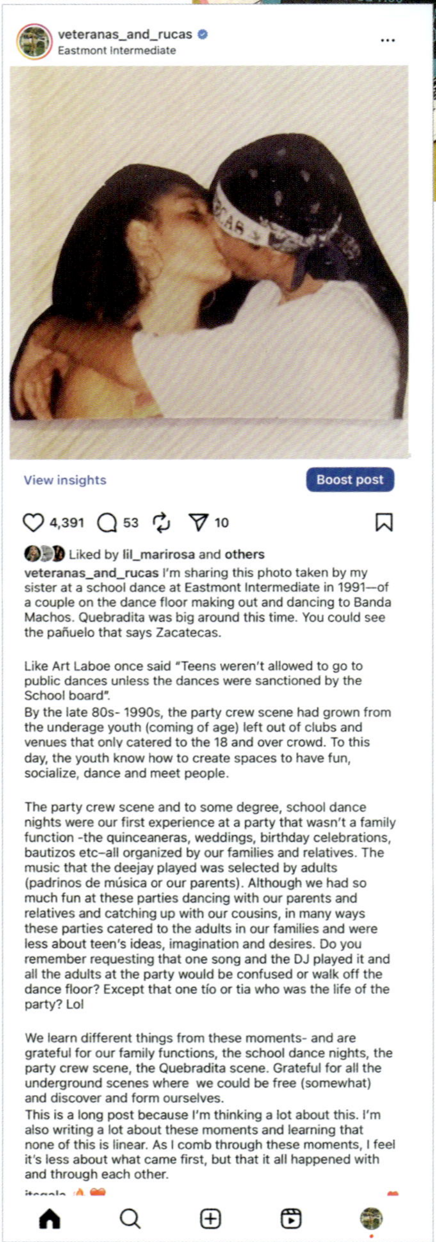

Post on *Veteranas and Rucas* highlighting the quebradita scene

the quebradita scene because it wasn't getting the recognition it deserved, and when I made my posts—the first post to request photos, and the second sharing a photo that my sister Maria had taken at a middle-school dance in 1991 or 1992—they became almost viral. Maybe it was also because young people could relate to this movement. We were seeing how modern narcocorridos or even Peso Pluma's music was rooted in this genre. Back in the '90s, las quebraditas were for people who felt left out of the party-crew scene, which was English-dominant, even though it was dominated by Latino youth. People felt prejudice: If you were a teenager who was first-generation or had moved to L.A. from Mexico and you didn't really speak English, there was a lot of prejudice against you. That's something that pushed people to start this underground scene: Flyers were similar to those for party crews, but in Spanish.

AS I CONTINUED building my work online, new opportunities opened up with Los

veteranas_and_rucas ...

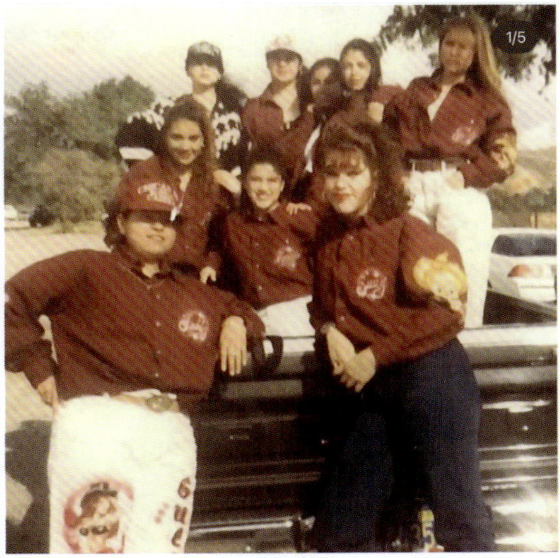

1,749 34 88

Liked by **quecholatanrica** and **others**

veteranas_and_rucas Flyers of La Quebradita backyard party scene

This is a long post because I see this coming back and many don't know it's history. More to discuss and I hope others can chime in and share their input and stories behind this scene

This is dedicated to 90s Quebradita and Banda music scene. La Quebradita was so prominent from the early-mid 1990s. This scene, or subculture or movement is an important milestone in LA youth history so I'm sharing original party flyers of this time. The club or crews were named after songs. Similarly to party crews, youth formed "clubs" whose members were united by a passion for dancing to Mexican banda music.

Quebradita (or Banda) music and corridos hit hard in LA in the 1990s, a time when many of us were listening to all sorts of music. Like the party crew and rave scene- Quebradita was the new explosion of music and style for the youth. They organized backyard parties in Los Angeles, specifically South and East LA. Strobe lights and fog machines, and Djs playing music- Banda Machos, Chalino Sanchez, Jorge Gamboa, Arcángel R15 just to name a few, this was the music echoed across the city day and night. The chalinitos tumbados, wearing their custom airbrushed T-shirts. A bandana hanging off the back pocket, representing their Mexican state embroidered on the bandada. The hats or tejanas low almost covering their eyes or tilted to the side.
We continue to influence and be influenced by different music genres-This is one that continues to influence our music today.
What's your fondest memory of this time?

westcoastdave I grew up in East LA during this era. Great memories.

January 29, 2024

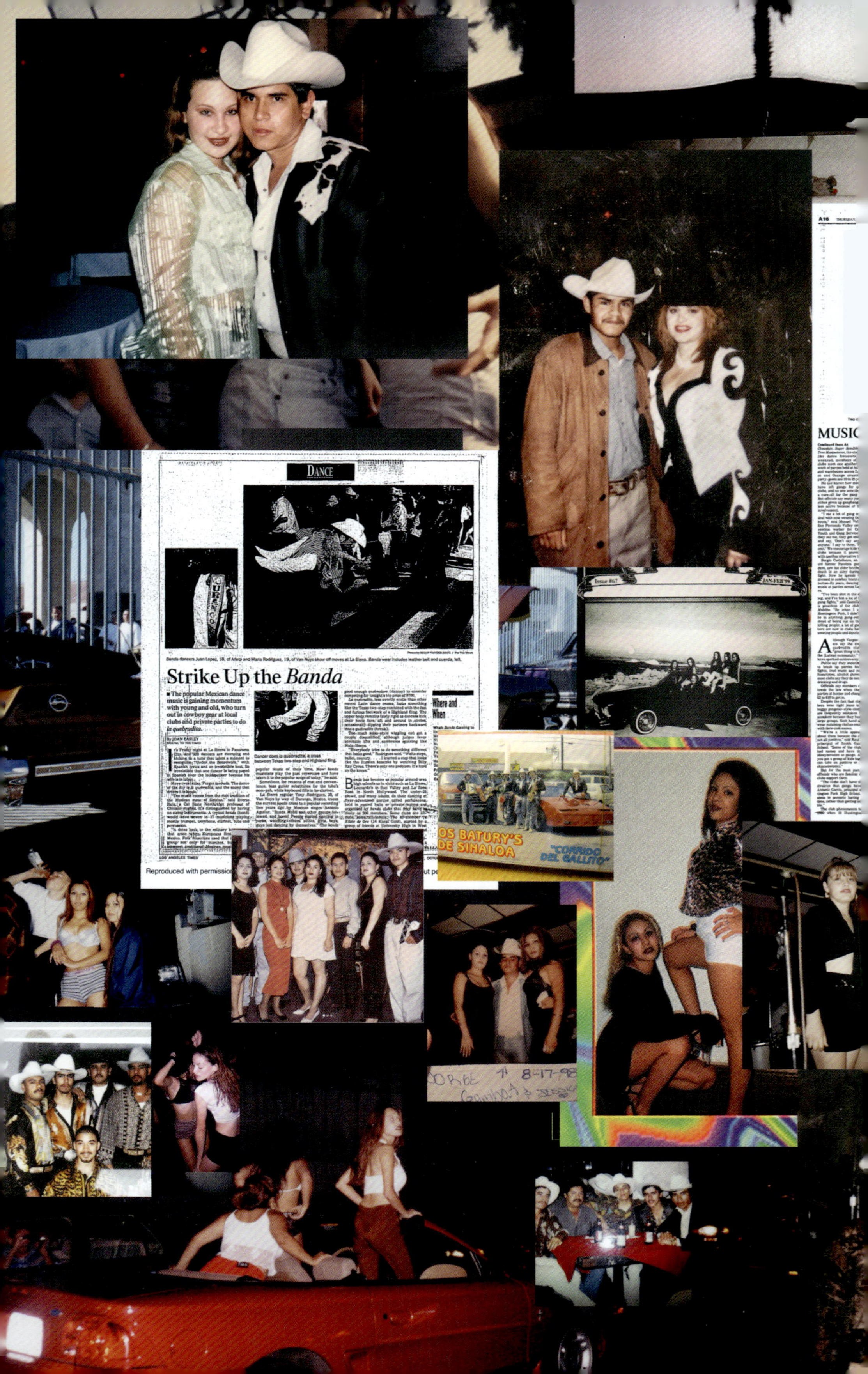
DANCE
Banda dancers Juan Lopez, 18, of Arleta and Maria Rodriguez, 19, of Van Nuys show off moves at La Sierra. Banda wear includes leather belt and cuerda, left.
Strike Up the *Banda*
The popular Mexican dance music is gaining momentum with young and old, who turn out in cowboy gear at local clubs and private parties to do *la quebradita.*
By JOAN EASLEY
Dancer does la quebradita, a cross between Texas two-step and Highland fling.
Where and When
LOS ANGELES TIMES
Reproduced with permission
Issue #67
JAN-FEB '99
OS BATURY'S
DE SINALOA
"CORRIDO DEL GALLITO"
MUSIC
A16
8-17-98

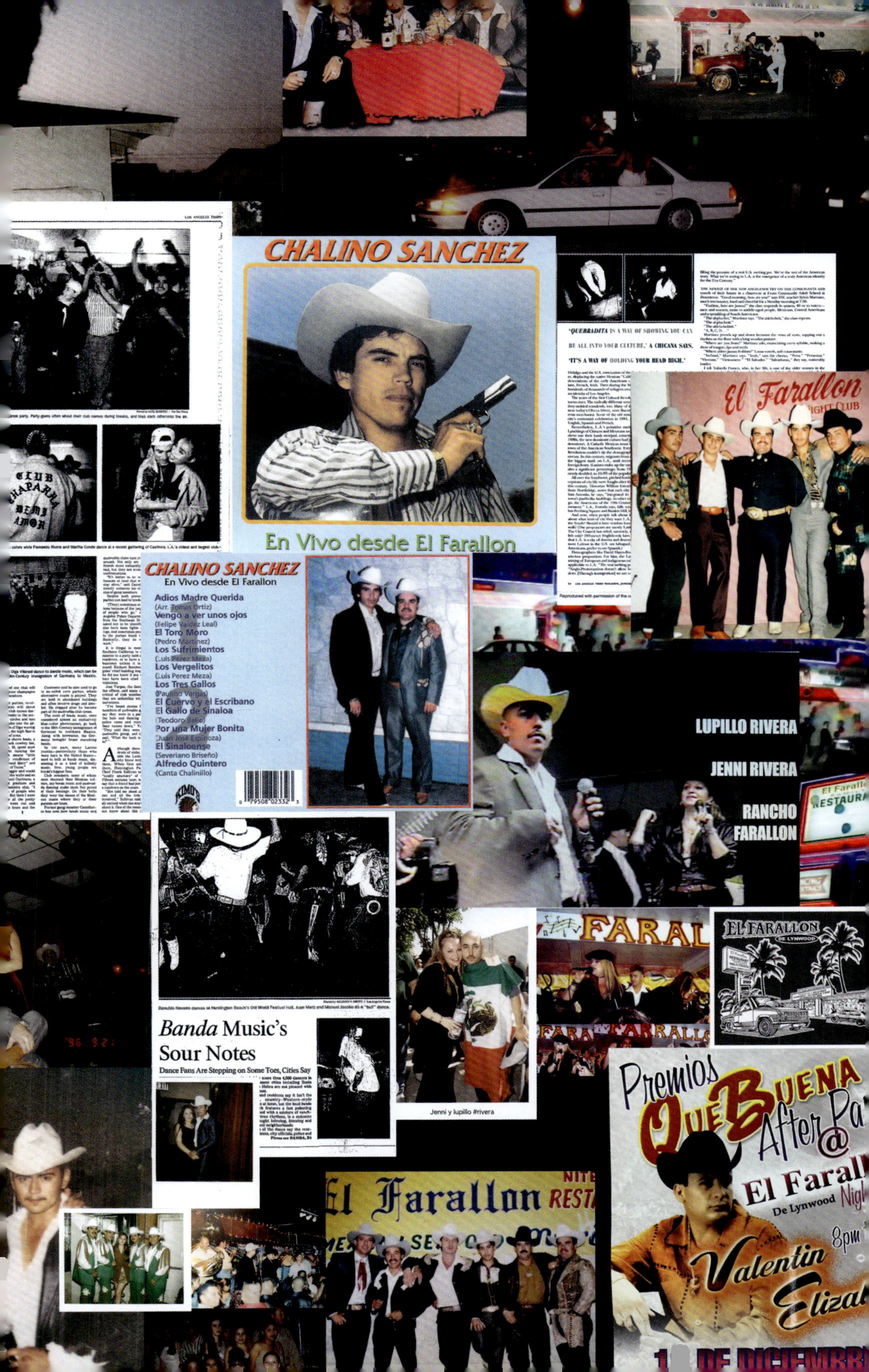
CHALINO SANCHEZ
En Vivo desde El Farallon
CHALINO SANCHEZ
En Vivo desde El Farallon
Adios Madre Querida
(Arr. Tomas Ortiz)
Vengo a ver unos ojos
(Felipe Valdez Leal)
El Toro Moro
(Pedro Martinez)
Los Sufrimientos
(Luis Perez Meza)
Los Vergelitos
(Luis Perez Meza)
Los Tres Gallos
(Paulino Vargas)
El Cuervo y el Escribano
El Gallo de Sinaloa
(Teodoro Bello)
Por una Mujer Bonita
(Juan José Espinoza)
El Sinaloense
(Severiano Briseño)
Alfredo Quintero
(Canta Chalinillo)
El Farallon
NIGHT CLUB
'QUEBRADITA IS A WAY OF SHOWING YOU CAN BE ALL INTO YOUR CULTURE,' A CHICANA SAYS. 'IT'S A WAY OF HOLDING YOUR HEAD HIGH.'
LUPILLO RIVERA
JENNI RIVERA
RANCHO FARALLON
Banda Music's Sour Notes
Dance Fans Are Stepping on Some Toes, Cities Say
Jenni y lupillo #rivera
FARAL
EL FARALLON
DE LYNWOOD
El Farallon
Premios
QueBuena
After Pa
@
El Faral
De Lynwood
8pm
Valentin
Eliza

Angeles institutions. In 2017, LACMA invited me to do an Instagram takeover as part of *Pacific Standard Time: LA/LA,* a citywide arts event celebrating the Latin American influence in L.A. They called me their first social media artist in residence. I had already done something similar with *The New Yorker* in 2016, when I took over their account for a week. But the LACMA experience felt different—it was where real life and social media truly merged.

For six weeks, I went to art events and exhibitions across the city and shared them on LACMA's Instagram page. I wasn't approaching it like a traditional art critic—I was speaking in my own voice. Instead of describing works the way a wall label would, I talked about how the art made me feel, what memories it sparked, and how I connected with it. Sometimes I brought my mother or a relative along, and I'd ask them what they thought about a piece, even if they had never heard of the artist. Those conversations reminded me that art didn't have to be intimidating—it could be about the connections we make with one another while looking at it.

While still in residence, I invited my nephew Joseph, Yesi's son, who was sixteen at the time, to come with me on a museum walkthrough for the exhibition *HOME—So Different, So Appealing,* curated by Chon Noriega, Mari Carmen Ramírez, and Pilar Tompkins Rivas. This was my second time seeing Pepón Osorio's work in person, and my nephew's first. This was also my nephew's first time at a museum or an art exhibition, and I couldn't have asked for a better introduction to the art world. Sharing that moment with him made it even more special.

This moment took me back to my own experience in 2013—when I saw Pepón's work for the first time and the impact his art made on me. My nephew and I stood in front of *Badge of Honor* for a good minute and talked. We paid attention to every detail of the bedroom he'd installed in the gallery space. We got close to the work and then stepped back to get a good look of the entire installation. My nephew shared with me that this work reminded him of his own bedroom: dresser, lamps, baseball cards, posters, trophies, clothes hamper, basketballs, mountain bike, computer . . . but most important, it reminded him of his relationship with his father.

Before leaving the museum, my nephew and I took some photos together, standing in front of the installation. We finally left the museum and drove back to our homes in East Los Angeles. So much of this

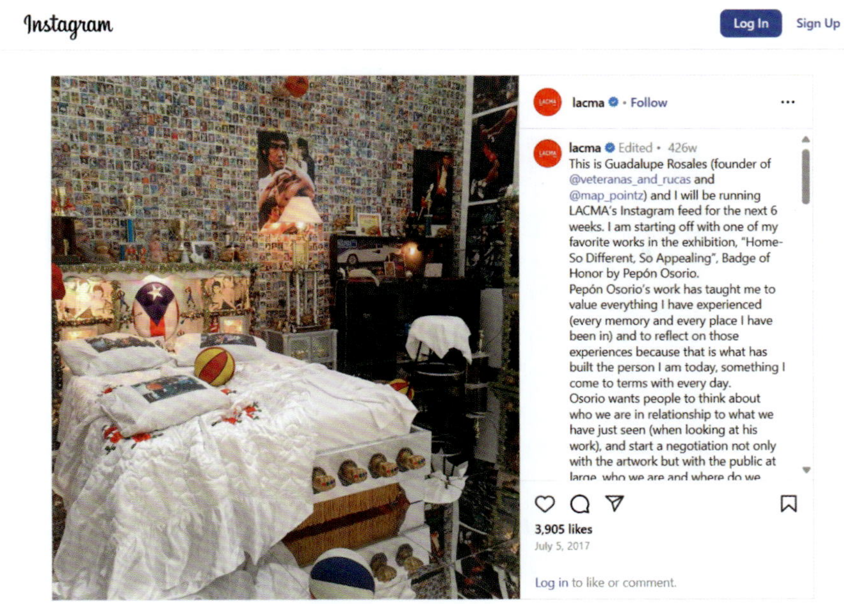

My takeover of LACMA's Instagram page

work felt personal to me and my nephew: a lived experience turned to art. Pepón Osorio made a big impact on both of us at different times of our lives. His work also gave me hope as an artist and a sense of belonging.

This is what I wrote as part of the Instagram post for LACMA:

> This is Guadalupe Rosales (founder of @veteranas_and_rucas and @map_pointz) and I will be running LACMA's Instagram feed for the next 6 weeks. I am starting off with one of my favorite works in the exhibition, "Home- So Different, So Appealing", Badge of Honor by Pepón Osorio.
>
> Pepón Osorio's work has taught me to value everything I have experienced (every memory and every place I have been in) and to reflect on those experiences because that is what has built the person I am today, something I come to terms with every day.
>
> Osorio wants people to think about who we are in relation to what we have just seen (when looking at his work), and start a negotiation not only with the artwork but with the public at large, who we are and where do we stand . . .
>
> "As you stand and you're not allowed to come in, then you

> need to reflect and you need to confront yourself almost as if I placed a giant mirror right in front of you."
>
> —*Pepón Osorio*

I find it helpful to watch or read about artists who I can relate with. We are constantly grappling for ways to talk about these things, because there isn't a starting point of departure for me, so we look at other artists to find words to describe our experience—like Pepón Osorio, Chavela Vargas, and other artists I've been introduced to or learned about along the way.

Through that experience with LACMA, I was finding my own way of making art accessible, bridging the world of museums with the language and experiences of everyday life. While I was doing this residency with LACMA, I learned about Sarah Charlesworth's work when I saw it at LACMA for the first time. I went home and googled her name. I watched an interview where some of her words stuck with me and inspired me.

> Part of my project was really to understand how to engage photography as a language—in other words, to understand how we talk about it, how we picture the world through it, how we orient ourselves to the universe through photography.
>
> I tried to make my artwork as though I were exploring this world—almost like an Alice in Wonderland. What is this strange world of pictures that I live in, and how do they affect me? How do they affect us?
>
> We speak this language, we're surrounded by it. Our sense of history, our sense of art history, our sense of the moon in outer space and under the sea is all informed through photography.

Hearing Sarah Charlesworth talk about photography as a language opened something up for me. She said that photography is how we come to understand places or things we may never experience in person. That stayed with me. I realized that the way we portray the world through an image becomes the way others will come to know it. This could be both good and bad. Good, because a photograph can offer people a glimpse into your way of thinking, into your world. Bad, because it all depended on who was holding the camera—whose perspective was being seen, and whose was left out. That realization pushed me to take more photographs, to trust my own ways of seeing, and to share them. Photography became not just a way of documenting, but of translating how I understood the world—so that others could see it, too.

I continued to photograph the sites in Los Angeles that had important meaning to me: Schurr High school, Arry's Burgers, the Simmons block, the Sixth Street Bridge, stores on Whittier Boulevard, Chronis, Nicola's strip club, and Hollenbeck Park, where I had my quince photoshoot in 1995. Years before, during my first visit to L.A. after many years away, I had started photographing the site where my cousin Ever had been killed. I wasn't looking for that perfect shot; old memories and trauma would stop me and make me nervous. It wasn't until much later that I went back and finally got a good shot of the site.

While working on *Made in L.A. 2023,* my friend Diego, who was also assisting me, and I decided to drive around Leonard and Whittier Boulevard after a long day in the studio. Every time I drove around this area, I made sure to have my camera with me. Days before while driving by myself, I saw a For Rent sign in the window of the apartment where the Rangels once lived.

On impulse, I called the number and asked to make an appointment to go see it with Diego. For the first few minutes, I walked around quietly, not saying anything. Then I told the guy showing me the place that years ago, in the 1990s, my friends had lived here, and this place held personal meaning for me. I asked if I could photograph it, and he kindly let me.

I finally stepped back into my childhood friend's apartment in East L.A.—and back in time. I could remember exactly where the furniture sat in the living room, the door in the back that led to the lot behind the building. A place where I'd kick it from sunset until the next morning—smoking weed, drinking beer, watching movies and music videos at midnight.

It was empty now.

Twenty-plus years later, I finally had access. I photographed everything—every corner, every room, every strike of light slipping through the cracks of the door and the windows.

. . .

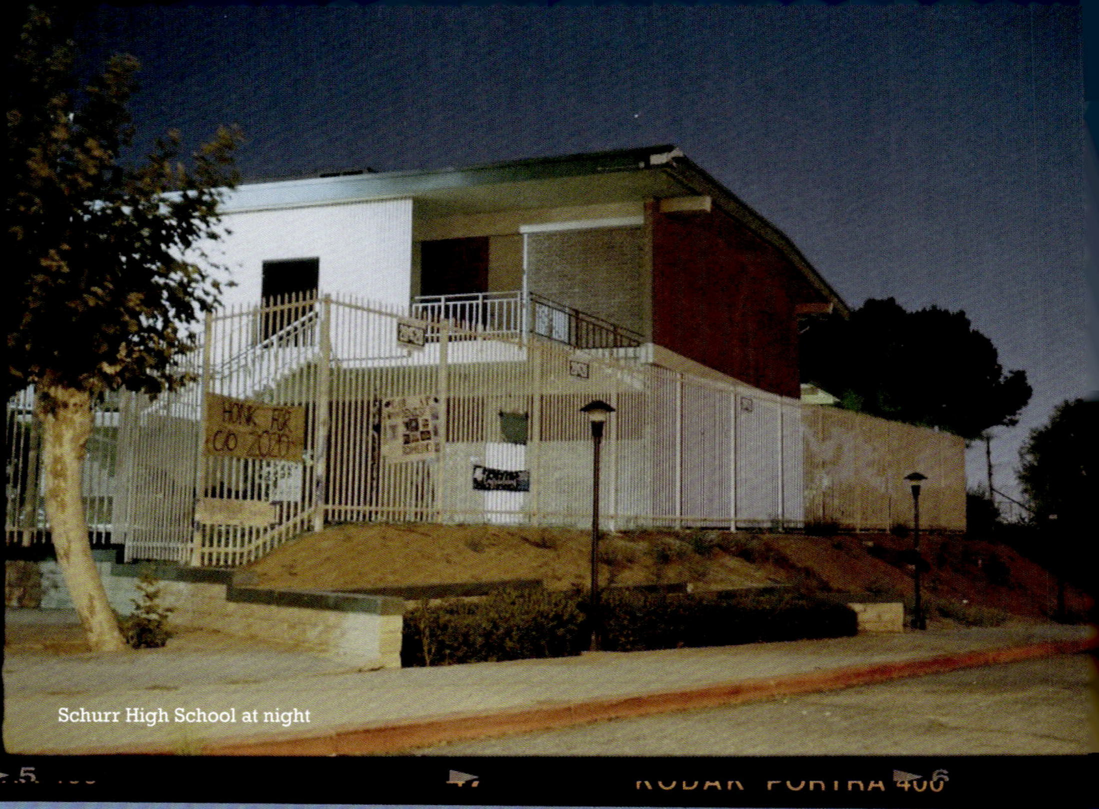

Schurr High School at night

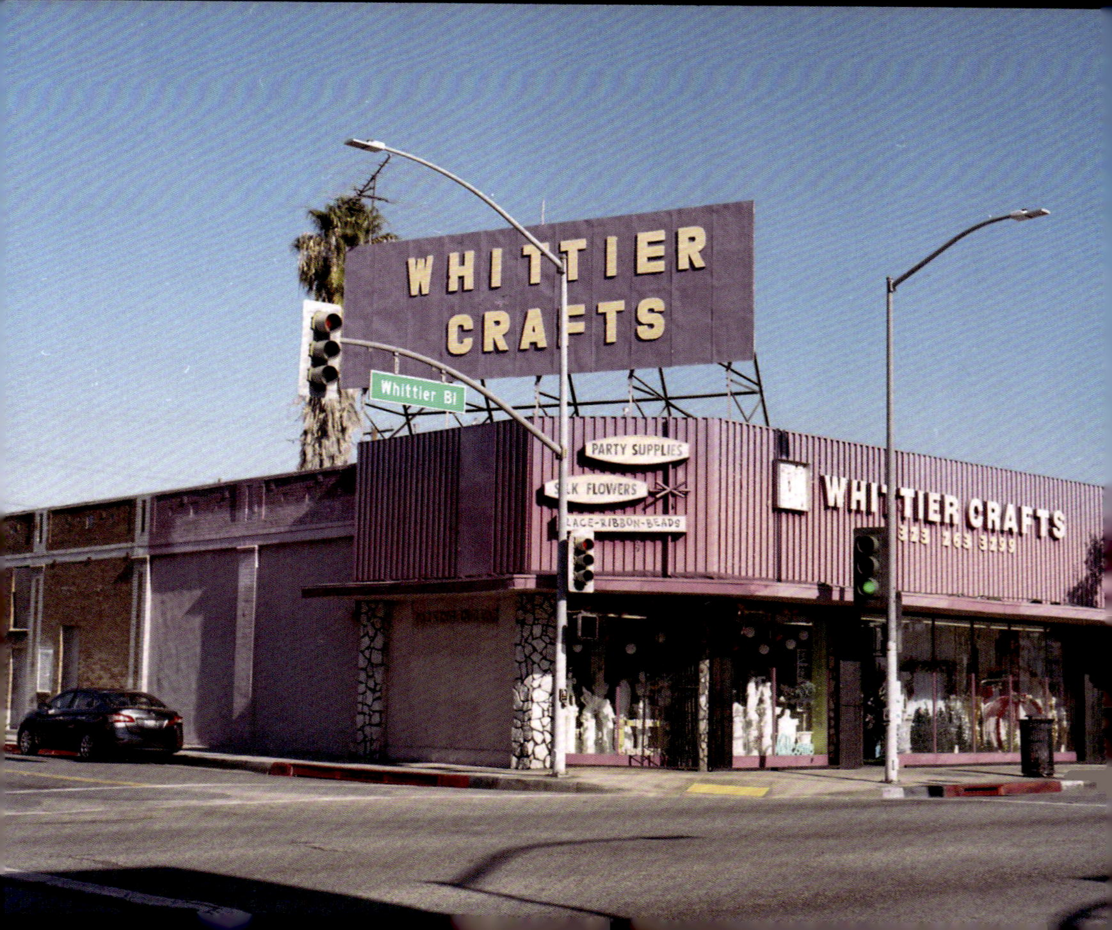

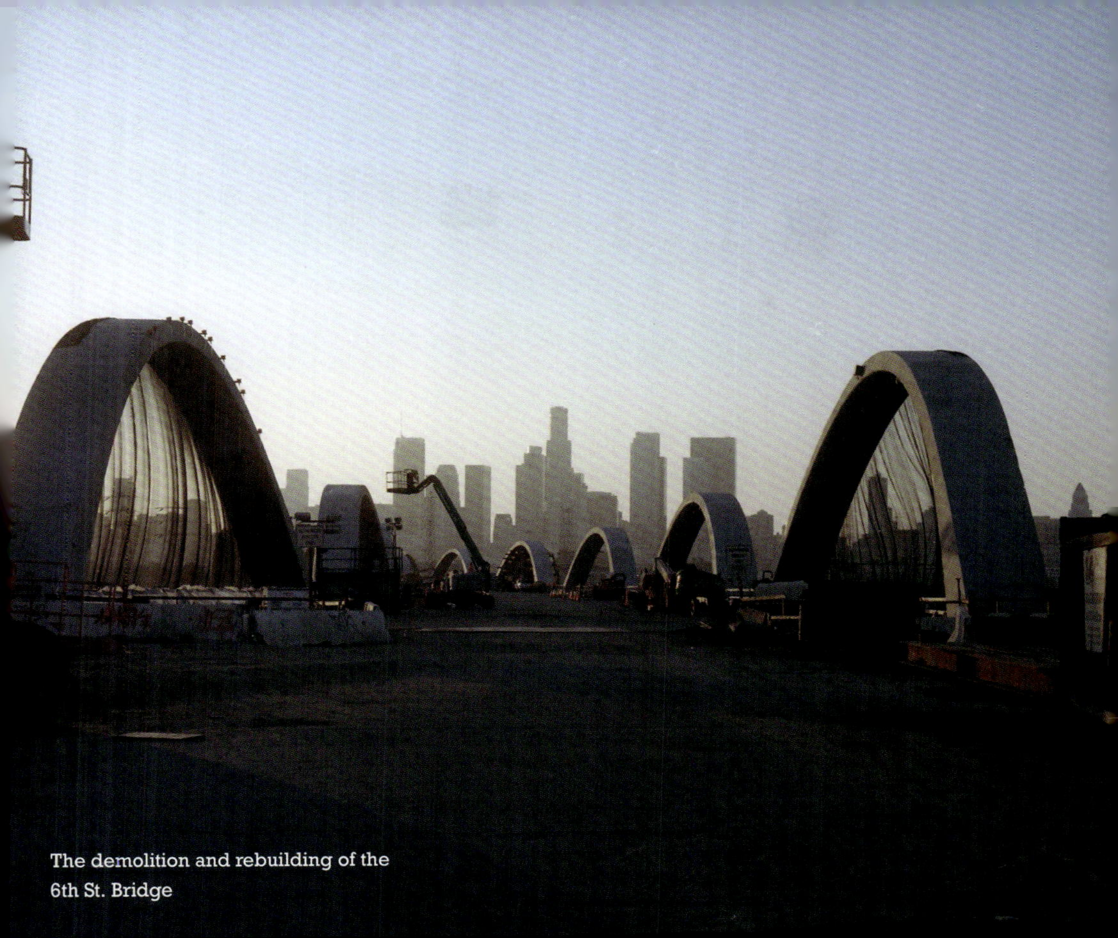

The demolition and rebuilding of the 6th St. Bridge

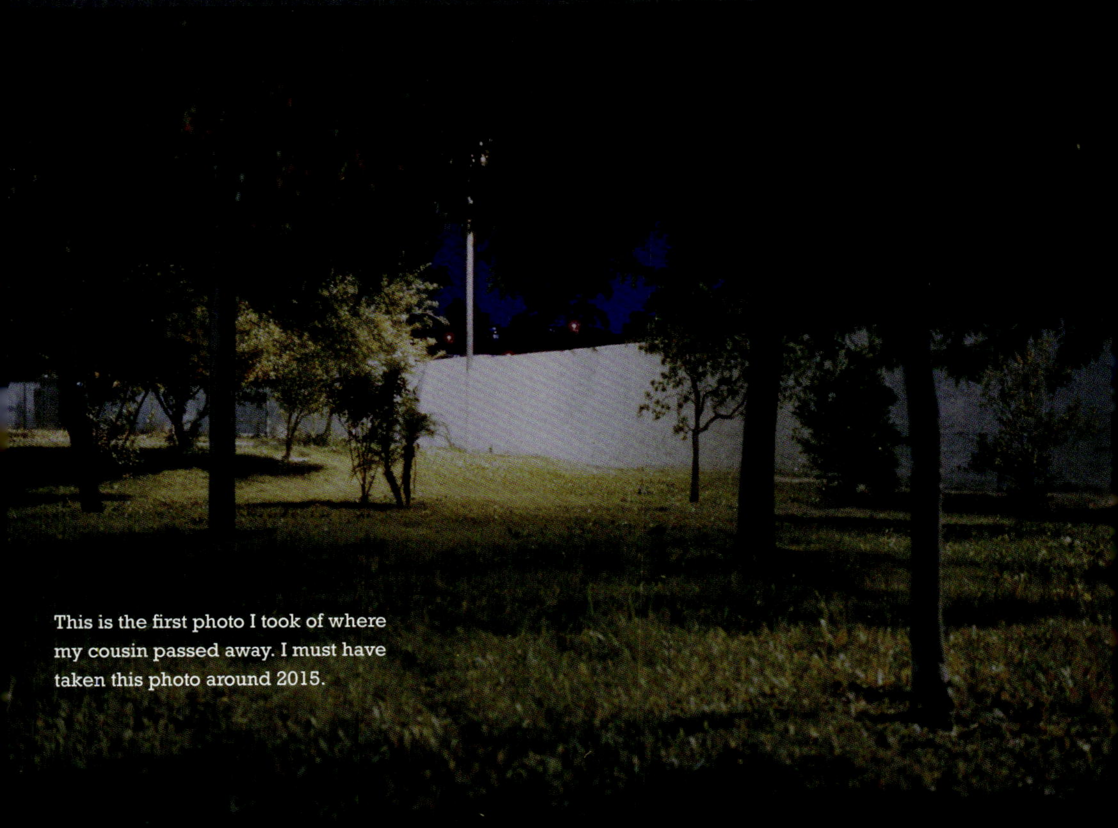

This is the first photo I took of where my cousin passed away. I must have taken this photo around 2015.

LOSING EVER AND wanting to celebrate his memory had been a motivation for me to start *Veteranas and Rucas,* but I also hesitated to write about him. In 2018, when I first shared his story and my memory of him on *Veteranas and Rucas,* I was afraid to open up out of fear that a rival gang would retaliate. I was even ashamed to have experienced so much violence in my life. But when I finally posted my cousin's story and described my grief, it felt like this weight was lifted off my chest, especially when people shared stories similar to mine while others expressed their condolences.

The act of sharing gave me a sense of being understood, and that I wasn't alone in this. Sometimes people who had known Ever left stories about him that I had never heard before. These public posts reminded me of those private drunken nights when family and friends gathered in my house to grieve together and to share stories about Ever that made us laugh and cry. I needed to do this because I wanted more to exist about him, not just a short paragraph in the *Los Angeles Times* describing him as a gang member who lost his life at a truce party. I also started mentioning him in interviews, so now, when you google his name, you'll find endless articles with his name in them. Not just the one from the crime section of the *Los Angeles Times* in 1996.

Although the thought of his death is always violent, what comforts me is knowing that the soil of this city absorbed my cousin's blood, on the night of the winter solstice when he was left to die. In that way, he is still here—in this city, in this world, with me.

As I continued to create work that blended photography with immersive and sculptural elements that transported viewers into the world I was creating, I was invited to exhibit at the Gordon Parks Foundation in Pleasantville, New York. The exhibition was part of my 2019 Gordon Parks Foundation Fellowship, for which I received an award to support projects reflecting themes of representation and social justice, inspired by Gordon Parks's legacy. Gordon Parks documented life in a way that was both candid and deeply human, something I connected to and saw as necessary. Photography has always been at the center of my practice because it allows us—especially people of color—to tell our own stories. It preserves our histories and communities that are often misrepresented, erased, or forgotten, whether those images come from family gatherings, protests, or moments of racial injustice like the L.A. Riots or Proposition 187.

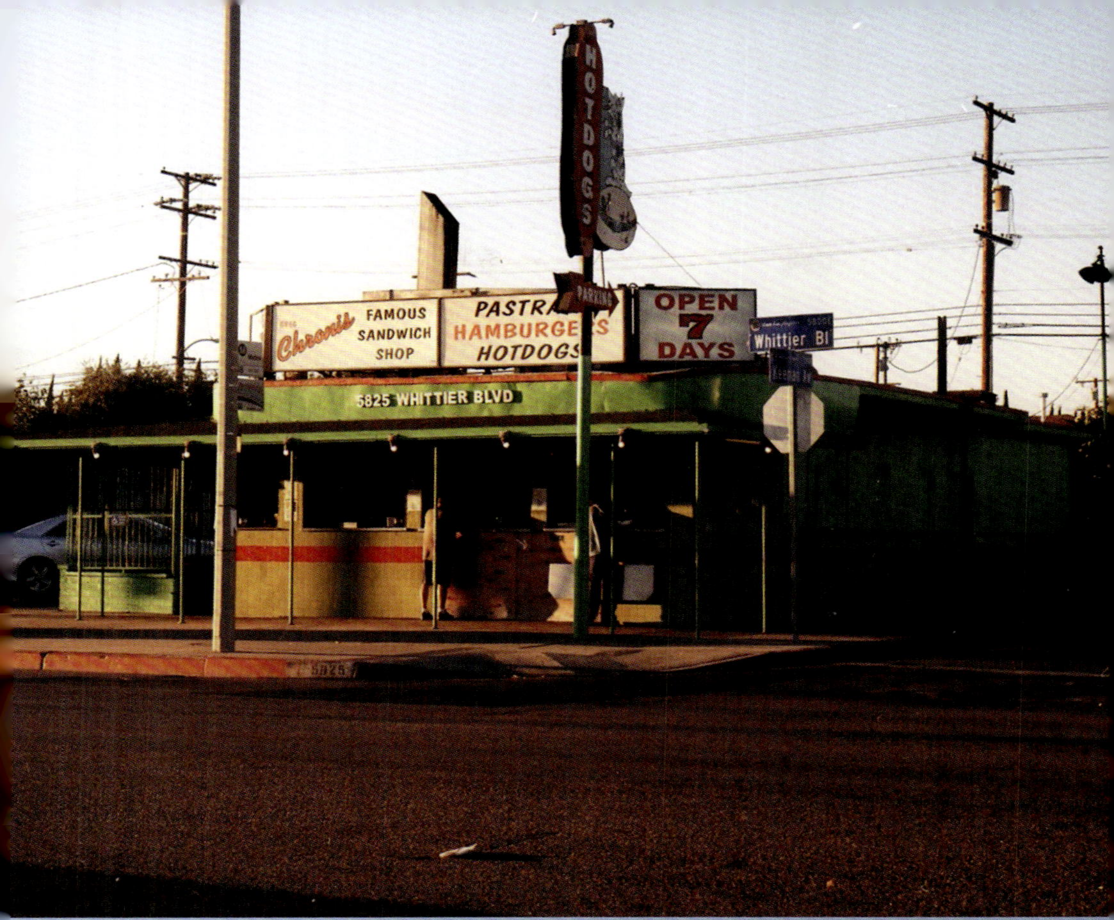
HOTDOGS
Chronis
FAMOUS
SANDWICH
SHOP
HOTDOGS
PARKING
OPEN
7
DAYS
Whittier Bl
5825 WHITTIER BLVD

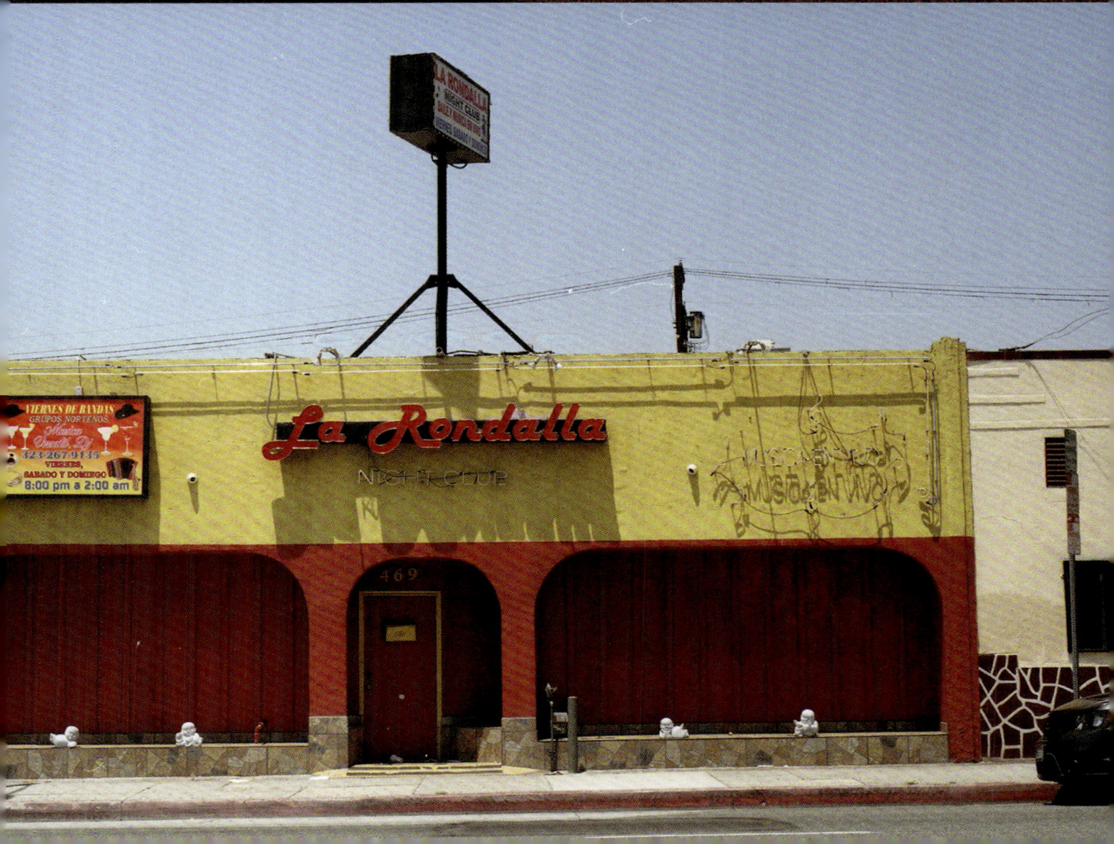
VIERNES DE BANDAS
SABADO Y DOMINGO
8:00 pm a 2:00 am
La Rondalla
NIGHT CLUB
469

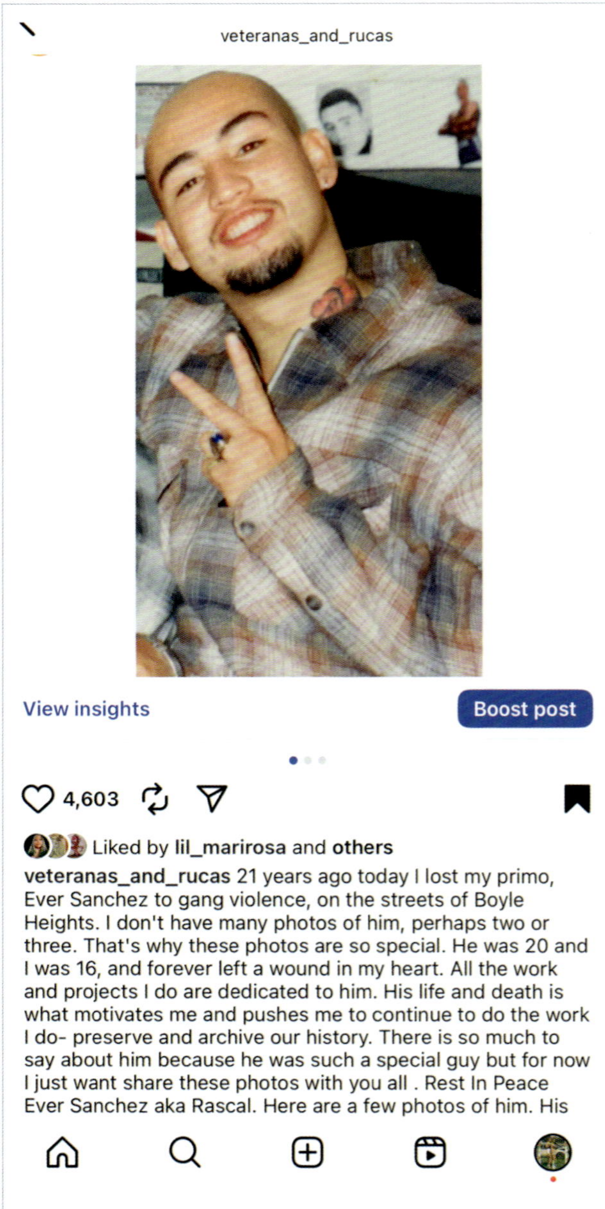

My work was being recognized, and I began weaving my social media practice with my art world experience into something that felt right—something less tangible but deeply connected. Now, at almost every show, people—especially young people—come up to me to thank me for showing work like mine in museums. It isn't so much about my work itself, but about what it reflects back to them: the experience of seeing themselves represented in that space.

I've seen entire families come together at my shows, standing in front of my work with a mix of excitement and emotion. A young woman once sent me a video of herself and her father visiting my exhibition at the Dallas Art Museum in 2022. In the video, they're looking closely at one of my sculptures, which combined etched glass, swap-meet finds, and drawings inspired by Chicano art like what you'd see in *Teen Angels* magazine. For them, it was a bonding moment, a way of connecting through the work. And for me, it was powerful to witness—two people sharing a beautiful experience in a museum where they had never felt like they belonged.

At the gala dinner in New York, I delivered a speech before an audience of hundreds, including artists, musicians, and other celebrities. Afterward, Alicia Keys approached me, introduced herself, and began following my Instagram page. I'll never forget what she said: "Your work spoke volumes. I am here to support one hundred percent." I followed her back, and that moment remains one of the most affirming experiences of my career.

SHAME LESS

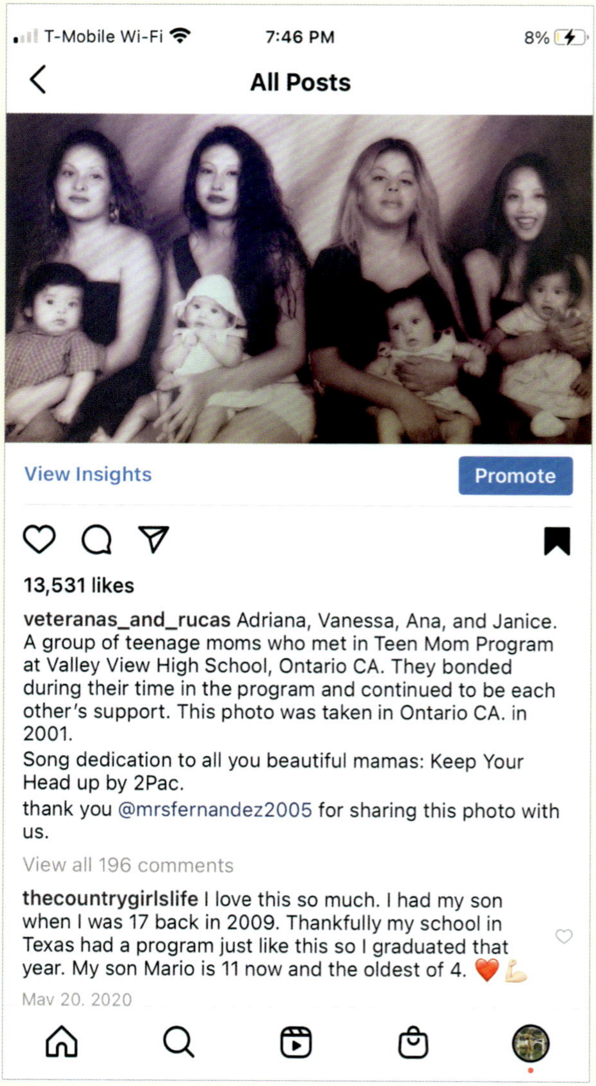

WHEN I RECEIVED this photo from Adriana, I felt like I must be doing something right. *We* were doing something right, because *Veteranas and Rucas* has always been a collaboration between me and my community. It put a smile on my face, and I felt excited to see this work evolve into a space where people from my community were starting to be recognized as something legit, as a place where it was okay to open up and take seriously and to use as a platform for empowerment through their own stories.

Adriana's DM felt like a reclamation. Stories like this had been overlooked or looked down on. Stories that many did not want to share, coming from the effects of a culture that shamed pregnancies at a young age, toxic masculinity, and the fear of slut- and body-shaming. But this was becoming a time when having a kid at a young age and bonding with other women with similar experiences was healing. In this post the women hold one another with a bond that seems indestructible, and over twenty years later, it is.

When I received photos like this through direct message, I would set up a conversation with the person who had submitted, to talk through getting to know each other. I let them know that their photo submissions are beautiful and important. If I can relate, I let them know that. It's important for people to know that they are talking to someone who had similar experiences. Then there is an opportunity to reminisce together. So when Adriana asked if I could share this photo of her and her four friends decades later, I realized that what we were doing collectively was more than empowerment. We were collectively creating a movement. This was also a reflection of what I was seeing in real life. In my own home and family. My close friends who I went to high school with. Many of us didn't have the opportunity to tell our side of things. Many of the stories shared were from a male perspective.

In moments like these, I was helping to facilitate conversations and dialogue that surround this often-overlooked piece of American history because these women had the courage to tell their stories. Posts like this one have been the foundation of *Veteranas and Rucas* and *Map Pointz:* women bonding over shared stories.

It is important to highlight these stories that were once seen as something to be ashamed of as empowering and brave and beautiful. In the comments, other women shared how they felt seen and how they were able to relate just by reading this story and post. Many women also shared that they had gone to this same school.

I get many submissions almost every day, mostly from women who now have the courage and pride to share their own stories. Since I've started this work, I have always encouraged others to share their stories, otherwise someone else will, most likely an outsider. Take a look at the mainstream media repeating the same stereotypes and not telling our complicated history. This is why it's taken us so long to do so because we have not been recognized or seen in a more beautiful light or representation. Many untold stories come with layers of beauty, pain, pride, vanity, grief, etc. Stories like my own. When I say "complicated" I mean it with so much love, pride, and complex beauty.

Another example are posts about our moments in school. Many of us took photo classes, some of the most interesting creative classes we had access to. I also took a photo class in high school and for a long time I thought my photos weren't worthy of sharing because I thought I wasn't a good photographer, but when people sent me theirs and I saw how beautiful they were, how much story and beauty they carried, I was inspired to share my own and to really appreciate those images decades later.

It was exciting to talk about this with a larger audience. What I appreciated most about these photos is how these images not just record a moment in time but also the imperfections, the attempts, the errors and beauty of learning analog photography as a teenager. Because we couldn't afford a good professional camera, we carried the school camera with us everywhere, to parties, kickbacks, cruise nights.

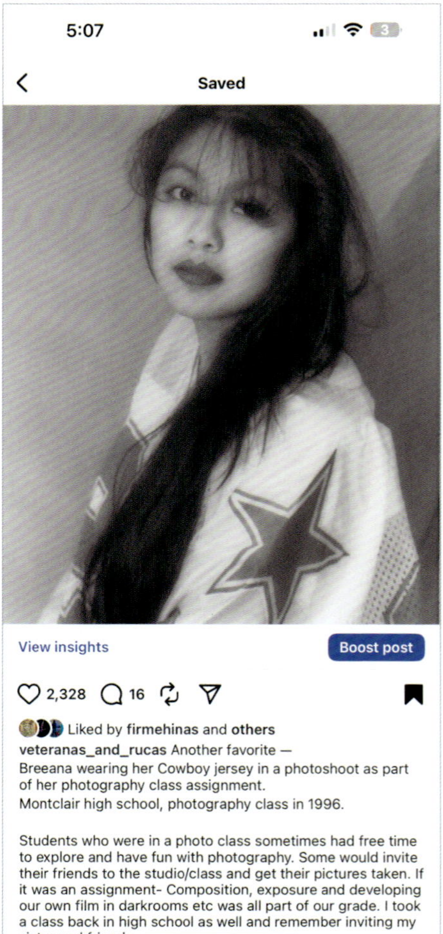

Veteranas and Rucas and *Map Pointz* were always sites where we collectively decriminalized and reframed the history of brown youth. Specifically, though, of young brown women who grew up in Southern California. My focus on women is especially poignant given the ways in which Latinas have been underrepresented and misrepresented, often in highly sexualized ways.

When I started these two projects my motive was always to amplify women's voices. I had noticed that when I started asking another woman (like my sister) about a particular memory it was always exciting to reminisce with them but there was always a moment of "Don't say that too loud because the kids could hear us" or "My husband doesn't know that part of my life" or "My parents slut-shamed me as a kid."

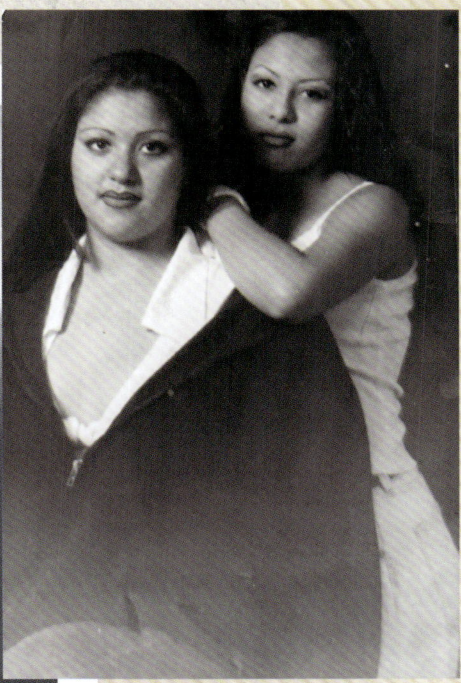

Maria and Paula as the subject for my photo class in 1997

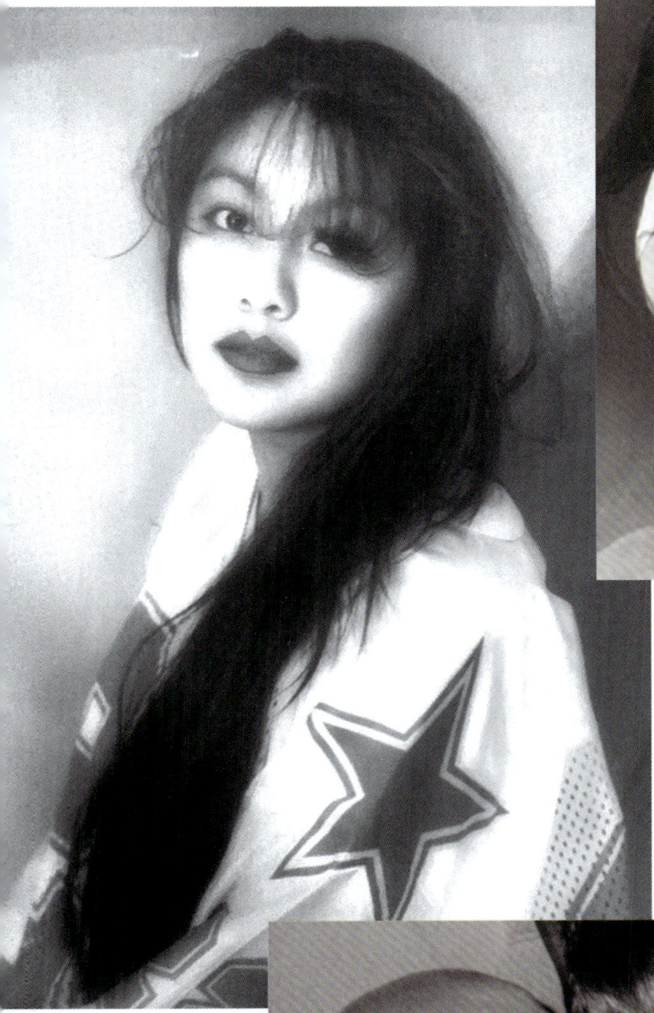

LEFT: One of Breeana's assigments was to take a self-portrait of herself using a timer.

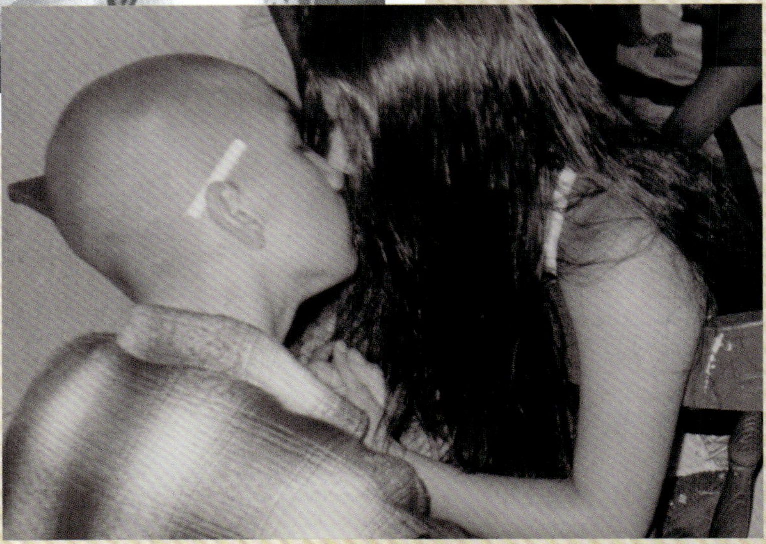

Photo I took of Maria getting a tattoo on her back at Coco's house. I took this with a camera I borrowed from my photo class. The camera was later stolen by Lil George.

As my page continued to grow, I noticed *Veteranas and Rucas* and *Map Pointz* began to get attention from important figures and celebrities—Becky G, BReal, Christina Ricci, among others. I also started building friendships with them; I was also in a photoshoot with Jessica Alba for Opening Ceremony, where we exchanged info and started following each other. Since Veteranas and Rucas was growing so much, I made posts to remind people to keep things respectful because this was a space for women to feel safe and able to share their personal stories.

When women in my life began to feel more comfortable sharing their stories, I knew there were many others who wanted to do the same. Myself included: I began to take out old photos, many of which I was still embarrassed to share but gradually I did. It was cute and funny to revisit these photos, especially reading the notes on the back. I was always attracted to photographs not just for their images, but also for those notes. They were like relics; they reconnected me to the people who gave them to me, and to the moment they were given. Over the years I've gotten so many emails and DMs from people thanking me, saying, "I'm so glad that there is something out there that represents a part of our culture." It's nice to hear that, of course, but it validates my belief that there was something missing—part of history.

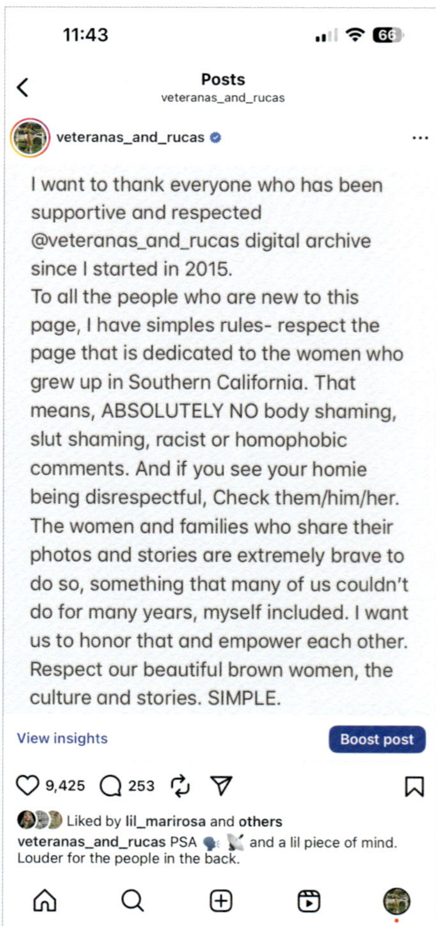

I have made posts to remind people to keep it respectful.

HUDDAS

ANOTHER PART OF OUR HISTORY THAT WE DIDN'T talk about enough was our interactions with the police, so I started to think about sharing those experiences publicly with the goal of acknowledging and addressing them or even healing them.

In my case, the first time I was intimidated by the police I was just seven years old, after my mom was arrested when my dad accused her of stabbing him. And my friends and I were targeted consistently throughout my youth and for many years I carried shame because of this; it made me feel less than. I believed that they were the good guys and that if we were being treated this way we weren't supposed to be out at night; we weren't supposed to get arrested.

Later on I realized that the police didn't go to our neighborhood to make sure we were safe. They came to profile us. It only happened in certain neighborhoods, it didn't happen in Beverly Hills. When the Rampart scandal happened it was similar to my experience. The people who were being targeted were the people who lived in those neighborhoods, meaning that we were poor.

I started understanding that it was a systemic problem when I started hearing other stories that sounded like mine.

When I was growing up, the local police knew my friends and me by our names or nicknames: Michael, Kiki, Lupe, Maria, and so on. To get around them, we created slang terms or codes to survive the streets and to communicate among our friends and family; we called the police “pigs,” “po-pos,” “black and white,” and “the huddas.”

As teenagers, every time a helicopter hovered over our heads at night, we made them chase us around the neighborhood with their beaming light aiming at us from the sky. Cutting through the bushes and trees, in alleyways and backyards casting silhouettes of us on the walls. Even if the helicopter chase wasn’t for us we still made them beam their lights at us just to confuse them. We laughed as we gasped for air from running around in circles. A dangerous game to play but at the time, this was fun for the kids of Los Angeles. We did not know if there were consequences. I was fourteen years old, naïve just like any kid our age and street-smart at the same time.

But sometimes we couldn’t escape them and their power became clear. The front of my house was my favorite hangout spot. Friends came by at any time of day or night. We leaned over and rested our arms on the chain-link fence as we greeted people passing by on their way to and from work. Our neighborhood friends came and sat with us on the stoop, sometimes for ten or fifteen mins, and other times ’til the sun came out again the next day.

One night, two policemen patrolling the block parked on the alleyway next to my house and got out of their car with their flashlights in hand, pointing them at us. As the police walked closer toward us, they got more aggressive. My sense was that they were afraid of us, so they wanted to intimidate us. Their flashlights were too bright for us to see their faces and they began to search us for no particular reason. They were male cops, but they didn’t care that we were underage girls. They patted us down while they had us on our knees with our hands behind our heads facing the wall. It was the wall from my house—the one with the faded orange-toned paint. As I stared at this wall, hearing the police go from being nice and trying to gain our trust to being aggressive, assertive, and rough, I was reminded that even in the place I called home, I was not safe. They didn’t find anything on us so they shoved us around, cursed at us, and told us to go home because it was past curfew. But we were home. The power they held over us—and how much they got away with—only fueled the fire I carried inside me.

In 2020, around the time when George Floyd was murdered by the police, I shared a post on Instagram of a teenage boy named Anthony Mosqueda Jr., who was shot and killed by the Montebello police in 1998.

Anthony and I went to high school together, and in the post I shared a photo along with my personal memory of him, a story that also humanized him. I was also reminded of Javier Quezada Jr. (D. 2003), murdered by the Pasadena police, and Jorge Jimenez (D. 2011), also killed by the Montebello Police, all of whom I had gone to school with. To see people I grew up with being murdered or harassed by the police angered me.

When I shared the post about Anthony, people opened up about their own personal experience with the police, about relatives, lovers, or friends killed by the police, and shared stories of Anthony.

Over the years, many people have described this Instagram

veteranas_and_rucas • Follow

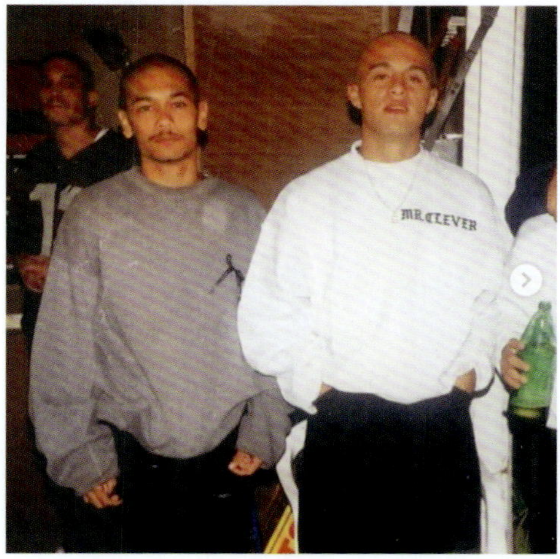

14,783 likes

veteranas_and_rucas I am looking up names of friends who were killed by the police. So many names I'm starting to lose count. This is Dreamer aka Anthony(grey sweatshirt) and his friend Clever. We went to high school together, he sat in front of me in history class. Quiet, mellow kid. In 1998, He was shot in the back multiple times by the Montebello Police. He was only 17 about to turn 18. He was a young teenage boy and it sickens me to think of this. Still can't wrap my mind on these murders. I want to remind us that the same system that continues to kill our relatives is the same system killing Black folks. For this reason we need to be united in this fight. We also need to stop criminalizing our own people (the media already does that for us) and start looking at the bigger picture- the

Claims Filed Against Police in Shooting Death of Boy, 17

L.A. Times Archives

Feb. 10, 1998 12 AM PT

<I> FROM A TIMES STAFF WRITER</I>

Parents of a 17-year-old youth who was shot to death by Montebello police Jan. 1 filed legal claims against the city Monday.

"I'm not ready to forgive. I'll never forget," the boy's father, Anthony Mosqueda Sr., told reporters in front of Montebello City Hall.

Anthony Mosqueda Jr. died after being shot by a Montebello police officer on South Spruce Street. Police said the youth pointed a rifle at two officers who had seen him beat on the window of an occupied car and chase the vehicle while armed.

Subscribe to Continue Reading

Subscribers ar

Dodgers Dugout: The 1 Dodger history

How Del Amitri rocker Parkinson's struggle in resilience

Cars are so expensive loans

Trump says he's firing opening new front in fi control

Apple TV+ is raising it 30%

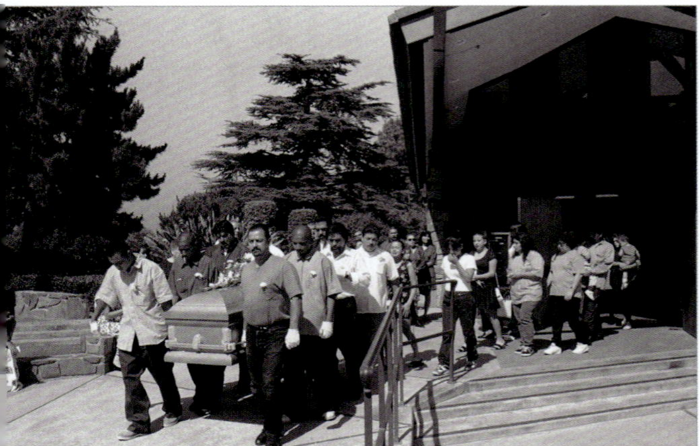

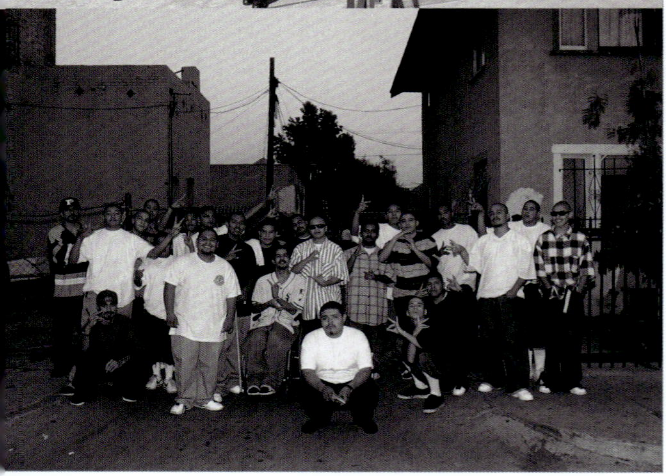

LEFT: Photos from Joseph's funeral, sent after I made the post below. These photos reminded me of my own experience when my cousin died.

page as a digital altar where people share stories in the comments. This is similar to leaving an offering. Many see the cycle of violence against black and brown people, especially men. After my post about Anthony, I received submissions from people who could relate to my post, like Joseph's sister, who has been a longtime follower and one I continue to stay in touch with.

Her brother's death at the hands of the notoriously corrupt Rampart division of

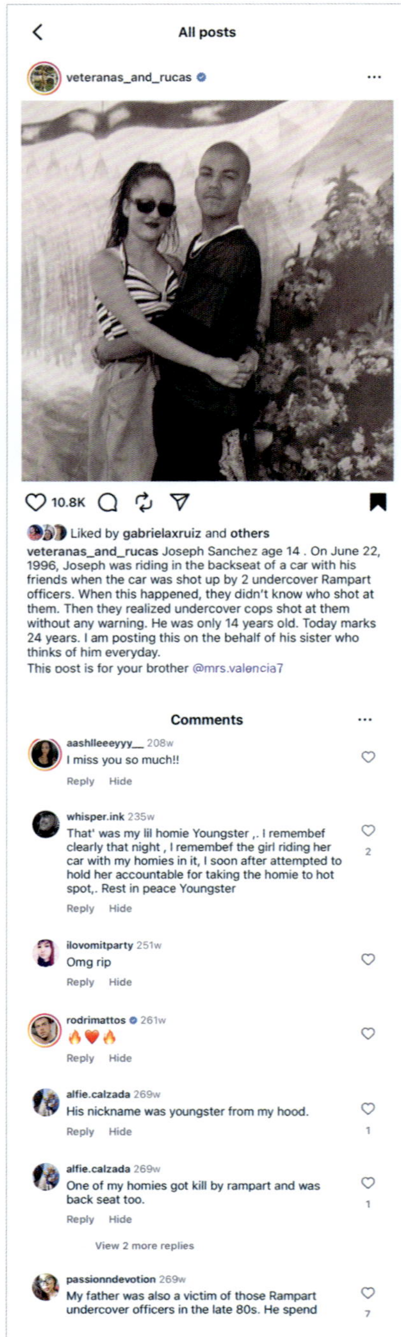

Post shared on behalf of Joseph's sister, who asked me to help raise awareness about police brutality and the lives lost to it

the LAPD had never been publicly acknowledged, and it was really important to her to share his story. I ended the post with the line, "I'm posting this on behalf of his sister who thinks of him every day." Many of us already knew the Rampart police were the most corrupt, and when I made this post, so much of this history resurfaced. People remembered, people spoke up. It wasn't a secret—it was an open wound that had never healed, a reminder that justice was never served.

A post I never imagined making was about suicide—specifically about men struggling with depression. When the family of a young man reached out and shared that their father had taken his own life, they asked me to post something in his memory. I wanted to honor their request in a way that raised awareness, while also offering resources to the community. In learning more, I found that men are at a higher risk

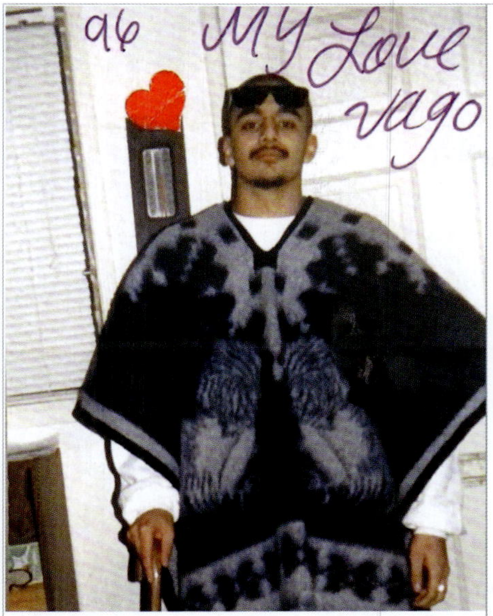

veteranas_and_rucas I would like to take this opportunity to share these photos of Sal aka Vago on the behalf of his family and express my condolence.

A few months ago I posted a photo submitted by @alysss96 , Sal's daughter-(second slide) a photo of her parents Lupe and Sal (Vago). This past Tuesday Sal passed away and the family is completely heartbroken. Sal struggled with depression and ended his life last Tuesday.
It is important for us to speak about depression and mental health issues in our communities. I know it's difficult but important. I also know that sometimes we don't even know how to speak about it or ask for help, especially for us who didn't grow up with enough resources. This is real and can affect anyone, men and women. This memorial post is for Sal and to bring awareness around mental health - depression, PTSD etc.

December 13, 2020

latinajunkie 244w
💔
Reply Hide

swishasandherb 244w · ❤ by author
Rip to the homie our raza needs to stand up more for each other when it comes to mental illness a lot of times it cause we don't have no one to turn to or get turned down by the it's all in your head saying but it's more then that I been down this road but I let my ego go and got help and was put on medication and not ashamed to say it it's turn my life around for the better and gave me my life back with also talk therapy I'm thankful everyday that I got help and I also pray to the most high don't wait till it's to late raza there's plenty of help out there
1

Sal, also known as Vago. His daughter shared this photo with me, along with his story of depression and suicide, hoping to raise awareness in our communities.

CALIFORNIA

Claim Filed in Fatal Shooting by Officer

By Daniel Hernandez
Feb. 22, 2003 12 AM PT

TIMES STAFF WRITER

The family of an East Los Angeles man shot and killed last month by a Pasadena policeman has filed a claim against that city seeking $10 million in damages.

Officer Steve Arcand shot Javier Quezada Jr., 22, several times Jan. 23 in the parking lot of Las Encinas Hospital after Quezada allegedly charged at the policeman with a pair of 9-inch scissors.

Quezada, who had been taking medication for depression for more than a year, was standing at the edge of the lot with his parents, who were trying to persuade him to go inside for a psychiatric screening, his family said.

Subscribe to Continue Reading

CALIFORNIA

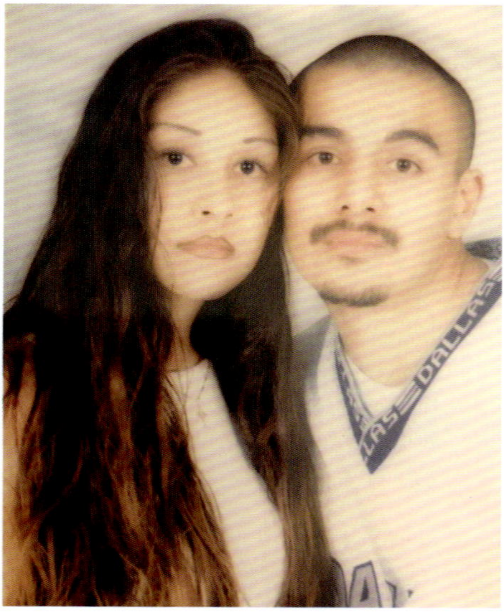

Sal and his girlfriend/wife in the ’90s

of suicide than women yet often face greater challenges when it comes to expressing their feelings or asking for help. Many men are raised to be tough, to hold back tears, and to not show emotion—but this can be more damaging than helpful. Sharing this post was my way of reminding people to check in with one another, especially with the men in our lives who may be suffering in silence. It was a reminder that the page was not just mine; it was being shaped by readers who were also contributors, who cared enough to share their painful stories alongside the happy ones.

I grew up during a period of extreme violence in Los Angeles, and my generation was always trying to figure out ways to escape—to find safety, to find joy. My Instagram accounts have given me the chance to celebrate those moments of joy and reconnect with others who lived through them, too. Most of the posts I share are actually pretty joyful: Mother’s Day dedications, people talking about where they shopped for their best ’fits on a budget—places like Santee Alley or the swap meet—or remembering the ritual of getting ready in the cutest looks just to take photos. Sometimes it only took an hour to get that perfect Starshot portrait, but you had to be fully present for it, no matter how violent the world outside was.

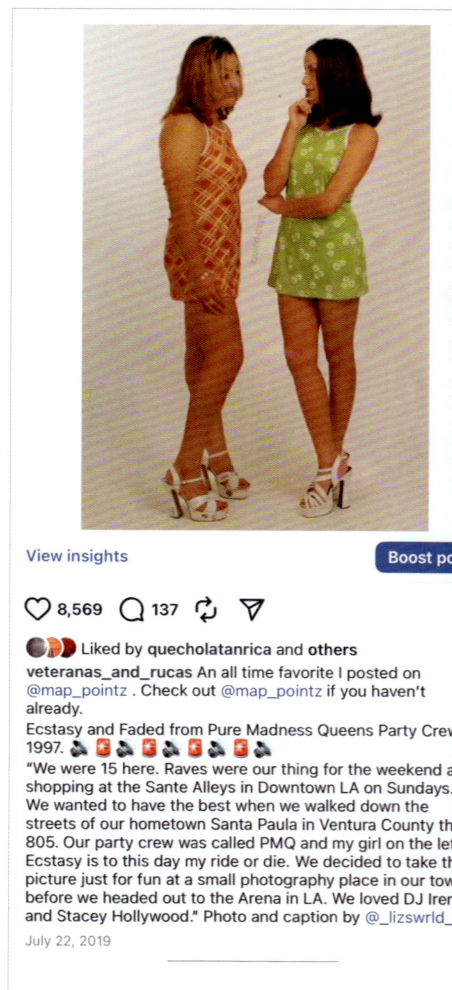

veteranas_and_rucas ...

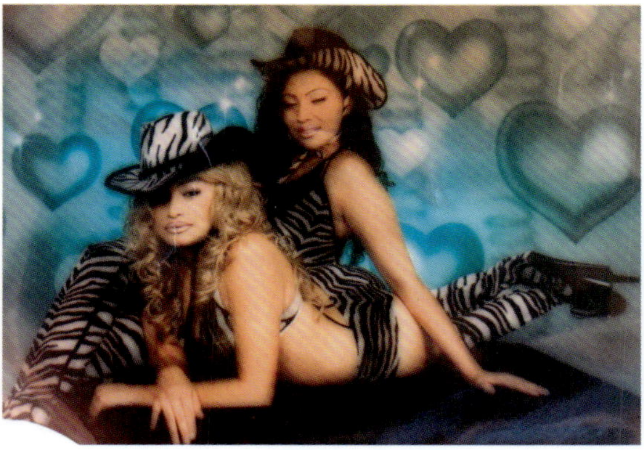

Liked by **anitaherrera_** and **17,428 others**

veteranas_and_rucas Sisters Mindi and Mandy, circa 1999, Riverside, Ca.

"When we went to the Tyler Mall to take this photo, a crowd gathered around and followed us." – Mindi (Watts,Ca raised)

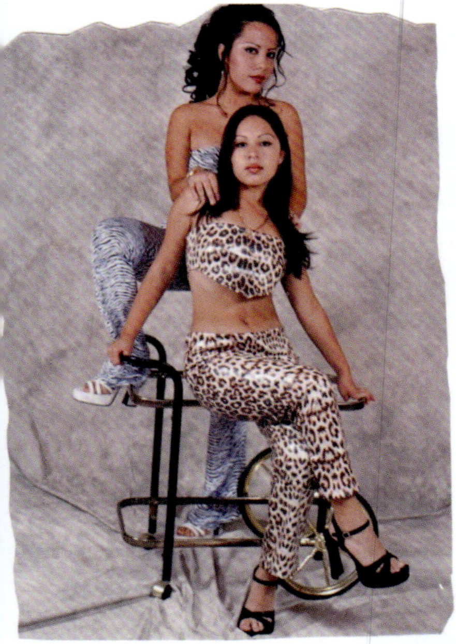

'iew insights Boost post

18.3K 205

Liked by **gabrielaxruiz** and **others**

'eteranas_and_rucas NOT YOUR MOOD BOARD

'his is Vere and Ericka in 2001.

.os Angeles CA

'hey worked in a mexican club in L.A called Rodeo as bottle jirls. A photographer called them up for this photoshoot. /ere (Zebra print) appeared in one of Lupillo Rivera's music 'ideos as one of the widowed girlfriends.

Enjoy your weekend everyone and keep on sending those 'irme photos!

Thank you @dayliadee !

Selection of positive posts

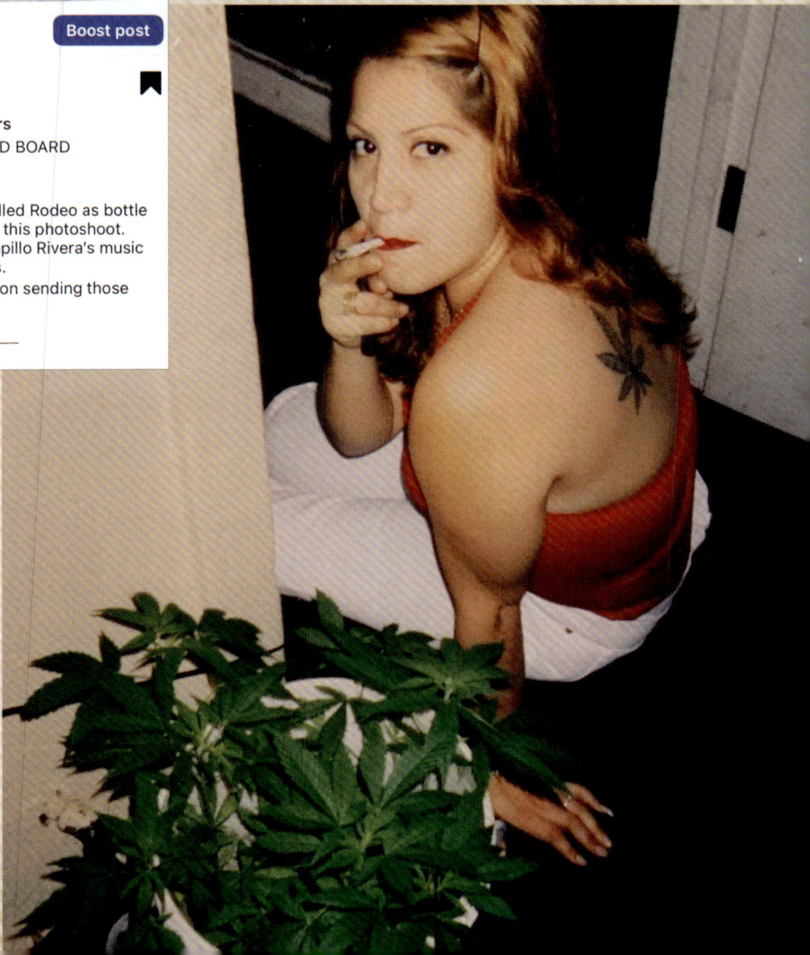

Patricia smoking weed

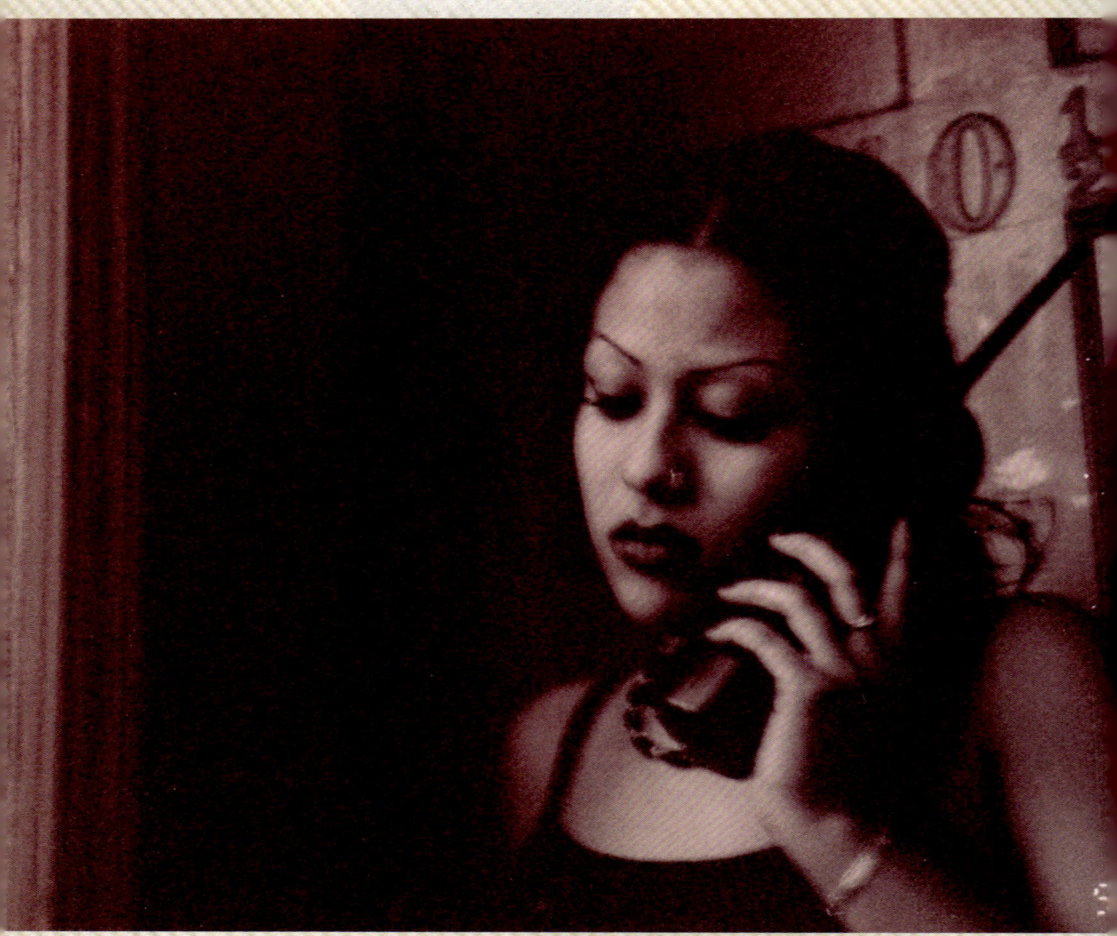

Maria on the phone in front of our house in 1999

PARTY LINE

BEYOND STYLE AND PHOTOGRAPHY, THERE were mental escapes, too, like the party lines that let us drift somewhere else, even if just for a while.

In 2020, the journalist Walter Thompson-Hernández invited me to be part of an episode of his podcast *California Love* celebrating party lines, a pre–social media way young people connected anonymously. We re-created the magic on that podcast and it took me back.

The party line was mostly made up of teenage boys and girls who had similar taste in music, fashion, and lifestyles and were in a similar location. Almost everyone who dialed in was a teenager eager to flirt and be silly and sometimes to start fights over the phone, especially those who were too shy to do it in person. Many, including myself, called in to step out of our comfort zone. It gave us an adrenaline high.

For the party line, we had to use all our senses and our imagination. We had to visualize the image the person on the other line was describing for us. What they were wearing, what cologne they used, what environment they were in when they called the line. You could hear if the other person was in an empty room, outside, or in a tight space like a closet or bathroom. Our senses were on high alert. On one occasion when I connected with this boy, we exchanged our personal numbers and got off the party line and he called me directly on the phone.

The song "I Only Have Eyes for You" by the Flamingos played on his line and I could hear it in the background. I could imagine an empty bedroom, probably with the lights off, just him and me talking peacefully on the phone. I could hear the phone close to his lips because his voice was clear, close to my ear. I could also tell he was by himself in the room because the music on his end sounded distant and like there was nothing else between us.

I closed my eyes and felt close to him, almost as if we were in the same room. Although I only knew what he had told me about himself and we never met in person, it felt very intimate. It was the same feeling I got when I hung out with a crush for the first time. This excitement of connecting and having all these cute fantasies of having a boyfriend. After the song "I Only Have Eyes for You" ended, another one played. "Blue Moon" by the Marcels.

I wish I remembered the boy's name because that moment was truly special. I had never felt so excited about someone. And perhaps this was the moment that taught me and showed me what flirting, talking to your crush, and maybe even falling in love could be like. While talking on the phone he told me he had been smoking weed and was a little faded, just like the music in the background.

He asked me if I smoked weed and said that if I did I should light one up while on the phone so I could be on the same level as him and to feel like I was there with him. I didn't smoke that night but did feel a contact high from afar. I had a few experiences like this, although these moments were rare because most of the time we only called the party line to talk to multiple people at once, just like we do when we're at a party.

This space was for the loners, the shy boys and shy girls. For the cholos and cholas, the ravers and groovers. The taggers, pretty boys, quebradita boys and girls. For the girls and boys looking for a fun hookup even if it's just over the phone. For the wild ones, the confident ones, and those who were good at holding up a conversation and flirting.

You could be your complete self or perform a completely different person, whatever you think the other person wanted to hear. About 50 percent of the kids calling these numbers made shit up. Our sexual energy and fantasies were high and many of us didn't know exactly what to do with it, which is why flirting over the phone with random people felt safe: We could be free.

We sifted through the calls and chats 'til we found people like us or whoever had a sexy voice that didn't sound like an adult. All over Los Angeles County, Orange County, and San Diego, kids spent hours dialing a free telephone number and jumping from one chat room to the next. Mostly late at night, Friday through Saturday was the busiest, and sometimes Sunday afternoons we spent hours flirting with strangers that perhaps we'd never meet in person.

These numbers were passed around at parties, at school, and on the boulevard. Some party crews created their own party lines. Party crews were taking over the virtual world, creating ways for us to connect and have fun not just in person but over the phone. There were many numbers out there but not all party lines were fun. The way this worked was to pick up the phone and dial a number. After dialing a number we were given instructions by an automated voice.

Numbers 1 through 9 were treated as "chat rooms." Some rooms may have had zero participants, while other rooms were full with more than ten people trying to have a conversation. When a room was this full, it could be fun but also overwhelming and chaotic, with everyone speaking over one another so much that it became a senseless noise. Each room had a different vibe, and if a room was empty and you liked the person you were trying to have a conversation with in a full room, the conversations could be taken to the empty room. Strangely this felt like you were in a hotel room or on a date but in pitch-darkness.

We started the conversation with "So what's up, what's your name, where do you live?" both of us being shy at first. These conversations often led to more personal questions like "What are you wearing? Where do you go to school?" Whether this went any further depended on if we were vibing each other. The voice was the first attraction. We asked the boys about their hair—"You got a shaved head? A fade? Buzz cut? Pretty-boy look?" Or "What cologne do you use? Do you wear hats? Do you bang?" Boys asked girls, "How long is your hair? What do you do for fun? Do you have a boyfriend? Are you from a party crew?"

Guys who banged, meaning started claiming gangs/neighborhoods and picking fights with rivals on the phone, could be hot but mostly annoying because it usually defeated the purpose of the party line. Some girls may have found this hot, especially if the boys banged on a rival gang and picked up on girls at the same time. Talking to someone from a gang usually ended up with a group of girls partying that same night of meeting up in a neighborhood.

. . .

NOT EVERYONE KEPT it real when it came to describing themselves over the phone but I believe most did. We could tell by their voice, their words and swag on the phone, and maybe a little instinct of ours: who had game and who didn't. Choosing your words and timing wisely. When to drop a good line. Everything had a rhythm. Sometimes, we couldn't trust them completely but this was all part of the game because most likely you'd never meet them in person. I never met anyone I spoke with on the phone in person and that's what was most thrilling.

On the *California Love* episode, a group of writers, poets, and artists who had been part of the party lines in the '90s got back together to re-create the magic of that time.

WALTER THOMPSON-HERNÁNDEZ: So look—in real life I was a goofy thirteen-year-old. But on the P-line, I was someone else. I was an eighteen-year-old mechanic who lived in Culver City.[. . .] I really thought that's what girls wanted to hear. The P-line gave me a rush, and to be honest, it's where I learned how to talk to girls for the first time. You see, I was pretty shy, I had a lisp—I still do. I stuttered, and I didn't have the courage to approach girls I liked. But on the P-line—I could be Little Brownie.

WALTER THOMPSON-HERNÁNDEZ: Damn you sound good. Where you stay at?

GUADALUPE ROSALES: Chaau— Hey, what's up? It's Lupe. Also known as Adorable (that was my nickname). From East L.A.'s Aztek Nation . . .

GUADALUPE ROSALES: I mean, I grew up in the fucking hood. So—this is a time when a lot of violence, a lot of like, incarcerations, gang violence, was on the rise, so we're already being criminalized. I'm already being, like, handcuffed by police. I do think that for most people the party line is a safe space. And we can be who we want to be. [. . .]

I don't even know if it's lying, like lying sounds like, "Oh, you did something bad. You're lying." It's more like this ideology of who we think we are or how much information we're going to put out there. As a fifteen- or sixteen-year old, I wasn't out. You know, as a brown queer person, I'm not out. So, I feel like my awkwardness, my shyness, stems from that because I am trying to be someone who I'm not. But I don't know this, you know what I mean? I don't know that I'm supposed to be someone else.

In retrospect, I realize that those party lines were a precursor to the internet communities that have been such an important part of my life. And when I started *Veteranas,* I was sort of hiding like I did on the party line, but over time, as my readers shared their stories, I became more and more empowered to share my own. And it felt important to do so, so that they could trust me at the same time that they entrusted me with their memories; that I had gone through some of the same experiences and that was part of why I cared.

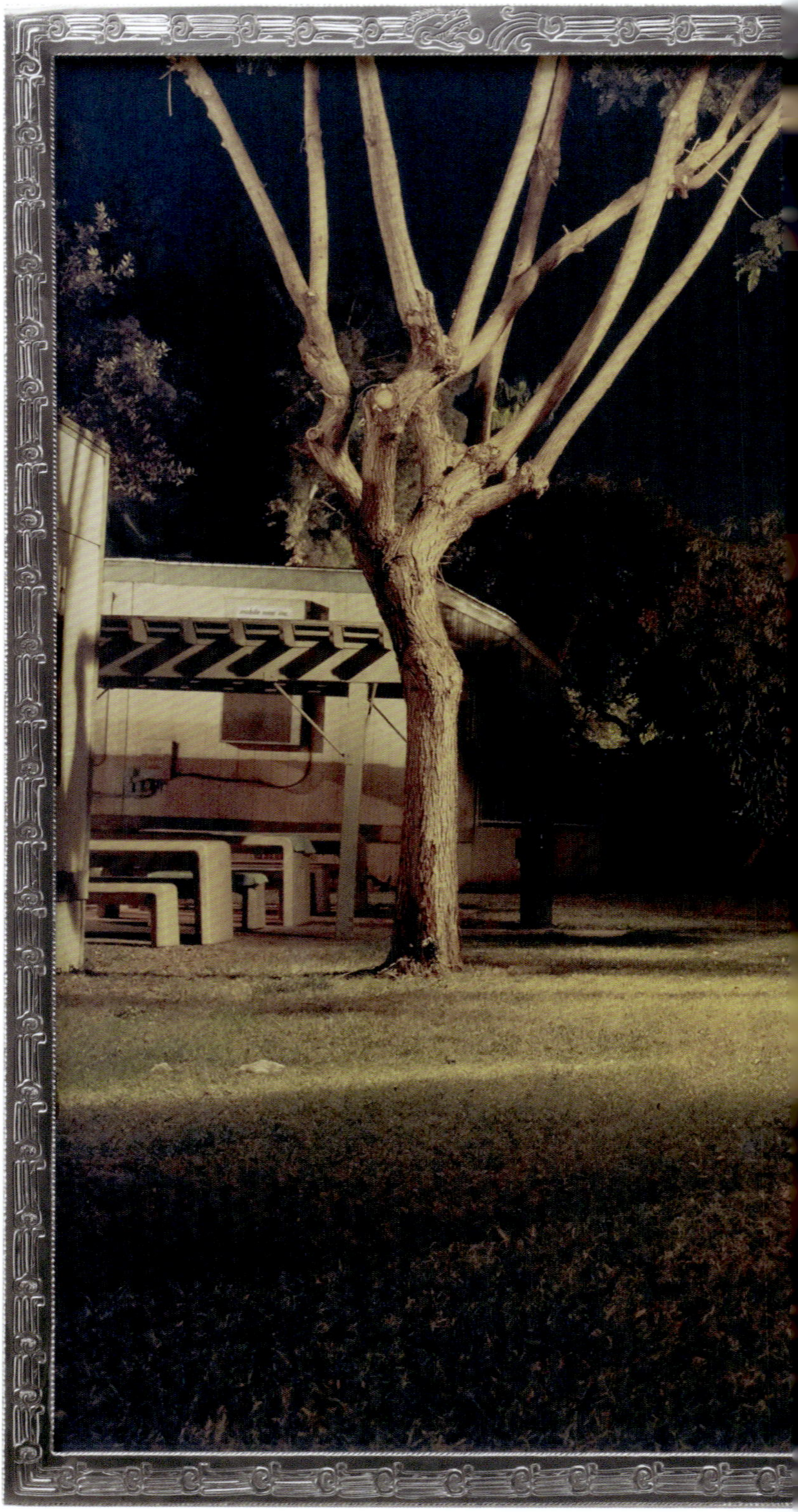

Winter Solstice/ Hazards, 2022

ARCHIVAL PIGMENT PRINT, UNIQUE HAND ENGRAVED ARTIST'S FRAME
48 X 62 IN; FRAMED: 51 X 65 X 2 IN

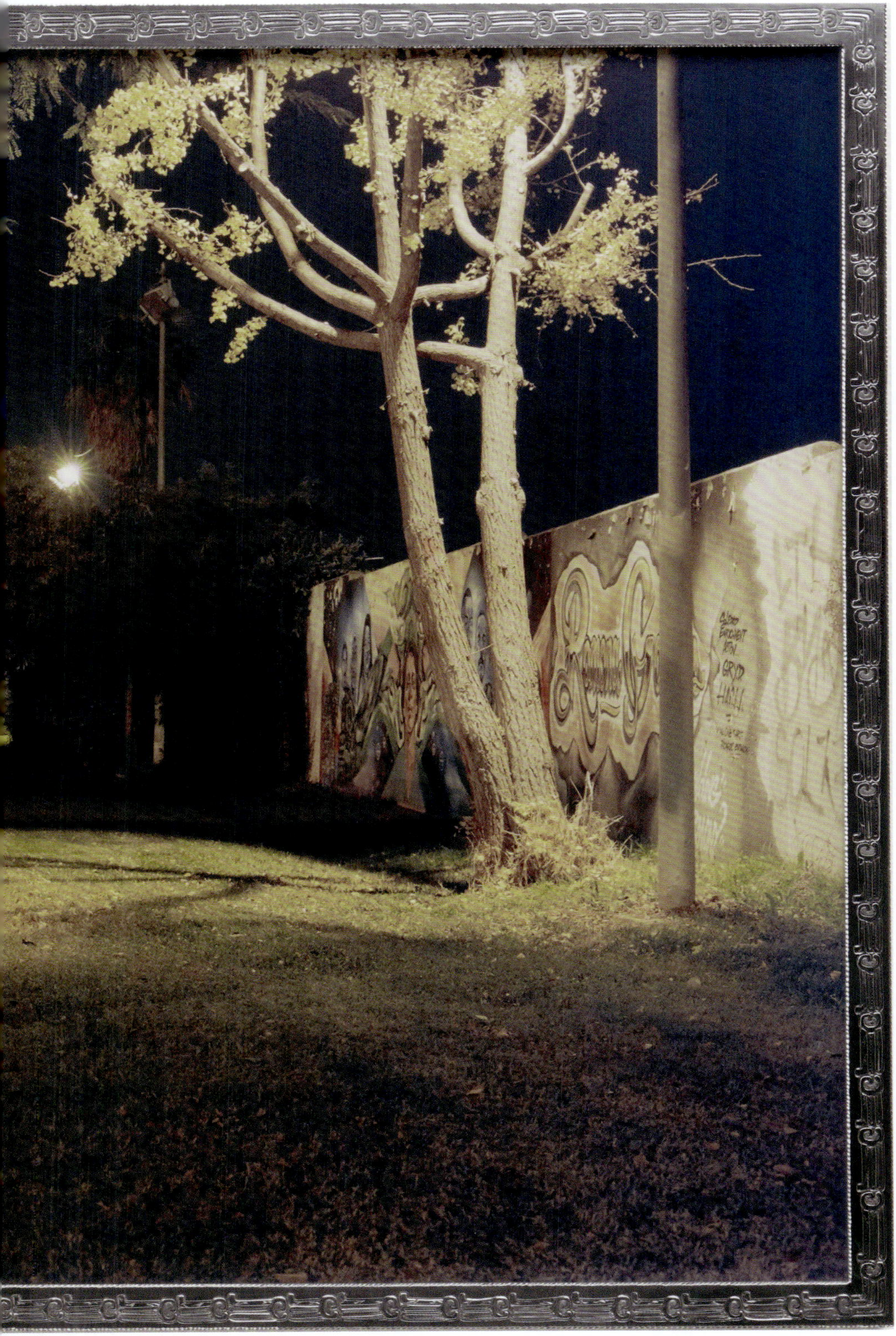

FULL CIRCLE

MY WORK AS AN ARTIST ALWAYS COMES BACK to belonging and memory. The photographs I showed in the Whitney Biennial were of landmarks and other meaningful sites from my childhood. My approach is very intentional—I pay attention to what it feels like when I return to those memories, standing in those places. I ask myself: Was the night hazy, hot, quiet? What was the energy of that moment, and how can I translate that into a photograph? My images are cinematic in that way. For me, this is the Los Angeles I know. It's the experience of being out at night, running the streets while the city sleeps.

In 2022, a series of these photographs were included in *Quiet as It's Kept,* at the Whitney Biennial. I focused on places that still carry memory for me—corners and landmarks of my youth, spaces that hold both joy and pain. Each image reflects how it felt to stand there again, and each decision was deliberate: the mood, the atmosphere, the temperature of the night. I wanted to make those feelings visible, turning them into something intimate, cinematic, alive with memory.

Looking back, I realize this was the first time I allowed myself to show these memories in such a public and institutional space. It was a way of saying: *This is my Los Angeles, this is the world that I grew up in.* The Biennial gave me a chance to root my work in the landscape of my youth and invite others to see the city through my eyes. To have the photographs seen in such an important museum, in New York, a place that has also been my home and where I became an artist, was a way of honoring both parts of myself.

Winter Solstice/Hazards (2022) shows a grassy section of Ramona Gardens Housing Projects, lit by a fluorescent yellow streetlight, marked with murals and the 10 freeway. This is the place where my cousin was killed, and every year I return on the winter solstice to honor him and confront the loss.

A Night to Remember (2022) traces the streaks of car lights across a dark cityscape, capturing the city at night with a police helicopter circling around the dark L.A. skies—its quiet, its motion, its invitation to dream. These images are my way of holding on to memory and understanding my past and are also deeply personal: portraits of the places where life, love, and loss intersect. I chose to capture the real L.A., the L.A. that I know. Not the L.A. with the Hollywood sign or beaches we see on television.

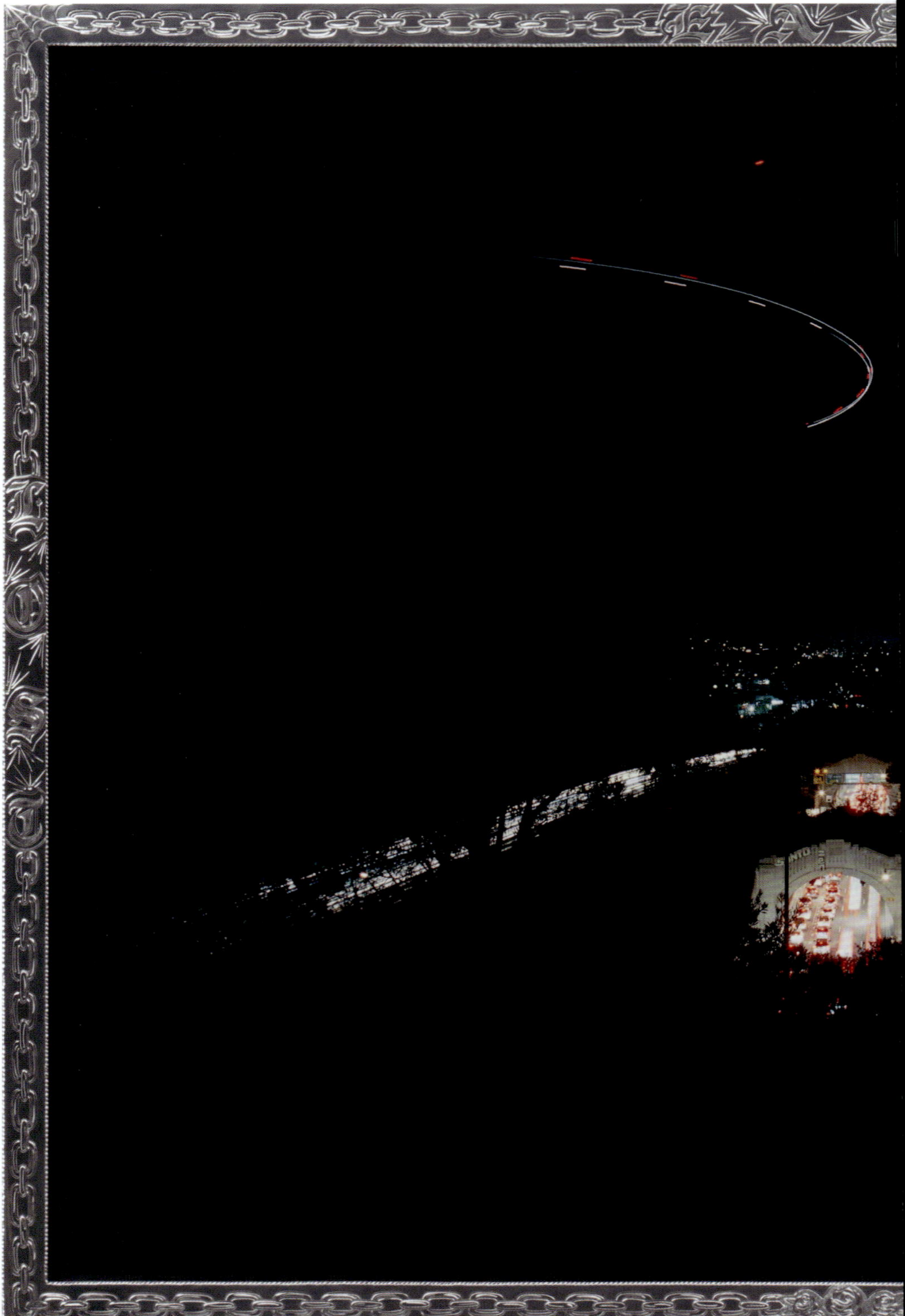

A night to remember, 2022

ARCHIVAL PIGMENT PRINT, UNIQUE HAND ENGRAVED ARTIST'S FRAME
48 X 62 IN; FRAMED: 51 X 65 X 2 IN

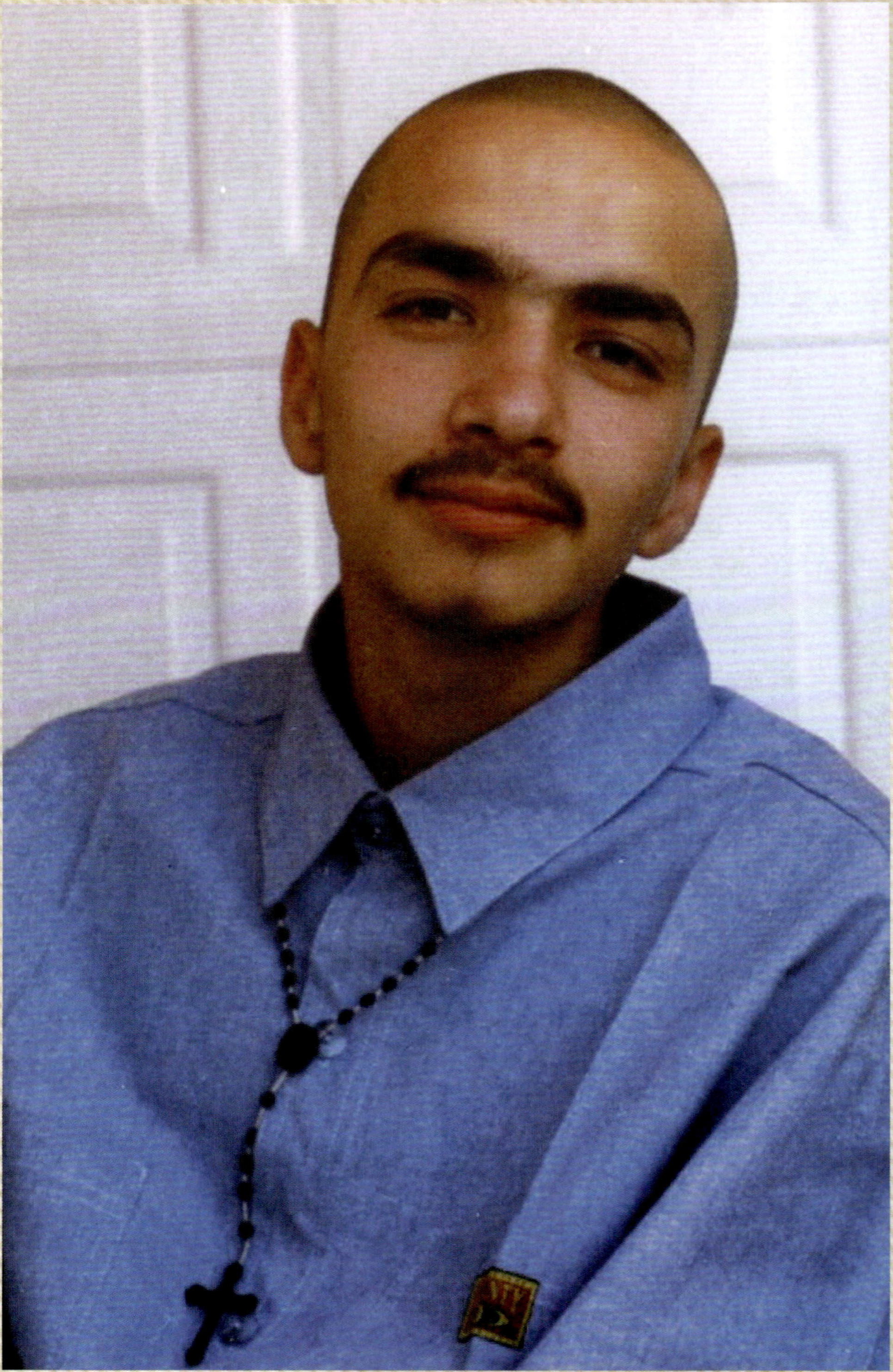

JERRY

WHEN I BEGAN WRITING THIS BOOK, MY FRIEND Jerry, whom I had known since we were both fifteen years old, died of an overdose. I hadn't seen him for some time, maybe a decade, but we had reconnected in 2016 over Facebook and we continued our communication online until he passed away. I wanted to remember him in the pages of this book.

Many people who are in prison have a very complicated relationship with "hope." Many don't want to give up on the idea that one day they will be released, especially if they are in prison for a crime they did not commit, or something so minor that it's possible to fight it.

I have many friends who went to jail in the '90s at a very young age and served or are serving more than a decade. Many were locked up for crimes that would be considered petty or minor, like smoking or having weed, or shoplifting, or even worse, innocently riding in a car that then became involved in something serious, like an armed robbery or drive-by shooting.

Jerry went to jail for robbery charges, but he always wanted the best for himself and his family. When he was in prison, he'd call me or message me with a burner phone; I had just moved back to Los Angeles. The conversations were very short. Just asking how I was, how my sister Maria was (she dated him around the time when Ever was killed). Then there were months of silence because his

OPPOSITE: Jerry in 1997

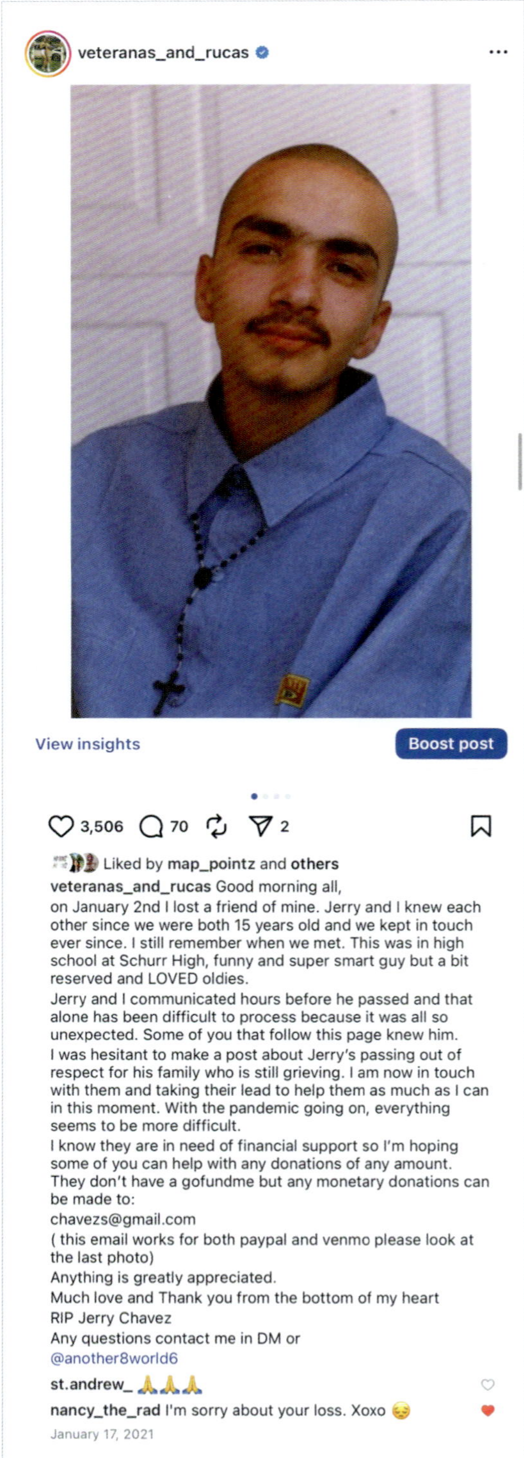

burner phone was confiscated. Even during that silence, his days continued. While Jerry was still incarcerated, he was part of a firefighter program, and he loved it. For a time, his days were spent outside. He slept on the earth, wrapped in the elements, falling asleep looking up at the sky and the stars. He worked on active fires and tended to the land. That experience mattered deeply to him. Even then, it allowed him to do work he loved.

He was proud of that work, just as he was proud of earning two associate degrees while inside—one in math and one in business. These were moments of dignity that existed alongside confinement. Jerry didn't do these things just to pass time. He did them for himself. He was always this way—someone who tried, who cared, who wanted more for his life. This is the Jerry I knew as far back as high school.

Jerry was finally released in 2020, and we reconnected again. He was living in West Covina and was excited to get his life together. He let me know he was working in construction, had his own apartment. (It was very clean and well-kept—he took pride in sending me photos through Facebook.) He told me he'd bought a truck and was excited to get his driver's license.

He sent me selfies of himself at work wearing a construction belt, his tools, and what he had been working on, like he wanted to be seen beyond the image of a cholo who had just been released from prison. He wanted to show his friends and family that he was more than the bad choices he had made in his life—he was a different man than before, a good man.

When Jerry was released he did not have any resources. All he knew was that he needed to get back on his feet and make money—get a job and work to survive. But what about resources for mental health, or even a professional he could speak with after prison to help him recover from the drug addiction he'd picked up in prison? I wish he'd been offered some kind of support when he was released, to help him function in the outside world.

I wanted to share Jerry's story in order to honor him specifically and also to give a window into how prisons, systemic racism, and oppression could intersect in one's life. I also wanted to celebrate the fact that despite these losses, we are a community of survivors. Memorials are essential to that survival: We need to honor the dead in order to move forward in life.

I was once told that I had a lot of deaths in my life. When I think about that comment, I must admit that it is true. I've gone to many funerals, and I've also known many people who have passed away throughout my life since I was sixteen years old. That's only true because my community is one that is deeply affected by poverty, which brings drugs, violence, and a lack of resources (health care, mental health awareness, etc.).

That comment left me feeling ashamed, like maybe my life was too "ghetto," and for years I kept things to myself about my upbringing and what I'd gone through. Compartmentalizing isn't ultimately good, but it did help me survive many tragedies.

I STAYED IN touch with Jerry's family after his passing, and we've been in conversation throughout the process of making this book. When I went to his funeral, they welcomed me into their grief and later shared something deeply personal—Jerry's scrapbook. It felt important to in-

FEB. '96

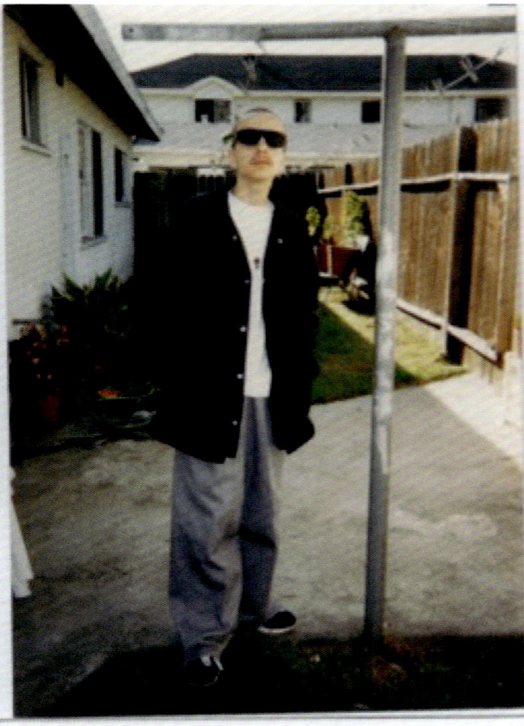

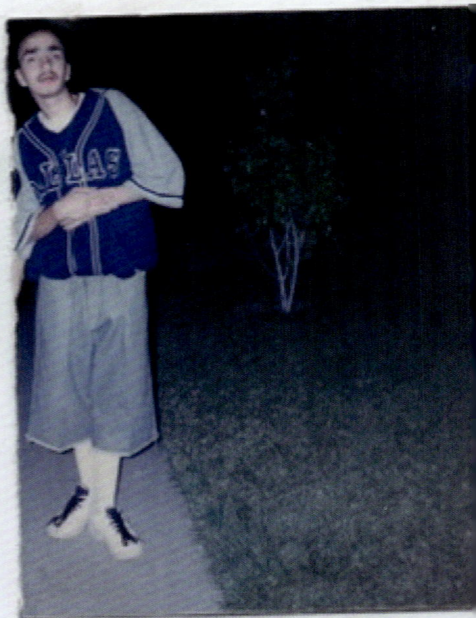

JUNE '97

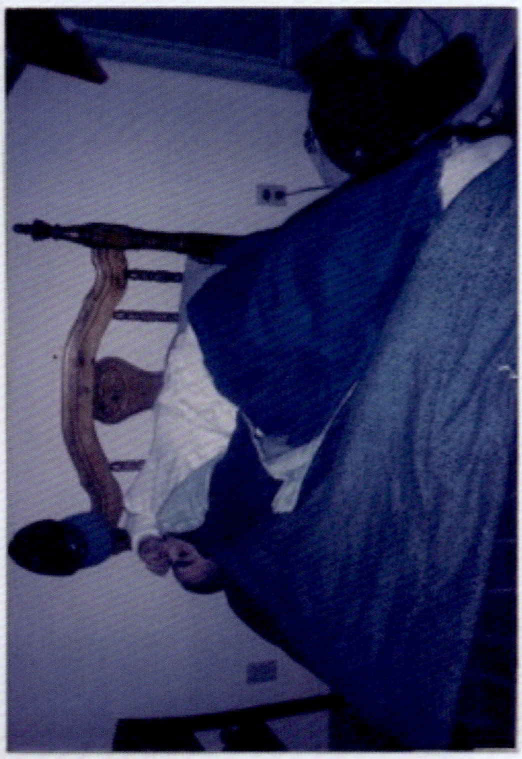

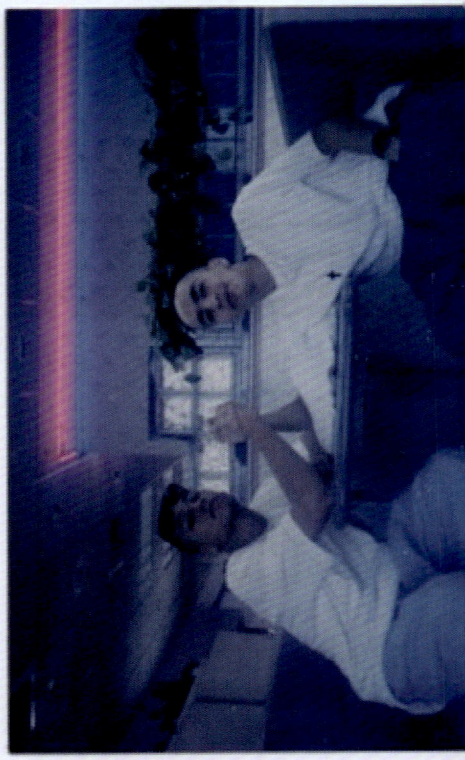

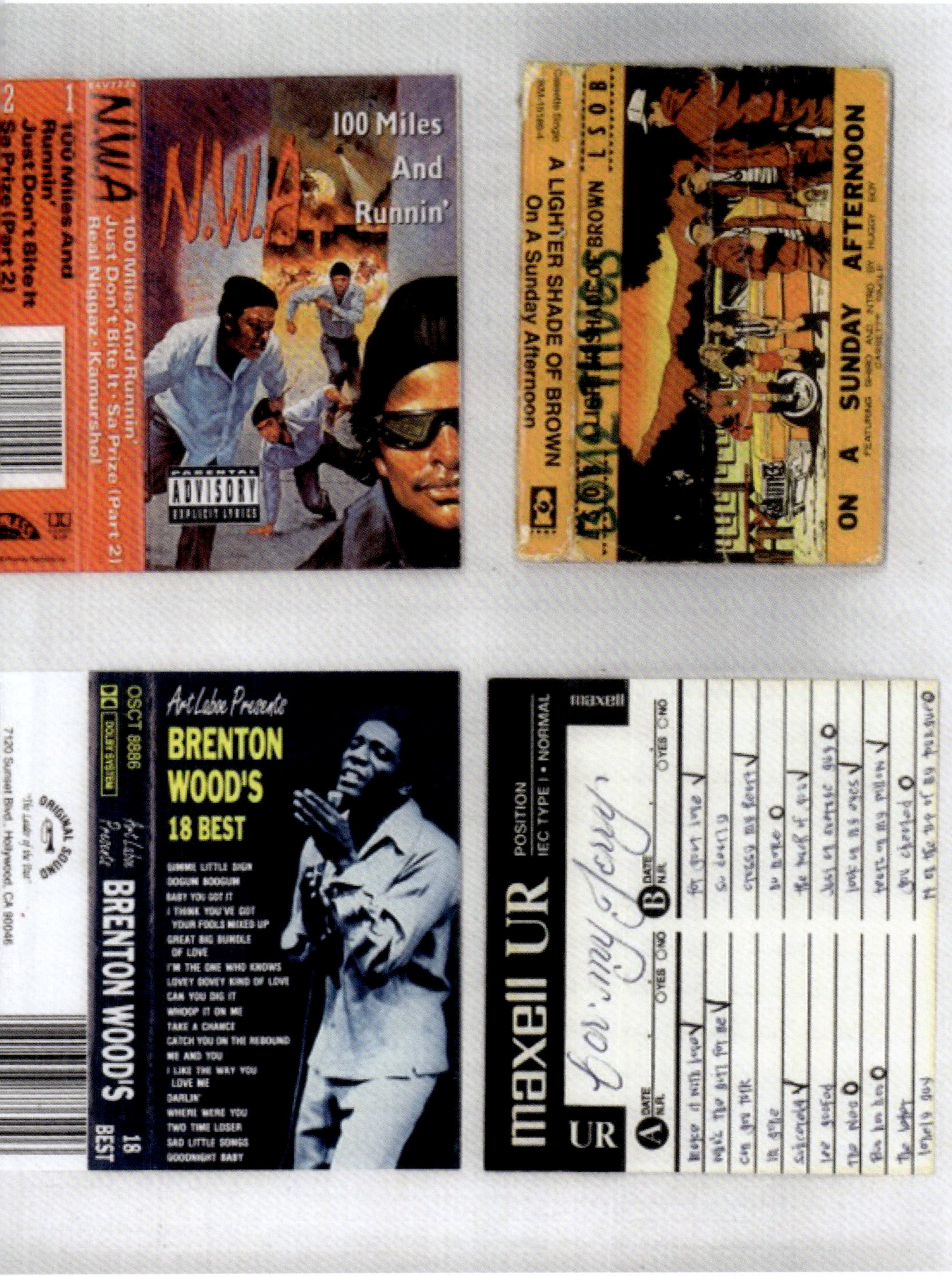

N.W.A
100 Miles And Runnin'
100 Miles And Runnin' · Just Don't Bite It · Sa Prize (Part 2) · Real Niggaz · Kamurshol
1 100 Miles And Runnin'
Just Don't Bite It
2 Sa Prize (Part 2)
PARENTAL ADVISORY EXPLICIT LYRICS
ON A SUNDAY AFTERNOON
A LIGHTER SHADE OF BROWN
On A Sunday Afternoon
Cassette Single
LSOB
Art Laboe Presents
BRENTON WOOD'S 18 BEST
GIMME LITTLE SIGN
OOGUM BOOGUM
BABY YOU GOT IT
I THINK YOU'VE GOT YOUR FOOLS MIXED UP
GREAT BIG BUNDLE OF LOVE
I'M THE ONE WHO KNOWS
LOVEY DOVEY KIND OF LOVE
CAN YOU DIG IT
WHOOP IT ON ME
TAKE A CHANCE
CATCH YOU ON THE REBOUND
ME AND YOU
I LIKE THE WAY YOU LOVE ME
DARLIN'
WHERE WERE YOU
TWO TIME LOSER
SAD LITTLE SONGS
GOODNIGHT BABY
OSCT 8886
DOLBY SYSTEM
ORIGINAL SOUND
"The Leader of the Beat"
7120 Sunset Blvd., Hollywood, CA 90046
maxell UR
POSITION
IEC TYPE I • NORMAL

G.O.G.I. Quote

- In the past, I felt I was a mistake rather than a person just making them. I am responsible for my future. I claim my past but I have learned from it. Experience is my strict and faithful companion. —Lee Smith GOGI.

- God is <u>Not</u> a "wishing well" - quote for kids.

- "As soon as you belive you know it ALL and decide to stop learning... It's time to die"

Stay away from the chismes DON'T REACT... don't show your feelings... just leave NEVER insult a female. Stay quiet and walk away... be the better man... They will get frustrated and you will look good... like a good man.

NORTH KERN STATE PRISON.

JANUARY 9th 2014

As I look out at the outside the tall (but 5' wide) (skinny) window [redacted] the sky is gloomy and lonely,

No-One can hear me, but I can hear echoing voices. Others like me that can't be seen or heard unless your in the belly of the machine.

I wasn't allways like this. Is this the end result? Life was supposed to be different. I was lied to. Is this the truth. This machine has made my heart pump gray. My love came and went away. What is left. A Concrete building to shut you up. Barbwire and towers. I guess it really don't matter if life is gray, any way.

clude it here, not only as a way of honoring him, but also as a way for others to see the beauty and reality of my dear friend. For me, sharing this page of his is my way of keeping his spirit present, a reminder of the life he lived and the memories we continue to carry.

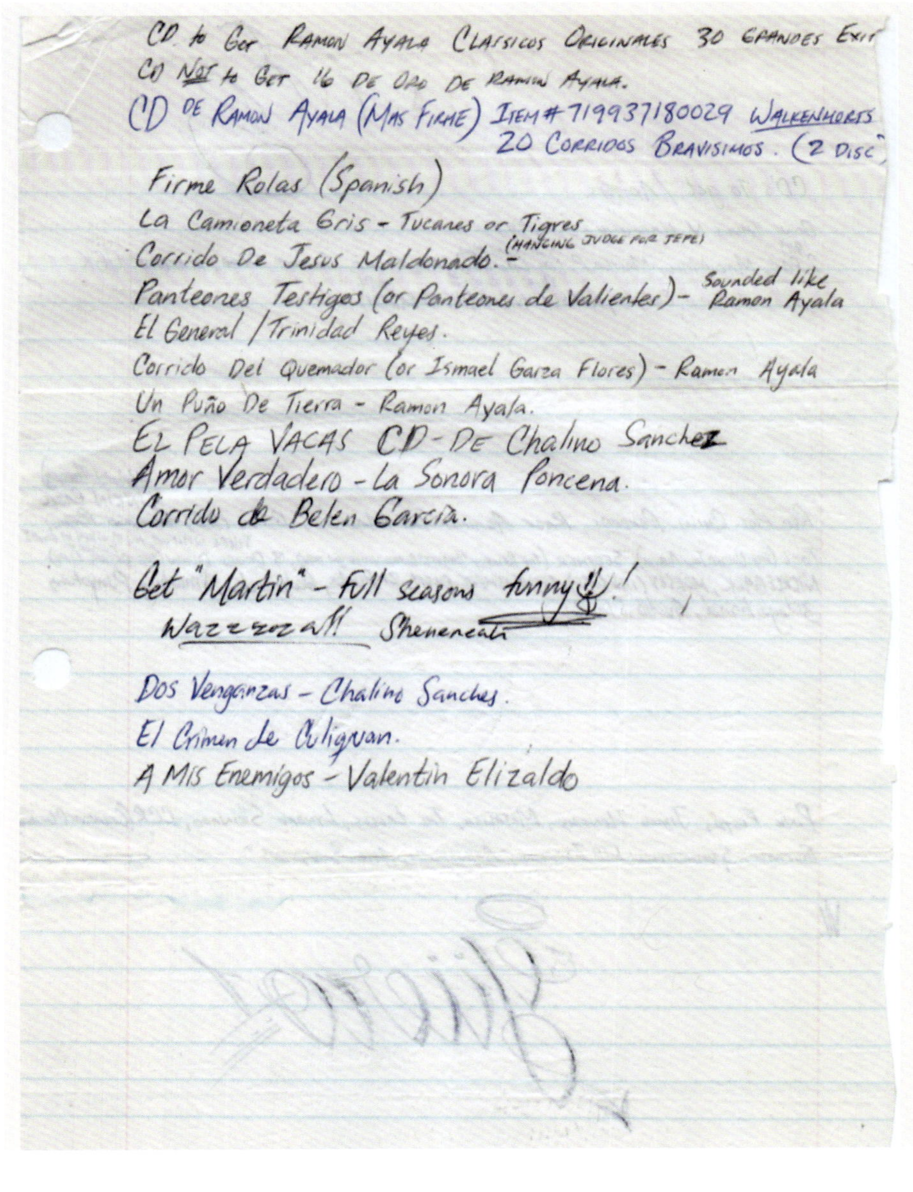

CD to Get Ramon Ayala Clasicos Originales 30 Grandes Exit
CD Not to Get 16 De Oro De Ramon Ayala.
CD De Ramon Ayala (Mas Firme) Item # 719937180029 Walkenhorsts
20 Corridos Bravisimos. (2 Disc)

Firme Rolas (Spanish)
La Camioneta Gris - Tucanes or Tigres
Corrido De Jesus Maldonado. - (Hanging Judge for Jefe)
Panteones Testigos (or Panteones de Valientes) - Sounded like Ramon Ayala
El General / Trinidad Reyes.
Corrido Del Quemador (or Ismael Garza Flores) - Ramon Ayala
Un Puño De Tierra - Ramon Ayala.
El Pela Vacas CD - De Chalino Sanchez
Amor Verdadero - La Sonora Poncena.
Corrido de Belen Garcia.

Get "Martin" - full seasons funny!!
Wazzzzzup!! Sheneneah

Dos Venganzas - Chalino Sanches.
El Crimen de Culiquan.
A Mis Enemigos - Valentin Elizaldo

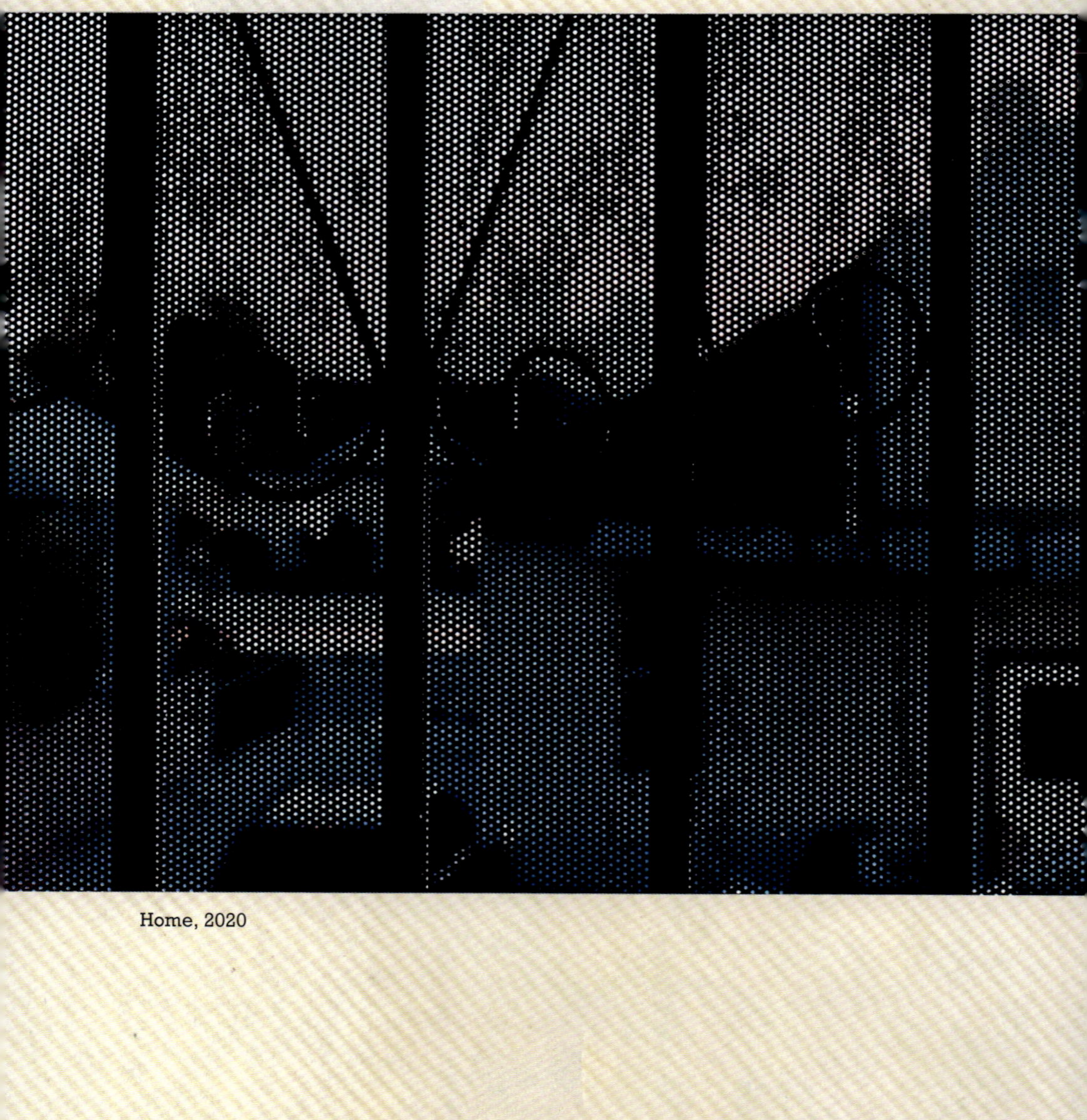
Home, 2020

BACK IN THE NEIGHBORHOOD

MY MOM IS A TRUE CANCER—TOUGH AS A NAIL, but emotional.

A few years after I had moved back, I met her for a birthday lunch at Mariscos El Paraiso in East Los Angeles, on Olympic and Gerhart, not far from Nicola's strip club. She wanted to meet at 11 A.M. A little too early for ceviche and aguachile, but that's what she was craving, so I agreed. After we finished eating, we took a walk around Belvedere Park. Mom calls this park "el parque de los patos"—there's a man-made lake right in the center of the park. The lake has an unnatural blue tint, with different types of ducks on the water. The blue pigmentation makes East Los Angeles seem like a place in a fictional story.

There is also East Los Angeles Library, where I would go to hang with my friends and sisters as a kid, the place where I first learned about the *Titanic*. Right across from the library is a courthouse and a beautiful building that houses a clinic. We call it "la clínica de colores" because it has these beautiful colored tiles depicting Aztec deities that wrap around the building.

This felt like my second home because we made many trips here—for court, welfare stuff, and therapy. On the outside, it is colorful and lively. On the inside, it is dull and monochromatic like all courthouses. In the park there is a sheriff's station. When I was a teenager, my mother made many trips here to pick us up after we got arrested for being out past curfew or whatever else.

Now, as we're walking around the little lake, Mom says to me, "¿Sabes cuántas veces las tuve que recoger de aquí? Muchas." (You know how many times I had to come pick you and your sisters up from here? Many.) She tells me, "There was one particular time when a sheriff yelled at me, accusing me of being a neglectful parent. He wanted to fine me for 'allowing' you to be out on the streets past curfew."

She laughs as she shares this memory with me, knowing too damn well this wasn't funny then. She continues, "No, mijita, yo le dije que ustedes tienen que pagar por ser tan vagas." Now I remember all those times we had to do community service but instead ended up hanging out at the boxing gym. After this conversation, I want to ask her more questions. I want to know her side of the story. What was her experience during our teenage years in the '90s?

I also ask my mother about her experience raising her kids and living in East L.A. Specifically, how it was for her to live there in the midst of violence. She tells me that sometimes it was like looking out the window for some good chisme, the gossip. There were people who would come out (instead of hiding) when they heard gunshots. It was like entertainment, she says as she shrugs her shoulders.

Drive-by shootings didn't faze her, she says, but I notice her thinking about the question as if she has never thought about it before. We've all had near-death experiences and I sometimes wonder how I am still here. These experiences are what made me street-smart, for better or worse . . . and suspicious of people walking behind me or cars that drive slowly in neighborhoods. I sometimes wonder what my life and my family's life would have been like if we had been raised in a different environment.

We end our walk with Mom reminiscing about her youth. I'm sure our parents have stories that are just like ours, but they have a harder time sharing them with us—because they can be a little old-school or traditional, but mostly because anything to do with sex or intimacy is still uncomfortable for them to talk about. I always ask my mom about her youth: What was it like to date? To hang out with friends? What did they do for fun? What was it like to have crushes? But every time I try to dig deeper, it's like pulling teeth. Sometimes I get half of a story or different versions of it, depending on her mood. Other times, she'll start sharing with excitement but then the details disappear, and all she'll say is, "I was a decent girl and didn't date much."

But the truth slips out in ways. Like on this walk, just talking about her experience raising us in East L.A., she tells me that she met Vicente Fernández in the '70s at one of his shows when she was a teenager. She was on a date with a guy, and he got them great seats at an intimate palenque in Michoacán. At the end of the night, when Vicente was singing his last song, he walked toward the audience and stopped in front of my mom. When he got close to her, he leaned in and asked for her hand. She reached out and he kissed it, and the boy she was with got jealous. She tells me, "Se puso bien celoso y pensó que me iba a ir con él." Mom and I start laughing. That little moment—that kind of magic—it's the kind of story I wish she'd share more, but she always pulls back, like there's something in those details that she's still not ready to let me see. Like many women in my family and on *Veteranas and Rucas*.

JUST LIKE MY mother's youth, and mine and my siblings', our adolescence was the time when we finally had a sense of freedom and independence—gradually learning how to carve out spaces of belonging in the *City of Angels,* using little to no money and limited resources—the streets, backyards, abandoned buildings, the L.A. River, Whittier Boulevard. We were creative kids using our imaginations, using what we could to find freedom.

Just like this neighborhood carries the blood of so many people we love who we've lost, it also carries the energy of our joy and our resilience. And every time I walk these streets, I notice something old and something new.

Just like these conversations, writing this book has helped me heal—and remember what was joyful and what wasn't. Recently, while I was deep in the writing, I talked with my little sister, Yesi. We were sharing memories, bouncing them back and forth, holding both the good times and the hard ones—like foster care. I told her about a moment I had written: one of my sisters crying at night, and me *wanting* to comfort her. And then she stopped me and said, "It was you, silly. Do you remember how much you cried at night in that foster home?" In that moment, the whole perspective shifted. I realized it was me—I was the one crying myself to sleep. And suddenly it made sense, because I still remember the pain in my chest, staring up at a dark ceiling, wide awake in the night.

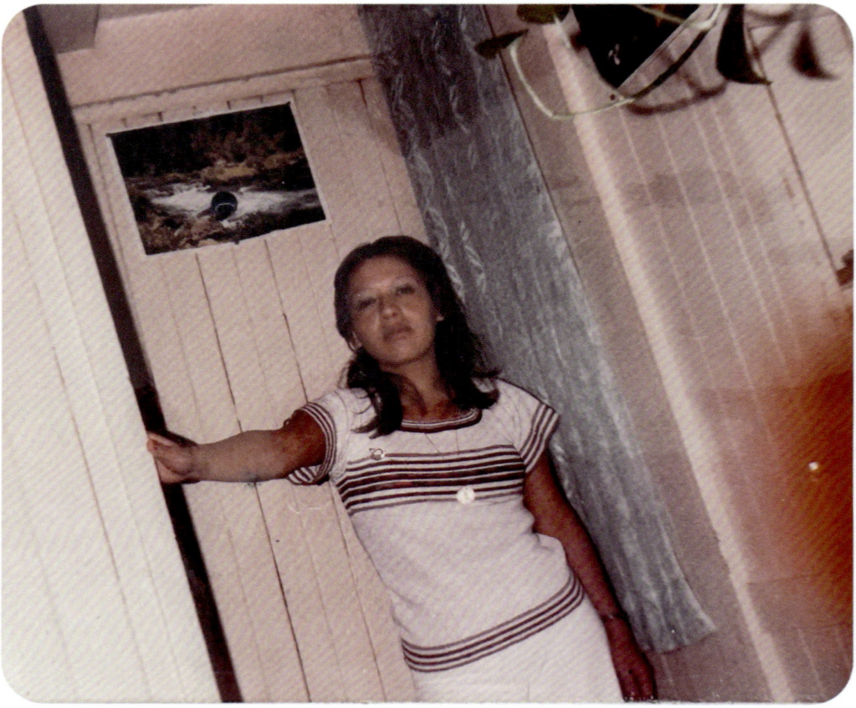

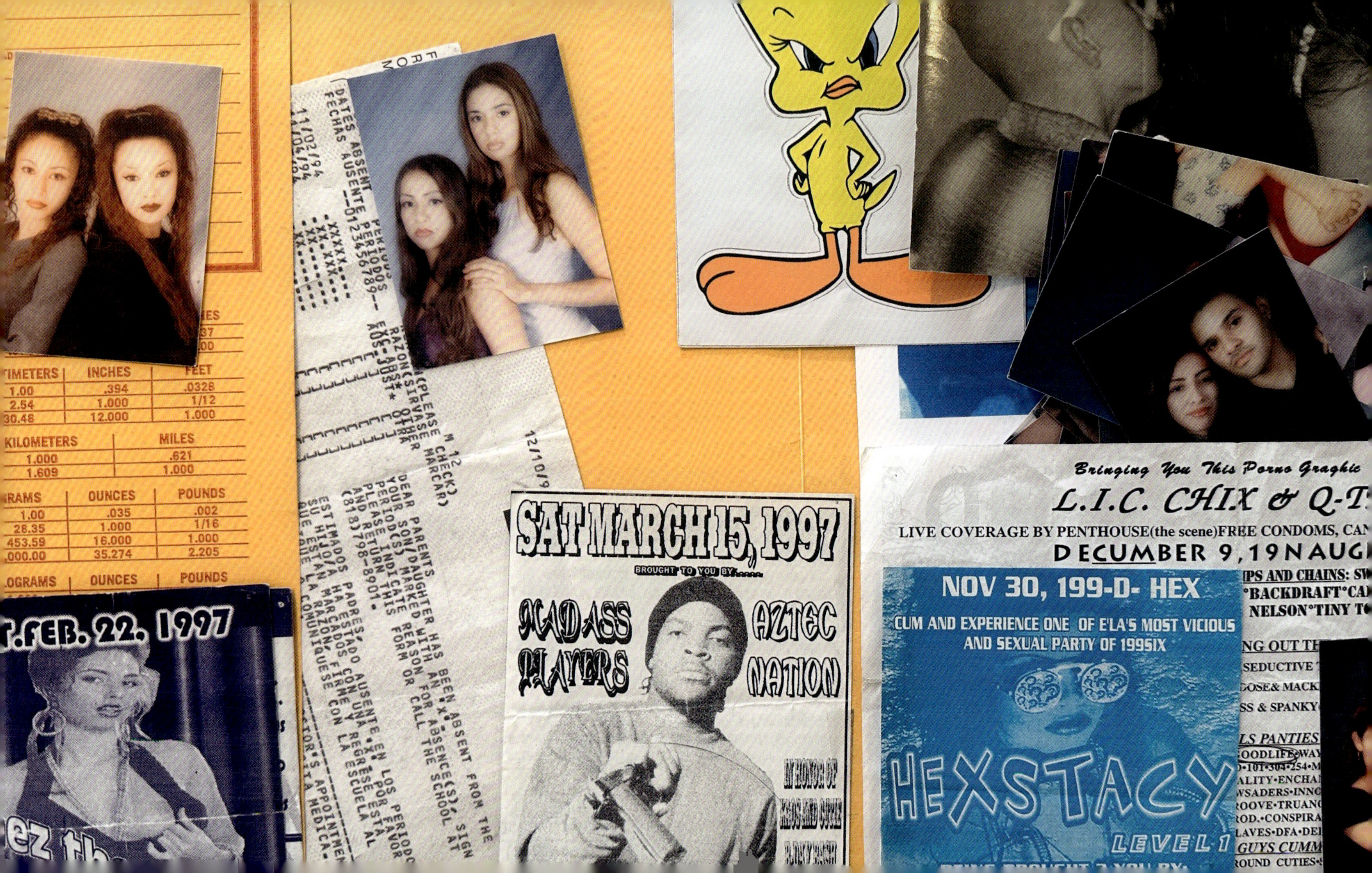

T.FEB. 22. 1997
SAT MARCH 15, 1997
BROUGHT TO YOU BY
MADASS PLAYERS
AZTEC NATION
DEAR PARENTS
YOUR SON/DAUGHTER HAS BEEN ABSENT FROM THE
PERIOD(S) MARKED WITH AN "X". ABSENCE(S), SIGN
PLEASE INDICATE REASON FOR OR CALL THE SCHOOL AT
AND RETURN THIS FORM
(818)798-8901.
DATES ABSENT
FECHAS AUSENTE
Bringing You This Porno Graphic
L.I.C. CHIX & Q-T
LIVE COVERAGE BY PENTHOUSE(the scene)FREE CONDOMS, CAN
DECUMBER 9,19NAUG
NOV 30, 199-D- HEX
CUM AND EXPERIENCE ONE OF E'LA'S MOST VICIOUS AND SEXUAL PARTY OF 1995IX
HEXSTACY
LEVEL 1

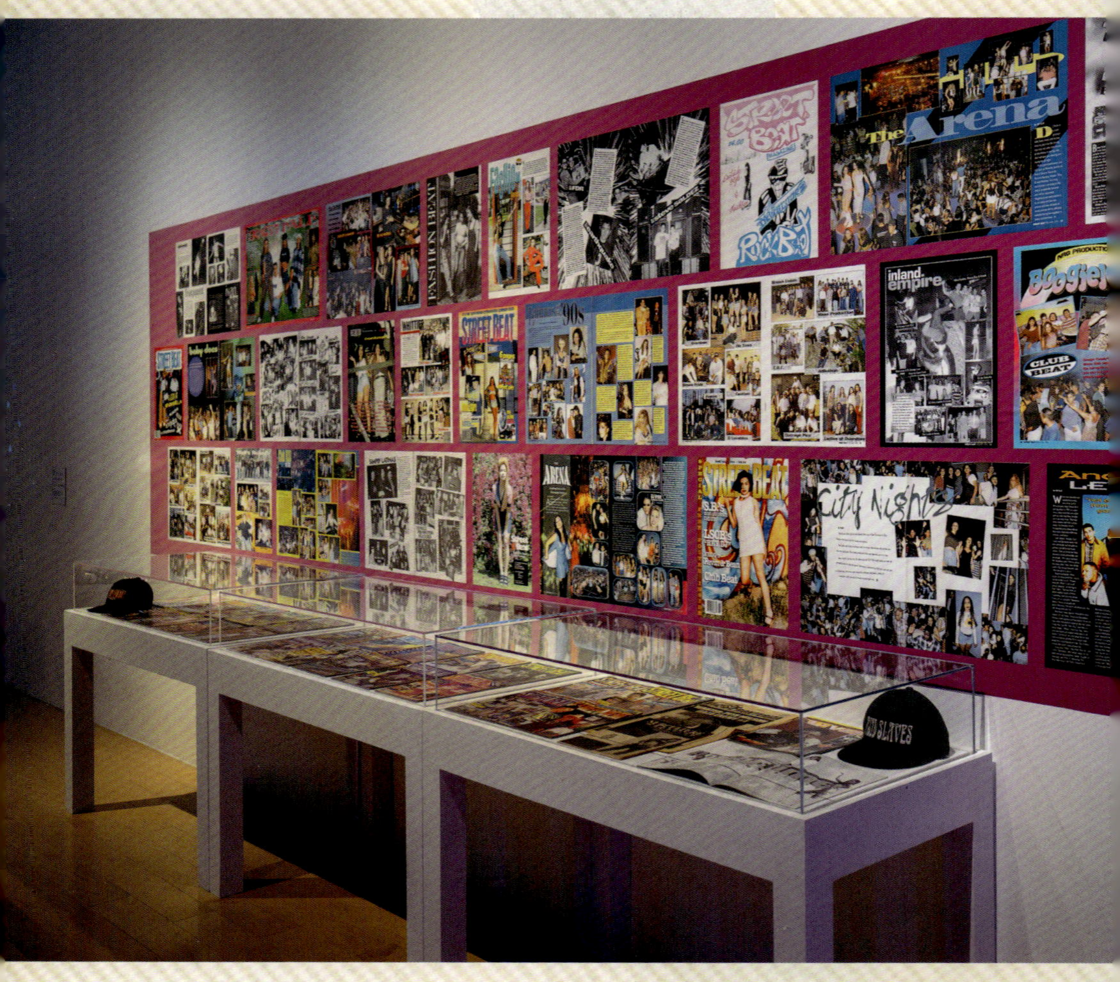
The Arena
STREET BEAT
inland empire
City Nights
CLUB BEAT

CONCLUSION

MY WORK WITH *VETERANAS AND RUCAS* AND *Map Pointz* and my art practice have connected me to a community of storytellers who, like me, understand that our histories cannot be left to institutions alone. We've always been our own archivists, keeping photos in shoeboxes, letters in drawers, and memories alive through stories passed down at the kitchen table. My goal has been to honor that tradition while creating new ways for these histories to breathe in the present and reach future generations.

But even as these archives grow, I remain aware of what is at stake. The continued gentrification of Los Angeles threatens not only the physical sites where our histories live, but also the cultural fabric of the city itself. The displacement of long-standing residents risks erasing the material evidence of our presence—our murals, our parks, our neighborhoods, the very spaces that raised us. This urgency is what pushes me to safeguard and share these stories, so that future generations will inherit not just fragments, but a living, breathing record of who we are.

As I reflect back on this journey—from my childhood in East Los Angeles to launching these archives in 2015 to seeing this work now in museums, classrooms, and conversations across the world—I am struck by how much it has transformed my life and how our stories are recognized. What began as a deeply personal act of urgency has grown into a living, collective archive that challenges erasure and celebrates resilience. It fills me with pride when teachers and students tell me that my work is being taught in classrooms—that our beautiful history is no longer hidden but studied, honored, and shared.

I never imagined this life. As a girl growing up amid poverty, violence, and grief, I could not have pictured myself as an artist, mentor, or storyteller. Yet it was precisely in those fragments of another time—old photos, letters, parties, and the everyday beauty of our lives—that the foundation was laid for what would become a movement of reclamation and empowerment.

Through interviews, exhibitions, books, and digital platforms, *Veteranas and Rucas* and *Map Pointz* have grown into archives that center women, honor working-class youth culture, and remind us that when our history is missing, we have the power to document and reclaim it ourselves. This work is not finished—it continues to grow with every contribution, every memory shared, every young person who decides to preserve their story.

For over a decade now, *Veteranas and Rucas* and *Map Pointz* have inspired and influenced countless people—artists, fashion brands, and future generations alike. Many look at this work and my creative practice and see themselves reflected back. They realize that they, too, can be artists, archivists, and storytellers. What began as digital archives has become a living space of remembrance and visibility, inspiring others to tell their stories and keep our culture alive.

This book marks a deeply personal moment in my journey—a reflection of more than a decade spent preserving and honoring collective memory. It carries the spirit of the archives but also the parts of me that needed to heal, remember, and begin again.

What I hope to leave behind is not only a record of my community but a legacy of self-representation, empowerment, and teaching—a reminder that we all hold archives in our homes and within ourselves. A reminder to the next generation that our stories are worth telling, protecting, and celebrating.

I am deeply grateful to all who have shared, supported, and trusted me along this journey. What began as fragments of memory has become a collective voice, a map of who we are. And as we move forward, the work continues—to keep learning, thriving, and celebrating who we are, together.

And now, here we are, holding a book in our hands—a physical object, born of experience and care. We return to the tangible, to something that can be touched, carried, and passed on.

I hope that this book brings healing and joy to my family, my friends, myself, and my community. Writing this book has been its own form of healing—an act of remembering, forgiving, and coming home to myself.

ACKNOWLEDGMENTS

TO MY FAMILY, THOSE WHO ARE HERE AND THOSE WHO HAVE passed. You are the heart of everything I do. Thank you for teaching me what love, resilience, and memory look like. For every story shared on our porch on Leonard Avenue and Whittier Boulevard, every photograph saved in a shoebox, and every moment of laughter through the pain.

To my mom, Alicia, for doing everything you could to be a good mother, even in the hardest times—when it felt like the world was against us. I know you carried your own pain when the system failed us all. I hope I'm making you proud. Thank you for sharing your stories—of your youth, of creating a family, of the beauty and heartbreak you've lived through. Your strength is the root of mine.

To my sister Maria, my almost twin. You've been my inspiration then and now, and your presence lives in these pages.

To my lil sister, Yesi—aka Lil One—we grew up fast and fearless. You taught me how to be brave, to fight for myself, and to move through the world without fear—or giving a fuck. I'll never forget our wild nights—riding in stolen cars, smoking weed with you and Danny, jumping fences, and laughing through it all.

To my primo Danny, there are moments when we go years without communication, especially when I was living in New York. I am glad I am back home. To be close with you and the family. Love you.

To my friends, my chosen family, thank you for holding me down, for believing in me, and for reminding me of the beauty in our chaos. To those who are no longer with us, your spirit continues to move through this work. I carry you with me always—Gabriela Ruiz, rafa esparza, Franc Fernandez, Adrian Rivas and Pilar Tompkins Rivas, Rita Gonzales. Bob Dominguez, for being a great friend and supporter. Javi and Joey of Paisa Boys, for always being down to collaborate on the sickest parties and merch drops.

To my wonderful partner, Ashley. I love you. Thank you for reading this over and over with me.

To the people I met through Instagram: Kim, Brandy, and Nancy of Firme Hinas. Thank you for your love and energy, and for helping build community in this digital world. To everyone I reconnected with from Schurr High and Eastmont, and to my friend Miros, thank you for reminding me of the stories, places, and moments that shaped who we are.

To everyone who trusted me with their stories and found the courage to share them with the world to make change for the better, *Veteranas and Rucas* and *Map Pointz* would not exist without you. To all the people I've met in real life—those who've come to my shows, events, talks, and panel discussions. Thank you for showing up, for your words, and for believing in this work.

For Jerry's family, though we reconnected under the weight of his loss, I hope this book, and his chapter within it, offer some comfort and keep his spirit and our friendship alive in memory and honor. It's an honor to include some of his most precious collections in this book—his scrapbook.

To the new followers and the ones who've been here since day one, back in 2015, thank you for growing with me and for keeping this community alive.

To Aztek Nation, my party crew. You were the ones I ran with, the crew I partied with, and my first real sense of belonging outside home. Those nights, the music, the chaos, all of it shaped how I see community today.

To the Commerce Shopping Center and every spot where I spent time growing up—thank you for being part of my story. The place where we'd hang for hours, just existing, talking, dreaming, watching life happen around us. Those small moments taught me as much as any classroom ever could.

To my friends in New York (you know who you are—the ones who truly believe in me), thank you for seeing me.

To my community, near and far, thank you for sharing your stories, your photos, your trust. You've turned these archives into something much larger than I could have ever imagined. You remind me that we're never alone in our remembering.

To Commonwealth and Council (Kibum Kim and Young Chung) for years of encouragement and support.

To the Chinati Foundation, for offering me a space to work in solitude. That time gave me the focus I needed to finish this book—and even the confidence to practice public readings during my residency with you.

At One World: Oma Beharry, Chris Jackson, Avideh Bashirrad, Jocelynn Pedro, Katryce Campbell, Michael Morris, and Greg Mollica. THANK YOU!

At PRH: Matthew Martin, Allison King, Simon Sullivan, Barbara Bachman, Rebecca Berlant, Allison Fox, Luke Epplin, Mark Birkey, Richard Elman, Linnea Knollmueller, Kelly Chian, Leah Sims, and Stuart Calderwood.

To Stephen Serrato, Gloria Ortega, Isvett Verde, Rayhané Sanders . . . We did it!

Last but not least, to my editor, Elizabeth Méndez Berry—this book wouldn't exist without you. Thank you for believing in me, in my work, and in my community. You saw something in me before I fully saw it in myself, and you guided me through a process I once thought was impossible. The opportunity to write a book—a memoir—is something I never could have imagined in a million years. Thank you for helping me find the words to tell our story with love, honesty, and soul.

This book is for all of us—for the ones who came before, the ones still here, and the ones yet to come.

ABOUT THE AUTHOR

GUADALUPE ROSALES is a multidisciplinary artist and educator best known for her community-generated archival projects, *Veteranas and Rucas* and *Map Pointz,* which can be found on social media. The archive explores ideas about how history and culture are framed and who does the framing. As a counterpoint, the archive celebrates, humanizes, and reflects the positive and honest attributes of shared culture. In her studio practice, Rosales works with sculpture, photography, video, sound, drawing, community-based projects and collaborations, and the archive.

veteranasandrucas.com

Instagram: veteranas_and_rucas

ABOUT THE TYPE

This book was set in Plantin, a classic roman typeface named after the famous sixteenth-century printer Christophe Plantin (c. 1520–89). Plantin was designed in 1913 by the Monotype Corporation, based on some sixteenth-century type designs of Robert Granjon (1513–89). Plantin's even strokes and lack of contrast make it a highly legible face. It was, later, the typeface from which Times New Roman was modeled.